Jesus in Memory

Jesus in Memory
Traditions in Oral and Scribal Perspectives

Werner H. Kelber
Samuel Byrskog
Editors

BAYLOR UNIVERSITY PRESS

© 2009 by Baylor University Press
Waco, Texas 76798-7363

All Rights Reserved. No part of this publication may be reproduced, stored in a retrieval system, or transmitted, in any form or by any means, electronic, mechanical, photocopying, recording or otherwise, without the prior permission in writing of Baylor University Press.

Scripture quotations, where not an author's own translation, are from the New Revised Standard Version Bible, copyright 1989, Division of Christian Education of the National Council of the Churches of Christ in the United States of America. Used by permission. All rights reserved.

Cover Design by Pamela Poll Graphic Design

The Library of Congress has cataloged the hardcover edition as follows:

Jesus in memory : traditions in oral and scribal perspectives / Werner H. Kelber and Samuel Byrskog, editors.
   p. cm.
  Includes bibliographical references (p.   ) and index.
  ISBN 978-1-60258-235-4 (hardback : alk. paper)
  1. Bible. N.T. Gospels--Criticism, Form. 2. Oral tradition. 3. Literature, Ancient--History and criticism. 4. Gerhardsson, Birger. Memory and manuscript. I. Kelber, Werner H. II. Byrskog, Samuel.
  BS2555.52.J475 2009
  226'.0663--dc22
                              2009020938

The ISBN for the 2017 paperback edition is 978-1-4813-0820-5.

Printed in the United States of America on acid-free paper.

Contents

Introduction *Samuel Byrskog*		1
1	Form Criticism *Christopher Tuckett*	21
2	The Jesus Tradition as Oral Tradition *Terence C. Mournet*	39
3	Jesus Tradition and the Pauline Letters *David E. Aune*	63
4	Honi the Circler in Manuscript and Memory: An Experiment in "Re-Oralizing" the Talmudic Text *Martin S. Jaffee*	87
5	Memory and Tradition in the Hellenistic Schools *Loveday Alexander*	113
6	Memory *Alan Kirk*	155
Conclusion: The Work of Birger Gerhardsson in Perspective *Werner H. Kelber*		173
Notes		207
Bibliography		261
List of Contributors		279
Index of Ancient Sources		281
Index of Modern Authors		288

Introduction

Samuel Byrskog

Memory and Tradition

The present book is about memory and tradition, and a host of related issues. The relationship between the two is far from evident. Modern society venerates various sites of artificial memory that distance traditional knowledge and information from human memory while turning our minds into a blur of diverging impressions and sensations. In the Western world the printed book page is the primary site of information, and it is perceived to represent the stability and durability of communication. Computerized information technology competes successfully in the arena of artificial memory and influences us in unforeseen ways. The plurality and fragmented character of its messages collides with our desire for stability and coherence in communication and threatens to collapse into an impressionistic fusion of fiction and reality. Human memory has been emptied of its structuring elements and become the battleground of a vast array of conflicting modes of information. It takes sustained and disciplined effort to lay open the existential and communicative importance of the mnemonic structures of the human mind and recover the inextricable bonds between memory and tradition.

Memory can be many things. At a time when writing was virtually unknown and everything depended on the spoken word, it was a venerated goddess. *Mnemosyne* was born when heaven and earth united and it was she who gave birth to the Muses (*Theog.* 53–63, 133–36). When Hermes discovered the lyre, he sang the story of the immortal gods and honored *Mnemosyne* as the first one among them (*Merc.* 429–30). During the legendary Golden Age kings and poets were endowed with the gift of *Mnemosyne* and privileged to enter into a special relationship with the Muses. The reasons for the prestige of this Greek Titaness were manifold. The absence of writing was a contributing factor as it precluded any sense of external, diachronic development and fostered a blending of past, present, and future that was mediated and negotiated mnemonically. Memory and tradition were symbiotically united in all aspects of life. Human memory was the structuring force of life in a world of myths.

This vital and mythical union was nourished especially in circles that were separate from the mainstream Greek polis-centered cult. Inscriptions of possibly Pythagorean origin on the so-called Orphic gold leaves indicate fascinating notions of how the dead were longing to drink from *Mnemosyne* and warned against forgetting.[1] A noteworthy, although not direct, analogy is Pausanias' description of the ancient underground oracle of Trophonius at Lebadea (western Boeotia). Visitors to the subterranean chasm, it was believed, were made to drink from the rivers of *Lethe* ("forgetfulness," "concealment") and *Mnemosyne*. After their ascent the priests placed them upon the chair of *Mnemosyne*, not far from the shrine, so that they may ask the visitors about all that they had seen or learned (9.39.8–13). Memory was the fountain of life for those who sought eagerly to experience the mysteries. To remember was to live, to forget was to die.

Memory became the essential link to the past. There emerged a never-ending struggle to protect it from distortion and to prevent the threat of forgetfulness. Plato feared that the invention of the alphabet would make students rely on external characters which, not being part of themselves, would discourage the use of memory within them (*Phaedr.* 275a). In his treatise *De Memoria et Reminiscentia* Aristotle insisted that true recollection arranges the past according to the sequential structures of images imprinted on the mind and creates a sense of temporal distance between the past and the present.

The rhetoricians made memory into a matter of honor and shame. Quintilian would not write anything which he did not intend to memorize (*Inst.* 10.7.32), and he shared with several other orators an interest—albeit somewhat reticent—in the old mnemo-technical repertoire believed to have originated with Simonides of Ceos in the sixth and fifth century B.C.E. The honor attached to it produced several exaggerated accounts. Seneca the Elder, a skilled rhetorician, boasts that in his youth he was able to repeat two thousand names that were read to him and that he could recite in reverse order over two hundred verses that his fellow student told him. To him, this was a true *miraculum* (*Controversiae* 1 pref. 2). His boasting is a reminder of the vital importance that anyone who wished to speak and write persuasively attached to a good and accurate memory. The well-informed Pliny the Elder likewise praises memory as the greatest gift of nature and tells several anecdotes about persons who had gained glory from "this most necessary boon of life" (*Nat.* 7.24.88). Forgetfulness, as he goes on to illustrate, was exceedingly embarrassing. At this point memory was not seen as the structuring feature of life in a world of myths, but rather as the grand vehicle of persuasive and successful oral performance. Memory and tradition were rhetorically united into forceful and glorious mnemonic performances.

Pliny died at Pompeii in 79 C.E. This was the time when the rabbis entered the arena of history. To them as well memory was a matter of honor and shame, but within a different sacred and scholarly context. The Mishnah records from the early days of the rabbinic movement how Yochanan ben Zakkai praised Eliezer ben Hyrkanos for his excellent memory and compared him with a plastered cistern which loses not a drop (*m. Abot* 2:8). Eliezer enjoyed a special and idealized reputation for his memory. The rabbis moved memory into the religious domain by developing it into the fundamental basis of a learned didactic discourse linked to a specific concept of sacred tradition. When they narrowed down tradition to items of the Torah, they focused on memory as the stable guarantee and medium of successful transmission in a chain of teachers and students. Hence they both enhanced the importance of memory and limited its reference. In their own scholarly way, they recovered it as a vital structuring principle of life and confined it to acts of memorization and transmission.

The early followers of Jesus thus lived in a milieu where memory and tradition were closely bound to each other in various sacred contexts and forms of communication. The Christian authors of the first two centuries—from Paul to Irenaeus—encoded into their writings different signs of mnemonic negotiation between the sacred past and the present to such an extent that written and oral tradition became words to live by and to die for. Modern scholars have assessed the significance of these signs in different ways. While memory studies were scarcely taken into account in New Testament scholarship during the last century, there has recently appeared a significant range of work dealing with the mnemonic dimension of the early Christian tradition. Memory and tradition are again seen to belong together and the scholarly world is seeking actively to recover the ancient bond between the two.

The Contribution of Birger Gerhardsson

Few scholars have influenced New Testament scholarship in the area of memory and tradition more profoundly than Birger Gerhardsson. Today, as memory and tradition have again been placed on the scholarly agenda, his pioneering work comes into new light. The contributors of the present book come from various academic and intellectual milieus and hold different views on a number of scholarly matters, but they have all willingly taken on the task of evaluating his contribution anew and bringing his insights up to date with the current debate. The discussion of his ideas, even where there is disagreement, is a manifestation of the crucial importance of his work.

Memory and Manuscript

At a time when form criticism tended decisively to dissolve the ancient relationship between memory and tradition and focus solely on the kerygmatic concerns of the early Christians, Gerhardsson launched his Uppsala dissertation *Memory and Manuscript*. It was published for the first time in 1961.[2] In his unpublished *Licentiatenarbeit* from 1956 entitled *Studier i Jakobsbrevets uppkomstmiljö*, he had discovered—contrary to Martin Dibelius—that the sayings of Jesus alluded to in the letter of James had been transmitted independently of their use in paraenesis. It was, however, with his dissertation that he confronted New Testament scholarship with a deeply erudite and original thesis about Christian origins.

Uppsala was a lively and stimulating center of biblical studies in the 1950s and early 1960s. Gerhardsson began his doctoral studies in 1952 under Anton Fridrichsen, the dynamic professor of New Testament in Uppsala from 1928 to 1953, and he served as his last *famulus*.[3] Fridrichsen knew the leading form critics well and entertained close contact especially with Rudolf Bultmann. He was positively inclined toward the form-critical program but addressed only sporadically the problem of tradition. Upon the death of Fridrichsen in 1953, Gerhardsson continued his doctoral studies under Harald Riesenfeld. It was, however, Ivan Engnell, the prolific professor of Old Testament in Uppsala from 1947 to 1963, that aroused his interest in oral and written tradition. Gerhardsson attended Engnell's seminar for eight years. He was surrounded by other scholars with a keen interest in various issues concerning orality and literacy, ancient schools and education, and tradition and transmission in different religious contexts. The investigations of these and related issues by G. W. Ahlström, Engnell, H. S. Nyberg, Helmer Ringgren, and, in a different way, Geo Widengren,[4] with their attention to prophetic disciples and traditionalist circles as well as oral and/or written tradition, made any simple recourse to popular and collective features of oral tradition problematic. Among New Testament scholars, Krister Stendahl had in his Uppsala dissertation of 1954 questioned Dibelius' central idea of the kerygmatic force behind early Christian tradition and focused on settings of scribes and schools.[5] Form criticism was indeed an object of discussion and critical scrutiny in Uppsala during the 1950s. Gerhardsson recognized the need to advance these inquiries and he was the first one in Scandinavia thoroughly to study tradition and transmission in rabbinic Judaism and early Christianity.[6]

The influential form-critical paradigm of the 1950s and early 1960s, with its proposed solution to the problem of the origins of the gospel tradition, was the starting point of Gerhardsson's dissertation. He introduces his work with some critical remarks on the form critics' emphasis on eschatology, their notions of Jesus' identity and ministry, their insistence on the pneumatic and nonliterary character of the early church, and their neglect to define the concept of tradition and transmission. Considerations such as these, he believed, make it necessary to determine the technical procedures that were implemented by the early church in its transmission of the gospel tradition and other material.

The Jewish Torah of the Tannaitic and Amoraic periods serves as the principal comparative material and constitutes the object of the first part of Gerhardsson's study. He is not discussing the Jewish law in the narrow sense of the term, but, as he emphatically points out, the Jews' sacred authoritative tradition (doctrine) in its entirety. Written Torah is not to be equated with the Pentateuch, whether standing on its own or in conjunction with the Prophets and the Writings. It is, rather, authoritative transmission in written form. Oral Torah is not merely the Mishnah. It is authoritative transmission in oral form and includes repetition and that which is repeated.

Gerhardsson's attention to rabbinic literature was deliberate. He defends it not by arguing for its roots in the pre-70 situation, as many of his critics have assumed, but by pointing to the fact that rabbinic Judaism was a most influential current at the beginning of the Christian era and in subsequent centuries. Moreover, the Oral Torah was sacred and authoritative to the extent that its transmission was methodologically regulated and described in the sources. While fully aware that the catastrophes of 70 and 135 C.E. brought with them changes in the rabbis' views and actions, he regards it unlikely that any radically new teaching methods were introduced after 70 C.E. It would be highly desirable, he says, to pay equal attention to the techniques of transmission within other groups in the Hellenistic world as well.

Gerhardsson had noticed the occurrence of both Jesus texts and the free proclamation and teaching about Jesus in the New Testament. Turning to the Jewish Torah, he discovers a similar duality between the preservation of the wording of the biblical texts and the imaginative use of sacred texts in the targums and the midrashic literature. This duality points to different contexts, he argues. He is aware of the dynamic adaptation of the text in various situations and intentionally narrows the perspective of his study to the specific situations in which the text was faithfully reproduced in its traditional state.

Three contexts of scriptural transmission are crucial. The primary one is the professional context. Here trained scholars methodologically preserved the text in unaltered fashion. The second context is educational. The Torah was passed on in elementary schools. The preservation of the text was not the main objective in education, but great importance was placed upon the accuracy of the text. The third context is liturgical. Here the sacred text was read unchanged in public worship.

Gerhardsson's major interest was the Oral Torah. It was transmitted in different places. The activity of the schools—Gerhardsson uses the term "college" for the *bet midrash*—was of primary importance. In this context trained specialists performed transmission programmatically and methodically. It is difficult, Gerhardsson maintains, to envision any alternative kind of oral transmission besides this regular and disciplined one. While transmission in a sense took place at all times and in all places and religious tradition had a broad basis among the people as a whole, it was the specialists who carried the tradition to the religious communities.

The transmission of the Oral Torah is, according to Gerhardsson, similar to the transmission of the Written Torah. The conviction that oral transmission was strongly stamped by the written word is the reason why he devotes a chapter to the Written Torah before turning to the Oral Torah. The Oral Torah interpreted, particularized, complemented, and occasionally modified the Written Torah, but both were carried and handed on by means of memorization. The only important difference was that in one case the text was a written text and must be learned from reading, while in the other case it was an oral text to be learned by repeating what the teacher said.

The teacher and his students memorized and interpreted the Torah in separate yet closely related activities. While Gerhardsson emphasizes that these two activities were held apart to the extent that memorization always should precede interpretation, he also refers to the critique of some rabbis against those traditionists who only memorized and failed to penetrate to the meaning of the tradition and to implement it in their lives. In the advanced college the memorized texts provided only elementary knowledge to be used in exposition and dialectical techniques. Occasionally the traditionists' text became the object of negative criticism, especially when it conflicted with the received Mishnah. The transmission of the Oral Torah took place on all school levels in such a way that the teacher or traditionist equipped the students with the oral text by repeating it several times and required them to interpret it. Knowledge of the Oral Torah was not complete, according to Gerhardsson, until it had been interpreted adequately, even if in a most rudimentary fashion. He spends considerable effort to show how the rather mechanical Mishnah teaching was carried out and memorized, being fully aware of its limited focus. But his frequent references to the interplay between solidity and flexibility in the transmission of the Oral Torah illustrate his sensitivity to the close relationship and interplay between that which was transmitted and current discussions and needs.

Gerhardsson divides the Oral Torah roughly into the sayings tradition and the narrative tradition. After describing in detail the techniques of memorization, he elaborates how additional inspired words and episodes concerning the deeds of the rabbis were introduced into the more rigid process of transmission and themselves became the object of transmission. Brief halakic statements were memorized together with new sayings, so that the same tradition could be carried forward in different forms. Haggadic material contained additional sayings which the teacher wished to place among other texts that the students had in mind.

The students' reverence for the teacher and their ambition to retain his every word led to the incorporation of further sayings into the tradition, as time went by including even relatively free and peripheral ones. The sayings were, according to Gerhardsson, often deduced from the narrative tradition. Just as all traditions in antiquity were tendentious, the narrative tradition in rabbinic Judaism had the intention of preserving and spreading the Torah in response to multiple life situations. Teachers and students knew that the Torah was learned by imitation. The narrative tradition, with the exception of the imaginative, legendary haggadah type, was mainly formulated when the eyewitnesses at a later point needed to illustrate a particular question that was posed to them. Gerhardsson's view of tradition and transmission thus reckons with and incorporates deliberate efforts to relate dynamically that which was memorized to new situations and questions.

The second part of the book deals with the delivery of the gospel tradition in early Christianity. Although employing insights from his study of rabbinic Judaism, Gerhardsson is cautious not to impose rigidly the methods of the rabbis on early Christianity. Instead of moving from rabbinic or other theories concerning the mnemonic character of tradition to early Christianity, he takes the testimony of the early Fathers as his point of departure.

The Fathers had a traditional conception of the origin of the Gospels and attached great importance to discipleship and memory. They were vague as to the literary category of the Gospels. The writing down of them was an emergency measure, Gerhardsson argues, reflecting the ancient skepticism toward the written word. The somewhat confusing way in which they use the Gospels shows also, according to Gerhardsson, that these writings were regarded as "Holy Word" or Oral (messianic) Torah. The history of the Gospel texts as it can be traced back to about 200 C.E. and the use of the codex form in the church already at the beginning of the second century corroborate the possibility that the literature was derived from notebooks and oral in character. Jesus' disciples came from Pharisaic circles which stressed the distinction between Oral and Written Torah, and they began to put together collections on the basis of oral tradition and with the help of written notes. Up to about the middle of the second century, the Gospels were regarded as sacred tradition rather than Scripture, and they functioned predominantly orally. The advanced discussions about Christian doctrine at this time indicate that gospel texts and tradition were transmitted mainly orally and from memory and with a sense of individual specificity.

Gerhardsson then moves to the Lukan author. Although apologetic and tendentious, the Lukan view is that of a doctrinal center in

Jerusalem, where the apostles bear witness to and teach the word of the Lord entrusted to them as its servants. The word of the Lord is kerygma as well as didache and entails everything that Christ did and taught and everything that happened to him. It is, according to Luke, midrashically expounded like the Oral Torah of the Jews.

The Lukan view is not to be equated with what emerged from Gerhardsson's study of rabbinic Judaism in the first part of the book. There are several similarities, but Gerhardsson insists that early Christianity was in essence Christocentric rather than Torah-centric. Just as the Lukan Jesus practices midrashic exegesis, so the apostles proceed either from texts in the Scriptures by way of christological interpretation or from the message of Christ as a means of examining the Scriptures.

The next main witness to the delivery of the gospel tradition in early Christianity is Paul. Gerhardsson depicts a situation which in broad terms agrees with the one in Acts. The tradition was a matter restricted to apostles and apostolic authority. Defending his apostolate as a parallel to Peter's, Paul claimed only to have received the elementary mission message—the kerygma—directly from the risen Lord and acknowledged the unity of the church and Jerusalem as its doctrinal center. His apostolic teaching—the didache—was drawn from the Scriptures and the authoritative tradition that he had received from the Jerusalem apostles.

Being a former Pharisee, Paul broke with the tradition of the elders and transmitted and interpreted tradition from and about the Lord as an authority not unlike that of the Oral Torah. He did so with power and spiritual insight. In a sense, all he said, wrote, and did in relation to a congregation was transmission. He was himself an apostolic doctrinal authority who embodied his teaching and produced his own doctrinal, ethical, and ecclesiastical "Talmud" on the basis of the Scriptures and the received "Mishnah" from and about the Lord. This "Mishnah" was the gospel tradition. There is evidence, Gerhardsson maintains, that it consisted of sections recorded in the Gospels and some oral or written equivalent of one of them.

Gerhardsson returns to the question of the origins of the gospel tradition. They are to be found in the torah of Jesus himself. To his early followers Jesus was indeed much more than an earthly teacher. Gerhardsson believes the high Christology among the early followers to have some connection with Jesus' own understanding of his ministry and with his position and person. But what was decisive, in Gerhardsson's view, was Jesus' attitude toward the Jewish Torah as it was reflected in his words and deeds. His teaching was deliberately stamped on the memories of the disciples. A comparison with the contemporary, historical situation suggests that he required them to memorize it.

In the early church the collegium of apostles in Jerusalem presented their message as eyewitness accounts and in connection with the Scriptures. The memorization which they practiced and taught to others was facilitated by the grouping of sayings in memorable units. In answer to questions posed to them they formulated narratives about Jesus' actions on the basis of what they remembered. There existed thus a distinct activity of transmission. Gerhardsson realizes that the tradition was used in many situations, but focuses on a distinct *Sitz im Leben* of transmission in which the traditionist or teacher passed on the material to the students by means of repetition followed by interpretation.

In the last paragraphs of his dissertation, Gerhardsson incorporates into his thesis the feature of variations between different parallel traditions. Although this discussion has rarely been noticed in the subsequent debate of his view, he explicitly points to the possibility that Jesus delivered the same teaching in varying form and that the gospel material belongs to the flexible haggadic category. He also mentions the existence of adaptations, complicated processes of translation, faulty memorization, and redaction. In his study he paid much attention to the technical aspects of transmission in separate and distinct activities, but he did so with full awareness of the intricate interplay between solidity and flexibility and of the various uses to which the transmitted material had been put.

It is of no little significance that Gerhardsson's magnum opus was purposely directed toward the paradigms of the most influential scholarly agenda of the time. In the late 1950s and early 1960s form criticism was, by and large, firmly established and exceedingly influential among biblical scholars. It had, as we saw, dissolved the intricate ancient relationship between memory and tradition and paid only scant attention—mostly in the work of Dibelius—to the mnemonic dimension of religious life and communication. Tradition was not negotiated mnemonically, form criticism implied, but arose and grew accumulatively through the shaping and development of styles and forms used almost entirely in the various activities of the creative religious community. This was also the time when redaction criticism became an important analytical tool in New Testament studies. It shared with form criticism the conviction that tradition reflects primarily the contemporary historical situation out of which it arose and within which it was handed down. The traditions were seen as sources that had been accumulated and sifted in various literary processes, finally to be redacted so as to serve the theologies of the gospel communities.

Gerhardsson did not entirely reject form and redaction criticism—he felt indebted to the early form critics. But he modified their work in significant ways. He turned the attention to the profoundly mnemonic character of written and, above all, oral tradition and introduced neglected diachronic aspects into the form-critical program. This he did fully aware that scholarly work shares in the even broader prevailing cultural currencies of its time. His keen awareness of how memory in his own time had been replaced effectively by books leading to "the dethronement of memory" in the culture of modern society[7] is testimony to the wide-ranging scope of his work.

Explanation and Elaboration

Gerhardsson's dissertation met with different reactions. The form critics were skeptical; others were enthusiastic.[8] Few books have received more diverse comments. He explained and elaborated his view in several later publications and gradually established his position in biblical scholarship. His contributions after his dissertation span over more than forty years. From his heated debate in 1964 with Morton Smith, who had dismissed his dissertation, to his critical remarks in 2004 and 2005 on James Dunn's reading of his work,[9] he continually felt the need to clarify the essential elements of his view and clear up misunderstandings.

After defending the conviction that Jesus appointed twelve disciples to be his authorized messengers,[10] he began to apply the insights from his dissertation to different sorts of material. His first study to this end from 1966—the fascicle was completed in 1963—was an attempt to investigate how learned Christians had elaborated the Jesus tradition in the haggadic Midrash concerning the testing of God's son.[11] Here he discovered the crucial importance of the triadic Shema in Deuteronomy 6:4-5 as a means of understanding how the Pharisaic followers of Jesus worked with the Scriptures and the tradition. He subsequently examined a number of New Testament passages in support of his argument that this ancient creed had been an influential factor in the making of these texts.[12] In yet other studies he dealt extensively with the parables—calling them "narrative meshalim"—and the mighty acts of Jesus in Matthew,[13] repeatedly explicating how the basic essentials of what he stated in his dissertation are to be implemented in detailed work on the gospel tradition. Less attention was paid to the Jesus sayings—the "aphoristic meshalim." Gerhardsson's interests have been wide ranging. He was professor of exegetical theology at Lund University, Sweden, from 1965 to 1992, and dealt extensively also with central theological issues.[14] But he has established his position in international scholarship first and foremost as the pioneering expert on tradition and transmission in early Christianity. Three essays in particular, now collected in *The Reliability of the Gospel Tradition*,[15] point to the elaboration of ideas that he had initially presented in his dissertation.

The essay entitled "The Origins of the Gospel Tradition" is based on a lecture given to students of theology in spring 1976 in Holzhausen, Germany.[16] Form criticism was still the major paradigm, although decreasing in influence. The German audience was thoroughly trained in its theories.[17] Gerhardsson's task was to discuss the origins and earliest history of the gospel tradition, not to trace the changes that he believed occurred in the Jesus traditions. To this end he criticized the form-critical scholars for not being sufficiently historical and for neglecting the question how the tradition was transmitted in the Jewish milieu of Palestine and elsewhere at the time of the New Testament.

In this lecture he reflects more fully than previously on the gospel tradition. The Gospels are not to be equated with the Jesus tradition that Paul passed on, and they are not copies of a complete and mechanically unaltered recording of Jesus' teaching and eyewitness reports. They betray, however, a genuine interest in the past which is detectable in the earliest pre-Easter material. The early Christians preserved the memory of a distinct segment of the past on which they relied for support in the present. This memory carried individual traits and linked up and interacted with various individual memories. The form-critical approach and the parallels from folklore do not, in Gerhardsson's view, pay sufficient attention to the rather short period of time between the death of Jesus and the writing of the Gospels and to the limited number of people involved in the early Christian movement.

One of the most perplexing aspects of the Jesus tradition, according to Gerhardsson, is its focus on the singular personality and teaching of one teacher. This suggests to him that it arose and was preserved independently of various situations of preaching, teaching, and admonition. The tradition commences at a point where Jesus presented meshalim which were memorized, discussed, and interpreted by the disciples. Expanded sayings traditions with brief narrative components were added to the memorized material. The narrative material proper is diverse but has its roots in the important deeds which Jesus performed in order to supplement his sayings.

The subsequent transition from oral tradition—Gerhardsson mentions also private notes—to writing was a drawn-out process. He reckons with a reciprocal interplay between the two media. The key feature of the development was the intricate and deliberate interaction between technical transmission and editorial alteration. The interpretive adaptations were not mechanical exercises unrelated to the needs of the early Christians, but had to do with the diversified and yet unified search for "the whole truth."

The second essay, "The Path of the Gospel Tradition," goes back to a lecture delivered in 1982 in Tübingen, Germany, at an international symposium on the theme "The Gospel and the Gospels."[18] In this contribution Gerhardsson specifies a number of points he had made in his earlier work. The notion of Jesus as the one and only teacher and the idea that the Jesus tradition was an independent and autonomous entity from the beginning form the basis of the article. To Gerhardsson this means, firstly, that the tradition manifests itself only in special documents which probably reflect special tradition; secondly, that it deals only with Jesus; and thirdly, that Jesus' disciples could not supplement his teaching with contributions under their own names. From the very start and throughout the entire period up until the writing of the Gospels, the Jesus tradition was treated as an autonomous tradition.

This suggests, moreover, that the form-critical idea of a close correlation between the text type and its *Sitz im Leben* is inadequate. Early Christianity was not a primitive and original movement—Gerhardsson again expresses his skepticism toward the use of parallels from folklore and popular tradition. All the forms were already established, he notices. Texts could be formulated without recourse to the way in which the form of the text originally may have arisen, and various genres could be employed side by side in the same setting.

A further corollary of the idea that transmission was an independent act is that texts proper were actively employed in worship services, perhaps catechetical instruction, and in regular study. The tradition is a text, he stresses, and it is important to realize that its preservation was separated from its use. In recurring situations the church did not need to have the entire preserved text read to the congregation, but only the decisive point of the text. As to oral transmission, which was more diverse than written transmission, Gerhardsson rehearses the three contexts, especially the professional one. He also expresses his regret that he did not previously discuss in greater detail the changes that could take place and defends himself against the charge of having made a simple comparison between the educational system of the rabbis and the activity of Jesus and early Christianity.

Jesus was the sole authority also in another sense. For Gerhardsson the synoptic tradition from Jesus to the evangelists cannot be adequately comprehended if we lose sight of the fact that Jesus was a unique figure whose crucifixion, resurrection, and salvific presence were central to his followers. Jesus' high self-consciousness and the exalted image of him were decisive motives for the transmission from the very beginning and gave the Jesus tradition a special dignity and uniqueness up to the time of the evangelists and further on.

From this perspective it will be possible to study the path of the gospel tradition. The sayings tradition consists of artful texts bearing the marks of poetic and narrative-technical skill. The speaker created a proper text which could be passed on and preserved. To a limited extent sayings were omitted, added, and changed in a prophetic spirit or in a more rational-didactic manner, but the archaic character of the Q material and the parables suggest that they were transmitted in fixed wording and with minimal editing.

The narrative traditions, which by necessity originated at further distance from Jesus, were open to more changes and influences from the kerygma and the post-Easter situation, but they were not entirely fluid. The narrative text was also handed down in memorized form and the changes were deliberate ones made by authoritative individuals for the purpose of clarification. Gerhardsson here realizes the censoring role of the social context and uses it to limit the range of creativity and additions. The group stimulated discussion but also functioned as an instrument of social control. For Gerhardsson this means that without its consent, no new or variegated form of a text would be generated. As to the passion story, he is skeptical about the idea that the narrative sequence in Mark 8–16 formed a primitive gospel already before 37 C.E. and indicates his view that it started as a Christian response to the official death sentence upon Jesus.

Not unlike his dissertation, the entire article undermines several central tenets of classical form criticism. As a sequence to his earlier discussion, he points out more clearly than before ten points at which form criticism is to be questioned:

(1) the distinction between Palestinian and Hellenistic;
(2) the idea of text form as a sociological fact;
(3) the link between text form and *Sitz im Leben*;
(4) the search for the pure form;
(5) the view of Jesus and early Christianity as unliterary;
(6) the idea of "first tradition then redaction";
(7) the separation of narrative entities in the tradition;
(8) the irrelevance of the traditionists;
(9) the neglect of written tradition; and
(10) the achievement of Mark.

Gerhardsson's latest major contribution to the investigation of memory and tradition is entitled "The Gospel Tradition" and was first presented in 1984 at a symposium in Jerusalem discussing the genetic relations between the Gospels.[19] At this time new notions of orality and textuality had recently entered the scholarly discussion and challenged the old discipline of form criticism from a fresh angle. Gerhardsson was aware of this debate.

His assignment was to discuss the oral prehistory of the Gospels. To this end he developed an approach to tradition in a more discursive way than previously. His model distinguishes between the inner and the outer tradition. The former are those fundamental convictions and intentions that express themselves in fellowship with others and generate tradition for the next generation. The latter is the outward form of the inner tradition. It externalizes itself in four ways: in verbal tradition using language; in behavioral tradition linking to the mechanism of imitation; in institutional tradition where fellowships immediately and gradually establish coherence and continuity; and in material tradition using inanimate objects.

Ideally the four interact, but often people with an insider perspective—those *intra muros*, in Gerhardsson's terminology—accept only parts of the outer tradition and people at the outside—those *extra muros*—encounter aspects of the inner tradition without comprehending their significance. The manifestations of the outer tradition depend themselves on rules of convention and as time goes by they tend to be used independently of the inner tradition. When the tradition is essentially new and permeates the existing realities, it may be labeled programmatic tradition. When it is old but still exists without being consciously accepted or rejected, it may be called de facto tradition. The programmatic tradition is usually the one receiving attention, while the de facto tradition occurs as old values and patterns of behavior unconsciously influencing the present situation.

This model can be applied both to the Torah-centric, ancient Jewish tradition and the Christ-centered, early Christian tradition. Gerhardsson gives a brief sketch of these traditions, but his focus is on the verbal aspect of early Christian tradition. He explicates his view on orality and textuality, mainly in discussion with Werner Kelber.[20]

While orality closely interfaces with the written word, because the written word was intended for the ear, the culture in which Jesus lived was no preliterary society, he points out, and the Jesus tradition was never "pure" orality. The relationship between oral and written transmission was more complex than appears from comparisons with oral cultures. Scholars have to take into account how written texts, especially those from the Scriptures, constantly interacted with oral performance in the ancient Jewish milieu closest to early Christianity. The appearance of both fixed and flexible elements in tradition runs across the division between written and oral material. Both could be flexible and both could be fixed. Free oral narration was a rare thing in the Jesus tradition. Jesus was a teacher and prophet, not a popular performer, and most narratives about him are terse and condensed to the extent that they must have been texts also at their oral stage. This does not mean that transmission was passive and without social engagement. Already in his dissertation, Gerhardsson points out, he wanted to take seriously the influence of the social life of even the most academic halakists among the rabbis.

Commenting on the origin of the gospel tradition, Gerhardsson pays less attention than previously to the Jewish Torah in Jesus' teaching and stresses, in accordance with his model, that early Christian tradition in the proper sense did not start until Jesus appeared publicly. The verbal gospel tradition originated when Jesus began to teach and gained disciples who accepted his message. The words were artistically formulated meshalim which were memorized, interpreted, and expounded in roughly the same way as Jewish meshalim. The mighty deeds of Jesus were mostly put into pointed narrative form after his departure. These narratives were memorized after the pattern of the sayings tradition. The Passion Narrative is a coherent chain of episodes and arose as Jesus' followers needed an explanation for the death of Jesus other than the official one.

Gerhardsson realizes that a number of questions remain to be answered before we have a clear picture of how the gospel tradition became text. The creation, reshaping, and compilation of texts remain to him enigmatic issues. He believes it will be possible to isolate the creation of a text from its various uses, but prefers to pose a number of questions as to how this technically came about. He is convinced, however, that the gradual synthesizing of the text material was a natural outcome of its intraecclesiastical character. His model of interaction between verbal and behavioral tradition and institutional tradition precludes the idea of a pluriform and multidirectional process. Institutional structures set the borders; they reduced the pluralism of traditions and increased the need for summaries and textual organization. The writing down itself might at first have been accidental—local circumstances or personal qualities of the first evangelist might have caused it—but was later occasioned by the need to preserve what the first eyewitnesses had conveyed, by the ongoing institutionalization, and by the fall of Jerusalem and the destruction of the temple.

At the end, the four evangelists created a rather unified and harmonious picture. There was, according to Gerhardsson, no question of one Gospel criticizing or intending to replace the other. The polyphonic—or tetraphonic—gospel is not a secondary fact but rather a manifestation of the four written Gospels being rooted in the same tradition. Gerhardsson relies again on his model and the institutional factors of the church. The oral gospel tradition *intra muros ecclesiae* was a plurality with a considerable homogeneity, and it remained so when it was put into writing.

The Present Scholarly Debate

Gerhardsson's long academic career, distinguished by a steadfast pursuit, elaboration, and explication of his understanding of the early Christian tradition, carries certain elements that recur largely unaltered and others that have been gradually clarified and developed. Throughout his writings, from his dissertation and onwards, he has remained convinced of the crucial importance of memory and memorization as the basic medium of preserving oral and written tradition from the past. His sensitivity to the mnemonic dimension of what was said and done by Jesus and of the gospel tradition has been the central core of his work in the area of tradition and transmission. Among his principal objectives also are the effort to modify form criticism, to point to the didactic dimension of Jesus' activity as well as to the learned and separate setting of transmission, and to focus on oral tradition and the close interaction between the oral Jesus tradition and the scribal activities of the transmitters. Memory and memorization in early Christianity were in his view deliberate and sophisticated acts of preservation and cannot be equated with models of mnemonic performances of a more popular kind.

Other ideas, only briefly mentioned in his dissertation, were elaborated in later publications. The readers whose knowledge of his ideas is limited to *Memory and Manuscript* might notice his references to both the solidity and the flexibility of the transmission of the Oral Torah, but they miss the studies which show in detail how he envisions the creative work of the learned Christian specialists to have taken place. It was after the publication of the dissertation that he discovered the extraordinary role that the Shema played in that creative work, and it was only later that he illustrated how the Shema influenced the formation of a number of texts in the New Testament.

Of special importance is his gradual development of the notion of tradition. From being mainly interested in the sayings tradition—and to some extent the behavioral tradition—he elaborated a more multifaceted view informed by insights from other disciplines. The sayings tradition with its relation to memory and memorization is still his primary interest, but other ranges of traditional phenomena are brought into his model and indicate an attempt to come to grips with the broader ramification of memory and tradition within the early ecclesiastical setting. The insider and outsider perspective on tradition relates to ecclesiastical concerns which determine the development of tradition.

Other matters remain, in Gerhardsson's own view, unexplored tasks for future investigations. He mentions several times the significance of the broader educational milieu of the Greco-Roman environment and considers it imperative to compare the outcome of such a study with the educational techniques of the rabbis. He is indeed aware that early Christianity cannot be seen only with the lenses of rabbinic Judaism and welcomes a larger perspective. Furthermore, he insists that the tradition and redaction of Jesus' aphoristic meshalim still remains to be investigated in detail. In his own work he focused on the mighty acts and the narrative meshalim. Moreover, his most recent major contribution spells out the need to specify exactly the ways in which the gospel tradition became text and was intraecclesiastically synthesized. The model of tradition that he presents there indicates—as did his previous studies—that he envisions significant overlappings between oral and scribal practices and that vigorous synthesizing factors were at play in early Christianity. Future investigations will have to work out the details of these areas and assess the possibility of implementing his perspective.

Recent scholarship has illuminated areas which touch significantly on essential aspects of Gerhardsson's most important ideas. This is a development that has cast his work into new light. Their implications have been discussed over the years with increasing recognition of the abiding relevance of his theses.[21] Research since the turn of the century has moved the debate further and calls for a fresh and broader assessment.

One of the crucial aspects of Gerhardsson's entire work is its critical discussion of the form-critical paradigm. Today form criticism is being challenged on several—if not all—of its basic tenets. Scholars have abandoned it or modified it into an analysis which looks at forms and literary types from the perspective of mnemonic signs or textual effect rather than their one-dimensional correlation with the *Sitz im Leben* of the early church. To some, it has developed into rhetorical criticism, bringing to light the communicative and persuasive dimension of tradition and text as well as the pragmatic force of mnemonic training in the Greco-Roman environment. Consequently, the notions of memory and tradition have undergone changes and elaboration. New Testament scholars today pay attention to memory as a psychological and social phenomenon—areas which always interested Gerhardsson. This includes considerations of the ranges of mnemonic negotiations and of the complex features and functions of memory. Recently the Jesus tradition has also been placed within a more developed sociological framework, and it has been reexamined with a view toward its complex oral and scribal textures and performances. Occasionally this research stands in contrast to Gerhardsson's conviction of the highly sophisticated and educational level of early Christian tradition and transmission. Furthermore, renewed interest in the ancient Greco-Roman school system has not only focused on the rhetorical training of the students, but also already brought to light the importance of teaching and transmission in philosophical and other schools, broadening Gerhardsson's focus on the special educational system of the rabbis by including a number of features that he himself could not fully develop. In addition, recent research in rabbinic Judaism and its Oral Torah widely acknowledges the importance of his pioneering contribution in this area. By introducing various notions of orality and scribality into the study of the Oral Torah and by discussing multiple forms of memorizations, scholarship has profiled the distinguishing features of rabbinic Judaism in relation to other forms of Judaism and the Greco-Roman environment. These are all developments that point to the scholarly relevance of Gerhardsson's ideas.

Thus the reconceptualization of form criticism, rhetorical criticism, notions of memory and of tradition, and the educational situation in the Greco-Roman world and in rabbinic Judaism are but some crucial areas in today's scholarly landscape that shed fresh light on Gerhardsson's contribution. His pioneering and lifelong work in the area of memory and tradition is still one of the most prolific statements in the field and deserves serious scrutiny from the perspective of new insights. In the chapters that follow experts in each of these areas will explore the manifold implications of his work.

Chapter 1

Form Criticism

Christopher Tuckett

Birger Gerhardsson is well known throughout the international New Testament scholarly world as a scholar of the highest repute. He has been accorded many honors, including being elected president of the international *Studiorum Novi Testamenti Societas* in 1990.[1] His major scholarly work, *Memory and Manuscript*, was first published in 1961,[2] and since then he has published a series of other books, articles, and essays over a long and productive scholarly career. His *Memory and Manuscript* constituted a highly significant challenge to many of the presuppositions and arguments of the discipline of form criticism, which was at the time a (if not the) dominant approach in gospel studies. In 1961, Gerhardsson was something of a lone voice (and as such a highly courageous one) in challenging many of the accepted scholarly norms of the day. But certainly since 1961, many other critical voices have been raised against several key aspects of the form-critical enterprise, and Gerhardsson's work was in a real sense seminal in opening up and generating debate and discussion in important areas. Gerhardsson himself has also returned to many of the subjects raised in his early book, especially as they relate to the alleged "results" of form criticism, in his further publications.[3] In this essay, I consider Gerhardsson's significant contributions in the discussions about form criticism and related topics, and then seek to analyze some other aspects of the discipline of form criticism, taking into account too Gerhardsson's own counterproposals to some of the suggestions put forward by the form critics.

THE WORK OF BIRGER GERHARDSSON

The discipline known as "form criticism" is a multifaceted enterprise with a number of different—and distinguishable—aspects. Over the years it has generated a great deal of discussion and debate, and perhaps no one has done more to invigorate and enrich that debate than Birger Gerhardsson. Gerhardsson's early magnum opus, *Memory and Manuscript*, makes it clear in the introduction that his study arises in a significant way out of the work of the early form critics (Martin Dibelius, Rudolf Bultmann) and, whilst acknowledging the great importance of their work, raises some critical questions about key aspects of the whole enterprise of form criticism.[4] Gerhardsson's great contribution has been above all to force New Testament scholars, and especially New Testament form critics, to think about the concrete process of transmission of traditions in early Christianity and especially of traditions about Jesus.[5] In order to appreciate Gerhardsson's contributions fully, we should first consider briefly some aspects of the work of the early form critics to which, in part at least, Gerhardsson's work provides an important response and possible correction.

The classic works of form criticism have generally been seen in the contributions of three German scholars—Karl Ludwig Schmidt, Martin Dibelius, and Rudolf Bultmann—working in the early part of the twentieth century.[6] As developed especially in the work of Dibelius and Bultmann, the main aim of form criticism as applied to the Gospels is to attempt to reach behind the present form of the Gospel stories about Jesus to identify the way(s) in which the traditions about Jesus circulated prior to the writing of our present Gospel accounts. In addition, the attempt is made to deduce how far the material might go back in the history of the tradition, in particular whether and how far it could confidently be traced back to Jesus himself.[7] In this approach, a number of basic assumptions were, and are, made.

The first of these is that prior to the writing of the Gospels the tradition consisted of individual separable units (stories, sayings, etc.), which may have been separated from each other at an earlier stage. The task of joining them all together into a connected whole was generally that of the evangelists themselves. This was above all the main thesis in the work of Schmidt. More significant, and certainly more debatable, were then the further moves made by Dibelius and Bultmann. Both went on to argue that many of the individual units of the tradition showed significant similarity with each other in terms of their structure or "form." Another fundamental assumption, taken almost as axiomatic, was that the traditions about Jesus were preserved and handed on because they were found to be useful in the ongoing lives of the early Christian communities (teaching, preaching, debates with opponents, cultic activities, etc.) and indeed were so used in those contexts. Further, the forms in which the traditions were cast reflected that use. Thus the individual stories and units of the tradition could be classified in relation to their form; then, on the basis of these forms, one could infer where and how the individual traditions might have been used in the early church, what the "setting in (the) life" of the early church was. The German phrase for this was *Sitz im Leben*, a phrase which has become as much part of English language scholarship as of German.[8]

It is at this point that Gerhardsson's work sets an important question mark against some of these fundamental assumptions of the work of the form critics. He has questioned whether the *Sitz im Leben* for the preservation and handing on of the Jesus tradition is really to be located in the ongoing lives of early Christians in the way the early form critics had suggested. In particular, Gerhardsson has appealed to the evidence we have from other early Christian writings. He refers, for example, to the letter of James, arguing that here we see a Christian writer engaged in paraenetical exhortations to other Christians, but the "form" employed is not to cite Jesus traditions. Traditions (of Jesus and/or others) may be alluded to, but the form is that of a writer speaking in his or her own name.[9] A similar phenomenon is found across the spectrum of early Christianity: for example, the writer of 1 John may well know Jesus traditions (probably the Gospel of John) but never quotes any traditions of this nature as such; the author of Acts (i.e., Luke) clearly knows large amounts of Jesus tradition but does not have his Christian preachers in Acts refer to it;[10] Paul knows Jesus traditions but rarely cites them as such. Gerhardsson thus refers to the phenomenon of what he calls the "isolation" of the Jesus tradition in early Christianity[11] and argues then that the primary *Sitz im Leben* for the preservation and handing on of Jesus tradition was not Christian paraenetical instruction: we see such activity taking place, we do not see Jesus tradition being developed or (explicitly) used.[12]

Gerhardsson's point about the absence of explicit references to Jesus traditions as *Jesus* traditions in early Christian teaching and paraenesis, is undoubtedly important, though perhaps one or two caveats are needed as well. Gerhardsson is careful not to overstate his case and he talks of the "primary" or "basic" *Sitz im Leben*.[13] He himself acknowledges that Jesus tradition was used in early Christian paraenetical instruction and elsewhere:[14] the difficulty is that, if it is, most of it is by way of allusion, and the very nature of nonexplicit allusions (rather than explicit quotations) is that it is not clear if such allusions are intended or not. Thus when Paul, say, appears to echo the teaching on Jesus (e.g., on blessing one's persecutors in Rom 12:14, cf. Matt 5:44), it is not clear whether he is giving his own teaching (which happens to coincide with teachings attributed to Jesus in the gospel traditions) or he is deliberately alluding to the teaching of Jesus (and if so whether he is thereby also claiming additional authority for what he says). The same problems recur at the level of Paul's readers/hearers: did they take what Paul said as Paul's own words, or did they recognize possible allusions to Jesus traditions? And if the allusions were intended and recognized, it is possible to argue that they virtually have the force of quotations, and Paul (and his readers) did not need to spell this out because it was so well known and could be taken as read.[15] So too one may note that, although explicit references to Jesus traditions in the form of quotations are rare in other early Christian writings, they are not entirely absent, at least in Pauline letters (cf. 1 Cor 7:9; possibly Rom 14:14).

Gerhardsson's argument here does however place a radical question mark against the assumption of the form critics that the *Sitz im Leben* of a tradition could be deduced from its "form," with a range of different forms in the Jesus tradition identified and assigned to different *Sitze im Leben*. In effect, Gerhardsson's argument is to claim that the very nature of Jesus traditions that are presented explicitly as traditions about Jesus (i.e., material explicitly ascribed to Jesus, rather than material which may happen to echo Jesus tradition but not explicitly claimed to be such) is the one relevant "form" in this discussion, and hence the transmission of (explicit) Jesus tradition has its own individual *Sitz im Leben* in the life of the early church. The Jesus tradition must then have been preserved and handed on in a quite separate *Sitz im Leben* from other early Christian activity.

Gerhardsson's own more positive suggestions about what the nature of such a *Sitz im Leben* might be derive in part from considerations of the social and religious context in Judaism within which the early Christian movement started and developed; in part, too, they derive from the evidence of early Christian sources outside the Gospels.[16] In particular, Gerhardsson argues that, whatever differences there may have been between the early Christians and their Jewish contemporaries in relation to their more "theological" claims and in relation to the nature and content of their traditions, there must have been common features of the broader culture which may cast light on the early Christians' traditioning process. Judaism clearly had a firm process for handing on traditions, both for the scriptural traditions themselves and for (later) rabbinic traditions giving the teachings and decisions of, as well as stories about, significant teachers and figures. While in no way denying the many distinctive features of Christian claims about Jesus and Christian tradition, vis-à-vis Judaism, Gerhardsson thus suggests that the process of transmitting the Jesus tradition may have been akin to that of the handing on of rabbinic traditions and Jewish scripture itself. Just as within Judaism the tradition was memorized and attempts were made to ensure that the tradition was handed on faithfully and accurately, the same process of memorization may have characterized the process of handing on the Jesus tradition. Further, this process was unlikely to have been the work of "'the' community," considered as some amorphous, undefined entity.[17] Rather, it is more likely to have been carefully controlled by a group of specific leaders or individuals within the community. In particular, Gerhardsson argues that the Twelve in Jerusalem may have acted as such a body, concerned (at least in part) to preserve the wording of the tradition faithfully. Thus built into the model is the presumption that a significant part of the aim (and perhaps the result)[18] of the traditioning process within early Christianity was to preserve the reliability of the tradition. Whether fairly or unfairly, the work of (certainly some of) the early form critics was regarded with considerable suspicion because it seemed to question the authenticity of the significant parts of the gospel tradition. The model of the (anonymous, amorphous) "community" (singular), which "used" the Jesus tradition, adapted it for its own purposes, and possibly at times created tradition for such purposes as well, is thus radically questioned in Gerhardsson's important proposals.

Gerhardsson's suggestions have in turn been the subject of critical analysis and evaluation.[19] His use of evidence from later rabbinic materials within Judaism to seek to illuminate earlier (pre-70) Christian developments formed the basis for a sharp (and perhaps intemperate) attack by Morton Smith, effectively accusing Gerhardsson of anachronism in his whole approach.[20] Gerhardsson responded in his short 1964 book,

Tradition and Transmission, making very clear just what he was claiming by way of continuity and similarity between the early Christian movement and (at times later) Jewish evidence and what he was not: hence the issue is primarily about the concrete process of handing on traditions, not necessarily the contents of the traditions themselves.[21]

Other critiques have focused on the way in which, it is claimed, the model proposed does not fit very well with the great variety and variation in the Jesus tradition (as evidenced perhaps in the different Gospels themselves).[22] Gerhardsson himself has never denied that variations in the Jesus tradition exist.[23] The issue is perhaps the nature and extent of such differences and changes. At times, Gerhardsson claims that these changes involve (primarily, perhaps only) "interpretive adaptations,"[24] and "the Gospels essentially provide us with a historically reliable picture of Jesus of Nazareth."[25] Certainly the general thrust of Gerhardsson's model has been taken (at least by others) to be one which almost inherently involves a quasi-guarantee of the reliability and authenticity of the traditions about Jesus in the Gospels. Whether this is quite fair to Gerhardsson is debatable;[26] but it is probably true to say that his model is more focused on "conserving" the tradition (and hence perhaps in one way "conservative") than the form-critical model of Christians creatively adapting (and possibly creating) traditions. Nevertheless, whatever the "primary" setting for the transmission of Jesus traditions, it is still clear that this tradition was used—and adapted—by (some) early Christians, at least to an extent. At the literary level, this is surely clear in the way Matthew and Luke have used and adapted Mark, at times quite extensively and radically.[27] At the pre-Markan stage, it is hard to deny this was happening at some points.[28] And in various passages where we have parallel versions of traditions, the same can be seen to have almost certainly been happening in the tradition prior to our Gospels.[29] The issue is then not a clear-cut either/or, but rather the degree to which this adaptation happened.

Gerhardsson's suggestion of the existence of a "college" based at Jerusalem under the leadership of the Twelve, seeking to hand on the Jesus tradition with great fidelity (and/or working on any "adaptations" being worked into the tradition), has also been seen by some as questionable. It seems more akin to Luke's presentation in Acts, but how far this picture reflects historical reality is less certain.[30] Further, the range of variation that one sees in the forms of the tradition which we now have (in our Gospels as well as sometimes in Paul's letters: cf. n. 29 above) also seems difficult to square with the model of a relatively centralized activity by a single group.

In sum, Gerhardsson's discussions and debates with the earlier form critics have raised some important question marks against key aspects of the whole form-critical enterprise, even if some of his own counterproposals have not been universally accepted and have raised (in the minds of others) other questions.

Form Criticism—Other Aspects

What though of the other aspects of form criticism? Over the years, form criticism has generated much debate and discussion.[31] Both the presuppositions and the methodology of the earlier form critics have often been analyzed and at times criticized. Some of these criticisms serve to reinforce the critiques of Gerhardsson's; some approach aspects of form criticism from a slightly different angle but still raise similar questions about some of the underlying presuppositions concerned.

As stated at the start of this essay, form criticism has a number of different and distinguishable aspects. As we have seen, an integral part of the discipline is to seek to determine the way(s) in which a tradition may have been used in the early Christian communities, perhaps by correlating this with its form. However, form criticism, certainly as practiced by scholars such as Dibelius and Bultmann, has always claimed a wider remit for itself. This may be reflected better by the German noun *Formgeschichte* (for which the English term "form criticism" has established itself as the standard translation equivalent). The German compound noun *Formgeschichte* (combining *Form* and *Geschichte*) might be more literally translated as "form history"; certainly the aspect of tracing out the possible history of the development of traditions in the New Testament has always been an integral part of *Formgeschichte*, at least for many (German) form critics. Thus scholars such as Bultmann and Dibelius sought to make claims not only about the way in which Jesus traditions were used in the early church, but also about the history of their development over time as well as their possible ultimate origin, that is, whether they could be regarded plausibly as having their origin in the life of Jesus himself or whether they might have been created by early Christians.[32] And it has very often been the claims that some Jesus traditions in the Gospels may have been created by early Christians that have provoked strong reactions to the discipline of form criticism.[33] However, perhaps we should distinguish carefully between two issues: the use of Jesus traditions in the early church and the origin of Jesus traditions. Both are important issues, but they need to be distinguished and should not be confused.[34] With this distinction in mind, some of the claims as well as some of the critiques of form criticism may be seen in a slightly different light.

As noted earlier, one of the basic presuppositions of form criticism relates to the separability of the individual units of the tradition. In general terms, this foundational claim of much form-critical study of the Gospels has stood the test of time well and is still widely accepted, even by those who are otherwise critical of other aspects of the form-critical enterprise.[35] There are, to be sure, some qualifications to put on the broad picture outlined here. For example, there have always been various theories about individual parts of the tradition, arguing that some individual units or pericopes may already have been joined together into larger units prior to the writing of the present Gospels.[36] Hence the model of a totally random set of individual pericopes, only being joined together for the first time in any way by Mark (and then subsequently by Matthew and Luke), is almost certainly too simplistic.[37] Nevertheless, the basic claim of the separability of individual pericopes is widely accepted.

An important corollary of this is that the chronological sequence and ordering of the events in the Gospels is the result of the later editing process at the stage of the production of the written Gospels. The Gospels do not therefore give us any reliable information about the chronological sequence of the events of Jesus' life and ministry. There are of course some obvious exceptions to any such general "rule," for example, some of the stories which constitute, and integrally belong to, the Passion Narrative where the relative ordering is clearly determined by their content.[38] Thus traditions about the Last Supper and the arrest, trial, and death of Jesus cannot come in any other order (though with the obvious potential for variation in some details). But it is now widely accepted that, at least prior to the Passion Narrative, the chronological ordering of the material in the Gospels is almost certainly due to secondary editing (whether by the evangelists themselves or, in some cases, by earlier editors or collectors). Occasional voices have sought to question this but have generally not been found to be persuasive.[39] For example, appeals to the speeches in Acts as evidence that early Christians may have preserved a primitive outline of the course of the ministry of Jesus are felt to be weakened now by the possibility (even probability) that these speeches may well reflect the influence of Luke's own hand as much as any early historical preaching by early Christians, and any possible vestiges of an outline of Jesus' ministry agreeing with the Markan outline (as, e.g., in Acts 10:37-38) may just as likely be a reflection of Luke's dependence on

Mark's gospel combined with (at least an element of) Lukan influence on the formulation of any speech placed on the lips of Peter or Paul in the Acts account.

It is then widely accepted that the order of much of the material in the Gospels cannot be relied upon to give reliable information about the chronology of the life and ministry of Jesus. The order of our present Gospels may tell us about how the evangelists chose to structure their materials into a single narrative and, as such, may provide important insights into their concerns. But we cannot reach very far behind the Gospels themselves (if at all) to an earlier ordered sequence of the material.[40]

More debated have been the further developments of form criticism, especially in the work of Dibelius and Bultmann, seeking to analyze the individual units of the tradition and making claims about their possible *Sitze im Leben* and origin. As noted earlier, one fundamental axiom of form criticism was that the form of a tradition and its *Sitz im Leben* can be correlated in a neat one-to-one correspondence. However, both Dibelius and Bultmann worked with a number of other shared presuppositions which characterized their approach. Both assumed, for example, that the tradition prior to the emergence of the earliest extant Gospel, Mark, was primarily oral tradition. This oral tradition was essentially unliterary, part of "folk" traditions which were preserved, adapted, and at times created by "the community" considered as an amorphous whole. Further, both Dibelius and Bultmann assumed that the Gospels themselves, as well as the oral tradition lying behind them, could be categorized as "popular." The Gospels showed no real sophistication or literary skill: they belonged to the category of *Kleinliteratur* rather than *Hochliteratur*.[41] There was thus a seamless transition from the oral tradition through to the written Gospels. The evangelists themselves were essentially "editors," collecting together traditions and putting them into a narrative sequence in a somewhat mechanical "cut and paste" manner, rather than self-conscious "authors"; also, the oral and written gospel traditions were so similar, the ways in which the oral tradition changed and developed could be deduced from the ways in which the written tradition developed (e.g., by the later synoptic evangelists using Mark).

Further, both Dibelius and Bultmann worked with a fairly firm distinction in mind between things (ideas, contexts, etc.) described as "Palestinian" versus "Hellenistic," coupling this with an implied chronological correlate whereby anything in the Gospels which was "Palestinian" was "early" and anything "Hellenistic" was "late."[42] In line with this, in relation to the issue of the ultimate origin of the material (i.e., whether it could and should be traced back to Jesus himself), the form critics tended to assign what was deemed to be Palestinian to the body of material which was most likely to be authentic. (For Dibelius and Bultmann this involved primarily the "paradigms" [Dibelius] or "apophthegms" [Bultmann] and some of the sayings material).[43] Anything which seemed to reflect Hellenistic influence, for example, the "miracle stories" as isolated by their form,[44] was judged to be more likely inauthentic.

One further assumption, at least for Dibelius and Bultmann, was that the units of the tradition started out in a "pure" form and further material was added at a secondary stage.[45] Extra elements disturbing the pure form were taken as later additions. This in turn provided a further criterion by which the history of the tradition could be identified and traced. Many of these assumptions and hypotheses have now been radically questioned.

The somewhat simplistic division of the material using categories of "Palestinian" and "Hellenistic" as virtually binary opposites with no overlap between them, and then using this to make judgments about historicity, is one point where the work of the early form critics is open to question.[46] Any distinction between "Palestinian" and "Hellenistic" has now been shown to be too crude, especially when coupled with any kind of geographical or chronological distinction (with a model of the Christian movement starting in a Palestinian environment which is "early" and then moving outside Palestine into a Hellenistic environment which is therefore deemed to be "late"). The work of Martin Hengel in particular has shown that first-century Palestine was deeply affected by Hellenism;[47] and in any case the simplistic model (of "Palestinian" implying "early" versus "Hellenistic" implying "late") has been undermined by the Dead Sea Scrolls, which have shown thought patterns and ideas sometimes identified previously as "Hellenistic" but now seen to be clearly present and at home in a first-century Palestinian Jewish context.

Further, the emphasis which Bultmann placed on the apophthegms as "Palestinian" (as opposed to "Hellenistic") was based on analogies which he found in rabbinic literature (rather than general "folk" literature),[48] and he failed to take account that the closest parallels to these stories are to be found in the *chreiai* which occur very widely in Greco-Roman literature.[49] Hence the closest formal analogies to the pericopes which both Bultmann and Dibelius saw as part of the bedrock of the most authentic Jesus tradition are in fact to be found in the Hellenistic world![50]

But in any case, in relation to form criticism and theories about historicity, any appeal to "Hellenistic" or "Palestinian" forms of the tradition to make deductions about historicity perhaps confuses the two separate issues of the use and the origin of a tradition, as noted earlier. A tradition may have been formulated in a form which made it suitable for use in an environment far removed from any setting in the life of Jesus, but that does not mean that the substance of the events concerned originated there. The issues of the origin of a tradition and its use by early Christians should be kept logically separate (cf. above).

Other critiques of form criticism have focused on the word "form." Some have pointed out that part (perhaps a substantial part) of the work of Dibelius and Bultmann fails really to deal with forms as such. For example, one of the categories isolated by both Dibelius and Bultmann was a group of stories labeled "Legends."[51] Dibelius defined these as "religious narratives of a saintly man in whose works and fate interest is taken."[52] It is, however, rather difficult to identify common formal features in these stories beyond the rather loose description of their content, and in any case any possible generalized *Sitz im Leben* for all such stories is probably hard to identify. Dibelius also isolated the Passion Narrative as a separate category.[53] But then, as a single entity, it is not really possible to see a "common" form here shared with other related narratives.[54] And many of the sayings of Jesus are divided into different categories often more on the basis of content than of form.[55]

However, any distinction between form and content is not easy to maintain rigidly, and the two inevitably overlap to a certain extent. Thus, as often as not, any attempt to identify the "form" of a tradition is based as much on its contents as well: there is no absolute clear dividing line between form and content (as if one could determine a form completely independent of the content). Hence, while some division of the material may be more content-based than more strictly form-based, such distinctions may still be valid and worthwhile to pursue. And even if the term "form" criticism for such an endeavor may be felt by some to be a slight misnomer, this does not necessarily invalidate the enterprise as such.

However, some of the other assumptions made by the early form critics, especially in relation to the oral nature of the tradition, the relationship between oral and written traditions, and the literary "level" of the tradition, have all been more radically questioned.[56]

I consider first briefly the use made of written Gospels by the form critics. In the history of Gospel scholarship, form criticism led on to redaction criticism, where attention was focused on the evangelists themselves who were seen now not as mere editors, but were much more authors with ideas of their own; and these ideas then influenced significantly the ways in which they told their stories. Hence the evangelists were no longer seen as so unsophisticated as the model of the early form critics had suggested. In one way, this might not have affected the basic assumptions of form criticism too severely. It would mean a more radical qualitative break being envisaged between the oral tradition and the written Gospels (and other possible written versions of the tradition, e.g., Q);[57] it would also raise a question mark against the procedure of using the written gospel tradition as a measure by which to gauge the ways the oral tradition developed (cf. below). But on its own, such a reassessment of the literary status of the written Gospels need not challenge many of the basic presuppositions and claims of form criticism.

More recently, however, other question marks have been raised about the assessment of the early form critics of the oral gospel tradition itself in a more radical way. In part this arises from a greater appreciation of oral tradition elsewhere and a deeper understanding of orality and oral cultures. Also, questions are now raised about whether "folklore" traditions comprise an appropriate body of traditions to compare with gospel traditions about Jesus. Thus in relation to the last point, several have pointed out that the time scales involved in the various sets of traditions are very different: folklore traditions evolve over long periods of time, perhaps several generations; in the case of the pre-gospel traditions about Jesus, we are dealing with a period of the tradition lasting approximately one single generation (from circa 30 C.E. to circa 70 C.E.).[58] Also the nature of the material differs significantly.

Further, questions have been raised from the side of studies of orality whether it really is the case that oral tradition should be regarded as quite as "low grade" as the early form critics considered it to be.[59] Rather, a greater appreciation of predominantly oral-based cultures and societies has led to the realization that oral forms and oral communication can be quite sophisticated and display a significant level of literary and rhetorical skill. In turn, this might raise doubts about the neat correspondence drawn by the form critics between the form of a tradition and its alleged *Sitz im Leben*. Bultmann had maintained strenuously that the "form" of a tradition was a sociological concept, not an aesthetic one.[60] But if forms arise as much from literary or rhetorical skills, they cannot so easily be tied down to one particular *Sitz im Leben*. As Samuel Byrskog says, "one of the most basic conditions of the practice of form criticism thus becomes seriously problematic."[61]

Serious doubts have also been raised about the way the form critics sought to delineate the history of the tradition. Bultmann and Dibelius both claimed that the tradition developed in regular and identifiable ways that could be "tracked" using various criteria. In this way, the earlier forms of the tradition could then be identified. In part, as noted above, they claimed that the laws of the development of the oral tradition could be derived from the ways in which the written tradition developed.[62]

Credit for mounting a major challenge to this aspect of the work of the form critics has often been given to the study of E. P. Sanders.[63] Sanders showed that no regular laws could in fact be established for the ways in which traditions developed. Basing himself on the later manuscript tradition of the canonical Gospels and on the noncanonical gospel tradition, he showed that the tradition displays no regular features in its development,[64] and hence any attempt to establish any laws of development or to use such laws to determine earlier stages in the tradition is fraught with difficulty and probably impossible to sustain.

Sanders' own work has itself been criticized for making the same assumption as the earlier form critics in presuming that the developments of oral tradition and developments of written traditions are indeed comparable.[65] Thus Sanders' investigation was directed solely to developments of written (Gospel) texts and hence may still not be alive to the very nature of oral tradition as oral.

As noted earlier, Bultmann and Dibelius also argued that, at the earliest stage, the tradition existed in "pure" forms, unadulterated by later developments (most frequently taken as additions).[66] Hence these later additions could be peeled away to reach back to the most primitive form of the tradition. However, the idea that a "pure" form of the tradition is necessarily more original has been questioned by many.[67] Others have raised more radical questions about whether the search for a more "original" form is in fact a misguided enterprise from the very start, failing to take seriously the oral nature of the tradition. Thus the model of peeling away later additions may be more determined by the editing of written texts (removing, e.g., "scribal" additions). But for oral tradition, any idea of an "original" form may be flawed. For it is of the nature of oral tradition not to be fixed (in the way that the act of writing fixes the tradition on a written page). Rather than there being a fixed "original" form of the tradition which is recoverable by modern investigators, there may have been variation from the very beginning and the variations are simply reflections of different (oral) "performances" of the tradition.[68]

These critiques of the form-critical "dream" of a "pure form" lying at the start of the tradition may be justifiable in general terms. However, it is not so clear that this can be pushed as far as, for example, James Dunn or Terence Mournet have done recently, arguing that many of the parallel versions of traditions in our written Gospels are to be explained as oral variants. Such claims effectively ignore the redactional activity of the evangelists (treating them as "editors" rather than "authors") by ascribing many differences between parallel versions to the evangelists simply reproducing the version known to them from (their own) oral tradition.[69] Also, it seems undeniable that, in some instances, the Markan tradition has grown by accretions and these can be "peeled away" to restore an earlier version of the tradition.[70]

Another point of fundamental criticism in relation to form criticism has focused on the strict one-to-one correspondence which form critics claimed to exist between a form and a *Sitz im Leben*. Such criticism can focus on a number of different aspects of the general issue. I have already noted earlier that a different assessment of the "literary" level of the oral tradition in societies where the bulk of communication takes place orally would cast questions on such a neat one-to-one correspondence.

Others too, referring to more general studies of oral traditions, have questioned whether traditions emerge quite so neatly from specific *Sitze im Leben* as the form critics had suggested.[71] The claims of form criticism here are similar to the theory of homeostasis proposed by some anthropologists, namely, that "societies and groups performing oral traditions censor the past and celebrate only those items of the tradition that are relevant to the present situation."[72] Jan Vansina and others have pointed to the presence of archaic features in some oral traditions as reflecting a greater historical awareness than might be suggested by the model presumed by form critics. In the work of Bultmann, the attempt was often made to deduce the *Sitz im Leben* of a tradition from the tradition itself.[73] Thus controversy stories involving Jesus and opponents reflected (all but identical) early church controversies with (very similar) opponents. Yet at times the "evidence" for the existence of such controversies in early Christianity arises solely from the Gospel evidence itself.[74] The possibility that the presence of such stories in the tradition might represent more of an "archaic feature" is ruled out by Bultmann almost a priori. The circularity inherent in the form-critical argument here might thus become a rather dangerous hermeneutical circle,[75] and the claim about the *Sitz im Leben* may in part be determined in advance by the methodological approach adopted.

Further, we must remember that not all traditions are necessarily preserved because they reflect positively the views of a community. As noted earlier, the early form critics tended to assume that traditions were preserved and handed on by collective (almost undifferentiated) groups ("*the* community"). Yet some traditions are generated, produced, handed down, and/or created not simply to reinforce (and reflect positively) existing community views. They may also be handed on by some in the community in order to address others in the (same) community. Traditions may be felt to be important because they speak to a group as well as speaking for a group.[76]

Other problems relating to a neat one-to-one correspondence between form and *Sitz im Leben* include the fact that a variety of different forms can be used in any one setting; conversely, the same form can be used in different settings. Thus the tradition of the Last Supper may have been used by early Christians in the setting of the cult (as a narrative repeated in the celebration of the Eucharist),[77] but it was also used by Paul as part of his ethical exhortations to the Corinthians about their behavior (1 Cor 11).[78] Equally it is clear that Christianity did not originate in a linguistic or cultural vacuum. Thus all the "forms" used by Christians were already in existence and well established. So too other groups (e.g., Jewish writers) could use a mixture of different "forms" side by side in the same text without difficulty. But then it is really inappropriate to suggest that a particular social setting in early Christianity was the sole generative force for the existence of a particular form in Christian oral traditions.[79]

There are then enormous difficulties in what was claimed at the time (by Bultmann) to be a fundamental aspect of form criticism, namely, deducing a specific *Sitz im Leben* from the form of a tradition.

How far this is fatal to the kind of analysis which those such as Bultmann and Dibelius actually undertook is however not quite so clear. In relation to the terms in which they set up their methodology, with their focus on "forms," the criticism is fully justified. However, as we have already noted, classifications of the material are often as much on the basis of content as of (strict) form, and in any case it is sometimes difficult to distinguish the two. Hence it may still be the case that traditions were used in the early church and do stem from a *Sitz im Leben*; and it may be possible to deduce something about this setting from the tradition considered in its totality, that is, its form and content (possibly even primarily its content). As often as not, this was the way which Bultmann in particular approached the material in his detailed analysis of individual pericopes.

This is also the broad approach of a more contemporary figure such as Gerd Theissen.[80] Theissen is fully aware of the problems of "classical" form criticism, but his work also involves real continuity with the work of the early form critics.[81] His work has focused more on individual traditions in the Gospels, suggesting situations in early Christianity which they may reflect. His suggestions about such possible settings are based not so much on literary forms, but on individual figures named, the ideological, geographical, and temporal perspective that is represented, as well as a consideration of the socio-political setting of the time[82] (hence, a considerably wider purview than that of the original form critics). It may well be that the use of the phrase *Sitz im Leben* to refer to the setting postulated in this way is a misnomer, since the phrase is really a sociological one, referring to a generalized situation covering a range of (various) similar but related texts; to use it in relation to an individual tradition and its setting is not really appropriate.[83] But for New Testament critics, the most important thing is presumably the value of the analysis, not the terminology used to refer to it! Thus in many respects, Theissen's work shows the potential value of still continuing the work of the classic form critics but taking seriously the questions raised against their specific proposals about forms.

A final problem to be mentioned briefly here (though it has arisen already, explicitly or implicitly, in earlier discussions) relates to the issue of which people might have been involved in the transmission of the Jesus tradition. Bultmann and Dibelius tended to postulate activity by a generalized, undifferentiated "community." Others however have suggested that this is inherently implausible.[84] Thus some have suggested that, instead of an anonymous, amorphous community, we should think of specific individuals (e.g., "teachers") with the particular responsibility of handing on the tradition to others. We have already noted that this was a key part of Gerhardsson's proposed model for the transmission of the Jesus tradition, with the Twelve in Jerusalem acting as a kind of collegium with responsibility for working with, and transmitting, the tradition.[85] Further, the issue has arisen over the precise relation of a tradition to any community: how far do traditions reflect positively the views of a community, and how far are traditions directed (perhaps by some within a community) at the views (of others) in a community? Suggestions that individuals within communities (rather than just "the community") were instrumental in handing on the Jesus tradition may in turn cast doubts on any claims to regularity or predictable laws governing the development of the tradition.[86]

In general terms, the critique of the older form critics' model is probably fully justified, though it is not quite so clear which model might or should replace this.[87] Thus one should probably place a big question mark against the picture of an amorphous community doing quite as much as the earlier form critics had suggested and doing so in a regular and predictable way. Gerhardsson and Byrskog are probably right then to press the case that we should think of individuals within the "community" or "communities" possibly acting in ways that are at times idiosyncratic and not so easily predictable. Whether we can be more precise is however less clear.

Conclusion

The various challenges and criticism which have been directed against the model of form criticism as developed by Dibelius and Bultmann are serious. That model, in precisely that form, is probably no longer sustainable. The dichotomy between "Palestinian" and "Hellenistic," the attempt to establish a one-to-one correspondence between form and *Sitz im Leben*, and the stress on the activity of "the community," are all now thrown into question, as Gerhardsson and others have clearly shown.

However, it is doubtful if we can simply turn the clock back nearly one hundred years and pretend that form criticism has contributed nothing.[88] That Jesus traditions were used and developed by early Christians in ways that related to their own concerns was one of the features highlighted by classic form criticism.[89] And this seems to be clearly evidenced in the gospel (and occasionally other) traditions themselves. Precisely how we can identify and clarify that usage and development is not always clear. Seeking to establish any generalized laws (or even tendencies) is probably no longer viable. Probably each tradition has to be considered in its own right.[90] The work of form criticism has opened our eyes to the need to do this work. If earlier form criticism did not provide all the answers, that does not mean that the questions are not still there. Certainly the issues raised by form criticism remain as challenging as ever for all those who would study the Gospels sympathetically and critically. In all his work on the Gospels, Birger Gerhardsson has exemplified that twin approach of being both sympathetic and critical. His tireless willingness to challenge accepted "wisdom" on so many questions, and to press issues about memory and tradition to the forefront of scholarly discussions, affects the very heart of so much of contemporary studies of early Christianity.[91]

Chapter 2

The Jesus Tradition as Oral Tradition

Terence C. Mournet

Birger Gerhardsson has made an inestimable impact on the field of New Testament studies. Our collective knowledge and understanding of the shape and texture of the Jesus tradition has been forever changed by his groundbreaking work which has deeply influenced countless colleagues through his forty-plus years of research, teaching, and graduate supervision. Not often does one individual make such a valuable and long-lasting contribution to a discipline. *Memory and Manuscript* remains a key work in the area of the transmission of tradition within both New Testament and rabbinical contexts.[1] Despite being written over forty-five years ago, *Memory and Manuscript* remains on the required reading list for all serious students of the New Testament, and every monograph and article written on the subject of the earliest stages of the Jesus tradition must, at the very least, engage thoughtfully the foundational work of this respected academician. Gerhardsson's former students have continued in his footsteps and their respective works reflect their ongoing indebtedness to their *Doktorvater*. As such, it is with great pleasure that I offer this work as a small token of gratitude for what Gerhardsson has already given us throughout his career.

There have been many summaries of Gerhardsson's work over the years, and no attempt will be made here to repeat in detail that journey undertaken in greater depth by others. Rather, we will first explore the character of the Jesus tradition as evidenced in the Synoptic Gospels. Second, we will summarize three major schools of thought in the area of the formation and transmission of the Jesus tradition and focus in more detail on the concept of oral tradition derived from the "orality model" with particular reference to research which has been built upon the work of Kenneth Bailey. Lastly, it is the aim of this current contribution to clarify some of the issues at stake in the discussion of the earliest stages of the Jesus tradition. While there are clear differences between the model of tradition transmission proposed by Gerhardsson and that forwarded below, there are also strong points of resonance which, through the process of clarification and refinement, might come to the fore and facilitate ongoing dialogue and continued synergy.

In assessing the work of Gerhardsson it is necessary to place his work within both its original and current academic context. When he wrote his *Memory and Manuscript* there were not as many potential models of the formation and transmission of the Jesus tradition to which one could appeal in comparison to today. At the time, the form-critical model dominated the academic landscape and its paradigm was widely used to frame the questions regarding the transmission of Jesus tradition.

For Rudolf Bultmann, the starting point for understanding the Gospels rests in the distinction between *Kleinliteratur* and *Hochliteratur*.[2] The labeling of the Gospels as *Kleinliteratur* carried with it a series of unvoiced and unjustified assumptions about the process of tradition transmission.[3] His assumed model of tradition transmission, which formed the basis for subsequent form-critical work, ran counter to the model which flowed from the historical context envisioned by Gerhardsson. While the form-critical model was, in theory, one built upon insights derived from various disciplines, it suffered from its alienation from the rich cultural and religious milieu in which Jesus the Jew lived and died. The form-critical work on the Gospels was informed by the texts and traditions of the Greco-Roman world apart from any meaningful interaction with the primary context of Jesus and his earliest disciples. While form critics such as Bultmann appealed, if in an indirect manner, to other disciplines to elucidate the Jesus tradition, the number of formal models to which one could appeal was limited at the time. Contrast this to today, where there are many diverse approaches to studying the Jesus tradition, some of which are themselves derivative of the form-critical model of tradition transmission.

It is admittedly difficult, if not impossible, to utilize entirely objective labels to describe each of these models. However, for our purpose, we will use the terms "literary model," "rabbinical model," and "orality model" to delineate three different perspectives on the Jesus tradition and their respective understanding of the process of tradition formation and transmission. While there is indeed overlap between these three models, each model has its own distinctive characteristics which will be elucidated in what follows. As it is beyond the scope of this chapter to interact with each of these models in detail, we will focus our attention on the "orality model," or more specifically, the model that Bailey has described as "the third way" between Bultmann and Gerhardsson.

Character of the Jesus Tradition

When examining the synoptic tradition, it becomes clear that the transmission history of the Jesus tradition is not easily recoverable. It is often a stated, or at least implied, goal to develop a simple and elegant model to account for the evidence in the Synoptic Gospels. Whether it is in an attempt to provide a working model of the synoptic problem or, in this case, a model for the transmission of the Jesus tradition, simplicity is a welcomed handmaiden to the task. Therefore, an appeal to the principle of parsimony, that is, Ockham's Razor,[4] does have a place in the humanities and social sciences. However, the complex character of the Jesus tradition is such that simple solutions inevitably "break down" quickly. As a model for the formation and transmission of the Jesus tradition is altered to account for evidence that does not fit easily into the proposed framework, the model grows, expands, and inevitably becomes more complex over time. Models that remain overly simplistic often come across as contrived as they do not take into account the inherently complex transmission history of the Jesus tradition.

Opting for a "media model" only makes the process more difficult.[5] Rather than dealing exclusively with texts, we now must deal with the Jesus tradition in multiple media and performance contexts including, but not limited to: oral tradition from the mouth of Jesus; written notes (notebooks); formalized didactic activity; written *logia* collections; the informal circulation of sayings, traditions, and teachings of and about Jesus; and the recirculation of the oral Jesus tradition back into written texts. In essence, we are forced to reckon with a circular process of tradition transmission whereby there is a complex interaction between the Jesus tradition in multiple forms, oral tradition informing and perhaps modifying the textual tradition, and the textual tradition informing and perhaps modifying the oral Jesus tradition. In sum, simple models of tradition transmission must be questioned once we account for the various media through which the Jesus tradition surely circulated both before, during, and after its initial inscription in the canonical Gospel of Mark and later when the Markan text was utilized by the authors of both Matthew and Luke.

The results of this complex process of tradition transmission have left their mark on the inscribed gospel tradition. I have found that both the terms "variability" and "stability" are helpful in describing the complex character of the Jesus tradition. Working under the general parameters of the two-source hypothesis, it becomes clear that the level of verbatim agreement varies greatly across both the double and triple tradition. Thomas Bergemann, in his examination of the so-called double tradition, shows that the level of verbatim agreement between Matthew and Luke varies from approximately 8 percent to 100 percent.[6] Robert Morgenthaler concludes that a large majority (78.5%) of the material assigned to Q ranges in levels of verbatim agreement between 20 percent and 80 percent; 13.2 percent of Q falls in the upper range of agreement (80%–98%), and 8.2 percent of Q falls within the lower range of 0–19 percent of agreement.[7] Theodore Rosché likewise concludes that only a limited percentage of Q has an average verbal correspondence above 54 percent and that 68 percent of what is commonly accepted as a part of Q exhibits less than the average degree of verbal correspondence.[8] Despite the differing conclusions of Bergemann, Morgenthaler, and Rosché, there is agreement among them that the level of verbatim agreement varies greatly across the double tradition material. That is, for our purposes, one of the primary characteristics of the Jesus tradition is that it is highly variable and multiform in its attestation in the inscribed Gospels.

While the level of variability in the multiform Jesus tradition is well documented, less attention has been directed toward the distribution of verbatim agreement within individual Gospel pericopes. That is, most statistical studies on the phenomena of verbatim agreement with the synoptic tradition assign each parallel pericope one single percentage of verbatim agreement. While helpful, this does not provide one with an accurate picture of the character of the agreement between parallel traditions. Using one single level of verbatim agreement assumes that the distribution of agreement is uniform across parallel traditions. However, as I have argued in more detail elsewhere,[9] many pericopes which have overall low levels of verbatim agreement exhibit uneven patterns of distribution of that agreement. In these cases, the agreement is often contained in a short section which constitutes a "core" of the tradition. Even in a pericope which exhibits an overall low level of verbatim agreement, the core of that tradition might exhibit high levels of concentrated agreement. In sum, not only is the Jesus tradition variable in character, but upon closer examination, the tradition reflects a level of stability whereby core elements of the tradition remain intact throughout the course of its transmission.

All three major models of traditional transmission, the "literary model," the "rabbinical model"—most clearly articulated by Gerhardsson—and the "orality model," are attempts to address both the variability and stability that characterizes the Jesus tradition. Each model has been formulated to account for these observable phenomena, and each model, understandably, suggests that it is able to do so in a coherent and plausible manner. We will now examine each of these three models in turn.

Literary Model

The "literary model" is founded upon what appears to be an entirely reasonable observation: the early Christian movement demonstrated interest in the production and consumption of texts. Early collections of Pauline epistles, the composition of written Gospels, scribal activity, the formation of the Christian canon—all of that activity has led us, as children of the Enlightenment, to a seemingly reasonable view that texts have always been at the very center of the early Christian movement. This is an understandable if perhaps misguided conclusion given that the primary historical attestations to the life of Jesus exist in the form of written texts. As has been demonstrated in more detail elsewhere, the privileged status given literary artifacts has had a profound impact on how we understand both the character of the Jesus tradition and how the tradents of the traditions carried out their task of passing down the story of Jesus to the next generation.[10] What we will focus on here is how, despite past efforts to appropriate oral tradition into a model of tradition transmission, the process has been largely viewed in literary terms—as a text to be excavated and a text to be redacted by means of tools themselves derived from the world of texts.

Although it is difficult to trace the origins of this perspective on the written gospel tradition down to one specific individual, it is safe to argue that the modern notions of the function of texts date back to the origins of the printing press itself.[11] Within New Testament circles this led to the examination of the Gospels apart from their original service to the needs of a predominantly oral society. Form critics functioned within a typographic society which privileged literacy and viewed the production of literary artifacts as attestation to the cultural supremacy of continental Europe.[12] This perspective on the importance of literary artifacts then extended beyond Europe to include all Western academia, including work undertaken in North America. Texts and literary compositions were perceived as the vehicle for accurate and reliable communication; oral forms of communication were viewed as inferior, less reliable, and less capable means of transmitting tradition. This broadly evolutionary perspective on both culture and tradition served to form the foundation upon which much of biblical scholarship in modernity has been built.

From this brief summary, it is possible to begin describing some of the characteristics which are shared by scholars operating within the literary paradigm. While all scholars work within the world of texts, not all scholars have seen the tradition through the same set of lenses. For those working within the literary model of tradition transmission, the process of transmission is conceptualized, theorized, and worked out from within an exclusively literary framework. Those most prone to adopting this particular perspective are typically scholars working with the so-called historical-critical tools of biblical scholarship. Textual critics work with multiple editions of texts, or fragments thereof; redaction critics examine texts to discern how authors utilized, adapted, or edited texts; source critics compare the Synoptic Gospels to detect evidence of literary activity—that is, the copying of one source text by another author; form critics examine the various subgenres of a text and attempt to recover early, original forms of texts and traditions. While each of these approaches is extremely helpful and is able to contribute much to our understanding of early Christianity, there is often an underlying presupposition regarding the role of oral communication and the process of tradition transmission that goes unvoiced—or even unrecognized—by many New Testament scholars; that is, the assumption that the same rules of tradition formation and transmission apply equally to either oral or literary tradition.[13] This then pushes the discussion on the oral stage of the Jesus tradition to the margins of the discussion. As we will illustrate below, even the early form critics who acknowledged the role of oral tradition in the formation of the Synoptic Gospels envisioned the medium of orality in largely literary terms.

Rudolf Bultmann and Martin Dibelius were both interested in the earliest stages of the Jesus tradition, and as such, both of them clearly recognized that the earliest literary works which attested to the life and work of Jesus were not solely created *de novo* from the creative work of the early Christians, but flowed from the earlier process of oral communication which characterized the ministry of Jesus himself. This observation is one which is, with few exceptions, still embraced to this day within the discipline. The problem for both Bultmann and Dibelius is that while they affirmed the existence of both oral traditions about Jesus and oral communication as the primary vehicle for those early Jesus traditions, they did not follow through with that fundamental assertion to explore in more detail the character of oral tradition, how those traditions were transmitted within the context of early Christianity, and what implications that might have for how we understand the extant literary artifacts produced by the early church.

Oral tradition was envisioned as adhering to the same "laws of transmission" as those which were posited for literary tradition. The tendencies of the tradition were toward growth and expansion, from simplicity to complexity, from disconnected, isolated pericopes to a larger, connected narrative.[14] The assumptions behind the early form-critical work on the Gospels were based upon the linear development of the Jesus tradition, an unbroken development from oral tradition to written text. However, if the medium of transmission did indeed have an impact on the dynamics of the process, then the so-called laws of transmission must be called into question.

In essence, the early form critics gave oral tradition "lip service" but did not allow that fundamental observation to impact their understanding of the tradition itself. To quote an excerpt from my *Oral Tradition and Literary Dependency*:

> [T]he difficulty in the theses of Bultmann and Dibelius lies not in their acknowledgment of the process of oral tradition formation—which is correct—but rather in their misunderstanding of the character of oral tradition and how the tradition was transmitted in its pre-textual, oral stage. Given their lack of interest in the question regarding the medium in which the tradition was transmitted, it is not surprising that the discussion developed in the way that it has. Bultmann accepted the oral character of the tradition, but was not sure how to deal with the material as orally transmitted. His uncertainty about how oral tradition functioned in the context of tradition formation and transmission led him ultimately to abandon any genuine pursuit of the role of orality in the development of the Synoptic Gospels. He therefore dealt with orality in a rather peripheral manner and the question of its possible impact upon the development of the Jesus tradition effectively dropped out of the discussion. Orality then became an unimportant side issue and was replaced by a more literary approach to the Jesus

tradition. Much is the same with Dibelius. He envisioned the Synoptic Gospels as the natural extension of the process of oral transmission. He understood the progression from orality to literacy as did Bultmann—it was simply the transcription of oral tradition into the textual medium.[15]

Bultmann and Dibelius are not the only scholars to work with texts and traditions without taking seriously the extent to which the world of antiquity was indebted to oral forms of discourse. Source critics and Q scholars have also traditionally worked with the Jesus tradition under the assumption that the process of Gospel formation was one with which a modern literary editor might be comfortable. For scholars working from this perspective, even when oral tradition is welcomed into the discussion, it is viewed as another source to be manipulated, largely under the rules and parameters derived from the world of texts. Differences between various literary editions of texts are envisioned to be the result of direct literary activity whereby one author consciously departs from his source, and these differences become explicable exclusively by means of the process of literary redaction.[16] Again, there are times when this understanding of the tradition is indeed an accurate reflection of the tradition history behind a particular text.[17] However, there are also times when the thesis of literary dependency and redactional activity is pushed beyond its limits.

RABBINICAL MODEL

Gerhardsson's contribution has to be understood and appreciated in light of its place within New Testament scholarship at the time. His *Memory and Manuscript* should be understood as providing a long-needed correction to the presuppositions, methods, and conclusions of Bultmann and those who adopted and applied his approach to the Gospel material.[18] From within this context, Gerhardsson's work was a magisterial contribution which encouraged the pendulum to swing back toward the center from the extreme limits to which it was pushed by means of the method of *Formgeschichte*. The form-critical method's approach to the Gospels left New Testament researchers with little reliable historical material from which one could evaluate the life and ministry of Jesus. The form-critical model attributed much of the gospel tradition to the retrospective, largely creative editors and compilers of the written Gospels. The written Gospels were records—not of the history of the life of Jesus—but of the history of the early church. According to this admittedly oversimplified characterization of form criticism, the task which faced the student of the Gospels was akin to that of an archaeologist working with texts and traditions rather than with the pick and shovel.[19] The form-critical assumption was that the Jesus tradition began as a pure form (*reine Gattung*) which was quickly obscured by the encrustations of theological strata, one layer built upon another.

Insights derived from a study of rabbinics provided Gerhardsson with the heuristic categories that enabled the Jesus tradition to be approached through new, less pessimistic lenses. While the form critics were quite reticent to attribute many of the sayings of Jesus to his own lips, Gerhardsson's work called into question these conclusions through an examination of rabbinic Judaism. For him, rabbinic Judaism provided the researcher with a more appropriate lens through which one could examine the early Jesus tradition and the traditions of early Christianity. After all, Jesus was described as a teacher and rabbi, and, according to our most reliable sources, surrounded himself with a group of disciples who learned about the kingdom of God through the methods and means which were commonplace during nascent rabbinic Judaism. Jesus engaged in intentional teaching with his disciples, and the evidence of such intentionality is, according to this model, accessible through the careful examination of our extant sources.

Among Gerhardsson's primary goals was to ask, "what was the technical procedure followed when the early Church *transmitted*, both gospel material and other material?"[20] He expressed the view that Jerusalem was the center of early Christianity and that members of the Jerusalem church and other early churches formed a collegium which included leading men as the official possessors and transmitters of the teaching of Jesus himself.[21] For Gerhardsson, the technical procedure was thoroughly indebted to the process of memorization, including the use of notebooks[22] as an *aide-mémoir* for the disciples. Jesus was the authoritative teacher who intentionally engaged in a teacher-student relationship with his disciples. In the course of the "technical procedure" envisaged by Gerhardsson, "reverence and care for the *ipsissima verba* of each authority remains unaltered."[23]

While some of the initial reviews of Gerhardsson's work were hypercritical and unfair,[24] they reflected more the state of both New Testament and rabbinic scholarship at the time than they did the contribution of Gerhardsson himself.[25] What was proposed by way of an appeal to rabbinic Judaism was nothing short of revolutionary, and as Eric Havelock has written, "a novel thesis requires a restricted emphasis to be put across."[26]

The major critiques of the approach advocated by Gerhardsson have centered on the charge of anachronism. Despite the ongoing debate over the particulars regarding the applicability of rabbinic Judaism to the Jesus tradition, there were no doubt elements within rabbinic Judaism that derived from their earlier usage during the first century C.E. While the rabbinic methods of pedagogy and tradition transmission were formalized and refined following the Jewish War and the destruction of the temple in 70 C.E., it would be fallacious to assume that these newly refined and/or adopted methods were created *ex nihilo* from within a cultural and historical vacuum. Just as the criteria of historicity demand that Jesus needed to have enough points of contact with his fellow Jewish contemporaries in order to be comprehensible and coherent, the didactic methods utilized by teachers during nascent rabbinic Judaism must have been, to some extent, continuous with those utilized by teachers and leaders during the time of Jesus himself. As such, the charge of anachronism should not lead one to reject Gerhardsson's model *in toto*.

The proposed appropriation of this new model into the New Testament landscape amounted to no less than a major paradigm shift, and, as is often the case with any paradigm shift, initial reactions are often polarizing and reflect the deep-rooted desire to defend and uphold the status quo being challenged at the time. The polarizing reactions against Gerhardsson's work would eventually soften—to the point which would allow one of his early vehement initial critics to write a very favorable defense of his work several decades later.[27] Gerhardsson's work reawakened awareness of the Jesus tradition's thoroughgoing indebtedness to Judaism and Jewish pedagogical practices which were present within the Gospel texts all along. This led to a more historically appropriate approach to the Jesus tradition, one which attempted to understand the activity of Jesus through the matrix of first-century Judaism. This perspective on the tradition, and the way in which it was handed down, led to an overall much more positive assessment of the historical reliability of our best and most reliable primary sources on Jesus.

Orality Model

As will become evident in the pages to follow, the "orality model" is a composite model derived from the contribution of scholars from various disciplines within the humanities. It is predicated upon an assumption which has been embraced by countless New Testament scholars over the decades: that the Jesus tradition was initially oral and Jesus was an individual who was at home within the oral performance arena. Through his use of oral forms of communication—*mashal,* proverb, and so forth—Jesus communicated to his diverse audiences through means which were both known to and appreciated by all. All of the approaches which fall under the rubric of "orality" are, in their own unique ways, attempts to reclaim for the twenty-first-century reader the power and dynamism of the performative arts which were integral to traditional society of Jesus' time.

The orality model is the most recent of the aforementioned models to be used in reference to the formation and transmission of the Jesus tradition and the one with which this present author has identified himself.[28] While the orality model has evolved over the years, it is largely attributable to the foundational work of Milman Parry and Albert Lord. Parry was a classicist who sought to determine whether the Homeric epics were the product of a literary genius or that of an oral performer.[29] Parry died before completing his work, and his student at the time, Albert Lord, continued in his footsteps, eventually shifting his focus to a comparative study of the Serbo-Croatian epic and other oral-traditional material. In *The Singer of Tales,*[30] Lord articulated a more fully formed theory of oral performance which would become known as the "oral-formulaic theory" and serve as fertile ground for an entire generation of scholars.

Lord's conclusions regarding the oral composition of oral poetry were profound indeed. He concluded that oral epic performance did not flow from a memorized, written source text, but rather that an oral performer drew from a collection of stock and set phrases which could be employed in a variety of ways to meet the needs of any given situation. Oral performance was not the wooden or rigid recitation of a text memorized verbatim, but the use of mnemonically appropriate phrases which could be used in varied fashion to meet the metrical and thematic needs in performance. Modern notions of a "word for word" and "line for line" rendition of a performance were not only inappropriate ways of describing the nature of an oral performance, but they were concepts foreign to both the performers and their audience.[31] While some scholars, including Lord himself, approached the Gospels through the lenses of the newly formed oral-formulaic theory,[32] most have suggested that the greatest avenue for exploration lies not in the specifics of Lord's thesis, but in the dynamics of orality and the numerous corollaries that flow from Lord's work on performance theory. John Foley in particular has worked extensively in the area pioneered by Lord, and he continues to make valuable contributions to both performance theory and orality studies.[33]

The next stage of development in the field of oral studies is attributable to the work of Walter Ong. His work was the genesis for a good deal of New Testament scholarship along the lines of orality studies.[34] Countless articles and monographs have been influenced by Ong's widely read *Orality and Literacy*.[35]

Ong's work proved instrumental in leading some New Testament scholars to a growing awareness of the role of oral communication in traditional cultures, including that of the ancient Mediterranean in which Jesus lived and functioned. The list of insights offered by his *Orality and Literacy* was extensive and has continued to influence recent work on early Christian tradition transmission. His chapter on the "psychodynamics of orality"[36] has been particularly influential on scholars across a wide spectrum of academic disciplines.

Ong posited a significant divide between orality and literacy, an approach which was embraced early on in the discussion of the Gospels, but one which, rightly so, has been adjusted to account for the high level of interaction between oral communication and written texts.[37] Arguments for the definitive presence of oral tradition within the gospel tradition have become more nuanced over time, following the recognition that many, if not all, of the "hallmarks" of oral communication such as syllabic meter, ring composition, chiasmus, and other types of "oral patterning" are equally at home in literary circles as they are in the world of orality and oral performance.[38]

The orality model is further developed by the extensive work undertaken on literacy and the role of texts in ancient society.[39] Texts were not foreign to the early Christian movement. What began as a spoken, verbalized tradition was now beginning to become inscribed and valued as a text.[40] Scribal activity was on the increase and copies of the Pauline corpus, the Gospels, and eventually the entire New Testament canon were being produced to satiate the ever-increasing need for Christian texts throughout the rapidly growing network of Christian congregations.[41]

However, despite the increasing production of texts during the first several centuries C.E., the impact of texts on the Christian movement was limited in scope, for the number of people who were able to interact directly with written texts remained small. The strong consensus as of late is that the vast majority of people in antiquity were illiterate, and a small percentage of people were, at best, marginally literate. These low literacy rates were not confined to one specific people group or even a narrow chronological period of time.

The influential and oft-cited work by William Harris suggested that less than 10 percent of the residents in an urban setting like Athens were literate during the time which Jesus lived.[42] As for the general population, which included women and slaves, the literacy rate was likely closer to 5 percent.[43] Subsequent work on the New Testament has concurred with Harris' findings and despite some recent attempts to demonstrate that literacy was more widespread than often envisaged,[44] the recent work by Catherine Hezser on Jewish literacy in Roman Palestine calls into question all precritical notions of high levels of Jewish literacy during the time of Jesus.[45] In sum, there appears to be developing a broadly held view within both New Testament and Hebrew Bible scholarship that the vast majority of people in antiquity, including the Jews in Roman Palestine, were at best marginally literate and that those who were literate were likely socially located within the political and cultural elite.[46]

Very few people in antiquity were able to interact directly with texts, and even when traditions were inscribed in textual form, they were not always valued in the same way as we take for granted today. Loveday Alexander has written on the use of the term *viva vox* in Greco-Roman society, and she concludes that "there is in the schools a strong tendency to see written texts as secondary to and subordinate to oral instruction. It is the 'living voice' of the teacher that has priority: the text both follows that voice (as a record of teaching already given) and stands in a subordinate position to it."[47]

While texts were indeed commonplace during the time of Jesus, they were often composed in conjunction with or informed by a living oral tradition.[48] Oral tradition served as sources for written texts, with numerous early Christian texts, including the *Didache, Acts of Paul*, Q, and the Apostolic Fathers, each exhibiting signs of their indebtedness to a living oral tradition which was available to their respective authors.[49] In addition, texts were written to be vocalized and aurally received with even the act of private, individual reading being a highly verbal and audible endeavor.[50] Throughout the Judeo-Christian tradition, including the corpora of the Hebrew Bible, New Testament, Pseudepigrapha, and Apocrypha, there is clear evidence that texts were read aloud to their intended recipients and, therefore, functioned as another oral/aural interface with the transmitted tradition.[51]

Informal Controlled Oral Tradition

Kenneth Bailey's contribution to the question of oral tradition and the formation of the Synoptic Gospels can be traced back to his 1991 publication of "Informal Controlled Oral Tradition."[52] N. T. Wright later, in his *Jesus and the Victory of God*, approvingly cited Bailey's work and proposed that it be adopted as a "working model."[53] James Dunn and this current author then spent a fruitful four years together (1999–2003), during which Dunn wrote his *Jesus Remembered* and I researched and wrote what would be subsequently published as *Oral Tradition and Literary Dependency*.[54] Both Dunn and I sought to follow through with the insights offered by Bailey, each of us in an attempt to take seriously the role of oral tradition in the formation of the Synoptic Gospels.

Bailey's anecdotal account of Middle Eastern tradition transmission derives from his thirty years of personal experience living in the Middle East. What is of importance for our current discussion is that Bailey polarizes the theses of Bultmann and Gerhardsson by placing them at opposite ends of the spectrum, describing Bultmann's view of tradition transmission as "informal uncontrolled" oral tradition and Gerhardsson's view as "formal controlled" oral tradition. Bailey then proceeds to outline his own model of tradition transmission which he defines as "informal controlled" oral tradition, whereby there was "no set teacher and no specifically identified student" and yet the community exercised control over the tradition.[55] Bailey continues to describe his theory of tradition transmission as follows:

> So there was continuity and flexibility. Not continuity and change. The distinction is important. Continuity and change could mean that the story teller could change say 15% of the story—any 15%. Thus after seven transmissions of the story theoretically all of the story could be changed. But continuity and flexibility mean that the main lines of the story cannot be changed at all. The story can endure one different transmission through a chain of a hundred and one different people and the inner core of the story remains intact. Within the structure, the storyteller has flexibility within limits to "tell his own way." But the basic story line remains the same. By telling and retelling, the story does not evolve from A to B to C. Rather the original structure of the story remains the same but it can be colored green or red or blue.[56]

Bailey proceeds to categorize the varying levels of flexibility within orally transmitted tradition: 1) no flexibility—in this category are included proverbs and poems, which Bailey suggests are not transmitted "with so much as a *word* out of place" or the storyteller will be "corrected by a chorus of voices";[57] 2) some flexibility—included in this category are parables and recollections of historical people and events which are of value to the self-identity of the telling community; and 3) total flexibility—in which are included jokes, casual news of the day, and what Bailey labels "atrocity stories."[58]

Bailey suggests that his "informal controlled oral tradition" model is able to account for these three categories of tradition, all of which are represented in the extant Jesus tradition. This description of what Bailey describes as "continuity and flexibility" is echoed in terminology used by Dunn, Mournet, and others.[59] This language resonates with many New Testament scholars,[60] for the evidence itself consists of synoptic passages which betray the authors' utilization of written sources external to the canonical Gospels as well as passages where a literary explanation of the similarities and differences seems to be lacking in strength.

The question which needs to be asked at this point is whether Bailey's characterization of Gerhardsson's thesis is entirely justified. Bailey is quick to label Gerhardsson's model as "formal controlled," thus implying that Gerhardsson's model does not take into account the variation within the tradition. However, as has been articulated by Gerhardsson himself and other supporters of his thesis, his work does allow room for varying levels of verbatim transmission of the Jesus tradition.[61] While it is true that Gerhardsson emphasizes the importance of the use of technical terminology in describing the process of tradition transmission (e.g., παράδοσις, παραλαμβάνειν, παραδιδόναι),[62] the process of "handing down" the Jesus tradition should not be understood exclusively in terms of verbatim transmission, nor should one assume that this was the only model of tradition transmission available within rabbinic circles.[63] What this suggests then is that views which juxtapose Gerhardsson's model over against more flexible models of tradition transmission, such as the orality model, might be arguing against a narrowly defined understanding of Gerhardsson's thesis rather than a holistic reading of his entire corpus of work.[64] Both Gerhardsson and so-called orality advocates recognize that the character of the inscribed Jesus tradition requires a deep appreciation for the dynamics of early Christian tradition transmission. While the models proposed by Gerhardsson and Bailey differ in some significant ways, they both recognize the "fixity" and "flexibility" inherent in the tradition and attempt to construct a cogent model to account for that diversity.

In advancing the model of tradition transmission advocated by Dunn and this current author, it is necessary to clarify some aspects of the model that have been challenged in the recent debate. Critics of the model suggest that Bailey's model of informal controlled oral tradition derives from an anecdotal study of twentieth-century Middle Eastern Arab culture and therefore is too far removed from the worldview of nascent Christianity to be at all helpful in more than very limited terms.

Excursus: The Value of Comparative Methodology

Gerhardsson, in his response to Dunn, echoes the most common critique of the orality model, that of the inapplicability of Bailey's model as a hermeneutical framework through which we can understand better the character of the Jesus tradition and the process by which that tradition was transmitted. He suggests that we must:

> respect the fact that they [i.e., the early Christians] were active as Jews in Hellenistic times in Palestine. To interpret them as examples of phenomena that are supposed to exist here, there, and everywhere in the world is to sacrifice their anchoring in their concrete historical milieu and instead advance by drawing on conditions in other parts of the world . . . Bailey's examples are after all from our own time and from an Arab peasant culture whose relation to the Jewish world is not clear, and he presupposes that similar customs existed among the Jews in NT times. This makes his comparisons somewhat precarious.[65]

This critique is a variation of the charge of "anachronism" voiced against Gerhardsson himself by his early critics.[66] The argument has been made on many occasions, is often revisited in each subsequent treatment of Gerhardsson's work, and is one which has now come to the fore once again. As for this charge, I have already addressed this in my earlier *Oral Tradition* and suggest that concern about anachronism should not, in theory, dissuade us from exploring the great body of research gathered from the study of various cultures around the world—the vast majority of it taking place outside the realm of New Testament scholarship.[67]

I have formulated two principles which I suggest can serve as guidelines for evaluating the potential difficulty of adopting a model from an admittedly different chronological period. The first is one which I believe characterizes the potential danger of anachronism which is inherent in the rabbinic model forwarded by Gerhardsson:

The *more closely* a parallel is tied to a specific cultural practice among a specific people-group at a specific time and place, the *more problematic* it is to use a non-contemporaneous parallel to interpret the events or settings under examination.[68]

The level of specificity drawn from the proposed rabbinic parallels requires that there is a high level of continuity between the parallels themselves and the context which they are intended to illuminate. So, despite the relatively short chronological gap between nascent Christianity and emerging rabbinic Judaism, there is a significant danger in the level of inference that is drawn from those parallels.

The second principle that I suggest is the converse of the former:

> The *less closely* a parallel is tied to a specific cultural practice among a specific people-group at a specific time and place, the *less problematic* it is to use a non-contemporaneous parallel to interpret the events or settings under examination.[69]

The informal controlled model should be evaluated according to this second principle. To rephrase this principle in more positive terms, the more widely applicable a phenomenon is among diverse people groups, the more useful it is, and subsequently less problematic to apply it to the Jesus tradition through a diachronic approach.[70]

While it is granted that there is a great chronological distance between the Mediterranean culture[71] of Jesus' time and that depicted by Bailey, this does not provide, in itself, justification for abandoning the model altogether. Such critiques do not adequately account for the fact that this model of tradition formation continues to be documented across the globe, in variegated contexts among disparate people groups. Such widespread and thoroughgoing support for this phenomenon across such a wide spectrum of human society suggests that the model is indeed capable of bearing the burden of the evidence within the canonical Gospels themselves. The model that Bailey has proposed and which has subsequently been appropriated by others, including this present author,[72] is living among countless people groups today, and is likely linked to aspects inherent in our human physiology. Human physiology is slow to change, and traditional societies, as has been pointed out by the early pioneers of the so-called orality movement, have strong homeostatic tendencies which translate into human patterns of interaction which remain, to this day, indebted to the psychodynamics of oral communication.[73] While the external skin of human cultures has clearly morphed into countless forms over the six thousand or so years of recorded human history, the internal skeleton remains largely intact. We are able to examine orally transmitted material—wisdom traditions, prophetic material, and legal types—and see that all of these forms have been and still are transmitted in ways that resonate with the thesis articulated by Bailey.

If we are to discard the findings of all the cultural anthropologists, folklorists, and other scholars working within related disciplines, we would also need to question both the usefulness and applicability of the many wide-reaching insights derived from all the social sciences—including social-scientific criticism and even the recent work on social memory. All ongoing examinations of the Jesus tradition draw upon theoretical models of tradition transmission external to the primary sources themselves. For Bultmann it was a theoretical model of expansion over time from a "pure," "original" tradition, for Vincent Taylor it was the studies he conducted among his university students, for Gerhardsson it is rabbinic Judaism, and for Dunn and Mournet it is the theoretical framework proposed by Bailey. Each of these models, in turn, functions external to the tradition itself. Simply put, there are no models of tradition formation and transmission which are able to completely avoid the question of anachronism and/or applicability. Ong's observations on the "temporary character" of orality and the spoken word continue to serve as a reminder that we will never be able to make a direct appeal to the "evidence" of oral performance,[74] but rather we must be content with positioning ourselves within the realm of probability and possibility that flows from theoretical models constructed from worlds outside of the biblical texts itself.

Gerhardsson, in his article "The Secret of the Transmission of the Unwritten Jesus Tradition," forwards a series of arguments against Dunn and his use of Bailey's informal controlled model of tradition transmission. After outlining four basic assertions, Gerhardsson summarizes Dunn's thesis under the heading "variation within the same."[75] Gerhardsson offers the following paragraph outlining what he perceives to be areas of essential agreement with Dunn (by way of Bailey):

> Dunn places strong confidence in the oral gospel tradition. He is convinced that it proceeds from Jesus himself and is preserved in a trustworthy way . . . it was handed over to the Christian communities when they were founded and played a fundamental role for the members by keeping insiders together and delimiting them from outsiders . . . Dunn thinks that the Jesus tradition was so limited, distinct, and familiar in the congregations that not much other material—e.g. from Jewish wisdom or early Christian prophecy—could be mixed with it.[76]

Following this general but significant agreement, Gerhardsson proceeds to articulate his points of fundamental disagreement with the orality model, as formulated by Dunn. It is at this point where the differences between the two approaches come to the fore. It will also become clear that again the so-called orality approach as framed by recent advocates of Bailey's model has been, at least within the context of this recent exchange, misunderstood.

Gerhardsson paints a portrait of "orality" whereby oral communication is "a popular telling, presented by singers or tellers to people gathered around them, and consisting of popular tales. Typical for these oral performances is that the presentation is constantly subject to change."[77] Lastly, in critiquing portraits of Jesus as a "cynic philosopher," "popular narrator," and so forth, Gerhardsson suggests, in reference to Dunn, that "no source indicates, for instance, that Jesus was a popular teller of tales who captivated disciples and throngs with variable performance."[78] While it is true that the Jesus tradition itself does not specifically depict Jesus as a "teller of tales," it does not take much imagination to envisage a context where this type of activity might take place and take place repeatedly.

Clearly, Jesus was, according to the Gospel sources themselves, a person who had no difficulty attracting attention and gaining popular support as he preached throughout the Galilean countryside. From the accounts of the miraculous feedings of large crowds, to the crowds surrounding Jesus as he preached, to the crowd which forced Jesus to preach from a boat—one is reminded time and time again that Jesus' message was not only popular, but that he was able to sustain the interest of large crowds. Further support for the popular ministry of Jesus can be found in the Markan notion of the "messianic secret." If the "messianic secret," as is commonly associated with William Wrede, is reflective of the historical Jesus himself, then this lends further support to the notion that Jesus was not only a teacher who taught those in his inner circle, but that he was popular enough that he needed to be concerned with the populace and their inherited messianic expectations. We are also reminded of the once abandoned but now revisited notion that Jesus likely preached and taught the same, or largely the same, material on multiple occasions.[79] Regardless of one's notion of the precise role of memorization in Jesus' ministry or the extent to which Jesus engaged in an intentional didactic process with his disciples, it is difficult, if not impossible, to avoid the conclusion that Jesus, being human, would have interacted in his various social contexts as a storyteller—through which he could teach, train, instruct, and yes, even entertain. Certainly not every social context in which Jesus was involved was formal and revolved around intentional didactic activity.

Jesus, according to Gerhardsson, "was not a link in a chain of tradition" but "spoke always in his own name, in his own authority. 'The only teacher' brought forward sayings of his own and nothing else. *Jesus was not a common traditionalist.* Even this simple fact strains the orality parallels."[80] The critique here is focused on the content of Jesus' messages (i.e., Jesus always "speaking in his own name"). However, the content of Jesus' message is not the pertinent issue. While Jesus might not have been a "common traditionalist," this does not mitigate the fact that Jesus needed to communicate the content of whatever tradition he desired to pass along to others and in its appropriate medium. Whether or not Jesus' teachings were "traditional" in the technical sense of the term is not at issue here. Jesus' ideas and concepts were integrally linked to the past, and as such, functioned as modifications or reconfigurations of existing traditional frameworks.

For documents such as the Gospels, the insider-outsider language and the often cryptic and obscure elements within the tradition are attributable to our social distance from the world in which Jesus lived. Texts convey meaning by connecting readers, or hearers, to the greater social world that exists outside of the text itself. We are reminded of John Foley's work on the concept of metonymic referencing, which he defines as "a mode of signification wherein the part stands for the whole."[81] In traditional society, elements of a performance (either oral or textual) reference a greater worldview and frame of reference than that which is clearly explicated from within the text itself. Only those approaching the text from an insider (i.e., *emic*) perspective are able to grasp the level on which the society at the time was indebted to the de facto means of communication. No individual, either during the time of Jesus or even today for that matter, functions without reference to their own metanarrative (used as the matrix through which they are able to make sense of their surroundings) from within a particular social context. For Jesus, the metanarrative was that of the story of Yahweh working through the patriarchs and his chosen people, and the greater social and communicative context in which that story was retold was the world of oral communication and oral performance. Jesus no doubt utilized his skills as an oral performer to present his message to others in a persuasive manner.

Conclusion

It is now necessary to examine the various threads which have been woven throughout the previous discussion and articulate, in conclusion, the main "thrust" of the orality model. While memory is at the heart of both the rabbinic and orality models,[82] it seems evident that the real crux of the disagreement lies in the envisioned level of didactic intentionality that advocates of both positions believe characterized the ministry of Jesus. The primary question which must be pursued further is this: to what extent was Jesus' didactic activity employed within a highly regulated, rabbinic context and carried out in an intentionally crafted and controlled environment?

The rabbinic model of tradition transmission advocated by Gerhardsson is one which argues for a consistently formalized didactic context within which Jesus himself functioned as a teacher, intentionally shaping and controlling the tradition as it was passed down to his small circle of disciples. Likewise, in subsequent further didactic contexts, Jesus' disciples and other "leading men" continued to ensure the accurate ongoing transmission of the tradition. From this perspective, differences in wording or phraseology within the synoptic tradition derive from the use of well-known and accepted rabbinic practices which were at work within nascent rabbinic Judaism. While it is recognized that memorization should not be understood exclusively as an attempt to transmit tradition verbatim, departure from verbatim transmission is explicable via an appeal to formalized, structured methods of transmission. That is, departure from the "text" of the tradition is explicable through the model of rabbinic expansions and ongoing interpretations modeled on how the rabbis interacted with their own textual traditions. From this perspective, the tradition, and its subsequent transmission, follows largely regulated paths of change and variation. Despite the recognition of the variable nature of the transmission of the early Jesus tradition, the process of tradition transmission which led to the final form of the Gospels is envisioned as the intentional departure from a more or less "fixed" exemplar—whether written or oral.

The orality model, by way of comparison, assumes a less structured and less formalized didactic context for the transmission of the early Jesus tradition. Even if the early Jesus tradition was originally handed down within a formalized quasi-rabbinic Jewish didactic context, such a context cannot be understood as exclusive to other less formalized transmission contexts. The significant question is whether an initial formal transmission context is able to describe fully the ongoing transmission process from the time of Jesus himself to the time in which the Synoptic Gospels were inscribed, copied, and transmitted throughout the Roman Empire.

Within a relatively short period of time the Jesus tradition would have spread far beyond the confines of Jesus' immediate circle of disciples. Jesus regularly interacted with people outside of his circle of disciples, and, if the testimony of the Synoptic Gospels is to be trusted, then the geographic locale of his influence and impact reached far beyond the environs of Jerusalem. Once the teachings, sermons, proverbs, parables, and sayings of Jesus extended beyond his immediate circle of students—and beyond the confines of Jerusalem itself—then neither Jesus nor his disciples would have been able to control the manner in which the tradition (loosely speaking) was transmitted. Numerous Jesus communities each received ongoing deposits into their respective collective pools of tradition. Some of that tradition might very well have come by means of "official" channels, delivered by teachers and ministers of the word.[83] However, even if such an argument was granted, that does not count against the argument for the ongoing role of oral tradition in those communities; for if Christian communities did receive such official tradition, their resources would certainly not have been exclusively restricted to such official channels.

Once the tradition circulated beyond its initial performative context, it would have been subject to the ongoing influence of the various Christian contexts, formed and shaped by that tradition, while also lending their own theological and communal contours to the tradition as well. What might have been thoroughly Jewish contexts were becoming more ethnically diverse. By the time the tradition is inscribed into one of its canonical forms, it has been exposed to the influence of oral communication within a context that is becoming more and more influenced by non-Jewish thought.

Rather than speaking of an ongoing, singular, formalized rabbinic context for transmission of the Jesus tradition, centered in Jerusalem, we must come to terms with the phenomenon of multiple Jesus communities, multiple tradition-transmission contexts, and the influx of Jesus tradition from numerous sources—in both textual and oral forms. When the Gospel writers proceeded to write their respective accounts of the life of Jesus, they were drawing from a river of tradition which itself was formed from the combined input of the diverse streams of Christian thought reflective of the variegated nature of early Christianity itself. They drew upon source texts which might have been at their disposal, such as Q, Mark, among others, and they no doubt also drew upon their individual and corporate recollections, that is, memories, which would have also had an unavoidable impact on the social dynamics involved in Gospel composition.

Such is the basic supposition of the "orality model." The only way in which we are able to dismiss the orality model of tradition transmission is if we are willing, and able, to argue for an undisturbed, unbroken, continuous chain of transmission and control exerted by Jesus himself, and continuing within a formalized context for several decades until the time of the writing of the Gospels themselves. Advocates of orality are unable to envision such a uniform, sustained process of tradition transmission. Despite the possible presence of early texts, *logia* collections, and other textual sources, oral tradition and oral performance would have continued to exert a powerful influence upon the final forms of the canonical Gospels.

The model of tradition transmission which found its genesis in the work of Bailey and which has been formulated with greater specificity by Dunn and Mournet has the benefit of being able to account for the complex character of the primary repository of the Jesus tradition, that is, the Synoptic Gospels themselves. The Jesus tradition exhibits both fixed and flexible characteristics and is the product of the complex interaction of both oral and textual traditions under the shaping influence of social memory and stability provided via eyewitness testimony and community self-regulation.[84] While each of the three models of tradition transmission described above is able to provide a theoretical explanation of the synoptic phenomena, it is proposed that the orality model is able to account for the character of the Jesus tradition, and to do so in a way that is both coherent and plausible within the historical context of first-century Mediterranean life.

Chapter 3

Jesus Tradition and the Pauline Letters

David E. Aune

This essay is written in honor of my friend and colleague, Birger Gerhardsson, a pioneer in the study of oral tradition in early Judaism and early Christianity. After reviewing the major contribution that Gerhardsson has made to New Testament scholarship, the essay will survey and critique some of the contributions to the problem of oral tradition in the Pauline letters, and then give a survey and critique of some discussions of Paul's use of Jesus traditions apart from the problem of how they were transmitted. Finally, I will turn to a discussion of Paul's letters as *lieux de mémoire,* that is, as "sites" or "artifacts of memory," in the Pauline letters.

THE PROJECT OF BIRGER GERHARDSSON

While Gerhardsson's *Memory and Manuscript* remains one of the classic works of the twentieth century, progress in scholarship along with the inevitable changes in perspective and methodology make it appropriate to reassess his great work forty-five years after its publication.[1] Gerhardsson's great achievement was to argue for the link between memory and tradition, and the recognition of this connection has sparked renewed interest in his work.

Gerhardsson's work centered on assembling what can be known of oral and written transmission in rabbinic Judaism from Tannaitic and Amoraic sources (ca. 70–500 C.E.). This model is then applied to the more fragmentary evidence for the oral transmission of Jesus traditions in first-century Christianity, primarily in Acts and Paul. Gerhardsson argued that, on analogy with the rabbinical model, the disciples of Jesus and their successors carefully memorized and even took notes about the words and deeds of Jesus (referred to by Gerhardsson as both "the Holy Word" and "the gospel tradition"), which they then accurately transmitted in relatively unchanged form.[2] This deposit of tradition was preserved and transmitted by duly constituted authorities, the twelve apostles, who constituted a collegium with supreme doctrinal authority in the early church (conceptions influenced by the influx of Pharisees into the church), and "are bearers, not only of the tradition concerning Christ, but also of the correct interpretation of the Scriptures."[3] One of Gerhardsson's primary purposes was to question the fundamental assumptions and methods of form criticism.[4]

Gerhardsson's monograph was subjected to thoroughgoing criticism by scholars such as W. D. Davies, Morton Smith, Jacob Neusner, Norman Perrin, and Werner Kelber,[5] with a relatively positive response early on by Joseph Fitzmyer,[6] and a more recent and positive critique by Richard Bauckham.[7] Gerhardsson has responded to many of the criticisms leveled against *Memory and Manuscript*,[8] often by claiming that he had been misinterpreted.[9] The most frequent objection to Gerhardsson's central thesis is that it is anachronistic to read rabbinic pedagogical techniques of 200 C.E. (and later) into Christianity of the pre-70 C.E. period.[10] Neusner, an early critic of Gerhardsson's anachronistic use of Tannaitic and Amoraic pedagogy as a model for understanding the transmission of Jesus tradition in early Christianity, has recently recanted and even written a positive introduction to the 1998 reprint of *Memory and Manuscript*.[11] According to Neusner, all that Gerhardsson was proposing was that

> comparison and contrast need not be synchronic and may under carefully controlled and justified circumstances take the route of diachrony. He went in search of a model of how oral formulation and oral tradition can have taken place. He did not claim that his model derived from, or attested to the practice of the period of his principal interest. He sought only knowledge of possible techniques. So he did not mean to say that the way they produced the Mishnah in the late second and early third century tells us how they produced the Gospels a century and a half earlier.[12]

Neusner thus sees the difference between Gerhardsson and his critics as the difference between "paradigmatic versus historical thinking," and the bulk of his introduction is devoted to this theme.[13]

The anachronistic use of rabbinic pedagogy as a model for understanding the transmission of Jesus tradition in early Christianity has grown more, rather than less, obvious since the early 1960s. While Gerhardsson frequently uses the term "Pharisaic-rabbinic," merging the pre-70 C.E. Pharisees with post-200 C.E. rabbinic sages, and uses the phrase Oral Torah of certain traditions in the pre-70 C.E. period, Martin Jaffee argues convincingly that there are no clear connections with the Pharisees and the later rabbinic sages and that there is an important distinction between traditions external to the Written Torah and the Oral Torah. Between the written sources of textual study and the oral-literary tradition within which the texts were interpreted was a development that belongs to the mid-third century C.E.[14] (parenthetically, Jaffee connects the Galilean sages' ideological commitment to the idea of Oral Torah as a conception developed in the circle around Rabbi Yohanan, where it functioned as an explanation and celebration of the master-disciple relationship, the distinctive social form of rabbinic community).[15] Further, though Gerhardsson uses the term *halakah* (i.e., "an orally transmitted tradition of laws derived from scriptural exegesis but not explicitly contained in the Torah") to refer to early Christian practices,[16] the term *halakah* is found neither in the Qumran literature nor in the surviving literature of the Second Temple period; its earliest appearance is in the Mishnah and Tosefta, rabbinic literature of the third century C.E.[17]

Interestingly, none of the earlier critiques of Gerhardsson's monograph touched the issue of the adequacy of his understanding of oral transmission in Tannaitic and Amoraic Judaism. Kelber was an exception. He criticized Gerhardsson for his thesis of "mechanical memorization," that is, of a "passive and authoritative transmission of traditions," implying that Gerhardsson had misread the rabbinic evidence.[18] More than two decades later, Kelber repeated the same criticism:

> Gerhardsson envisioned a mechanical commitment of materials to memory and a passive transmission by way of continual repetition. Changes that did occur in the processing of traditional items remain confined to interpretive adaptations. On the whole, the work of memory as a key arbiter of tradition was, therefore, characterized by fixity, stability and continuity, and the primary purpose of transmission was the deliberate act of communicating the legacy of Jesus for its own sake.[19]

Gerhardsson himself later raised the issue of whether or not the rules for memorized oral transmission were actually used in practice.[20] That is, what the rabbis say they do may be quite different from what they actually do. Norman Perrin was an early critic who observed that "the most successful part of the work is the study of 'oral tradition and written transmission' in rabbinic Judaism, to which Gerhardsson has clearly devoted a great deal of time."[21] Neusner himself has investigated the theme of oral tradition in Judaism in great detail, focusing on the highly formal, patterned speech that characterizes the Mishnah. He argues that these are mnemonic patterns indicating that the Mishnah was constructed to be memorized. The Mishnah, then, is "not the result of a long process of oral formulation and oral transmission. It clearly is meant to inaugurate a long process of oral transmission or oral tradition."[22] The rabbis themselves claimed to have accurately passed on the traditions they received, claiming "not merely essential accuracy but exact verbal correspondence with what was originally stated by the authorities standing behind the traditions."[23] Philip Alexander has observed, however, that though Neusner is able to account for the creation of intermediate units, or "chapters" in the Mishnah, he provides no formal rules explaining the combination of "chapters" into tractates and tractates into orders.[24] He also notes that while the rabbis claim to have preserved the traditions they received verbatim, by imposing a standard formulaic structure on the words of a sage when juxtaposed to the opinions of other sages, they effectively destroyed his *ipsissima verba*.[25] Despite the claims made in rabbinic literature for verbal accuracy in transmission, multiple attestations of the same tradition reveal substantial textual variation, indicating that the transmission was variable and dynamic rather than static.[26]

The Problem of Paul and Oral Tradition

There is no evidence that Paul, unlike the framers of the Mishnah, wrote his letters with the intention that they be subject to oral transmission. There is evidence to suggest that Paul, like many others, dictated his letters to a secretary or amanuensis, who was actually responsible for writing the letters.[27] There is striking confirmation of this widely known ancient practice at the conclusion of Romans: "I Tertius, the writer of this letter, greet you in the Lord" (Rom 16:22), and confirmation in a different way toward the end of Galatians, when Paul claims, "See what large letters I make when I am writing with my own hand!" (Gal 6:11).

Further, Paul's letters would have been read aloud to the congregations to which they were directed, and since he was aware of this it is likely that he would have unconsciously designed them for oral recitation. There can be little doubt that much is lost in the written transcription of an oral discourse, such as gestures, intonation, and emphasis, all of which contribute to meaning. Yet it should by no means be assumed that Paul's oral recital was transformed into a static written product. During the early transmission history of the various works making up the New Testament, it is widely recognized that scribes took the freedom to add, subtract, and modify the texts that they were copying.[28] Thus each new "copy" of an exemplar was itself a performance in its own right, raising the question of the extent to which the traditional text-critical goal of reconstructing the "original" text is an achievable enterprise. In my own work on a commentary on the *Testament of Solomon*, it became evident early on that the "original text" of this second-century document cannot be reconstructed.[29] This raises the important question about the purpose of such a commentary. In the case of the *Testament of Solomon*, I decided to base the commentary on a single manuscript "performance" of the text, bringing in a discussion of some of the extensive variants only when such a discussion seemed warranted.

Two sorts of evidence for early Christian orality are arguably present in the Pauline letters. First, Paul occasionally refers to various aspects of oral tradition directly when he refers to such concepts as "tradition" and "the Word of God." Second, it is inherently likely that patterns of oral composition as well as particular units of oral tradition have been incorporated by Paul into his letters, whether consciously or unconsciously. The problem here is that of distinguishing with any confidence between genuine "oral footprints" and between patterns of composition that are used both orally and textually (as we shall see below in our discussion of Harvey).

In the remainder of this section, I will summarize Gerhardsson's discussion of Paul and oral tradition, followed by a synthesis and critique of three scholars who have treated the issue of Paul and oral tradition in some detail, Werner Kelber (1983), Traugott Holtz (1991), and John D. Harvey (1998).[30]

Birger Gerhardsson

Toward the end of *Memory and Manuscript*, Gerhardsson devoted fifty-one pages to a discussion of "The Evidence of Paul."[31] In part one of his monograph, Gerhardsson discussed the transmission of Written and Oral Torah in rabbinic Judaism from the Tannaitic and Amoraic periods, circa 70–500 C.E. (pp. 17–189). In part two, he turns to evidence for the transmission of the gospel tradition in early Christianity, using his construction of rabbinic pedagogical methods as a model for understanding the oral transmission of Jesus traditions beginning with the post-apostolic church (pp. 194–207), the evidence found in Acts (pp. 208–61), the evidence found in Paul (pp. 262–323), and finally, "The Origins and Transmission of the Gospel Tradition" (pp. 324–35).

Gerhardsson begins with an emphasis on Paul's status as an apostle, an equal to the accepted apostolic status of Peter, since he has been commissioned by the risen Lord (Gal 1–2). According to Paul, the Christian message had been revealed in two forms, Paul's "gospel of circumcision" and Peter's "gospel of uncircumcision," both variations on the one gospel. Paul maintained that the church of Christ was a unity with its center in Jerusalem, with the circle of the Twelve as the highest doctrinal authority (emphasized on pp. 274–80). Paul therefore uses traditions that originated from this doctrinal center in Jerusalem. His relationship to the collegium of the apostles is analogous to that between an individual rabbi and his colleagues (*haburim*). Gerhardsson emphasizes the roles of the apostles as both eyewitnesses of what Jesus did and taught as well as of his resurrection (pp. 280–88). Since Paul claims to be an eyewitness of the resurrection only, and not the words and deeds of Jesus, he necessarily had to rely on authoritative tradition. Scripture is now understood christologically in a way principally revealed to the apostles (p. 285). Gerhardsson claims that Paul can say that he received his gospel by revelation (Gal 1), since "the message of salvation" (*kerygma*) does not include everything called "the word of God" (*didache*). In his teaching, Paul's arguments are not drawn from personal revelations, but from Scripture and the authoritative "tradition of the Lord."

Turning to the subject of Paul and tradition, Gerhardsson first discusses the terminology for tradition used by Paul and argues for the existence of an authoritative body of "tradition" functionally equivalent to the "oral torah" of Judaism (pp. 288–89). What Paul refers to as "tradition" is the authoritative material (consisting of both words and actions) that he passed on to the congregations he founded, making conscious use of apostolic authority to transmit authoritative doctrine. Thus "the word of God" that Paul passes on to his congregations proceeds from Jerusalem (p. 296). Gerhardsson asks: "What was the nature of the fundamental authoritative material which Paul passed on to his congregations before writing his epistles to them?"[32] That which Paul passed on to the congregations with which he interacted centered in a corpus of sayings of and about Christ, that Gerhardsson labels "the Gospel tradition."[33] Yet he maintains that

> At all events, this Christ-tradition seems to occupy a self-evident position as a basis, focus and point of departure for the work of the Apostle Paul. It is evident that he attempts to provide a firm basis in this centre even for what appear to be peripheral rules. But he does not pass on this focal tradition in his epistles. He *presupposes* it constantly, since it has already been delivered.[34]

The single most important section in the Pauline letters indicating the content of the word of God is 1 Corinthians 15:3-8, which clearly demonstrates that Paul received authoritative tradition about the death and resurrection of Christ (pp. 299–300). In Gerhardsson's brief analysis of 1 Corinthians 15:3-8, he argues that the passage consists of a series of *simanim* (a Hebrew transliteration of the Greek word σημεῖον, "sign"), in which each line or *siman* is a short designation for some passage in the gospel tradition about Christ.[35] In rabbinic literature, a *siman* is a device designed to help a student remember a complex ruling or retain the order of the main parts of a talmudic argument; a *siman* could be a verse of Scripture (*m. Abod. Zar.* 1:3) or a series of keywords based on the text (*b. Ber.* 57b), though the latter are found only in the Gemara of the Babylonian Talmud.[36] It is not clear that the later mnemonic use of *simanim* is directly relevant to interpreting such passages as 1 Corinthians 15:3-8, however, since the same could be said of all the creed-like passages in the New Testament and even of the missionary speeches in Acts (e.g., Acts 10:34-43). In the case of 1 Corinthians 15:3-8, Gerhardsson claims that "we have good reason to suppose that he derived this tradition—directly or indirectly—from the college of Apostles in Jerusalem,"[37] though such a supposition is speculative but not impossible. Gerhardsson then turns to the matter of the relationship of Paul to Jesus and to the college of apostles in Jerusalem. When the author of Colossians enjoins the recipients: "As therefore you received Christ Jesus the Lord, so walk in him" (Col 2:6), Gerhardsson construes this reference to "Christ Jesus the Lord" as "the transmitted Christ," referring not to the gospel, but to "a collection of traditions which he regarded as being a unity: some oral or written equivalent of one of our Gospels."[38]

Gerhardsson compares the central role that the gospel tradition played for Paul as a sort of "Mishnah," with Paul's own teaching and "legislation" as a "Talmud."[39] This important move is based on his rabbinic model in which orally formulated texts in fixed forms provide the basis for more fluid textual forms, corresponding to "Mishnah" and "Gemara."[40] This means that Gerhardsson is prepared to deal with both the fixity and fluidity of the gospel tradition. Gerhardsson discusses Paul's "Talmud" (or tradition) under three headings: doctrine, ethics, and ecclesiology. Examples of doctrine include 1 Corinthians 15 on the resurrection and several passages on circumcision (1 Cor 7:19; Gal 5:6; 6:15). Examples of ethics include 1 Thessalonians 4:1-8 on rules for Christian living and 1 Corinthians 4:17, the "ways" in which Paul taught. Examples of ecclesiology, dealing with directions about such matters as public worship, teaching, and church discipline, include 1 Corinthians 11:23-25 (the institution of the Last Supper), 1 Corinthians 5 (church discipline), and 1 Corinthians 14 (silence of women in church). Finally, Gerhardsson discusses a series of issues in which Paul alludes to sayings of Jesus, including 1 Corinthians 7:10-12 (divorce), the problem of clean and unclean (1 Cor 8; Rom 14:20; cf. Mark 7:14), 1 Corinthians 9:4-18 (support for apostles), and 1 Corinthians 11:23-25 (the institution of the Last Supper).[41]

Werner Kelber

In *The Oral and the Written Gospel*, Werner Kelber produced a monograph that introduced New Testament scholars to some of the implications of research in orality that the guild had ignored. Throughout the monograph, Kelber shows little direct concern for models of oral transmission or the specific evidence for oral composition and transmission found in the New Testament. His chapter on "Orality and Textuality in Paul" is no exception.[42] Here, as in the rest of the monograph, the author implicitly valorizes oral over written communication, a valorization that he reads into Paul.[43] Kelber associates letter writing with oral language, making Robert Funk's identification and functional description of the Pauline travelogue, with its emphasis on oral words and personal presence, the basis of his discussion.[44]

Kelber discusses four main issues: (1) "The Oral Gospel," where he calls attention to "Paul's partiality toward oral discourse that pervades his treatment of gospel, faith, and obedience";[45] (2) "The Written Law," treating Paul's aversion toward the objectified, written word evident in his polemic against the law; (3) "The Oral Matrix of the Righteousness of God," that is, the antithesis of law and gospel as a conflict between *verbum scriptum* and *viva vox*; and (4) "The Rupture of the Oral Synthesis," Paul's message as it is available in written documents.

Kelber's discussion of "The Oral Gospel" calls attention to the fact that the term "gospel" occurs more than fifty times in the Pauline letters and is typically associated with the act of speaking as the master metaphor that pervades Paul's program. Kelber argues that, from a broad hermeneutical perspective, "spoken words are experienced personally and more directly than written words."[46] "Gospel in Pauline hermeneutics," argues Kelber, "is not subject to formal definition" but is "an operational term;" it does not equal "the transformation of plural oral traditions into narrative linearity, stretching from birth through a powerful life on earth to death and resurrection" (i.e., Paul's gospel is not analogous to what is found in the missionary sermons of Acts, e.g., Acts 10:34-43, or to the amplified story found in the Gospel of Mark).[47] Kelber is certainly correct that Paul's oral proclamation of the gospel was his central preoccupation. But then, of course, oral interaction remains the central function of modern pastors and teachers.

Kelber has prepared the reader for "The Written Law," a section in which he argues that there are subtle linguistic cues that Paul had a fundamental anxiety toward the law as written authority. Though he does not label it as such, this section is an exercise in *Sachkritik*, that is, what Paul really means is masked by much of what he says. For Kelber, "This written complexification of the Word appears to be contrary to the personalized communication fostered by the oral gospel and faith that come from hearing."[48] The Pauline antithesis of "spirit" and "letter" (2 Cor 3:1-6) is construed as an antithesis between the oral gospel and the written law, rather than the more common understanding as an antithesis between faith and works. Though it is not possible to deal with this issue here, it is in fact more likely that "spirit" and "letter" mask Paul's concern with the universality of the gospel over against particularism represented by the Jewish law.[49] Kelber also finds in 2 Corinthians 3:1-6 a repudiation of "Divine Man hermeneutics," that is, the conviction that the written word served as carrier of the Spirit, while Paul as an oral traditionalist disconnects "spirit" from "letter" and reconnects the Spirit of the living God with "word in its internal personalizing efficaciousness (3:2-3)."[50] Rightly or wrongly, this calls to mind Luther's description of Scripture (*die Biblia*) as "des Heiligen Geistes eigen, sonderlich Buch, Schrift und Wort," that is, as "the Holy Spirit's own special book, writ, and word."[51] The term "word" here refers to Luther's emphasis on the *viva vox* of the gospel, that is, "a vivid sense of the living spoken word of God that is communicated both in Christian preaching and the reading of Scripture."[52] (Luther spoke of "the ears alone" as "the organs of the Christian."[53]) In the history of Lutheranism, the *viva vox* of Luther found its antithesis in Lutheran orthodoxy (which flourished from 1580 to 1675), the chief enterprise of which was the formulation of a doctrine of Holy Scripture that could serve as the foundation of pure doctrine.

In "The Oral Matrix of the Righteousness of God," Kelber argues that for Paul, gospel, faith, and obedience function in a linguistic and auditory sphere, and that his theology of language is such that "the righteousness of God" is an act or event rather than a principle or concept.[54] As such, the active character of righteousness makes it inappropriate for propositional explication. Finally, in "The Rupture of the Oral Synthesis," Kelber suggests that by using the written medium of letters, Paul distanced himself from the act of primary speech.[55] Paul was apparently aware that the eruption of enthusiasm among the Thessalonians was in part a product of his oral gospel,[56] and in 1 Corinthians he polemicizes against the oral powers of wisdom.[57] Consequently, "when faced with the extreme consequences of oral wisdom, Paul, preacher of the oral gospel, is here compelled to reconsider his hermeneutical priorities and to invoke the norm of Scripture."[58] Thus, following Kelber's narrative, Paul in the end suffers from a failure of nerve.

In the end however, Paul's failure of nerve is the result of Kelber's use of *Sachkritik* to impose an orality versus textuality ideology on Paul where it simply does not do justice to the texts that he considers. In the end, despite Kelber's broad familiarity with modern oral studies, he does nothing to advance the use of models of oral transmission to explicate the role of memory in Paul's use of tradition.

Traugott Holtz

Traugott Holtz contributed an essay on "Paul and the Oral Gospel Tradition" in the second of two conferences on Jesus and the oral gospel tradition, organized by David L. Dungan, William Farmer, Birger Gerhardsson, and Henry Wansbrough.[59] The first was held in Dublin in 1989 and the second in Gazzada, Italy, in 1990. The papers presented at both conferences were revised, edited by Henry Wansbrough, and published in 1991 by the JSOT Press under the title *Jesus and the Oral Gospel Tradition*. The present author attended both conferences and presented a paper at each of them.

Holtz begins with a consideration of the Jesus tradition in the Synoptic Gospels, arguing that sayings of Jesus were transmitted side-by-side in verbal fixed form and extremely free presentations.[60] Paul had access to oral Jesus traditions exhibiting both fixed and free formulations. First Corinthians 11:23-25 (the institution of the Last Supper), introduced by the technical verbs of transmission παραλαμβάλειν, "to receive traditional instruction," and παραδίδοναι, "to hand over to" (1 Cor 11:23a), is an example of a verbally fixed form of tradition (cf. Luke 22:19-20).[61] This is the only instance in the Pauline letters or the other New Testament letters that a saying of Jesus is transmitted in a verbally fixed form. Paul alludes a few more times to Jesus traditions (clear examples include 1 Cor 7:10-11; 9:14; cf. 1 Thess 4:13–5:11), reproducing the general content though not the fixed form of sayings of Jesus known from the Synoptic Gospels. Holtz suggests that there are probably many allusions to the Jesus tradition in the Pauline letters that remain unrecognizable to us.[62] He then points to several passages in the Pauline letters in which Paul consciously alludes to Jesus traditions, though certainty in identifying these is not possible:[63] (1) nothing is in itself unclean (Rom 14:14; cf. Mark 7:15 and par.; Luke 11:41 and par.); (2) the whole law is fulfilled in the command of love of neighbor (Gal 5:14; Rom 13:8-10; cf. Mark 12:28-34); (3) give to all what is due to them (Rom 13:7; cf. Mark 12:17 and par.); and (4) bless those who persecute you (Rom 12:14; 1 Cor 4:12-13; cf. Matt 5:43-44; Luke 6:27-28; *Did.* 1:3).

What accounts for the disparity between fixed and fluid Jesus traditions in the Pauline letters? Holtz only hints at a solution. In the last sentence of his essay, he observes that tradents "in the early period obviously possessed the freedom to put the sayings of Jesus known to it into its own words addressed to the present time, and in this way lend the words such forceful authority."[64] Thus Holtz seems to favor a theory of the development of Jesus traditions, which are used in looser formulation in the "early period," but are used in a more fixed form at a "later period."[65]

John D. Harvey

The most extensive discussion of oral tradition in the Pauline letters is the published dissertation of John D. Harvey. Harvey provides a succinct review of modern research on orality in the ancient world, epistolary analysis, and Pauline rhetoric, though unfortunately he studiously refrains from critiquing the views he surveys even though some of them are mutually contradictory. Harvey then identifies "oral patterning" in Greco-Roman literature and the Septuagint,[66] focusing on eight compositional patterns: chiasmus, inversion, alteration, inclusion, ring composition, word chain, refrain, and concentric symmetry.[67] The author then identifies occurrences of these compositional patterns in those Pauline letters that are widely agreed to be authentic (Romans, 1 Corinthians, 2 Corinthians, Galatians, Philippians, 1 Thessalonians, and Philemon).[68]

Harvey never comes to grips with the central problem bedeviling anyone who claims that oral patterns are present in written texts: all of the evidence is contained in written texts. To a certain extent the oral-formulaic theory formulated by Milman Parry and Albert Lord escapes this hermeneutical circle on account of the convincing modern analogy of oral epic composition among Yugoslavian and Bulgarian bards (studied in situ by Parry and Lord in the 1930s and by Lord in the 1950s),[69] though even this has failed to convince some eminent classicists of the validity of oral-formulaic theory. Unfortunately, the oral-formulaic theory of the Homeric epics has no relevance for analyzing the Pauline letters, since Paul did not compose his letters in a manner analogous to the anonymous oral poets and Harvey makes no claims that he did. While it is impossible to disprove that compositional techniques have a proximate oral origin, neither is it possible to prove that they actually do. The reason is simply that there is a revolving door between oral and written composition. Virtually all of the compositional techniques used originally in oral composition made a seamless transition into the stylistics of written composition. It is therefore far from clear what Harvey means by "oral" in the phrase "oral patterning." Since, according to Harvey, Paul learned many "oral patterns" from written sources, such as the Septuagint,[70] what significance does the term "oral" retain? Ring composition is one of Harvey's "oral patterns" that appears in Paul's letters.[71] Ian Worthington has argued that, in classical Greece, when orations originally delivered orally are revised and written down for posterity, the structural complexity of the speech is frequently increased, including a more complex use of ring composition.[72] What Harvey has accomplished is to provide an inventory of some Pauline stylistic techniques, an important contribution to the neglected study of Greek style in the New Testament.

Paul and the Jesus Tradition

In the previous section I focused on studies that explicitly treat the problem of Paul and oral tradition. In this section, I turn to scholars who have focused on Paul's use of Jesus tradition but have not directly addressed the problem of oral transmission.

One perennial issue in assessing the relationship between Paul and Jesus, and one which our brief review of the article by Holtz has thematized, is the problem of "why Paul, along with the whole early Christian epistolary literature, did not make use of the Gospel tradition."[73] Since Paul died circa 64 C.E., none of the canonical Gospels existed in written form (though it is likely that a written version of the Q document was in circulation),[74] meaning that any quotations of or allusions to Jesus traditions would have to be derived from oral tradition. Though the amount of literature on this subject is enormous, very few scholars have followed the approach of Holtz and directly addressed the issue of the role and character of oral tradition. The extent of the literature on the issue of Jesus traditions in Paul makes it possible only to provide a sample of the discussion and then offer a few concluding reflections.

While many New Testament scholars have puzzled over the apparent neglect of Jesus traditions in the Pauline letters, the prize for having ferreted out the most allusions to the synoptic tradition in Paul must be awarded to Alfred Resch, who claimed to have identified 792 allusions to the canonical Gospels in the seven generally accepted Pauline letters (Romans, 1–2 Corinthians, Galatians, 1 Thessalonians, Philippians, and Philemon).[75] Justly skeptical of Resch's optimistic list of allusions to the Gospels in Paul, W. D. Davies suggested that, in addition to the few clear references to sayings of Jesus (1 Cor 7:10; 9:14; 11:23-25; 1 Thess 4:15-16; 1 Cor 14:37),[76] Paul has interwoven the words of Jesus almost unconsciously in his letters. Davies singled out twenty-five clear parallels to the Synoptic Gospels in Romans, 1 Thessalonians, and Colossians, indicating how Paul is steeped in the mind and words of his Lord.[77] The view that Paul alludes to Jesus traditions almost unconsciously is one of the major solutions to the problem of the apparent neglect of Jesus traditions in Paul.

In 1982 Dale Allison devoted an important and creative essay to the problem of allusions to the Jesus tradition in the Pauline letters, arguing that they tended to cluster in 1 Thessalonians 4–5, Colossians 3–4, and 1 Corinthians (a point made by other scholars). Allison argued that Paul must have known the sources behind Mark 9:33-50, Luke 6:27-38, and Mark 6:6b-13 and parallel passages, along with the Passion Narrative and a collection of conflict stories.[78]

Nicholas Walter addressed the issue of "Paulus und die urchristliche Jesustradition" in 1985.[79] Walter argued that the Pauline letters betray no knowledge of the narrative elements of the Jesus tradition, nor did Paul allude to the sayings of Jesus in connection with his exposition of the central themes of his gospel. Like others before him, Walter observes that the most recognizable allusions to the sayings of Jesus are found in Paul's epistolary paraenesis (an issue that is treated in detail by Allison, among others).

The most detailed discussion of the evidence relating to the use of Jesus traditions in the Pauline letters is the 1986 article by Franz Neirynck, "Paul and the Sayings of Jesus."[80] In a characteristically detailed, methodologically sophisticated and incisive way, Neirynck deals almost exhaustively with the secondary literature through 1984. His procedure is to list some of the proposed allusions to the Jesus tradition in Romans, 1 Corinthians, and 1 Thessalonians suggested by Allison and to discuss the viability of each.[81] In the conclusion, Neirynck maintains that 1 Corinthians 7:10-11 and 9:14 are not "quotations" in the strict sense, but Pauline "halakhic" formulations based on sayings of Jesus. He continues:

> Elsewhere in the Pauline letters there is no certain trace of a conscious use of sayings of Jesus. Possible allusions to Gospel sayings can be noted on the basis of similarity of form and context but a direct use of a Gospel saying in the form it has been preserved in the synoptic Gospels is hardly provable.[82]

Neirynck's use of the phrase "no certain trace of a conscious use of sayings of Jesus" leaves the door open a crack for the presence of such traditional material.

More recently, David Wenham has treated this issue at some length.[83] Wenham observes that "one of the most embarrassing facts for those who see Paul as a follower of Jesus is his failure to refer much to Jesus' life or teaching."[84] One obvious reason for this state of affairs, and one with which Wenham disagrees, is that Paul was not particularly interested in the ministry of Jesus before the passion. Another possible reason is that Paul takes knowledge of the message of Jesus for granted; both he and his readers have been taught it and know it well. The fact that there are numerous possible or probable allusions to the teaching of Jesus in the Pauline letters is just what one would expect if the teaching of Jesus were presupposed. Later in the book, Wenham deals in more detail with this problem. He begins with what he describes as the "massive overlap" between the teaching of Jesus and Paul:

> At the heart of Jesus' teaching and of Pauline theology is the conviction that God has intervened and is intervening to save his people and the world. This divine intervention is the fulfillment of OT promises and it is associated particularly with Jesus' own coming and sacrificial death. God's salvation is not just for the religious or the righteous, but is for sinners and outsiders. They are gathered into the restored Israel—the community of those who receive the word and have faith in Jesus. That community is God's new temple and is called to live in perfect love, thus fulfilling and surpassing the OT law, and in expectancy of the Lord's return to judge and to complete his saving work.[85]

On closer inspection, this "massive overlap" turns out to be a very general and abstract description of the default theological perspective that permeated early Christianity, with the truly distinctive features of both the teaching of Jesus and the theology of Paul omitted.

James D. G. Dunn has argued that since the Jesus tradition was known intimately by both Paul and those to whom he wrote, it would have been unnecessary for him to refer explicitly to sayings of Jesus in a verbally formal way.[86] In fact, he maintains, had Paul explicitly cited the authority of Jesus every time he mentioned something that Jesus said or did, he would have weakened the force of the allusion.[87] This is surely a case of special pleading. Dunn concludes that "knowledge of and interest in the life and ministry of Jesus was an integral part of [Paul's] theology, albeit referred to only *sotto voce* in his written theology,"[88] a close parallel to Davies' claim that Paul used the words of Jesus almost unconsciously. Dunn emphasizes the fact that echoes or allusions to the teaching of Jesus are all to be found in Paul's paraenesis, for example, Romans 12:14 (Luke 6:27-28; Matt 5:44), Romans 14:14 (Mark 7:15); 1 Corinthians 13:2 (Matt 17:20); 1 Thessalonians 5:2, 4 (Matt 24:43); 1 Thessalonians 5:13 (Mark 9:50).[89]

Among the central concerns of Detlef Häusser in his dissertation, *Christusbekenntnis und Jesusüberlieferung bei Paulus*,[90] is a discussion of the relationship between Jesus and Paul and the way in which Jesus traditions have been taken up in several pre-Pauline passages: 1 Corinthians 15:3-8; Romans 1:3-4; Philippians 2:6-11; Galatians 4:4-5 (perhaps also 6). Häusser approaches the issue of the presence of Jesus traditions in Paul from a very different angle. Rather than focusing on quotations or allusions to the Jesus tradition in Paul, he centers his discussion on primary units of pre-Pauline tradition found in the Pauline letters and on what they reveal of Paul's knowledge of Jesus. The monograph is complex, and the following summary remarks do not do it justice.

According to Häusser, Paul was certainly (*mit Sicherheit*) aware of the eucharistic words of Jesus (1 Cor 11:23-25), the ransom saying of Jesus (Mark 10:45 and par.), the self-designation of Jesus as Son of Man, the crucifixion of Jesus, his burial, the discovery of the empty tomb and various appearances of Jesus; the appearance before the Twelve (connected with Luke 24) and before the apostles (connected with Acts 1) is probable but not certain.[91] In connection with Häusser's discussion of 1 Corinthians 15:3-8, it is important to mention the fact that he adopts Gerhardsson's proposal that the passage consists of a chain of *simanim* with each line being connected with a passage from the gospel tradition,[92] passages that Häusser carefully explores.[93]

Paul probably (*wahrscheinlich*) knew the synoptic saying on humiliation and exaltation (e.g., Luke 14:11), the "I have come" and "I was sent" sayings, particularly the sending formula, the temptation of Jesus, the controversy saying on the son of God and the son of David and the trial of Jesus, including Jesus' confession before the Sanhedrin (Mark 14:61-62); he also knew that Jesus addressed God as father, but it is only a possibility that this is connected with the Lord's Prayer or the prayer of Jesus in Gethsemane.[94]

Finally, Häusser thinks it possible (*möglich*) that Paul knew parts of the infancy tradition, including the announcement of the birth of Jesus (Luke 1:30-35), and the presentation of Jesus in the temple (Luke 2:21-51), as well as the passion predictions, the parable of the wicked husbandmen, and the appearance of Jesus in Nazareth (Luke 4:18-30).[95] Moreover, Häusser suggests that Paul was familiar with the Lukan special tradition (Luke 1:32-35 has a possible connection to Romans 1; Luke 1:30-35; 2:21ff.; and 4:18-21 have points of contact with Galatians 4; and Luke 24:7, 34, 36ff. are reflected in 1 Corinthians 15).[96] He suggests that 1 Corinthians 15:3-8 and Romans 1:3-4 originated in Jerusalem, Philippians 2:6-11 in Judea (or even Jerusalem), and Galatians 4:4-5 was transmitted in Jewish Christian circles, while the Hebraizing Lukan special tradition was probably connected with conservative Jewish Christian circles in Judaism. He also proposes that Jesus traditions were transmitted to Paul directly from Peter (Gal 1:18) and James (Gal 1:19) in Jerusalem, and he perhaps received further traditions also during later stops in Jerusalem; two other localities where he may have gotten knowledge of Jesus traditions include Damascus and Antioch.[97]

Paul's Letters as *aides-mémoire* and *lieux de mémoire*

In the previous sections of this chapter, I have dealt with the memory of the Jesus tradition in Paul's letters, but in this final section I argue that Paul's letters themselves served as memorial texts, first as *aides-mémoire* (in the sense of mnemonic devices that serve as aids to communal memory) and then finally and more lastingly as *lieux de mémoire*, "sites of memory," or "realms of memory," from the time they were written until the present day. The Pauline letters initially functioned as *aides-mémoire* in the specific sense that they provided a summary of Paul's (and his associates') contacts and conversations with the local Christian communities to whom he addressed letters. With the passing of that first generation of Christians, the Pauline letters each community treasured could no longer function as *aides-mémoire* for communal memory, but were rather transformed into *lieux de mémoire*, that is, texts that generated and transformed communal memory. Further, this process was intensified by the gradual collection of Pauline letters, making it possible for Pauline churches to have access to letters addressed to communities other than their own. This meant that their original function as *aides-memoire* specific to each community could no longer maintain that purpose. These two factors, then, the passing of the generation of those who had experienced the ministry of Paul and the collection and distribution of Pauline letters throughout the Christian world, combined to transform the Pauline letters into *lieux de mémoire* that served to generate a compound communal memory of Paul and his ministry.

The phrase *lieux de mémoire* is borrowed from Pierre Nora's seven-volume edited work *Les Lieux de mémoire*, published in 1984–1992,[98] where it functions as the primary analytical concept in a new historiographical approach to French national history. Nola derived the phrase *lieux de mémoire* from the Latin rhetorical phrase *loci memoriae* ("memory places") discussed in detail by Frances Yates in her classic work *The Art of Memory*;[99] he is also in debt to Maurice Halbwachs' influential work *The Collective Memory*.[100] In the preface to the English-language edition of his magisterial project, Nora provides a succinct definition of *lieu de mémoire*:

> If the expression *lieu de mémoire* must have an official definition, it should be this: a *lieu de mémoire* is any significant entity, whether material or non-material in nature, which by dint of human will or the work of time has become a symbolic element in the memorial heritage of any community (in this case the French community).[101]

Examples of *lieux de mémoire* may include places (archives, museums, cathedrals, palaces, cemeteries, memorials), concepts and practices (commemorations, mottos, rituals), and objects (inherited property, commemorative monuments, manuals, emblems, basic texts, symbols).

Though Nora argues that *lieux de mémoire* are phenomena that belong exclusively to the modern world, in which constructed history replaces real memory,[102] a case can be made, mutatis mutandis, for applying his model to the ancient world. I want to argue, then, that the Pauline letters (with a focus on the Thessalonian correspondence), both those which were actually penned by Paul as well as those which were written in his name by others, have served the ancient Christian communities that first received them and those communities that transmitted them to subsequent generations initially as *aides-mémoire*, during the initial stages of communal memory, but were later transformed into *lieux de mémoire*, providing a basis for the creation of oral history and tradition. The Pauline letters, to use the words of Nora, function as *lieux de mémoire* constituting "a circle within which everything counts, everything is symbolic, everything is significant."[103] Further, just as *lieux de mémoire* in the view of Nora and his fellow contributors provide the basis for collective identity, it is clear that the Pauline letters, no less than the growing canon of New Testament writings from the second to the fourth centuries C.E., provided a narrative foundation for early Christian social identity as well as the basis for divergent construals of social identity.

Paul sometimes wrote letters to churches that he and his colleagues had visited, if not founded. These letters functioned to commemorate as well as strengthen and consolidate the impact of these visits. In those autobiographical sections of his letters in which Paul comments on his reception by particular Christian communities, he puts a certain spin on these interactions appropriate for his rhetorical intentions (e.g., 1 Thess 1:2–3:13; Gal 1:11–2:21; 2 Cor 1:12–2:17; Phil 3:4-16).[104] In other words, even when first written, these autobiographical sections are subjective rather than objective accounts of Paul's relationship with local communities. Initially, then, Paul's letters will have served to reshape and refocus the social memory of his past influence on the lives of his addressees. What is even more striking, however, is that these letters have continued to function in an even broader sense as universal artifacts shaping Christian social memory of Christian origins to the present day. In the case of the pseudepigraphical Pauline letters (2 Thessalonians, Ephesians, Colossians, and the Pastorals), the intentional reshaping of the Christian social memory of Paul is surely one of the primary intentions of the unknown authors. It is impressive to sit in one of the major Orthodox churches in modern Thessaloniki, the second largest city in Greece, and hear lections chanted from 1 and 2 Thessalonians during the fifteen weekdays of the twenty-third through twenty-fifth weeks after Pentecost, nearly two millennia after they were addressed to the Christian community in this Greek city. These letters, through their iterative reading, quickly became ritual objects with an iconic significance.

The rhetoric of Paul's letters is such that "some assembly is required," that is, they are clearly designed to be read before congregations and, thus functioning as surrogates of Paul's oral ministry of preaching and teaching, live on to the present day. This reading and rereading of Paul's letters in the social context of Christian worship goes back to Paul's own intentions in writing letters to congregations from whom he was unavoidably separated (Col 4:16; 1 Thess 5:27). As a liturgical act, this reading constitutes a commemoration of Paul's relationship to the communities who originally received these letters as well as an imaginative commemoration of Paul's ministry when read in worship contexts by other communities.

The language of memory pervades the Pauline letters both explicitly and implicitly. Explicitly, Paul used words translated as "memory" and "to remember" with some frequency. These often occur within the Pauline epistolary autobiographical narratives mentioned above, involving shared experiences with those to whom he addressed letters. A brief survey of Paul's use of "memory" vocabulary turns up the following results. There are first of all eight different words in the Pauline corpus derived from the morpheme μνάομαι,[105] all dealing with cognitive memory and all belonging to the semantic subdomain of memory and recall,[106] including ἀναμιμνῄσκω ("to cause to remember," three times: 1 Cor 4:17; 2 Cor 7:15; 2 Tim 1:6), ἀνάμνησις ("reminder," two times: 1 Cor 11:24, 25), ἐπαναμιμνῄσκω ("to remind," Rom 15:15), μιμνῄσκομαι ("to remember," two times: 1 Cor 11:2; 2 Tim 1:4), μνεία ("memory, remembrance," six times: Rom 1:9; Phil 1:3; 1 Thess 1:2; 3:6; 2 Tim 1:3; Eph 1:16), μνημονεύω ("to recall, remember," seven times: Gal 2:10; Eph 2:11; Col 4:18; 1 Thess 1:3; 2:9; 2 Thess 2:5; 2 Tim 2:8), ὑπομιμνῄσκω ("to remind," two times: 2 Tim 2:14; Tit 3:1), and ὑπόμνησις ("reminding," 2 Tim 1:5).

The emphasis that Paul (and the deuteropauline tradition) places on remembering is a commemorative process that is replicated when the letters are read and reread. First Thessalonians 3:6 contains evidence that Paul's emphasis on memory has had concrete results among the

Thessalonians; Timothy, upon returning from a visit to the congregation, can report to Paul that "you always remember us kindly and long to see us—just as we long to see you." Remembering is a two-way street, of course, and Paul assures the Thessalonians that he mentions them in prayer, "constantly remembering before our God and Father your work of faith and labor of love and steadfastness of hope in our Lord Jesus Christ" (1 Thess 1:2-3).

The realm of "behavioral memory" (i.e., learning by doing) is mentioned by Paul using several terms based on the morpheme μιμέομαι ("imitate," two times: 2 Thess 3:7, 9), including μιμητής ("imitator," five times: 1 Cor 4:16; 11:1; 1 Thess 1:6; 2:14; Eph 5:1) and συμμιμητής ("joint imitator," Phil 3:17). Paul's emphasis on behavioral memory is, of course, not limited to passages in which μιμέομαι and cognates are found. In 1 Thessalonians 4:1, Paul enjoins the Thessalonians: "We ask and urge you in the Lord Jesus that, as you learned [παρελάβετε] from us how you ought to live and to please God (as, in fact, you are doing), you should do so more and more." Paul's gospel message therefore involves exemplary living, which Paul summarizes under the rubric of "sanctification" (1 Thess 4:3).

Perhaps less obvious is the relevance of Paul's ubiquitous use of the verb οἶδα, used once with the meaning "to remember, recall, recollect" (1 Cor 1:16), but more frequently used in the semantic subdomain "know," frequently with the meaning "to know about, to have knowledge of."[107] Paul often uses the verb οἶδα in the second-person plural form οἴδατε ("you know," often in the phrase οὐκ οἴδατε, "do you not know") or the first-person plural form οἴδαμεν ("we know") or the plural participial form οἰδότες ("knowing"), all indicating knowledge that he shares with his recipients, that is, knowledge that he knows they have (alluding to what he shared with them when he was present with them), a fact of which he now reminds them. Here are some examples:

> Romans 7:14: "For *we know* that the law is spiritual."
>
> 1 Corinthians 6:2: "[Or] *do you not know* that the saints will judge the world?"
>
> 1 Corinthians 6:15: "*Do you not know* that your bodies are members of Christ?"
>
> 1 Thessalonians 1:5: "*Just as you know* what kind of persons we proved to be among you for your sake"
>
> 1 Thessalonians 3:4: "We told you beforehand that we were to suffer persecution; so it turned out, *as you know*"

1 Thessalonians 4:2: "*For you know* what instructions we gave you through the Lord Jesus"[108]

The mnemonic force of these statements is clear; all these references deal with shared memories or experiences, many clearly dealing with social memory (e.g., "For *we know* that the law is spiritual," and "Or *do you not know* that the saints will judge the world?").

Of course, not all of the letters attributed to Paul in the New Testament are thought to be authentic by critical scholars. These pseudepigraphical letters,[109] sometimes attributed to disciples of Paul or even to "the school of Paul," functioned, at least initially, in slightly different ways than letters actually written by Paul. Perhaps their most obvious function, however, since they were never intended to serve as *aides-mémoire*, is rather as *lieux de mémoire* for many of the images of Paul that had developed in the early postapostolic church as well as for the images of Paul's Jesus that were part of that overall development. Second Thessalonians in particular, a pseudepigraphical work, reflects the transformation of 1 Thessalonians into a *lieu de mémoire*, evident in the close verbal similarity of the two letters. One of the central functions of 2 Thessalonians appears to be to underscore the importance of what Paul transmitted to this community in 1 Thessalonians as well as provide a corrective.

In 1 Thessalonians, there are several references to a "tradition" or a "body of teaching" that the Thessalonians had received from Paul. One of the terms that Paul and the Pauline tradition uses for the process of transmission is παραλαμβάνω ("to learn from someone" or "be taught by," occurs eleven times: 1 Cor 11:23; 15:1, 3; Gal 1:9, 12; Phil 4:9; Col 2:6; 4:17; 1 Thess 2:13; 4:1; 2 Thess 3:6). The use of this lexeme in 1 Thessalonians 2:13 (part of an autobiographical passage) is particularly important: "We also constantly give thanks to God for this, that when you received [παραλαβόντες] the word of God that you heard from us, you accepted it not as a human word but as what it really is, God's word, which is also at work in you believers." In 2 Thessalonians 3:6, Paul enjoins believers "to keep away from believers who are living in idleness and not according to the tradition [παράδοσιν] that they received [παρελάβοσαν] from us."

The term παράδοσις, "tradition," that is, "the content of instruction that has been handed down," occurs five times in Paul and the Pauline tradition (1 Cor 11:2; Gal 1:14; Col 2:8; 2 Thess 2:15; 3:6). In the passage just quoted, 2 Thessalonians 3:6, it is clear that the παράδοσις referred to by pseudo-Paul refers to moral teaching exemplified by those who were involved in its transmission. The term also occurs in 2 Thessalonians 2:15, where the recipients are enjoined to "stand firm and hold fast to the traditions that you were taught [ἐδιδάχθητε] by us, either by word of mouth or by our letter." Here the earlier ministry of Paul reflected in 1 Thessalonians, together with that letter itself, is categorized as παράδοσις, and the verb διδάσκω ("to teach") is used as a synonym of παραλαμβάνω ("to learn from someone," "be taught by"). The term διδάσκω itself ("to teach") is found fifteen times in Paul (Rom 2:21; 12:7; 1 Cor 4:17; 11:14; Gal 1:12; Eph 4:21; Col 1:28; 2:7; 3:16; 2 Thess 2:15; 1 Tim 2:12; 4:11; 6:2; 2 Tim 2:2; Titus 1:11). The fact that παραλαμβάνω and διδάσκω are synonyms in the Pauline letters implies that παραλαμβάνω should not be regarded as a technical term for an institutional form of transmitting oral tradition, as it is frequently understood.

At this point, emphasizing the model of *lieux de mémoire* for the continuing function of the Pauline letters in the early Christian communities among which they circulated, I would like to turn to perhaps the most important *crux interpretum* in 1 Thessalonians for those concerned with Paul's use of the sayings of Jesus: 1 Thessalonians 4:15-17. This passage begins with these words, "For this we declare to you by the word of the Lord . . . ," followed by a Parousia scenario.[110] As we have noted above, various scholars have argued whether or not Paul was transmitting a saying of the historical Jesus, have speculated over the possible relationship between this passage and the canonical Gospels, or have speculated that Paul was transmitting a saying of the exalted Jesus mediated by an early Christian prophet.[111] No matter how this passage is interpreted, it must surely constitute an example of the tradition (παράδοσις) that Paul consciously transmitted to the churches he founded.

The *aide-mémoire* and *lieux de mémoire* model suggests another approach to the problem. As the earliest Pauline letter, 1 Thessalonians probably was written circa 49 C.E., long before the appearance of any of the written Gospels. The Q document, if in fact it existed in an early redaction by 49 C.E. (which in itself is uncertain), was half a world away from the Greek peninsula. There can be little doubt, however, that sayings and stories about Jesus were circulating throughout Christian communities in the entire eastern Mediterranean theater. When the members of the Christian community in Thessaloniki read 1 Thessalonians, I suggest that they would have had little doubt that, when Paul used the introductory phrase, "For this we declare to you by the word of the Lord . . . ," he was in fact referring to a saying of the earthly Jesus, not a saying of the heavenly Lord, nor a quotation from a written text. The citation itself is as follows (1 Thess 4:15-17):

> "we who are alive, who are left until the coming of the Lord, will by no means precede those who have died. For the Lord himself, with a cry of command, with the archangel's call and with the sound of God's trumpet, will descend from heaven, and the dead in Christ will rise first. Then when we who are alive, who are left, will be caught up in the clouds together with them to meet the Lord in the air."

Despite the freedom Paul uses in transforming this saying into the third person, this saying was doubtless accepted at face value as a saying of Jesus. It is well known that one of the earliest stages of the process out of which a stable canon of New Testament documents emerged by the fourth century was the inherent authority of the sayings of Jesus, whether oral or written (if written, the text in which such sayings were embedded would not have shared the intrinsic authority of the sayings themselves).[112] While it is usually assumed that belief in the authority of the sayings of Jesus was guaranteed by apostolic witness, 1 Thessalonians 4:15-17, in the context of the entire letter, suggests the reverse: the apostolic witness was guaranteed by the inherent authority of the words of Jesus, an authority at least equal to, and probably even greater than, the authority of the Septuagint itself among early Christians. The fact that 1 Thessalonians 4:15-17 has no close parallels among the words of Jesus preserved in the canonical Gospels and the *Gospel of Thomas*, while a problem for modern scholars, is an anachronistic issue for the Thessalonians who were the original recipients of 1 Thessalonians. The great variation that must have existed among orally transmitted versions of the sayings of Jesus and which has been frozen by the compilation of the four canonical Gospels is still visible in the variety found in quotations and allusions to the oral (and sometimes written) sayings tradition in the Apostolic Fathers and in the *Gospel of Thomas*.[113] Thus, 1 Thessalonians 4:15-17 must have functioned initially as an *aide-mémoire* for the early Christian community at Thessaloniki, who would have understood it as the high point of the letter.

Already by the second generation of Thessalonian Christians, if not earlier, the communal memories preserving the experience of the Pauline ministry would have faded, only to be gradually replaced by 1 Thessalonians, no longer functioning as an *aide-mémoire,* but transformed into a cenotaph for living memories and gradually supplanting them as a source for generating new communal memories. According to Nola, "*Lieux de mémoire* exist because there are no longer any *milieux de mémoire*, settings in which memory is a real part of everyday experience."[114] The same process must have occurred in much the same way throughout the Pauline churches, as the other genuine Pauline letters became sources for a secondhand social memory. The collection of the Pauline letters, first in smaller groups and then reaching the final stages of a group of ten and then thirteen letters,[115] may be construed as a search for the *lieux* that were thought to embody collective memories of the Pauline gospel. The availability of larger and more comprehensive collections of Pauline letters enriched the collective memory of the Christian communities in the circum-Mediterranean region by providing a basis for secondary constructions of communal memory. In many respects this tendency to reconstruct the irretrievable memories of the past is represented by the several deuteropauline letters (Ephesians, Colossians, 2 Thessalonians, and the Pastorals). Their very existence testifies to the fossilization of the genuine Pauline letters as *lieux de mémoire*. The existence of genuine Pauline letters (or letters that were taken for genuine) was particularly crucial for the production of Ephesians and 2 Thessalonians. The origin of the Pastorals is more complex, for although not largely dependent on a particular Pauline letter (as Ephesians was on Colossians and as 2 Thessalonians was on 1 Thessalonians), they reflect dependence on several Pauline letters, but were even more dependent on the appropriation of what the author took to be Pauline traditions.[116]

Chapter 4

Honi the Circler in Manuscript and Memory
An Experiment in "Re-Oralizing" the Talmudic Text

Martin S. Jaffee

B irger Gerhardsson's classic, *Memory and Manuscript: Oral Tradition and Written Transmission in Rabbinic Judaism and Early Christianity*, has inspired and shaped my work since I first encountered it in graduate school in the late 1970s. I have dipped into it repeatedly since then, as my own thinking about rabbinic textuality has developed, and with each dipping, I have retrieved fresh and vivifying waters from this marvelous fountain of learning.

To a degree unmatched by any prior scholar working with rabbinic texts, Gerhardsson appreciated the close connection between the rabbinic tradition's cultivation of an oral-performative *techne* and its proclamation of a soteriological *mythos* grounded in the dual revelation of Torah at Sinai. As Jacob Neusner would later develop the point, rabbinic performance of a memorized text from tradition is the central ritual act that mediates, through the symbol of "Sinai" and the narratives of revelation, the continuity of Scripture's "kingdom of priests and a holy nation" with rabbinic Israel.[1] Thus, any literary-historical consideration of the rabbinic corpus must in some way take account of the *Sitz im Leben* of its production—the discipleship community's oral-performative rehearsal of the Oral Torah that "Moses received on Sinai and transmitted to Joshua" (*m. Abot* 1:1).

Theorizing the "Orality" of Oral Torah: Working Back from Manuscript to Memory

"Oralist" students of rabbinic literature share with their colleagues in other ancient literary studies a common practical difficulty: how does one study the living process of orally transmitted literature on the basis of written manuscripts?[2] It seems probable that the scribes responsible for the surviving medieval manuscript copies of the extant anthologies of rabbinic tradition,[3] such as the Mishnah (compiled ca. 200 C.E. in the Galilee), the Tosefta (a supplement to the Mishnah from the mid-third century C.E.), the *midrashim* (compilations of rabbinic scriptural-exegetical traditions, ca. 350–425 C.E.), and the *talmudim* (of Palestine, edited, ca. 375–425 C.E.; of Babylonia, ca. 500–600 C.E.), copied them with relative care from written exemplars, but also felt free to correct texts that seemed corrupt or miscopied.[4] The earliest fragments of these can be dated no earlier than the eighth or ninth century and most are from the eleventh through thirteenth centuries.[5] Moreover, the manuscripts seem to emerge fully formed from the dark tunnel that connects the textual practices of medieval Ashkenazic, Sephardic, and Oriental Jewish communities to the Palestinian and Mesopotamian scribalism of late antiquity and the early Geonic authorities (ca. 700–900 C.E.) who disseminated the talmudic textual tradition from Islamic to Christian lands. What can medieval copies—themselves several centuries removed from the hypothetical first written versions—tell us about rabbinic textual practices, either at the beginning of the tradition or at the various stages along the way?

Indeed, most questions about the role of writing in the shaping of rabbinic oral tradition have, for lack of unambiguous evidence from late antiquity, only speculative answers. What sorts of textual material, for example, did scribes who produced the earliest written copies of the works now called the Mishnah or the Talmuds have in front of their eyes as they wrote? Did they feel constrained to record such texts more or less as they received them? How closely did the first scribal editors seek to replicate the shape and form of the tradition that preceded their work? In what ways did the very act of anthologizing tradition—whether performed by orally managed techniques or written notation—force a reshaping or reframing of the constituent traditions themselves, such that their prehistory is no longer recoverable?

In the absence of the discovery of a cache of rabbinic manuscripts from late antiquity comparable to the Dead Sea Scrolls of the Second Temple period, answers to questions such as these must remain hypothetical, heavily dependent upon theoretical constructions grounded in a comparison of the oral-performative remnants of rabbinic texts with those better attested in other literatures. One ray of light, explored with excellent results in Gerhardsson's own pioneering study, concerns the way the social world of rabbinic learning is represented in the texts through various reports about the conventions of textual learning among rabbinic disciples.[6] Another concerns the technical aspect of the composition of rabbinic texts, namely, the loosely structured, agglutinative patterns by which virtually all surviving rabbinic texts are compiled (see n. 3). In my view, both the presentation of the substance of rabbinic learning—as a series of discrete "learning paragraphs" that follow more or less explicit mnemonic technologies—and the textual representation of the method of rabbinic learning—as a process of memorization-for-performance[7]— suggest the essentially performative character of the rabbinic textual tradition in the centuries of its formation and flowering.

The depictions of rabbinic learning that pepper rabbinic texts from late antiquity assume that the mastery of literary tradition involved memorization of highly formulaic texts (such as those found now in the extant Tannaitic collections and the *baraitot*[8] of the Talmuds) and the ability to criticize them and expound them in a formal disquisition before various types of audiences[9]—the single teacher,[10] the study group under a given sage,[11] the favored study partner who served as both critic and enabler of one's rendition of the tradition,[12] the community of text memorizers (also called "Tannaim"),[13] whose multiple rehearsals of memorized texts constituted the "critical apparatus" against which any disputed recension could be measured.

Rabbinic writing, as best we can tell from the surviving medieval renderings, retrieved these texts from a primary performance setting of face-to-face study, where the texts lived in the minds of students within the medium of embodied discourse, for reworking in the secondary performance setting of the manuscript, where a written rendition of the texts (outside the minds of students) was stored as the basic model or point of departure for further oral-performative presentations. The time and place of the earliest written renderings of rabbinic tradition probably varies for each specific rabbinic genre; and in no case can we be certain how closely the scribal renderings of these oral-performative texts replicates what we might call the "oral/aural" form of the traditions. The best we can say is that the written manuscripts were "scripts" that supported the texts' return from the written surface back to the oral/aural milieu that was the preferred context of study and teaching. On the basis of this model of the performative character of rabbinic text making, amply supplied in the many descriptions of the oral-learning session of generations of rabbinic disciple circles, it is possible to make some educated guesses about the writing processes that might have supported, enhanced, or even emerged from such oral-performative settings.

I imagine the production of the earliest rabbinic manuscripts[14] as a kind of "text-processing" activity in which written texts (viewed now with the eye) and remembered texts (recalled with the ear) merged in the literary activity of the scribe as he vocalized texts in the course of composing his own rendition of the received discourse of his particular circle of disciples. If we understand written textual production as a variant of oral-performative textual transmission,[15] then we can imagine the early rabbinic text makers to have written, so to speak, with their ears, not so much copying the texts they transmitted, but rehear(s)ing them in memory as they rendered them visibly in new configurations on the page.[16]

There is, in this appreciation of the performativity of the classic written rabbinic text, an important—and to some degree, sobering—implication for textual interpretation. If the written text is, as it were, snatched out of the air in the process of composition, much of its meaning remains in the air—where it is necessarily lost to us, unless the happy existence of a parallel formulation in some other written compilation or a manuscript variant enables us to use the fuller text as a commentary on the one more spare.[17] That is to say, the oralist textual scholar is in a sense engaged in an effort to "restage" the oral-performative milieu of the textual tradition by comparing various written testimonies to the shaping of the texts and enabling the contemporary reader of the finished texts to "rehear" them in their multiple versions.

Precisely this sort of restaging or rehearing is what I have in mind in this contribution in honor of Gerhardsson. I offer an attempt to represent in writing (and translation) the written text of Oral Torah in such a way as to highlight the traces of oral forms of transmission in the products of scribal production itself: to imitate visually the multivocal quality of the living tradition of oral-performative literary discourse captured in the amber-like texts of the Oral Torah as it was transmitted in late antiquity and preserved in medieval manuscripts. I select for the experiment an example from the most recent "layer" of the classic rabbinic oral-performative literary canon, the Babylonian Talmud (the Bavli). As the transformative nexus of all stages of the rabbinic literary enterprise in both its Palestinian and Mesopotamian centers, the Bavli is the richest source for exploring the variety of modes of textuality embodied in classical rabbinic literature.

A Problem in Restorative Method: Imitating a Talmudic Manuscript in English Translation

Before us is a rendering of about thirty lines of the Munich manuscript's version[18] of the tale of Honi the Circler, the most famous of a number of Second Temple holy men whose feats are recounted in the rabbinic literature.[19] The text, copied in France circa 1342, corresponds to that found on folio 23a of the standard Vilna edition of the Bavli's tractate, first printed in the 1880s. The editor of the Vilna page introduces the passage with a brief citation of *m. Taan.* 3:8 (appearing in full on *b. Taan.* 19a) that represents the Mishnah's version of the Honi legend.[20] As we shall see, the Bavli will cite, paraphrase, and amplify virtually all of the Mishnah in the course of its own discussion. The many significant differences between the versions of *m. Taan.* 3:8 found in medieval manuscripts and later editions of the Mishnah and that cited in the Bavli will be noted for the reader at the appropriate time, and their significance for our understanding of rabbinic oral-performative tradition will be assessed in at least a cursory way.[21]

In order to illustrate the degree to which written versions of talmudic tradition conceal and dominate the oral-performative tradition that is the source of their vitality, I will present the Bavli's text in two versions. The first imitates MS Munich's chirographic scribal format, attempting to represent in English what a reader of the manuscript finds in the published facsimile edition: line after undifferentiated line of text without any of the normal cues of punctuation that would signal to a reader how to vocalize the text. The second rendering attempts to represent visually the various oral-performative sources of textual tradition that are manifested in the editorial shaping of the material but concealed by the scribal format of the manuscript. My goal is to permit the reader to grasp the fundamental ways in which the linear, scribal version of the Talmud neutralizes the oral-performative traces of the transmitted text even as it becomes the very condition of the recovery of the text's oral life.

Imitating the Chirographic Text: The Manuscript Representation of Bavli Taanit 23a

So let us begin with the legend of Honi as preserved in MS Munich, rendered so as to imitate as far as possible the visual appearance of the manuscript:[22]

> Our masters transmitted a tradition: One time, most of Adar[23] had passed, yet the rains had still to fall. They said to Honi the Circler: Pray that the rains may fall! He prayed. But the rains did not fall. He inscribed a circle and stood within it, the way that the prophet Habakkuk had done, as it is said: "I will stand on my watch, set myself at my post (and wait to see what He will say to me)." He said before Him: Master of the World! Your children have turned their faces to me, for I am like a family member to You! I swear by Your Great Name that I shall not move from here until You will have mercy on your children! The rains began to sprinkle. His disciples said to him: Rabbi! We see you yet we remain alive! It seems to us that the rains are falling only to relieve you from your vow! He said to them: You have seen me, and did not die. He said: This is not what I asked for! But rains to fill cisterns, trenches, and caves! The rains began to storm, until every drop was as big as the mouth of a barrel. And Sages measured the size of a drop as not less than a liter. His disciples said to him: Rabbi! We see you yet we remain alive! It seems to us that the rains are falling only in order to destroy the World! He said to them: You have seen me, and did not die. He said: This is not what I asked for! But rains of compassion, blessing, and bounty. They fell as he had specified, until Israel went up from Jerusalem to the Temple Mount because of the rains. They said to him: Rabbi! Just as you prayed that they come, now pray that they go! He said to them: Thus have I received [as a tradition]—That one does not pray on account of too much good. Nevertheless, bring me a bull for a Thanksgiving. They brought him a bull for a Thanksgiving. And he leaned both of his hands upon it and said: Master of the World! Your people, Israel, whom you brought out of Egypt, can bear neither too much evil nor too much retribution! You were angry with them, they could not take it; you showered good upon them, they could not take it. May it be Your will that the rains cease, and there be calm in the Land. Immediately, the wind blew and the clouds were dispersed. The sun shone and the earth dried out. And the people went out to the field and brought for themselves mushrooms and truffles.[24]   Shimon b. Shetah sent for him. Were you not Honi, I would condemn you to excommunication! For if these years were as the years of Elijah, when the keys to the rains were in the hands of Elijah, wouldn't the Name of Heaven have been desecrated by you? But what can I do to you? For you act like a brat before the Infinite, and He makes your desire His desire. As a son acts like a brat before his father, yet his father does whatever he asks! And he says, Abba! Bathe me in hot water! Rinse me in cold water! Feed me nuts, almonds, peaches, and pomegranates, and he gives! Of you says Scripture: "Your father and your mother

will rejoice; she who bore you will exult!"²⁵   Rav Nahman b. Rav Hisda expounded:²⁶ What did the people of the Chamber of Carved Stone send to Honi the Circler? "You will decree and it will be fulfilled, and upon your paths the light will shine." "You will decree and it will be fulfilled."—You have decreed from below, and the Holy One fulfills your utterance from above. "And upon your paths the light will shine"—a generation in darkness have you illumined with your prayer. "When they sink, you shall explain it as pride"—a lowly generation have you raised up through your prayer. "The downcast of eye shall he spare"—a generation sunk in its iniquity you spared with your prayer. "He will deliver the impure"—a generation that was impure did your prayer deliver. "And he will be delivered through the cleanness of your hands"—they will be delivered through the innocent deeds of your hands.²⁷   Said Rabbi Yohanan: All his life that Saint puzzled over this verse: "A song of Ascents: When God returned the Remnant of Zion, we were as dreamers." He said: Can someone sleep for 70 years and dream? One day he was walking along and he saw a certain man planting a carob tree. He said: How many years will that take to bear? He said: Up to 70 years. He said: It's obvious to you that you'll live 70 years? He said: I found the world with carobs in it, because my ancestors planted it; now I plant for my children! He sat and ate some bread. Sleep overcame him. A grotto grew around him and concealed him, and he slept for 70 years. When he awoke, he saw a certain man picking from the tree. He said: Did you plant it? He said: I am his grandson. He said: Am I to infer that I've slept for 70 years? He saw that his donkey had given birth to foals. He went to his house. He said: Is the son of Honi the Circler still alive? They said: His son's gone, but his grandson lives. He said: I am Honi the Circler! They did not believe him. He went to the house of study. He heard the disciples saying: These traditions are as clear as they were in the days of Honi the Circler! For when he entered the house of study he would solve any problem the disciples posed. He said to them: I am he! They didn't believe him and didn't extend to him the proper courtesies. He fell into despair and prayed for the mercy of death. Said Rava: As people say—give me a partner or give me death!²⁸

The textual communities within which manuscripts such as MS Munich circulated already knew these texts intimately and would have found the manuscript versions to be signaling helpful mnemonic cues²⁹—rather than the intimidating barriers to understanding that they represent to those of us who first come to them as academic practitioners. The words inscribed on parchment would, under their trained eyes, have been perceived aurally as a weave of highly differentiated textual "voices," each audible at its own frequency.³⁰ It is unlikely that moderns, even with the aid of accessibly edited versions of these texts in the original languages, can hear this chorus of textual voices as it would have sounded in the ears of those for whom the written manuscript served as a mnemonic cue to texts already stored in memory on the basis of constant repetition and rehearsal in the course of study. But it is possible to offer an estimate by resorting to a "re-oralization" of the text by altering its visible form in translation.

A Second Problem in Restorative Method: Re-Oralizing the Manuscript

I offer such a "re-oralization" below. The very first step in transforming the lines of the rabbinic manuscript into something approaching the oral-performative realities of the vocalized text is to recognize the significance of a simple fact: from an oral-performative point of view, the discourse of rabbinic literature is far closer to classic poetic discourse than to contemporary academic prose. That is to say, it is composed of collections of phrases that conform to and exploit the strengths and limitations of the human mouth, tongue, and lungs; in short, virtually all rabbinic traditions of whatever sort can be broken down into collections of phrases that take roughly a breath to enunciate.[31] In the "re-oralizing" translation offered in the second textual sample below, I break all texts into smaller stichs to offer a visual representation of such "breath-units."

A translation that hopes to capture the oral-performative dimension of rabbinic texts must reflect this basic reality. Even though English is more cumbersome than Hebrew or Aramaic in this regard, it is nevertheless possible to render rabbinic texts in translation in a way that preserves not only the underlying mnemonic cues provided by stereotypical textual formalism,[32] but also the oral-performative, formulaic phrasing that characterizes virtually all orally transmitted literatures.[33] Thus, a representation of a written manuscript looks like this:

> They said to Honi the Circler: Pray that the rains may fall! He prayed. But the rains did not fall. He inscribed a circle and stood within it, the way that the prophet Habakkuk had done, as it is said: "I will stand on my watch, set myself at my post (and wait to see what He will say to me)."

Its "re-oralized" counterpart, however, divided into "breath-units," looks like this:

> They said to Honi the Circler: Pray that the rains may fall![34]
> He prayed. But the rains did not fall.
> He inscribed a circle and stood within it,
> The way that the prophet Habakkuk had done,
> As it is said: "I will stand on my watch, set myself at my post
> and wait to see what He will say to me."

Building upon this fundamental foundation of the rabbinic text as a series of breath-units geared to an oral-performative setting, it is necessary to give the text oral "depth" or "resonance" by distinguishing the various "voices" embedded in the texts as they draw to themselves new elements in the course of literary transmission. One useful way of doing this, since it conforms to the Bavli's own persistent concern to isolate for analysis various sources of tradition, is to focus on the native literary-historical categories of the Talmud itself, namely its distinction between Tannaitic and Amoraic layers of textual tradition.

The earliest oral-performative textual "voice" recognized in the Talmud echoes in citations of materials in classical rabbinic Hebrew that, for the most part, are either paralleled in such Tannaitic compilations as the Mishnah, the Tosefta, and related works or appear to intersect with these Tannaitic texts as exegetical companions, thematic supplements, or alternate versions (i.e., the so-called *baraitot* [viz., "traditions external to the canonical Mishnah"]). Most of these materials can be assumed to have circulated as memorized tradition[35] by around the early to mid-third century, among both Palestinian and Babylonian masters of the rabbinic tradition.

In the various disciple circles of rabbinic Mesopotamia, this Tannaitic textual voice was transmitted till the early sixth century among Amoraic performance specialists (also called "Tannaim"; see n. 13). Sometimes the Amoraim[36] consciously or unconsciously reworked discrete passages of Tannaitic materials (often called *matnyta'* ["repeated tradition"] as opposed to *matnytyn* ["*our* repeated tradition," viz., the Mishnah]) as they transmitted and commented on them in diverse settings. At other times, as in the case of the Amora, Mar Shmuel, a key figure in the early third-century development of the Babylonian rabbinic curriculum, they composed explicit, running commentaries on Mishnaic texts.[37] In both the Palestinian and Babylonian Talmuds, it is common to distinguish the Amoraic comments on the Tannaitic tradition from the Tannaitic tradition itself by use of both routine citational formulae that serve to introduce Tannaitic material (e.g., "Our Rabbis taught as tradition": *tenu rabbanan*) and a distinctly rabbinic blend of middle Hebrew and Aramaic for the formulation of the Amoraic comments.

Most scholars now agree that the Babylonian Gemara (viz., "learned tradition" now codified in the texts of the Talmud) is not in its present form composed by the Amoraim (whose names and statements constitute the bulk of most talmudic compositions). Rather the Gemara appears to have reached its decisive shape due to the labors of the anonymous sixth- and seventh-century rabbinic editors of tradition now usually referred to as Stammaim.[38] These Stammaim, the theory holds, are the basic architects of the Talmud's literary project. Using the Mishnah as an organizational spine and a cue for summoning up related Amoraic and Tannaitic traditions, the Stammaim composed wide-ranging literary discourses (*sugyot*) that drew upon the rhetorical and discursive forms of Amoraic Gemara and formed complex arrangements of Tannaitic and Amoraic traditions about the entire range of matters that could conceivably arise from reflection upon the Mishnah.

As heirs of several generations of Amoraic discussion and amplification of the Mishnaic text and several less-formally compiled recensions of Tannaitic tradition, it is the Stammaim who stamped their seal on the Gemara of current versions of the Talmud. Inheriting orally mediated models of classic Amoraic discourses on Tannaitic tradition, the Stammaim contemplated a given Mishnaic passage and decided which series of Tannaitic texts and Amoraic discursive traditions would serve as important intertexts for analysis and inquiry. The Stammaim, like the Amoraim, employed conventional Aramaic citation formulae for introducing material ascribed to the Tannaim. They quoted traditional Amoraic teachings—normally apodictic legal statements or brief comments—and shaped them for the purposes of their own literary project. They punctuated the resulting compositions of traditions with their own editorial interventions as well, often using the house of study's agonistic forms of debate and challenge as the rhetorical framework of their own compositional work.[39]

Virtually all of the Bavli is created out of these materials. To "read" the Talmud "orally" is at least in part to be aware of ways in which the now-written texts resolve themselves into textual subunits that conform, first of all, to the requirements of performance, and only secondarily are shaped in writing to the needs of a given halakhic or aggadic editorial agenda. How closely will this reading strategy bring us to the ways in which the Stammaim of Sasanian Babylonia heard the traditions they received and transformed? No one can say, unless and until a substantial piece of talmudic writing from, say, the sixth century or earlier emerges from a neglected drawer in a forgotten library or, less likely still, from some as-yet-unexcavated *tel* in Iraq. But at the very least, the medieval manuscripts still retain echoes of the living textual voices that resonated in the ancient rabbinic academies before they were frozen into the scripted discourses of the medieval manuscript. The "oralist" scholar attempts to retrieve and savor them.

In what follows, I attempt to identify and disentangle these several voices. My first strategy is to employ distinct typefaces to represent specific, chronologically identifiable "voices" in the text. All material in italics represents rabbinic Hebrew texts likely to derive from the Tannaitic stratum of tradition (ca. early third century C.E.). I identify these texts as Tannaitic on the grounds that they are introduced by the editors of the Gemara either with explicit citational formula (e.g., "Our masters transmitted a [Tannaitic] tradition") or because they are closely paralleled in extant collections of Tannaitic traditions, such as the Mishnah and the Tosefta.

Amoraic contributions in Hebrew to Tannaitic citations, which probably stem from the mid-third through late fifth centuries, appear in plain type (rather than italics). Contributions framed principally in Aramaic, and which seem to be specifically of Amoraic venue, are represented in capital letters. The key indications that a given contribution stems from Amoraic circles is that it is transmitted in the name of an Amora or, where anonymous, it is framed in the mixture of Hebrew and Aramaic distinctive to the post-Tannaitic materials of the Talmud.

Materials that, in my judgment, derive from post-fifth-century Stammaitic editorial interventions are represented in bold face. We will encounter three types of Stammaitic interventions. Those in bold face and plain type represent Stammaitic insertions, in rabbinic Hebrew, into earlier Tannaitic traditions. We identify such materials as Stammaitic particularly when they introduce into Tannaitic citations issues or ideas elsewhere clearly attested to Stammaitic discussions.

The Stammaitic architects of the *sugya* also supply citation formulae for adducing Tannaitic material. I represent the one example before us in underlined, boldfaced capital letters. It is the ubiquitous Aramaic formula, "Our masters transmitted a tradition" (*tenu rabbanan*).

The Stammaim also select Amoraic traditions that illustrate the various modes of analysis prized in the rabbinic academy, link them to the Tannaitic tradition, and then add their own editorial materials to the mix. These contributions, which normally represent literary stylizations of the rhetorical combat of the house of study, appear below in boldfaced capital letters.

To sum up, the typefaces and the oral-performative contributions they represent are as follows:

Italics: Tannaitic traditions of the Mishnah, Tosefta, or selected *baraitot* ("external" traditions of Tannaitic provenance). These are taken to be the earliest literary foundations of the Talmud.

Plain type: Amoraic supplements to or modifications of Tannaitic traditions in Hebrew.

CAPITAL LETTERS: Amoraic discussions in Aramaic (rather than Hebrew).

Boldfaced plain type: Stammaitic insertions, in rabbinic Hebrew, into earlier Tannaitic traditions.

UNDERLINED, BOLDFACED CAPITAL LETTERS: Stammaitic citation formulae for adducing Tannaitic material.

BOLDFACED CAPITAL LETTERS: Stammaitic editorial supplements linked to the rhetoric of the house of study.

How did this orally managed material come together in its present form? At present it is not possible to reconstruct the literary-editorial-transmissional processes by which all this material was brought together in the composition before us. It is likely, for example, that Tannaitic compilations—such as the Mishnah and the Tosefta—reached their literary completion through a rather different mode of composition-performance than the Amoraic traditions that entwine and preserve them. By the flowering of the Amoraic period (let us say around the late third century), there can be little doubt that the Mishnah and the corpora of Tannaitic traditions among which it circulated were memorized as a fixed-text tradition.[40] In contrast, the Amoraic and post-Amoraic discussions of the Talmud undoubtedly circulated in a free-text format (memorized for "gist" rather than for word-for-word accuracy) for quite some time until the "redaction" (however that may be imagined) of such texts as the Talmud Yerushalmi and the Talmud Bavli. I am very hesitant to posit any more definition of the editorial-transmissional activity that yields the talmudic text for the simple reason that the work of reconstructing the textualizing process within the frame of oral-traditional models remains in its early infancy despite well over a century of literary studies of talmudic redaction.

Representing the Oral-Performative Text: *b. Taan.* 23a "Re-Oralized"

Let us now return to our text. Bringing these diverse reading strategies—dissection into breath-units and graphic depictions of hypothetical textual strata—to the text of MS Munich, we get something like the following "re-oralizing" rendition of the first of the text's three basic compositional units.[41] Echoing the citational protocols of the Amoraic study house, the *stam* begins by citing a Tannaitic tradition strikingly similar to *m. Taan.* 3:8.

Note the various layers apparent in the ensuing discussion of what the Stammaitic editor represents as the citation of a single Tannaitic source:

OUR MASTERS TRANSMITTED A TRADITION:
One time, most of Adar had passed,
Yet the rains had still to fall.[42]

They said to Honi the Circler: Pray that the rains may fall![43]
He prayed. But the rains did not fall.
He inscribed a circle and stood within it,

The way that the prophet Habakkuk had done,
As it is said: "I will stand on my watch, set myself at my post
and wait to see what He will say to me" (Hab 2:1)[44]

He said before Him: Master of the World!
Your children have turned their faces to me,
For I am like a family member to You!
I swear by Your Great Name that I shall not move from here
Until You will have mercy on your children!
The rains began to sprinkle.

His disciples said to him: Rabbi![45] We see you
Yet we remain alive!
It seems to us that the rains are falling
Only to relieve you from your vow![46]
He said to them: You have seen me, but did not die![47]

He said: This is not what I asked for!
But rains to fill cisterns, trenches, and caves!
The rains began to storm.

Until every drop was as big as the mouth of a barrel.
And Sages measured the size of a drop as not less than a liter.[48]

His disciples said to him: Rabbi![49] We see you
Yet we remain alive!
It seems to us that the rains are falling
Only in order to destroy the World![50]
He said to them: You have seen me, but did not die![51]

He said: This is not what I asked for!
But rains of compassion, blessing, and bounty.
They fell as he had specified,
Until Israel went up from Jerusalem to the Temple Mount,
Because of the rains.
They said to him: **Rabbi!**[52] *Just as you prayed that they come,*
Now pray that they go![53]

He said to them: Thus have I received [as a tradition]—
That one does not pray on account of too much good.[54]

Nevertheless, bring me a bull for Thanksgiving.[55]
They brought him a bull for a Thanksgiving.
And he leaned both of his hands upon it and said:
Master of the World! Your people, Israel,
Whom you brought out of Egypt,
Can bear neither too much evil nor too much retribution!
You were angry with them, they could not take it;
You showered good upon them, they could not take it.
May it be Your will that the rains cease,
And there be calm in the Land.
Immediately, the wind blew and the clouds were dispersed,
The sun shone and the earth dried out.
And the people went out to the field
And brought for themselves mushrooms and truffles.

Shimon b. Shetah said to him.
Were you not Honi, I would condemn you to excommunication!

For if these years were as the years of Elijah,
When the keys to the rains were in the hands of Elijah,
Wouldn't the Name of Heaven have been desecrated by you?[56]

But what can I do to you?
For you act like a brat before the Infinite,

And He makes your desire His desire.

As a son acts like a brat before his father,
Yet his father does whatever he asks!

And he says, Abba! Bathe me in hot water!
Rinse me in cold water!
Feed me nuts, almonds, peaches, and pomegranates,
And he gives!

Of you says Scripture:
"Your father and your mother will rejoice;
She who bore you will exult!" (Prov 23:25)

This unit—the only one of the three in which Tannaitic materials appear—is built around the core narrative of *m. Taan.* 3:8. In fact, if one strings together the italicized lines, ignoring all other typographical elements, one has a nearly verbatim citation of the Mishnah. Except for one most obvious difference: namely, the Bavli's tradition-reciter introduces Honi with the phrase:

One time, most of Adar had passed,
Yet the rains had still to fall.

But the Mishnah reads:

To avert any calamity that befalls the community,
They blow the shofar—except for too much rain.

The Mishnah's introduction perhaps is more successful at highlighting the theme of the narrative that follows, insofar as, in this light, we are urged to see the story of Honi as a precedent explaining that Honi himself was wary of praying for rains to end. On the other hand, the Bavli's introduction, by indicating that the spring month of Adar is the setting for the tale, drives home the impending emergency into which Honi is asked to intervene with his power. The Palestinian Amoraic transmission of this material, at *y. Taan.* 66d, omits this introduction entirely. I am inclined, therefore, to view these lines as a Babylonian Amoraic refashioning of the Mishnah's Honi narrative that dramatizes the rainmaker's success by clarifying the dire circumstances of his summoning.

Certainly, as it stands, the Bavli's version has been generously supplemented during its passage from Palestine to Babylonia. In the unit we have just examined, virtually all the materials not paralleled verbatim in *m. Taan.* 3:8 stem from contributions of Amoraic and Stammaitic tradents of the Mishnah, as its version of the tradition passed repeatedly through the oral-performative renditions of the discipleship circles of Palestine and Babylonia.

After the introductory lines of the *baraita*, the next firmly Amoraic addition seems to be the interpolation of Honi's prayer over the bull of thanksgiving, with which he responds to the petitions to cause the rain to cease. This passage seems part of the "rabbinizing" *Tendenz* of the Bavli, noted by recent students of this passage such as William Scott Green and Jeffrey Rubenstein,[57] since it links Honi to a legitimate public institution—the Temple (conceived by the sages to have been controlled by their ancestors)[58]—and further reinforces the impression that it is God's will, not Honi's antics, that account for his powers.[59]

This is not the first appearance of the bull of thanksgiving in the Honi tradition. An almost identical version appears at *y. Taan.* 67a. There, however, it is tightly woven into the Yerushalmi's rendition of Honi's reference, in the Mishnah, to the Claimants' Stone:

> He said to them: Go and see if the Claimants' Stone has melted.
> (*m. Taan.* 3:8)
> He said to them: Just as it's impossible for this stone to melt from the world,
> So too is it impossible to pray for the rains to go!
> Rather, go and bring me a bull for a Thanksgiving . . .

It seems to have survived passage into the Babylonian performative tradition intact precisely because its attempt to soften Honi's charismatic image proved congenial to the interests of the Babylonian sages as well. Indeed, precisely this concern dominates those additions to the text that seem likely to stem from the redactional activities of the Babylonian Stammaim responsible for the present version of *b. Taan.* 23a.[60]

Other Stammaitic incursions into the Honi tradition before us seem entirely devoted to legitimating Honi's activities in light of precedents respected by the rabbinic communities. Sages, who viewed themselves as inheriting the line of prophetic tradition (e.g., *m. Peah* 2:6), immediately link Honi's circle-drawing technique to a rather elusive verse in Habakkuk. Rabbis, who defined their roles in Jewish society as the "raising up of many disciples" (*m. Abot* 1:1), repeatedly represent Honi as a master of disciples who inquire after the reasons for his actions and address him as "Rabbi." And masters of the Oral Torah, who pride themselves on their capacity to "receive" and "transmit" traditions intact, have Honi announce to his disciples in the time-honored rabbinic form: "Thus have I received [*mequbalni*: e.g., *m. Peah* 2:6, *m. Yeb.* 16:7, *m. Yad.* 4:2]—that one does not pray on account of too much good!"

The final Amoraic and Stammaitic contributions to the Honi story come at the very end, interpolated seamlessly into Shimon b. Shetah's confession that he is at a loss to know how to deal with this rain-making "brat." Shimon b. Shetah figures as a looming Hasmonean-era presence in the Mishnah's chain of oral tradition from Moses to Rabbi Yehudah haNasi and his heirs (*m. Abot* 1:8-9). His teaching is Torah with a capital T. Yet he must rely on the unlettered Honi to bring life back to the parched Land! And even worse, Honi not only brings the rain, he has God customize it and, contrary to the Mishnah's own introductory statement, prays for it to cease![61]

Let us for a moment review Shimon b. Shetah's tirade as he confronts Honi:

Shimon b. Shetah sent for him.
Were you not Honi, I would condemn you to excommunication!
For if these years were as the years of Elijah,
When the keys to the rains were in the hands of Elijah,
Wouldn't the Name of Heaven have been desecrated by you?
But what can I do to you?
For you act like a brat before the Infinite,
And He makes your desire His desire.

As a son acts like a brat before his father,
Yet his father does whatever he asks!

And he says, Abba! Bathe me in hot water!
Rinse me in cold water!
Feed me nuts, almonds, peaches, and pomegranates,
And he gives!

Of you says Scripture:
"Your father and your mother will rejoice;
She who bore you will exult!" (Prov 23:25)

The Amoraic material, first attested in the Yerushalmi, alludes to the three years of drought that prevailed in the days of the prophet Elijah (1 Kgs 17). Had Honi sought to make rain in those days, he would have run up against prophetic authority instead of that of the rabbinic heirs. Thus displaying his ability to manipulate the divine decree of drought would have "desecrated the Name of Heaven."[62] The Stammaitic material builds upon this point: there is something about Honi that eludes even the prophet's closeness with God. The brattier he gets, the more likely he is to get his way.

In order to make sense of these last observations, we need to recall that the Honi being chastised here in *b. Taan.* 23a is not the Honi of *m. Taan.* 3:8. The latter is figured as an unlettered Hasmonean-era shaman; the former is described as a model rabbinic sage, with disciples who call him "Rabbi" and to whom he transmits oral traditions. The performers of the Stammaitic version of this tale, then, no longer imagine Honi as the charismatic counter-sage of Hasmonean times known to the Tannaitic sources. Rather, they view him, from a sixth-century C.E. vantage, as the consummate model of the perfected rabbinic saint (*zaddiq*) who joins in himself not only great learning in Torah but, precisely as a result of his Torah, great powers to influence the will of God.[63]

Our discussion clearly discloses the heavy hand of Stammaitic editing in the Honi *baraita'* that parallels *m. Taan.* 3:8. Before summarizing our observations, one additional point is in order. The Stammaim make their presence known not only by what they add to the received oral-performative tradition, but also by what they delete from it. Specifically, in the Mishnah, the very first thing Honi says after being summoned to pray for rain is "Go out and bring in your Passover ovens so they don't melt!" This line is missing in the Bavli. The reason is anticipated in the Yerushalmi's parallel at *y. Taan.* 66d. There the reason for Honi's initial failure to bring rain is explained (by the Palestinian Amora, Rabbi Yose b. Rabbi Bun) as follows: "Since he didn't come with humility." That is, in approaching his task, Honi failed to exhibit the humility appropriate to the rabbinic sage, whose archetype of self-abnegation originates with Moses himself (Num 12:3) and attains its classic dimensions in the traditions about the mild humility of Hillel the Elder (*Abot R. Nat.* A:15; *b. Shab.* 31a).

Similarly, after Honi is petitioned to cause the rain to cease, the Mishnah credits him with an enigmatic phrase: "He said to them: Go see if the Claimant's stone has melted." Why does the Bavli delete this phrase from its version? Again a glance at the earlier Talmud Yerushalmi offers a clue. The Palestinian reciters of the Honi tradition did not delete this line; rather, they interpreted it. Apparently, they heard Honi's stipulation as a kind of arrogance—as if he were saying: "I'll make the rain leave when I'm good and ready, that is, when boulders have melted!" Accordingly, the Yerushalmi's version of the Mishnah has Honi explain:

Just as it's impossible for this stone to melt from the world, so too is it impossible to pray for the rains to go.

This elegantly transforms Honi's Mishnaic boast into a concession to the consensual view, spelled out in the Mishnah's introductory clause, that one should never pray for rain to stop.[64]

To sum up our observations thus far: the *baraita'* of *b. Taan.* 23a is a prime example of the transformative dimension of rabbinic oral-performative tradition. The *baraita'* began its oral-performative life within a tradition of wonder-working narratives, one of which was selected for incorporation into the Mishnaic oral curriculum at *m. Taan.* 3:8. But in its course through Amoraic performances it both lost and acquired textual elements. The result is a reconfiguration of the Mishnaic "source" into a recognizably "different" text, one that, at the time of the editing of the Babylonian Gemara, could now stand as an independent testimony about Honi, distinct from but intimately linked to the corresponding Mishnaic narrative that "our Rabbis transmitted as a tradition."

This observation adds a new dimension to Green's and Rubenstein's earlier observations about the "rabbinization" of Honi. The "rabbinization" of Honi coincides with the canonical transformation of "our Mishnah" itself into a memorized work that is no longer under active construction, one that only permits a place for other performance-grounded reworkings of the text outside "our Mishnah's" own canonical frame. In other words, the freedom with which the Stammaitic editor reworks the performed "Tannaitic" text testifies to his own sense of the "fixed" (canonical) status of the Mishnah, in light of which his own repetition is framed as "external" to the Mishnaic corpus and, therefore, still malleable in performance. This *baraita'* is not memorized by its transmitter, but is composed by him. It is "memorized" only after the reformulation of the text as manuscript tradition in that "dark text-transformative tunnel" that connects the work of the Stammaim to the Geonic sponsors of the earliest talmudic manuscripts (whoever they may have been and whenever they did their work).

The second and third units of the Babylonian *sugya* are much simpler to account for. Section II, in its entirety an Amoraic construction,[65] is cited now to support the previous unit's depiction of Honi as a man who could manipulate the will of God.

> Rav Nahman b. Rav Hisda[66] expounded:
> What did the people of the Chamber of Carved Stone send to Honi the Circler?
> "You will decree and it will be fulfilled,
> And upon your paths the light will shine." (Job 22:28)
> "You will decree and it will be fulfilled"—
> You have decreed from below,
> And the Holy One fulfills your utterance from above.
> "And upon your paths the light will shine"—
> A generation in darkness have you illumined with your prayer.
> "When they sink, you shall explain it as pride"—
> A lowly generation have you raised up through your prayer.
> "The downcast of eye shall he spare"—
> A generation sunk in its iniquity you spared with your prayer.
> "He will deliver the impure"—
> A generation that was impure did your prayer deliver.
> "And he will be delivered through the cleanness of your hands"—
> They will be delivered through the innocent deeds of your hands.

The reference to the "people of the Chamber of Carved Stone" expresses the rabbinic conception that the Sanhedrin was a rabbinic institution that had its main convocation in the Temple's Chamber of Carved Stone (*lishkat hagazit*). Their message to him is clear: his efforts to force God to overturn His decrees are not only legitimate; they are even forecast in scriptural prophecy. Indeed, even in a sinful generation, God's saints are able to avert catastrophe from Israel.

Finally, in unit III, the editors of the Gemara supply the story for which Honi is perhaps most well known—as the "Rip Van Winkle" of rabbinic folklore. The unit is built upon two Amoraic foundations, Rabbi Yohanan's association of Honi—here termed a "saint" (*zaddiq*)—with a verse from Psalm 127, and a tale about his rude awakening after a sleep of seventy years.

> Said Rabbi Yohanan:[67] All his life that Saint puzzled over this verse:
> "A song of Ascents: When God returned the Remnant of Zion, we were as dreamers." (Ps 127:1)

HE SAID: CAN SOMEONE SLEEP FOR 70 YEARS AND DREAM?
ONE DAY HE WAS WALKING ALONG.
HE SAW A CERTAIN MAN PLANTING A CAROB TREE.
HE SAID: HOW MANY YEARS WILL THAT TAKE TO BEAR?
HE SAID: UP TO 70 YEARS.
HE SAID: **IT'S OBVIOUS TO YOU THAT** YOU'LL LIVE 70 YEARS?
HE SAID: I FOUND THE WORLD WITH CAROBS IN IT,
BECAUSE MY ANCESTORS PLANTED IT;
NOW I PLANT FOR MY CHILDREN!
HE SAT AND ATE SOME BREAD.
SLEEP OVERCAME HIM.
A GROTTO GREW AROUND HIM AND CONCEALED HIM,
AND HE SLEPT FOR 70 YEARS.
WHEN HE AWOKE, HE SAW A CERTAIN MAN PICKING FROM THE TREE.
HE SAID: DID YOU PLANT IT?
HE SAID: I AM HIS GRANDSON.
HE SAID: **AM I TO INFER THAT** I'VE SLEPT FOR 70 YEARS?
HE SAW THAT HIS DONKEY HAD GIVEN BIRTH TO FOALS.
HE WENT TO HIS HOUSE.
HE SAID: IS THE SON OF HONI THE CIRCLER STILL ALIVE?
THEY SAID: HIS SON'S GONE, BUT HIS GRANDSON LIVES.
HE SAID: I AM HONI THE CIRCLER!
THEY DID NOT BELIEVE HIM.
HE WENT TO THE HOUSE OF STUDY.
HE HEARD THE DISCIPLES SAYING:
THESE TRADITIONS ARE AS CLEAR AS THEY WERE
IN THE DAYS OF HONI THE CIRCLER!
FOR WHEN HE ENTERED THE HOUSE OF STUDY
HE WOULD SOLVE ANY PROBLEM THE DISCIPLES POSED.
HE SAID TO THEM: I AM HE!

THEY DIDN'T BELIEVE HIM
AND DIDN'T EXTEND TO HIM THE PROPER COURTESIES.
HE FELL INTO DESPAIR
AND PRAYED FOR THE MERCY OF DEATH.
SAID RAVA: AS PEOPLE SAY—
GIVE ME A PARTNER OR GIVE ME DEATH!

The Stammaitic contributions are purely redactional. The first, which articulates the question that plagued Honi, establishes the relevance of the story of Honi's seventy-year sleep to the independent tradition of Rabbi Yohanan's association of Honi and Psalm 127's dreamers. That is, his experience helped him to explain the verse.

The Yerushalmi as well knows of a link between Honi and Psalm 127, but records it in an entirely different narrative setting, right after Honi's first failure to bring rain:

SAID RABBI YUDAN THE CONVERT:
THAT HONI THE CIRCLER [OF M. 3:8] WAS
THE GRANDSON OF HONI THE CIRCLER
WHO LIVED NEAR THE TIME
OF THE DESTRUCTION OF THE [FIRST] TEMPLE.
HE WENT OUT TO THE MOUNTAINS WITH WORKERS
AND THEN IT RAINED.
HE ENTERED A CAVE.
WHILE WAITING, HE FELL ASLEEP.
HE WAS SUNK IN HIS SLEEP FOR 70 YEARS
UNTIL THE TEMPLE WAS DESTROYED
AND REBUILT A SECOND TIME.
AFTER 70 YEARS
HE AWOKE FROM HIS SLUMBER.
HE LEFT THE CAVE
AND FOUND THE WORLD IN DISARRAY.
PLACES THAT HAD BEEN VINEYARDS
NOW GREW OLIVES;
WHERE OLIVES ONCE GREW,
FIELDS WERE NOW SEEDED.
HE ASKED THE LOCALS:
WHAT HAPPENED TO THE WORLD?
THEY REPLIED: DON'T YOU KNOW
WHAT HAPPENED TO THE WORLD?

HE REPLIED: NO!
THEY SAID TO HIM: WHO ARE YOU?
HE REPLIED: HONI THE CIRCLER!
THEY SAID TO HIM:
WE HEARD THAT WHENEVER HE'D GO UP TO THE
    TEMPLE COURT
IT WOULD BE ILLUMINED BY HIS LIGHT,
AND HE APPLIED TO HIMSELF THIS VERSE:
WHEN GOD RETURNED THE REMNANT OF ZION, WE
    WERE AS DREAMERS (Ps 127).

Nothing of this survives in the Bavli version except for the idea that the dreamers of Psalm 127 are somehow connected to Honi's seventy years of sleep. The Yerushalmi offers scant precedent for the Babylonian tale that uses the verse to build up Honi's rabbinic credentials.

The remaining Stammaitic additions all tie Honi—now firmly accorded the status of a *zaddiq*—tightly to the rabbinic estate. Not only does Honi walk the rabbinic walk, he talks the rabbinic talk. When conversing with the man who plants the carob, for example, Honi employs a common rhetorical formula of the house of study, normally used in the analysis of halakhic arguments: *peshita' lakh*, "It's obvious to you?" Moreover, upon his awakening, he employs a standard scholarly rhetorical term used for deducing a legal principle from a text: *shma` minah*, "Am I to infer?"[68] Finally, the concluding Stammaitic materials establish Honi firmly as a mainstay of the local rabbinic academy and portray his untimely death as a result of despair over having been denied the collegial deference due to one of his rank.[69] In context, then, the concluding citation of folk wisdom by the mid-fourth-century Babylonian Amora, Rava—"Give me a partner or give me death"—is likely to imply something that any veteran academic—rabbinic or tenured—could certainly echo: "I'd rather drop dead than be treated like a nobody by junior colleagues!"

Conclusion

To Gerhardsson goes the lion's share of the credit for placing the oral-performative dimension of rabbinic literature at the center of the study of this literary corpus. The intervening decades have produced fine and detailed literary studies of rabbinic texts and much discussion of their oral character in particular. But there remain no editions and very few (partial) translations that attempt to render the texts "on the page" in ways that call attention to their oral-performative characteristics. Even the incisive, pioneering, form-critical studies of Neusner on the Mishnah and the Tosefta, or the extensive scholarship inspired by David Weiss-Halivni's formulation of the significance of the Stammaitic contribution to the Babylonian Talmud, normally make little effort to present the texts in a way that draws the reader into the performative life that sustained their written transmission.

The main intention of this essay, accordingly, has been to offer an experiment in "re-oralizing" the talmudic text. To this end, I have used the standard redaction- and source-critical methods routinely applied to the study of ancient texts. These remain the first step in determining the precise relationship of the diverse textual units that structure a given rabbinic passage. An "oralist" reading of rabbinic texts then moves a step further. It reminds the reader that the written manuscript is not the text itself, but the storage space for that part of the text that can be represented in fixed, visual form. Thus, the written text must be (mis)represented in a manner that points at all moments beyond the actual written words to the oral-performative milieu from which they emerged and to the evidence of other inter-texts not formally present in the words of the manuscript copy.

I have pointed out that the fundamental fact of oral performance is that the text in question is mediated in speech from memory (even if memory is itself tutored by reference to written versions of the text). Thus the "re-oralized" text attempts to imitate the relation of breath to phrasing that is fundamental to textual performance. Most renderings of rabbinic texts in scholarly essays, not to mention full-fledged editions and translations, imitate the long, undifferentiated lines of the manuscripts, thus hiding precisely what the manuscripts themselves conceal—the fact that the oral text is deployed *in time* to the ears of an audience rather than *in space* to the eyes of readers.[70] Lines in the text that are keyed to the needs of human breathing, therefore, subvert the impressions left by manuscripts and permit the reader to "hear" the text in new ways.

The second key contribution of this experiment in "re-oralization" involves the attempt to present the manuscript text in a way that calls attention to the diverse "textual voices" that are coordinated by various editorial composers and transmitters. For the Talmud Bavli in particular, the paragraphing and selective fonts within which the texts are rendered attempt to employ visual cues to represent the distinctive achievement of talmudic editing, namely, the orchestration of the performing voices of Tannaitic memorizers, Amoraic expounders, and, of course, the Stammaitic editors responsible for the *sugya*, into a single textual "performance" that calls forth yet a final performative initiative from the contemporary "performative transmitter" of the text—the reader.

What is the *sugya* if not an artificially constructed literary image of the oral give and take of the disciple circle? *Torah shebe`al peh*—Torah delivered from memory in a performance that qualifies the performer to be numbered among those who not only received Torah from Sinai, but also stand firmly in the chain of its holy transmitters—is concealed in the rabbinic manuscript. It is the job of "oralist" studies of Oral Torah to restore to the inscribed texts of Oral Torah the living voices that, in the rabbinic *bet midrash*, brought the disciple as close as he might ever come to hearing the Voice that spoke to Moses out of the cloud at Sinai.[71]

Chapter 5

Memory and Tradition in the Hellenistic Schools

Loveday Alexander

Critical attention on Birger Gerhardsson's *Memory and Manuscript* has focused largely on the parallels between early Christian practice and the practice of the rabbinic academies. But Gerhardsson points out that the appeal to tradition is also a feature deeply rooted in the Hellenistic world, "in schools for philosophers, rhetoricians, lawyers and even doctors!"[1] In this paper I intend to explore this neglected insight, examining Justin's allusions to the "*Apomnemoneumata* of the Apostles" in the light of ancient school practice in the Hellenistic world.

GERHARDSSON AND THE *Collegium apostolorum*

"History is what you can remember," said the authors of that very English work of comic genius, *1066 And All That*,[2] more truly perhaps than they knew: for as the raw material of history increases in bulk, we are more conscious than ever that the virtual databanks of information are just that, not history but raw data, inert and inoperative until retrieved and reactivated as part of a living memory system. And in an era when information is treated as a form of technology, it is salutary to be reminded that the prime carriers of information between one human generation and another—even in the modern university—are still people. Even (perhaps increasingly) in a technological age, social memory—the events and mechanisms that serve to pass on social capital from one generation to another—is vital for the well-being of all forms of human society.³

The reinstatement of memory as a core activity in the construction of early Christianity is one of the lasting contributions of Gerhardsson's work, and it is a privilege to be associated with this tribute. The particular area of Gerhardsson's work that I want to focus on is the role of the *collegium apostolorum* as described in *Memory and Manuscript*, chapter 14, and especially on the Lukan understanding of the "ministry of the Word" (ἡ διακονία τοῦ λόγου) as the essential apostolic task:

> The principal tasks of the Apostles were to pray and to serve the Word. The latter task, διακονία τοῦ λόγου, seems to be practically identical with what Luke calls διδαχὴ τῶν ἀποστόλων. By this is meant, not mere proclamation, but *teaching*: a doctrinal work based on the Scriptures and the tradition of Christ. This work with the logos was regarded by the early Church as being of such vital importance, and has such scope, that on one definite occasion the Apostles were solemnly exempted from certain other tasks, important in themselves, in order that they might be able to concentrate uninterruptedly—"night and day," metaphorically speaking—on that task and on prayer.⁴

As Gerhardsson rightly observes, the post-Easter task of the apostles is very carefully defined in Luke–Acts. Their central task is the ministry of the word, διακονία τοῦ λόγου, and this is a task that requires both disciplined attentiveness and the voluntary shedding of other responsibilities (Acts 6:1-6).⁵ From this point on, the apostles follow a more and more narrowly defined role in Acts, a role distinct from both the ἐκκλησία and the elders. In its initial stages, their ministry is tied closely to Jerusalem—though even the Jerusalem apostles adopt an increasingly itinerant role from chapter 8 onward.⁶ But they continue to provide a key link between the fast-expanding church and the story and teachings of Jesus: the apostles in Acts are the prime (though not the sole) bearers of the Jesus tradition.

Although the form critics tended to speak of the apostolic task in terms of kerygma, "preaching," the key verbs Luke uses to describe their activity are "bearing witness" and "teaching."⁷ The medieval illuminators who depicted the apostles in the early chapters of Acts as a "school of Christ" were following a sound exegetical instinct.⁸ It is implicit in the whole structure of Luke's story that the apostles are themselves disciples (μαθηταί, students) of the one teacher, Jesus, and that their task is to pass on his teaching, not their own.⁹ Hence this explains the central importance for Luke's whole structure of the instruction given by the risen Christ to the disciples in Luke 24 and Acts 1. The content of this instruction is not spelled out in detail, but there is a clear implication that it forms the basis of the teaching Luke presents through the medium of the apostolic speeches in Acts 2 through 13. The focus of the apostolic teaching on Jesus is reinforced continually through the marturi/a word-group ("You shall be *my* witnesses," i.e., witnesses *of me*) and through the apostles' insistence, when challenged, on teaching "in the name of Jesus"—a form of words that echoes rabbinic teaching formulae.[10]

Where can we find a plausible social model for the patterns of memory and tradition Luke ascribes to the Jerusalem apostles? Gerhardsson works chiefly with rabbinic parallels but recognizes the importance of putting these in a wider Hellenistic framework:

> During the centuries around the beginning of the Christian era it was not only among the Jews that the appeal to tradition was made: in the mystery religions and similar currents, in schools for philosophers, rhetoricians, lawyers and even doctors! The technique of transmission in these groups would be worth investigating.[11]

In an earlier chapter, Gerhardsson also notes the importance of examining the role of memory and tradition in the education systems of the Hellenistic and Roman worlds.[12] There is a fundamental insight here, the significance of which has been eclipsed by the more extensive coverage of rabbinic material in Gerhardsson's work. The Hellenistic schools have immense potential as a social model (complementary to that of the rabbinic schools) for understanding the functioning of memory and tradition within early Christianity, and I believe that it would be an immensely valuable task to revisit this material in light of the explosion of more recent studies of Greco-Roman education and of the Hellenistic schools.[13] Here I can do no more than sketch an approach to this material, focusing on Justin's famous designation of the Gospels as the "*Apomnemoneumata* of the Apostles."

Apostolic Memories: Justin, Papias, and the *Apomnemoneumata*

It is well known that Justin's preferred term for the "so-called gospels" which are read every Sunday in Christian assemblies (τὰ λεγόμενα εὐαγγέλια) is the "ἀπομνημονεύματα of the Apostles" (1 *Apol.* 66.3). Justin implies that εὐαγγέλια is insider-language, a technical term used within the Christian sect, whereas ἀπομνημονεύματα ("reminiscences" or "memoirs") is the term he expects a wider audience to understand. Εὐαγγέλιον in fact only occurs three times in the extant writings of Justin (1 *Apol.* 66.3; *Dial.* 10.2; *Dial.* 100.1), whereas variants on τὰ ἀπομνημονεύματα τῶν ἀποστόλων occur fourteen times, with the cognate participial form οἱ ἀπομνημονεύσαντες πάντα τά περὶ τοῦ σωτῆρος ἡμῶν once at 1 *Apol.* 33.5.[14] Two things emerge clearly from these passages: first, that Justin is referring to written texts, texts that are "read aloud" to the assembled Christian congregation on Sundays alongside the "writings of the prophets" (1 *Apol.* 67.3); and second, that these texts are known internally as εὐαγγέλια (1 *Apol.* 66.3).[15]

What precisely Justin means by the term ἀπομνημονεύματα is less clear. Clearly the genitive τῶν ἀποστόλων is subjective, rather than objective: the apostles are the authors/originators of these texts, and Jesus is their object, not their author (cf. *Dial.* 88.3; 1 *Apol.* 33.5). Verbs used cover the normal range of scholastic discourse in this period: "writing," "teaching," "showing"; once Justin varies the phrase to highlight what he himself has "learnt" from these memoirs (*Dial.* 105.5). Unlike Papias, Justin shows little interest in the authors of these texts: they are cited to bear witness to the words and deeds of Jesus, and all that matters is that they derive from "his apostles" or their followers (*Dial.* 103.8). Interestingly, the distinction between apostles and "followers" does not appear to be of apologetic interest to Justin: traditions related by "those who followed them" (τῶν ἐκείνοις παρακολουθηκουσάντων) are no less authentic than those of the apostles themselves. In other words, Justin's conception of apostolic tradition works with a built-in assumption both of catholicity and of continuity. Only at one point (*Dial.* 106.3) is there a possible hint of a named tradent—possibly a reference to Peter.[16] Justin tends to paraphrase and conflate his gospel quotations, with the result that it is not always easy to identify precisely which gospel texts he is alluding to. It is clear however that Justin is drawing primarily on synoptic materials here, albeit in a paraphrastic form which reflects the relatively fluid nature of gospel tradition at this period.[17]

It is equally well recognized that Papias, a couple of decades earlier than Justin, uses the cognate verb ἀπομνημονεύω to refer to Peter's teaching activity in Rome. Papias is aware that the generation of the apostles—and even of those who can claim to have heard the apostles in person, the πρεσβύτεροι—is dying out and is conscious that he himself belongs to a third generation, neither a hearer nor an eyewitness. But he shows sufficient antiquarian interest to take steps to bridge the gap, seeking out and questioning visitors, collecting and passing on traditions about gospel authors and tradents. Papias himself conceived the ambitious project of putting together an "interpretation" of dominical sayings (Λογίων κυριακῶν ἐξηγήσεως) in five books (Eusebius, *Hist. eccl.* 3.39.1–4), and it is from the preface to that collection that Eusebius quotes the well-known statement about the composition of Mark's gospel:

> Μάρκος μὲν ἑρμηνευτὴς Πέτρου γενόμενος, ὅσα ἐμνημόνευσεν, ἀκριβῶς ἔγραψεν, οὐ μέντοι τάξει τὰ ὑπὸ τοῦ κυρίου ἢ λεχθέντα ἢ πραχθέντα. Οὔτε γὰρ ἤκουσεν τοῦ κυρίου οὔτε παρηκολούθησεν αὐτῷ, ὕστερον δέ, ὡς ἔφην, Πέτρῳ· ὃς πρὸς τὰς χρείας ἐποιεῖτο τὰς διδασκαλίας, ἀλλ' οὐχ ὥσπερ σύνταξιν τῶν κυριακῶν ποιούμενος λογίων, ὥστε οὐδὲν ἥμαρτεν Μάρκος οὕτως ἔνια γράψας ὡς ἀπεμνημόνευσεν. Ἑνὸς γὰρ ἐποιήσατο πρόνοιαν, τοῦ μηδὲν ὧν ἤκουσεν παραλιπεῖν ἢ ψεύσασθαί τι ἐν αὐτοῖς. (Eusebius, *Hist. eccl.* 3.39.15)

> Mark became Peter's interpreter and wrote accurately all that he remembered (ὅσα ἐμνημόνευσεν), not, indeed, in order, of the things said or done by the Lord. For he had not heard the Lord, nor had he followed him, but later on, as I said, followed Peter, who used to give teaching as necessity demanded (πρὸς τὰς χρείας) but not making, as it were, an arrangement of the Lord's oracles, so that Mark did nothing wrong in thus writing down single points as he remembered them (ὡς ἀπεμνημόνευσεν). For to one thing he gave attention, to leave out nothing of what he had heard and to make no false statements in them. (*Eusebius*, vol. 2, p. 297, LCL)

Eusebius tells us explicitly that he found these words in the προοίμιον of Papias' five-volume collection (*Hist. eccl.* 3.39.2), and this provides an important key to unpicking the rhetoric of this remarkable statement. Such prefaces regularly include information both on the sources of the present work and on its literary predecessors, often with a veiled critique which implicitly justifies the author's own project.[18] Papias is being careful to distance his own project from Mark's, but the words he uses to say what Mark and Matthew were not doing pick up key words from his own title, as if to say, "What I am trying here is something that my predecessors have not even attempted." Matthew put together a collection of *logia* (τὰ λόγια συνετάξατο), just as Papias is doing, but (besides being in "Hebrew"), this collection left the interpretation to the reader, that is, it did not contain the ἐξήγησις on which Papias prides himself (*Hist. eccl.* 3.39.16). Mark, on the other hand, did not even attempt to rise to the heights of a systematic collection of dominical sayings (οὐχ ὥσπερ σύνταξιν τῶν κυριακῶν ποιούμενος λογίων), but simply sought to provide a faithful written version of the Lord's words and deeds, "not in order" (οὐ μέντοι τάξει), but following the oral pattern of Peter's teaching, οὕτως ἔνια γράψας ὡς ἀπεμνημόνευσεν.

All this is well known. What is less often observed is that Papias' words conceal a persistent ambiguity that is habitually ignored in translation. The μνημονεύω word-group occurs twice in this passage (ὅσα ἐμνημόνευσεν / ὡς ἀπεμνημόνευσεν) and in both places is usually translated "as he [sc. Mark] remembered." But it makes equal if not more sense to translate "as he [sc. Peter] recounted," giving the verbs the sense they commonly bear of "recounting" or "making mention," whether orally or in writing (as in Eusebius' reference to Irenaeus' "making mention" of Papias' work at 3.39.1 or in Papias' reference to "those who recount the commandments of others" at 3.39.3). Read this way, the passage is not a comment on what Mark "remembered" so much as on what Peter "recounted"—in other words, on the process of memorializing, the formal codification of memory. The focus is on the verbal processes that ultimately lead to the production of written *Apomnemoneumata*—and the final sentence reinforces this by stressing that Mark made it his paramount concern not to omit or falsify anything of what he had heard, namely, Peter's verbal recounting (ὡς ἀπεμνημόνευσεν) of the Jesus tradition.[19]

The verb ἀπομνημονεύω, like the simplex form μνημονεύω, shares a triple semantic ambiguity with many memory words in Greek and other languages, covering the full range from "remembering" as a mental act, through "making mention" as a verbal act, to "memorial" as a physical or textual record. This triple ambiguity is evident from a glance at the entry Μνήμη in the Liddell-Scott-Jones lexicon,[20] which covers "memory, remembrance of a person or thing"; "memory as a power of the mind"; "memorial, record"; and "mention, notice of a thing." Similarly, μνημονεύω covers both "call to mind, remember, think of," and "call to another's mind, make mention of, say"—with no necessary connection with personal memory.[21] Compounds and cognates retain the ambiguity, varying the balance between the mental act of memory and the verbal act of memorializing: διαμνημονεύω is weighted more toward the mental act of remembering, while ἀπομνημονεύω and its cognates lay more weight on the verbal act of relating from memory (ἀπομνημόνευσις, "recounting, summarizing; commemoration") or its written deposit (ἀπομνημόνευμα, "memorial, record; memorandum; memoirs").[22]

Bearing in mind this simple semantic observation, we can begin to see that Justin's designation of the Gospels as *Apomnemoneumata* opens up three distinct but overlapping modes of relation between the written text and its precursors in early Christianity. If we translate the phrase as "memories of the apostles," we place the emphasis on the eyewitness recollection of the apostles. The prime focus here is on the origins of the tradition, legitimating where it comes from. This apologetic issue seems to be of interest to Papias, but is less obviously so to Justin. If we translate the phrase as "anecdotes of the apostles," the focus shifts to the performance of tradition: memory codified, fossilized, structured, and performed as anecdote, memoir. Here oral transmission becomes a process in its own right, a process which can be studied even though it is no longer accessible to us. For Justin, on the other hand, the expression "Memoirs of the Apostles" clearly designates a text, the written deposit of this tradition—though still, it should be noted, a text accessed primarily through the ear, read aloud in public performance, rather than through the eye, in the privacy of the scholar's library.

Justin's ἀπομνημονεύματα τῶν ἀποστόλων thus nicely encapsulate the threefold nature of gospel transmission, and the three models that have dominated the study of the gospel tradition throughout the twentieth century. (1) Traditional synoptic criticism, with its successors in redaction and narrative criticism, has focused (and continues to focus) on the written deposit of the gospel tradition, identifying sources and quotations, or simply concentrating on the final form of the written Gospels as all that is accessible to our analytical tools. (2) The oral tradition model recognizes that the "memorizing" (or better, "memorializing") of tradition is itself a structured process, and looks to find different ancient models of oral transmission between the recollection of an event and the written text, seeking to understand the processes of the formalization and structuring of oral tradition, raising questions about the process of tradition itself: What is it for? How is it used? How is it controlled and formalized? One of the dominant threads in this research is the search for some kind of intermediate model between "controlled" and "uncontrolled" models of oral tradition, avoiding the twin extremes of classic form criticism (which drew heavily on a folk-tradition model) and of Gerhardsson's rabbinic model of transmission, which postulates a more controlled medium of formalization and transmission within the framework of a school.[23] Particular interest in recent studies has focused on Kenneth Bailey's model of "controlled informal" traditioning (based on traditional practice in the villages of the Middle East), as offering a *via media* between the "informal uncontrolled" transmission of jokes or casual memories and the "formal controlled" retention of memorized texts.[24] (3) More recently, Samuel Byrskog has proposed an oral history model focusing on memory as a mental act, and on the validity or otherwise of the claim to be based on authentic eyewitness testimony.[25] Richard Bauckham's recent study of *Jesus and the Eyewitnesses* takes this further: for him, memory is located primarily in the recollective powers of the individual, rather than in collective community processes, and is increasingly conceived as moving in a more or less unmediated form from personal memory to written record, minimalizing the transmission stage or cutting it out altogether.[26] All three models appeal in one way or another to Justin and Papias; and all of them can be illustrated from the Hellenistic school tradition.

In the remainder of this chapter, I intend to examine the role of *Apomnemoneumata* in the Hellenistic school tradition. I shall argue (1) that the Hellenistic school tradition provides a valuable ancient model for the gospel tradition and deserves to be considered on the same footing as the rabbinic tradition, (2) that the Hellenistic school model offers an ancient *via media* of controlled informal traditioning to set alongside Bailey's modern Middle Eastern parallel, and (3) that the key to avoiding the sterile standoff between eyewitness tradition and folk tradition may lie in Gerhardsson's concept of the "*collegium* of the apostles." Since the tradition is only accessible to us in its written deposit, we need to work backwards, looking first at memory as text (*Apomnemoneumata* as literary phenomenon), then at memory as performance (*Apomnemoneumata* as oral event), and finally at memory as tradition *(Apomnemoneumata* as the art of recollection).

Memory as Text: *Apomnemoneumata* as Literary Phenomenon

As we have seen, Justin's *Apomnemoneumata* clearly refers to a written text. Why does Justin choose this term, and what kind of text is he thinking of? Karl Ludwig Schmidt argued that Justin's use of the term should be discounted as an apologetically motivated allusion to Xenophon's *Apomnemoneumata* of Socrates.[27] Justin does in fact quote Xenophon (1 *Apol.* 2.11) and cites the unjust prosecution of Socrates as a parallel to the imperial persecution of Christians (1 *Apol.* 18, 46; 2 *Apol.* 3, 7, 10). But he does not give any title to Xenophon's work, and there is no obvious connection between these passages and his references to the *Apomnemoneumata of the Apostles*. To substantiate Schmidt's argument, we would have to show that the title was unique to Xenophon, or at least was so intimately connected with the Socratic tradition as to evoke it without further explanation. R. G. Heard, by contrast, dismisses the parallel with Xenophon as "not a true parallel," and claims that "Xenophon's title stands alone; the term is not elsewhere used as the definite title of a work."[28] He therefore goes on to argue that Justin, "using documents that had no titles," adapted the phrase from Papias. Both of these approaches are seriously misleading and have perpetuated the confusion that has prevented a full critical appreciation of Justin's term precisely as a way of conceptualizing the gospel traditions that makes sense within the context of the second-century Hellenistic schools.

Xenophon's *Apomnemoneumata* was written to defend Socrates' reputation after his death and claims to be based on Xenophon's own memories of Socrates: "In order to support my opinion that he benefited his companions, alike by actions that revealed his character and by his conversation, I will set down what I recollect of these" (ὁπόσα ἂν διαμνημονεύσω: Xenophon, *Mem.* 1.3.1). The Latin title *Memorabilia Socratis* is not attested before 1569, but the Greek title *Apomnemoneumata Xenophontis* is certainly ancient.[29] Diogenes Laertius knows the work under this title (2.48, 57; 3.34), as do at least two earlier writers: Harpocration, in *Lexeis of the Ten Orators* (early second century C.E.), and Theon, in *Progymnasmata* (late first or early second century C.E.).[30] Xenophon could justly claim to be writing on the basis of his own personal recollection of Socrates. But a glance at Xenophon's work makes it clear from the outset that even within one generation, memory, however personal in origin, is already molded by the literary forms and expectations of the larger society. Xenophon's work combines apologetic (echoing the trial format of Plato's *Apology* and forged in the heat of the reputation wars that broke out over Socrates' memory after his death) with anecdotes (e.g., 3.14) and more extended dialogues of the Platonic type.

However, Xenophon's work is not the only work to bear this title in antiquity and is in many ways untypical of the *Apomnemoneumata* literature known to Justin and his contemporaries. One of the earliest known works with this title is the *Apomnemoneumata* of Lynceus of Samos, a collection of Athenian wit and repartee from the late fourth century B.C.E., surviving only in fragments and liberally cited by the erudite dinner guests of Athenaeus' *Deipnosophistae*.[31] Lynceus' anecdotes belong to two worlds: the celebrity subculture of Athens in the late fourth and early third centuries B.C.E. ("playwrights, professional comics, intelligent and independent women, prostitutes, even a few political figures, foreign royalty") and the "shelf-load of gossip and reminiscence of Alexander's court."[32] Some of this material is recorded by near-contemporaries, like Lynceus himself or the Alexander historians, to be quoted five centuries later by Athenaeus; some of it is passed down in oral tradition and "surfaces, unattributed, in Plutarch, in Quintus Curtius, and even in Arrian."[33]

Thus the emergence of the anecdote collection as a written genre can be traced back at least to the fourth-century Lyceum. Lynceus was a student of Theophrastus, and two earlier collectors, Callisthenes and Clearchus of Soli, were students of Aristotle himself.[34] Andrew Dalby plausibly links the emergence of the new genre with two key literary shifts at the end of the fourth century:

> The first is the codification of existing Greek culture: the making of classics and cultural heroes. This grew out of the need for maintaining, even asserting, Greekness in those vast eastern realms with their new, largely Greek, wholly Greek-speaking élites; in spite of migration Greeks were spread thin, at first, till gradually more people began to become Greek. Hellenism had to be held on to. The second is that at this period some more genres turn from being purely oral in their manifestation to forming the basis of literary texts. To us this means that they appear to be "new genres" because ancient Greek oral literature is, except in some sidelong way, unknowable to us.[35]

Both phenomena coincide in an anecdote demonstrating Philip of Macedonia's overpowering urge to "own" the cream of Attic culture:

> They met in the Diomean temple of Heracles, sixty in number, and that is what they were called in town: "The Sixty said so-and-so," "I've been with the Sixty." Among them were Callimedon "Crayfish" and Deinias, and again Mnasigeiton and Menaechmus, according to Telephanes in his *On the City*. Their wit was so famous that Philip the Macedonian, when he heard of them, sent a talent to have their jokes written up and sent to him. (Athenaeus, *Deipnosophistae* 14.614d)

This anecdote highlights the important role of formalization, memorialization, and verbal codification in the composition of anecdotes. These mini-pods of Athenian wit and wisdom were not stray reminiscences but carefully honed samples of an oral performance culture that took pride in verbal craftsmanship. But the story also shows how the literary genre of the anecdote collection is perched on the cusp between orality and writing, coming into existence precisely at the point where external circumstances (here, the combination of physical distance and royal patronage) create a demand to codify, record, and capture a culturally significant performance of verbal wit and transport it to a different social and geographical location.[36] And of course, as Plato famously observes (*Phaedr.* 275d–e), once this step has been taken the written record has a potential afterlife of its own: Philip could hardly have envisaged that his simple request would have provided a resource for the learned dinnertalk of the Second Sophistic some five centuries later.

The process of collecting and recording this quintessentially Hellenic performance art seems to have continued spasmodically through the Hellenistic period and comes to a head in the period of the Second Sophistic, when the burgeoning classicism of the second and third centuries C.E. leads to a new interest in the collecting, recording, and comparing of the oral traditions—perhaps even the rival streams of oral tradition—that capture the essence of what it means to be "Greek."[37] The epitome of this essentially scholastic activity is Diogenes Laertius, whose mammoth third-century compilation, *The Lives and Opinions of the Philosophers,* is one of our major sources for the Hellenistic anecdotal tradition. Just as Justin clearly refers to the *Apomnemoneumata of the Apostles* as preexistent written texts, so Diogenes Laertius cites (and draws freely on) earlier collections of *Apomnemoneumata* by Zeno (7.4), Persaeus (7.36, cf. Athenaeus, *Deipnosophistae* 4.162), Ariston (7.163), Dioscourides (1.63, cf. Athenaeus, *Deipnosophistae* 11.116), and Favorinus (2.39; 3.20).[38] The bulk of these date from the Hellenistic period; the latest, Favorinus, dates from the second century C.E. and seems to have been simply a collection of assorted "memorable facts" (*Lesefrüchte*), garnered from earlier collections going back to the pre-Roman period.[39]

Diogenes Laertius provides a unique entrée into this complex and vigorous anecdotal tradition. His work is essentially "a kind of coffee-table book, with just the information that the educated person needs to know," and he himself comes across as "an erudite amateur, isolated and without personal connections with the contemporary schools of learning."[40] What he writes is not narrative so much as scholastic discourse, a fascinating combination of the learned and the frivolous. Much of it seems a textbook example of the "useless erudition" that Plutarch deprecates in the biographer (Plutarch, *Nic.* 1.524a). It is a third-order academic discourse that constantly draws attention to its own sources and structures and to the observing, recording self which has assembled so much learned material. There is no attempt to construct a seamless narrative or to conceal the debates and disagreements of the sources: Diogenes prefers to draw attention to the whole scholarly enterprise, citing his sources by name (at least when he disagrees with them) and cheerfully labeling the separate elements which make up his *Lives.*[41] Among these components, anecdotes play a major role, and this material opens a window into one of the most important of the underground streams of the Hellenistic tradition from which Diogenes is drawing.[42] Even within

Diogenes, it is clear that some of the anecdotes he recounts have an independent existence, as the same anecdote turns up in more than one place attached to different protagonists. Many of them are known from a range of compilations both earlier and later than Diogenes (Athenaeus, Aulus Gellius, Plutarch, Stobaeus): the easiest way to see this material synoptically is in the *Testimonia* sections of all the major scholarly editions of philosophical fragments. Similar (often identical) anecdotes appear in the *Progymnasmata* of the rhetorical theorists: thus the famous *chreia* attributed to Isocrates by Hermogenes in *Progymnasmata* 3 ("The roots of education are bitter but the fruit is sweet") turns up in Diogenes Laertius (5.18) as a saying of Aristotle. Similar anecdotes (again, often the same ones) appear independently in the "biographical" papyri.[43]

Though it seems clear that the primary vehicle for transmission of much of this material was oral, by the time of Diogenes there were, as we have seen, many different kinds of written collections in existence. The simplest is the "sayings collection," an assemblage of γνῶμαι or aphorisms encapsulating the teaching of a school in its most compressed form and often used as the basis for preliminary instruction. Some of these were generic collections of gnomic wisdom (often associated with the fabled Seven Sages).[44] Others provided an induction into the teachings of a particular master: the Hippocratic *Aphorisms* and the *Kuriai Doxai* of Epicurus provide two of the most famous examples of this method of teaching in antiquity.[45] A collection of anecdotes could serve a similar function, condensing the essence of a teacher's lifestyle or βίος into a string of compressed anecdotes: many of Diogenes' *Lives* consist of little more than a sequence of disconnected anecdotes, and Lucian's *Life of Demonax* shows how easily such a collection could be given a rudimentary biographical format by the addition of a preface and conclusion. Many of the so-called biographical papyri are of this form, catenae of disconnected anecdotes about Socrates or Diogenes: they may be school texts (or teacher's handbooks) containing the raw anecdotal material on which the students would have to go to work.[46] We might compare the notebooks (*volumina*) compiled by Roman authors to provide a repertoire of historical or mythological *exempla* to be used by students or orators in composing speeches.[47] But such compilations need not follow a biographical format: they could equally be arranged thematically, like the *Memorable Deeds and Sayings* of Valerius Maximus, designed by its author to "save his readers the trouble of going to historical sources to search out illustrative anecdotes."[48] These collections function as cultural databanks for the educated public speaker, for whom anecdotes were an essential resource in moral and cultural formation, to be cited liberally in speeches or letters and endlessly re-oralized in the table-talk of the *literati*.[49]

Anecdotes also play an important role in the paratextual repertoire of Hellenistic scholarship, part of "the hard currency of biography in the hellenistic schools: sequences and catalogues, floating anecdotes and sayings, a name attached to a teacher, a name or an anecdote attached to a doctrine or discovery, archival collections of letters or wills."[50] Once again, however, it is important to note that this material does not necessarily follow a narrative sequence. Jørgen Mejer lists four main literary genres in the historiography of the Hellenistic schools: "Successions" (Διαδοχαί), the *Haireseis*-literature, doxography, and the *bios* of an individual philosopher.[51] Of these, the first is by far the most comprehensive, covering philosophical schools of all periods and ranging philosophers in διαδοχαί from one teacher to another. They are predominantly plural in form (the history of a single school is much less common) and deal with each philosopher under standard headings (place of origin, family relations, chronology, death, bibliography), using anecdotes along the way to illustrate this information and to characterize the philosopher.[52] The *Haireseis*-literature offers a guide to the doctrines of each school and does not give detailed information on the lives and writings of individual philosophers.[53] Doxography (a modern term) is a multifarious tradition spanning many literary genres and going back to the roots of Greek philosophy; it provides a history of ideas rather than of individuals, but may well cite individual anecdotes or apophthegms as evidence for a particular thinker's ideas.[54] In fact, such anecdotes may turn up at any point in "the three major loci for biographical interest in the Hellenistic schools: sequencing and chronology; doxography/bibliography; and ethics."[55] Amid all this intense scholarly activity, the decision to combine a series of anecdotes into a biographical sequence to create a laudatory *Life* of an individual philosopher is by no means an inevitable progression.[56] From earliest times, such *Lives* were arranged in collections (lives of philosophers, lives of the poets, lives of the orators), and many were composed with hostile intent as an attack on a rival school.

Two points emerge from this brief survey. First, despite the strong interest of the schools in biographical anecdotes, the *bios*-format itself was only one—and by no means the most common—of the literary forms in which anecdotes might be collected. Even where a rich anecdotal tradition exists, there was no necessity for this scattered material to be combined into a single biography at all: there were a thousand

and one other things you could do with anecdotes, and weaving them together into a connected narrative was by no means the most obvious. Both Socrates and Diogenes generated a rich anecdotal tradition, and both created hugely influential lifestyle paradigms, without inspiring a definitive narrative biography.[57] Secondly, even within the biographical format, creating a sequential narrative seems to have been rather low on the list of priorities. Plutarch's *Lives* show that it could be done, but the narrative description of historical exploits in biographical form is associated much more strongly with political biography than with intellectual, and with Roman literary practice than with Greek. The historiographical tradition of connected narrative of events is largely missing in the anecdotal tradition of philosophical biography represented by Diogenes Laertius and is severely curtailed even where good historical sources exist—as for example in Diogenes' *Life of Xenophon* (2.48–59).

Memory as Performance: *Apomnemoneumata* as Oral Event

Apomnemoneumata effectively collapse the artificial distinction between "literate" and "oral" societies. The people fashioning and preserving these anecdotes in Hellenic culture are highly literate people, but they still value the art of oral performance. This is brought out beautifully in an anecdote recounted of Aristotle:

> Διογένους ἰσχάδ' αὐτῷ διδόντος νοήσας ὅτι, εἰ μὴ λάβοι, χρείαν εἴη μεμελετηκώς, λαβὼν ἔφη Διογένην μετὰ τῆς χρείας καὶ τὴν ἰσχάδα ἀπολελωκέναι. (D.L. 5.18)

> When Diogenes offered him dried figs, he saw that he had prepared something caustic to say (χρείαν εἴη μεμελετηκώς) if he did not take them; so he took them said that Diogenes had lost his figs and his jest into the bargain (μετὰ τῆς χρείς καὶ τὴν ἰσχάδα ἀπολελωκέναι). (*Diogenes Laertius*, vol. 1, p. 461, LCL)

The *chreia* here is a piece of verbal wit, repartee, designed for oral performance (scoring a point off a rival philosopher) in a particular setting. It is also the end-product of a careful and conscious process of mental composition (χρείαν εἴη μεμελετηκώς), the fashioning of a *mot juste* carefully crafted and perfectly matched to the situation—though trumped here by Aristotle's quick-thinking riposte. This is precisely the kind of sophisticated verbal art that Lynceus' collection values and preserves. The exchange is preserved in a mini-narrative, an ἀπομνημόνευμα that skillfully condenses the whole encounter into a single sentence and forms part of a list of "exceedingly happy sayings" (ἀποφθέγματα κάλλιστα) attributed to Aristotle:

> To the question, "What do people gain by telling lies?" his answer was, "Just this, that when they speak the truth they are not believed." Being once reproved for giving alms to a bad man, he rejoined, "It was the man and not his character that I pitied." He used constantly to say to his friends and pupils, whenever or wherever he happened to be lecturing, "As sight takes in light from the surrounding air, so does the soul from mathematics." Beauty he declared to be a greater recommendation than any letter of introduction. Others attribute this saying to Diogenes. When someone accused him of having given a subscription to a dishonest man—for the story is also told in this form—"It was not the man," said he, "that I assisted, but humanity." To the question, how we should behave to friends, he answered, "As we should wish them to behave to us." Justice he defined as a virtue of soul which distributes according to merit. Education he declared to be the best provision for old age. Favorinus in the second book of his *Memorabilia* (ἐν τῷ δευτέρῳ τῶν Ἀπομνημονευμάτων) mentions as one of his habitual sayings, that "He who has friends can have no true friend." Further, this is found in the seventh book of the *Ethics*.[58] These then are the sayings attributed to him. (D.L. 5.17–21)

How much of this material Diogenes drew from written collections like Favorinus' *Apomnemoneumata* is unclear. What is clear is that he treats it as a fluid, composite stream of oral tradition, part of a live performance culture of *apophthegmata* keeping alive the memory of the great philosophers of the past by recounting their sayings and deeds, a stream of oral tradition (ἀγράφου φωνῆς) distinct from (but of equal value to) the written works of the philosopher himself (D.L. 5.34).[59] In many cases (notably Diogenes the Cynic in book 6), the anecdotal tradition comprises virtually the sum of his information on a particular philosopher.[60]

Where does this material come from? Anecdotes do not circulate like bacteria, in the air we breathe. They are designed, in Plutarch's words, to be useful, and they will survive only in social contexts where those uses remain operative.[61] Fortunately we have a solid starting point for reconstructing those social locations in the rhetorical *Progymnasmata*, which provide indispensable definitions for *Apomnemoneumata* and related speech forms in the culture of antiquity.[62] At first sight, anecdote and *chreia* form part of a carefully defined hierarchy of speech events within the training of the rhetorical schools. The fundamental distinction is between the γνώμη, the maxim or saying, passed on as a pure nugget of gnomic wisdom unattached to any narrative situation, and the ἀπομνημόνευμα, in which the morceau of wit or wisdom is attached to a particular person and occasion and located within a minimal narrative framework:

> A χρεία is a brief saying or action making a point, attributed to some specified person or something corresponding to a person, and maxim (γνώμη) and reminiscence (ἀπομνημόνευμα) are connected with it. Every brief maxim attributed to a person creates a χρεία. An ἀπομνημόνευμα is an action or a saying useful for life. The γνώμη, however, differs from the χρεία in four ways: the χρεία is always attributed to a person, the γνώμη not always; the χρεία sometimes states a universal, sometimes a particular, the γνώμη only a universal; furthermore, sometimes the χρεία is a pleasantry not useful for life, the γνώμη is always about something useful in life; fourth, the χρεία is an action or a saying, the γνώμη is only a saying. The ἀπομνημόνευμα is distinguished from the χρεία in two ways: the χρεία is brief, the ἀπομνημόνευμα is sometimes extended, and the χρεία is attributed to a particular person, while the ἀπομνημόνευμα is also remembered for its own sake. (Theon, *Progymnasmata* 96–97)[63]

In practice, however, the rhetors' neat definitions cannot match the cheerful chaos of extracurricular linguistic usage: outside the schools, the categories are more fluid, and the functional term χρεία covers a wide range of gnomic and anecdotal material.[64] We should perhaps think more of a sliding scale of narrative complexity, with the pure unattributed maxim at one end and the more substantial narrative anecdote at the other; we would need to place somewhere in between the two extremes the saying attributed to a named σοφός ("Isocrates used to say") or the rudimentary narrative context provided by the question-and-answer format ("When asked [ἐρωτηθείς] . . . , he replied . . .").[65] Some ἀπομνημονεύματα depend for their point on an exchange with a historical figure, like Diogenes' famous encounter with Alexander the Great; others evoke a series of encounters with stock figures: a student's father, an Ethiopian, a woman.[66] But with all their variety, these anecdotes fall into a recognizable narrative pattern, identifying the speaker and the situation with a minimum of contextual detail and typically (at least in the rhetorical handbooks) compressed into a single period.

Their most familiar use—and the one for which the term χρεία was, I suspect, originally coined—is as a school exercise. Quintilian (*Inst.* 1.9.2–6) assigns the *chreia* to the sphere of the *grammaticus*, the secondary stage of education, and sees its use chiefly as an exercise in grammatical declension: you took the whole sentence and declined it through all possible permutations of number, gender, and case (no wonder Greek and Latin writers are so good at *oratio obliqua*!).[67] This was an exercise designed to initiate the student not into everyday linguistic usage but into all the intricate possibilities of the classical language in its high Attic form: the dual had effectively dropped out of use by the time of the handbooks, but school students still had to decline "Isocrates said that the fruits of education were bitter . . ." in the dual ("The two Isocrateses said . . .") and so on. The popularity of this pervasive grammatical exercise may account for the routine compression of the *chreia* into a single period; to put it another way, we may fairly surmise that the single-period ἀπομνημόνευμα is most likely to have got that way through repeated reiteration as a grammatical *chreia*. The Greek handbooks, however, assign the *chreia* to the sphere of the rhetor, the tertiary level of Greek education, and use the same anecdotes as a basis for a whole series of exercises in composition and dialectic: "The ways we can use the *chreia* for exercise are: recitation; inflexion; comment; and objection. We also expand and condense the *chreia*. In addition, we refute and confirm it."[68] For Hermogenes, the grammatical exercises have disappeared, and the "chief matter" is the "elaboration" or ἐργασία of the *chreia*, which means encomium; paraphrase; rationale.[69]

But all the rhetorical handbooks insist that the *chreia* also has a moral function: it is βιωφελής, "useful for life."[70] This is the kind of use Plutarch has in mind when he describes his apophthegms as "the common offerings of the firstfruits that come from philosophy" (*Mor.* 172c), a phrase that recalls Socrates' hymn to the Seven Wise Men whose wisdom consisted of "short memorable sentences," like the well-known Delphic inscriptions, "Know thyself" and "Nothing in excess."[71] The philosophical teachers were not interested in declining Isocrates (or even Aristotle) in the dual, but they were interested in the wisdom contained in these compact mini-narratives and highly valued the art of compressing a great deal of truth into very few words. Isocrates' maxim that "The root of education is bitter but its fruit is sweet" has its own intrinsic educational value, and the *chreia* form adds the barest possible narrative framework: *Dixit ille, aut dicere solebat,* as Quintilian puts it (*Inst.* 1.9.4).[72] Much of the anecdotal material in Diogenes Laertius is of this type.

But the *chreia* does not have to be a saying to be morally improving: it can also be an action (*Etiam in ipsorum factis esse chriam putant*: Quint. *Inst.* 1.9.5); and while some actions simply express their author's wit or wisdom in practical form ("Diogenes, seeing an ill-educated child, beat his paedagogus"), others have a more obviously exemplary function.[73] Quintilian uses the Greek word *ethologia* for these (*Inst.* 1.9.3).[74] Seneca ascribes the term (which must have been current among Greek rhetors in republican and early imperial Rome) to Posidonius:

> He remarks that it will also be useful to illustrate each particular virtue; this science Posidonius calls *ethologia*, while others call it *characterismos*. It gives the signs and marks which belong to each virtue and vice, so that by them

> distinction may be drawn between like things. Its function is the same as that of precept. For he who utters precept says, "If you would have self-control, act thus and so!" He who illustrates says, "The man who acts thus and so, and refrains from other things, possesses self-control." If you ask what the difference here is, I say that the one gives the precepts of virtue, the other its embodiment (*exemplar*). The illustrations, or, to use a commercial term, these samples (*iconismos*) have, I confess, a certain utility (*ex usu esse confiteor*); just put them up for exhibition well recommended, and you will find men to copy them. (Seneca, *Ep.* 95.65–66, LCL)

This form of moral teaching by exemplar might restrict itself to types, like the *Characters* of Theophrastus or the unnamed (or autobiographical) narrative *exempla* used by Galen to illustrate the passions.[75] But it is clear that Seneca has real people in mind for his *iconismos*: "it will be helpful not only to state what is the usual quality of such men, and to outline their figures and features, but also to relate and set forth what men there have been of this kind" (*quales fuerint narrare et exponere*: Seneca, *Ep.* 95.72). So the letter finishes with a list of exemplars of the ancient Roman *virtus*: "We might picture that last and bravest wound of Cato's, through which freedom breathed her last; or the wise Laelius and his harmonious life with his friend Scipio; or the noble deeds of the elder Cato at home or abroad." And the beneficial effect is not limited to those of whom many such *facta* can be reported or to "noble deeds" in the standard historiographical sense. Seneca's final example is a single scene from the life of Tubero:

> ... or the wooden couches of Tubero, spread at a public feast, goatskins instead of tapestry, and vessels of earthenware set out for the banquet before the very shrine of Jupiter. What else was this except consecrating poverty on the Capitol? Though I know no other deed of his for which to rank him with the Catos, is this one not enough? It was a censorship, not a banquet. How lamentably do those who covet glory fail to understand what glory is, or in what way it should be sought! On that day the Roman populace viewed the furniture of many men; it marvelled only at that of one! The gold and silver of all the others has been broken up and melted down times without number; but Tubero's earthenware will endure throughout eternity. (Seneca, *Ep.* 95.72–73)

Tubero, in Seneca's mini-gallery of *imagines*, is like the many minor philosophers of whom Diogenes Laertius has only one anecdote to record, but that one is still sufficient to act as a basis for moral exhortation.

Seneca makes it clear in his letters that the use of concrete moral exemplars was fundamental to the ethical teaching of the Stoics:

> The miser, the swindler, the bully, the cheat, who would do you a lot of harm by simply being near you, are actually inside you. Move to better

company; live with the Catos, with Laelius, with Tubero. If you like Greek company too, attach yourself to Socrates and Zeno: the one would teach you how to die should it be forced upon you, the other how to die before it is forced upon you. Live with Chrysippus, live with Posidonius; they will give you a knowledge of man and the universe; they will tell you to be a practical philosopher: not just to entertain your listeners to a clever display of language, but to steel your spirit and brace it against whatever threatens. (Seneca, *Ep.* 104.21-22)[76]

It is this belief—the belief that the βίος or lifestyle of a teacher is just as important as his verbal teachings—that gives the biographical anecdote its underlying seriousness. Even the most trivial details may have something to teach the willing student. The collection and transmission of anecdotes about great teachers is about something far more important than the "historical background" to their doctrine: these anecdotes embody the essence of the man himself.[77] And in the case of a philosopher, that means that they are "samples and primal elements" (ὥσπερ δείγματα τῶν βίων καὶ σπέρματα, lit. "seeds") of the philosophic βίος itself (Plutarch, *Mor.* 172e): capable, by implication, of generating new instantiations of the philosophic way of life in those in whom they are planted.

It would be a mistake, however, to assume that the usefulness of anecdotes was confined to the ethical teaching of the schools. Even the rhetorical teachers admit that it is hard to find a serious moral function for every *chreia*: some are simply there to amuse.[78] Ancient biography has a strong element of the gossip column about it, and much of it is simply frivolous.[79] As Mary Lefkowitz shows, one of the underlying motives of the anecdotes that make up the *Lives of the Poets* is to cut the great men down to size, "in order to make the poet's achievement seem more comprehensible and accessible."[80] There is a whole category of anecdotes (like the story of Thales falling down the well) that do the same thing for the philosophers.[81] Many of the more salacious anecdotes in Diogenes Laertius belong in this category. Some of these may, as Werner Jaeger argued, be genuinely popular stories: some clearly go back to the comic poets. If we were to identify a social function within the schools for these comic or derogatory anecdotes, it should probably be sought within the inter-school polemic which characterized the tradition from the fourth century onwards and which spawned the first philosophical biographies. As the trial of Socrates shows, the lifestyle of a philosopher could as well be used against him as in his favor and might in its turn inspire a crop of favorable anecdotes in refutation:

> Such was his own character: how then could he have led others into impiety, crime, gluttony, lust, or sloth? On the contrary, he cured these vices in many, by putting into them a desire for goodness, and by giving them confidence that self-discipline would make them gentlemen. To be sure he never professed to teach this; but by letting his own light shine, he led his disciples to hope that they through imitation of him would attain to such excellence. (Xenophon, *Mem.* 1.2.2–3)

Philodemus' *Rhetorica* contains a nice example of a whole polemical argument built around an anecdote of Aristotle, though not, in this case, an intrinsically hostile anecdote.[82] The starting point here is the apparently harmless witticism that Aristotle "taught rhetoric in the afternoon, saying, 'It is a shame to be silent and allow Isocrates to speak.'"[83] This "opinion" (κρίσις) of Aristotle's is then put into a fuller context: it is all of a piece, Philodemus avers, with Aristotle's writing treatises on rhetoric and politics (both subjects which in Epicurean opinion had nothing to do with philosophy) and with the arguments put forward by Aristotle for engaging in politics. The underlying insinuation is that Aristotle's motives for branching out from philosophy into rhetoric and other subjects had more to do with courting popularity among fee-paying parents than with philosophical principle. An exposition of the Epicurean denunciation of rhetoric leads back to a syllogistic deconstruction of the original apophthegm: "Consequently Aristotle's practice and remark were not philosophic."[84] The crunch is that the anecdote shows Aristotle as falling away from his own philosophical principles: "when Aristotle . . . took to rhetoric, he became a deserter from philosophy in its Epicurean sense of a quiet contemplative life."[85] The debate is all about the βίος (lifestyle) of the philosopher: about the consistency of Aristotle's own practice with his stated principles, and about the competing definitions of the true philosophical βίος. The anecdote is central to the debate: but it is a debate about the way of life, not a biographical narrative.

Memory as Tradition: *Apomnemoneumata* and the Art of Recollection

The relationship between *apomnemoneumata* and personal recollection is probably the least well-theorized area in the study of the anecdotal tradition in the Hellenistic schools. Earlier generations of classical scholarship, like their biblical counterparts, tended to approach this material as a purely literary phenomenon, studying texts with an eye to source and redaction criticism. More recent studies have begun to focus more on the performative aspect, looking especially at the role of the *chreia* in rhetorical education. But issues of orality have scarcely begun to impact the study of the anecdotal tradition—specifically, for our purposes, the question of the operation of memory in the whole process of transmission and preservation of this material. The Hellenistic schools offer rich material in this field which would repay further study; here we can do no more than to single out three areas of initial interest: social memory, techniques of memorization, and the role of personal reminiscence.

Apomnemoneumata never quite lost their semantic connection with memory. Their function was first and foremost to preserve and relay sayings or deeds "worthy of memory," ἄξια μνήμης: compare the variant ways of introducing the *chreia* listed by Theon in *Progymnasmata* (102).[86] And there is clearly a mnemonic element in the verbal formalization of these anecdotes: like all good jokes, they are designed to be easy to remember and repeat.[87] Diogenes Laertius describes how Diogenes the Cynic formulated his own teachings in this easy-to-memorize form for the children to whom he was acting as a private tutor:

> And the boys retained [in their memory] many [sayings] of poets and prose writers, and of Diogenes himself; and he used to practise every means of giving them a concise statement in order to make things easy to memorize. (D.L. 6.30)[88]

This method of teaching was especially suited to Cynicism, where so much of the school's teaching was encoded in the *Apomnemoneumata* of Diogenes and his disciples (cf. D.L. 6.20–83). But it is not a Cynic peculiarity. All ancient educationalists regard the power of memory as fundamental to a good education, one of the five natural faculties that mark a child's potential for education, "the treasury of education" and "the mother of the Muses."[89]

> Memory was the foundation of all knowledge in a world that could not rely on easily consulted books, tables of contents and indexes, library catalogues, and electronic search tools. Exercises of mental gymnastics practiced at every level of education aimed at strengthening the student's natural capacity for retention to levels unheard of in the modern world. Higher education was particularly concerned with developing a student's "artificial" memory, thus not only improving his capacity to memorize content word for word but also strengthening his capacity to build rapid and effective systems for learning. The art of memory created by Simonides and Aristotle was adopted by the Romans: arguments and subjects were located under "places" in the mind (*topoi, loci*), such as buildings or settings. The ancients' experience of these memory-images was much more vivid and intense than our own.[90]

Within such a culture, it is not hard to see how the ἀπομνημονεύματα, shaped and formalized for easy memorization and readily adapted for internal appropriation by the students who used them in the rhetorical exercises, came to play a significant role in the social memory of the Hellenistic schools. The highly literate and sophisticated world of the Greek polis remained, as we have seen, a world that valued spontaneous verbal wit and repartee and developed a complex repertoire of mnemonic capsules for preserving and passing on this oral wisdom in the form of maxim and anecdote. In its varied written repositories, in live performance, and in the interchange between the two, the anecdotal tradition was a treasury of cultural memory, passed on in a variety of social locations. These maxims and anecdotes are not just memorable sayings but sayings of the cultural heroes of Greek *paideia*, set in the lost social world of the fifth-century polis. Inevitably, they enshrine the values and aspirations of their teachers, but they also enshrine the distance between the elite, those who had the time and money for the full ἐγκύκλιος παιδεία, and the rest.[91] Similarly in the philosophical and medical schools, biographical anecdotes and apophthegms encode the school's social memory of the founder's values and lifestyle. It is no coincidence that they play a particularly important role in constructing the social memory of the nonwriting philosophers, principally Socrates and Diogenes, charismatic founding figures whose philosophy is encapsulated in their life and actions.

The universal use of the *chreia* in the schools ensured that this cultural memory was built into the educational system at every level. The *chreia* forms one of the most basic elements of Greco-Roman education:

> The rhetorical educational circle was built on skills and elements of knowledge developed since primary education. *Chreiai*, for instance, were already a part of previous educational stages: novices memorized and copied them and used them to practice reading and writing. Rhetorical education purposely pulled *chreiai* out of their elementary context and made them into something more elaborate, in which students could recognize familiar elements while measuring their advancement.[92]

It is thus somewhat misleading when theorists tell us that the use of the *chreia* presupposes a rhetorical education. The appropriation of the *chreia* by the rhetor marks a deliberate annexation—for good pedagogic reasons—of a form of exercise already familiar from the grammarian's schoolroom. This was all part of the process by which the most advanced students moved from passive learning (memorizing, reading, and copying) to active, learning to articulate for themselves what they had previously learned by rote: "What the pupil was told without negotiation by means of gnomai, his rhetorical training now constrains him to articulate, equally without negotiation, for himself."[93] This marks "a watershed in *enkyklios paideia*," the point at which the student "articulates what he has learned in his own words, asserting both his claim to what he speaks and his acceptance of it."[94] Nevertheless, Teresa Morgan argues, "by casting his first articulations in the form of paraphrases of other authors, he places himself in a cultural tradition, while rearticulating the tradition for his own time and place."[95] The fact that the same material (mythic and epic tales paraphrased from poetic texts, alongside the gnomic *chreia* tradition) spans both stages of the process reinforces the cultural continuity that lies at the heart of ancient education.

The endemic use of paraphrase as a rhetorical exercise also tells us something about the tension between stability and fluidity built into this model of tradition. On the one hand, anecdotes are valued as "potted histories," capsules of social memory that link the speaker with the cultural heroes of Hellenism. Along with the favorite literary texts of the school canon, they tie the speaker into a shared past as well as enshrining the more abstract values of paideia.[96] The texts and maxims chosen for paraphrase belonged to the literary canon (almost certainly the origin of our use of the term "canon").[97] These were iconic texts within Greek literary culture. But their very importance for paideia makes them vulnerable to alteration: in an educational context, pupils were continually being encouraged to rewrite them in their own words. "This suggests that texts oscillated between two statuses: that of the particular canonical version of the story, and that of a tool which could be used and altered."[98]

The anecdotal tradition thus contains within itself the tension between the two poles of "philology" and "performance" that Gregory Nagy sees as endemic to Greek literary education.[99] Philology, in this sense, focuses on the classic texts as part of the past, texts from an ancient culture, requiring explication, glossing, historical research. Much of the ancient biographical tradition is weighted toward this end of the spectrum: it is part and parcel of the relentless historical and pinacographic activity of the Alexandrian librarians. Yet this material is never without its performative context: even pinacography arises out of the practical need of the Alexandrian librarians to classify and authenticate the separate items in their ever-growing collection, and the erudition of Athenaeus' dinner guests is a direct response to present needs in the era of the Second Sophistic, above all the overpowering need for the literate elite to display the cultural markers of Greek identity.[100] Even the most trivial or subversive anecdotes are not just funny stories, but stories about people who matter in the present: specifically, people from the classical golden age of fifth- and fourth-century Athens which retains an abiding and historically disproportionate significance within Hellenistic culture. Knowing about these people is part of the cultural formation of the educated, part of what paideia is about. By continual immersion in this material, students were exposed not only to the whole textual repertoire of classical literature but to a common set of values, "arguments and views which were commonly recognised."[101] Even the most rudimentary exercises, as Theon recognizes, served "to imprint a score of examples on the soul for the individual to draw on later for his own compositions."[102] Right through the educational process, the classic texts of Greek *paideia* were both revered and studied as written texts and simultaneously subject to a process of re-oralization within the performative framework of the classroom—a performative context that was reinforced at all levels of adult life.

The symposia of Athenaeus or Aulus Gellius exemplify the quintessential showground for this kind of cultural competition, where the guests strive to excel in their recondite knowledge of lost Attic treasures, displaying their capacity to act as walking libraries or "living books" in a constantly changing cultural environment.[103] For this cultural colonialism to work, it is essential to have a certain minimum of accuracy and stability within the tradition. Thus it occasions no surprise that Athenaeus' dinner guests at the end of the second century C.E. are able to cite—and to cite accurately—ἀπομνημονεύματα recorded by Lynceus from the Athenian smart set of the fourth century B.C.E., and that these should be accepted by historians as reasonably reliable reminiscences from the Macedonian court.[104] Yet the memory thus preserved is a memory of "gist" rather than of exact verbal recall.[105] In the *chreia* tradition, stories and sayings are reduced to their essential core so that they can easily be retold in a variety of different words. Verbal variation is built into the model—but a variation within limits: the rhetorical handbooks are quite prescriptive in defining the stylistically acceptable formulae to be used in the ἐργασία of the *chreia*.[106]

How does memory function in the higher echelons of the Hellenistic school system? The rhetorical schools (especially in Rome) had adopted a sophisticated system of mnemotechnics to aid in the mental processes of composition and performance of lengthy speeches.[107] But as Jocelyn Small points out, the increasing complexity of the world of books in antiquity made the arts of memory more, not less, important as time went on: "Memory became *the* classical means of cognitively organizing and, most significantly, retrieving words."[108] Even for the highly literate protagonists of Athenaeus' symposium, memory is an essential component in the process of retrieval and re-oralization: without memory, it would be impossible to index and access all the vast reserves of Hellenistic learning, written and oral. So for Athenaeus' dinner guests, "Memory is located between writing and orality, between the material archive (books and libraries) and the mental technique."[109] Memory is the "key factor" that helps the Deipnosophists to navigate a fluid and complex hypertext, "reading a large and heterogeneous collection of texts, deciding to link such and such key words or fragments, deconstructing the cohesiveness of texts in order to follow the thread of a lexical search or of a thematic investigation," creating "'a fluid network of verbal elements' that was temporarily fixed in a new written form."[110]

Memory was equally valued in the more technical schools. We only have to look at the prefaces to technical manuals across a whole range of disciplines to see that ease of memory, and fidelity to tradition, were highly valued in a teaching manual (cf. the partiality in prefaces for variants on εὐμνημόνευτος).[111] Among the medical schools, the Empiricist school particularly attracted the sobriquet μνημονευτικός.[112] What is interesting here is that Galen implies that one of the sects is associated in the popular mind with memory in a particular and unusual way, even acquiring the nickname "the memory men." What does this mean? In this case, Galen is not talking about biographical memory—and certainly not Hippocratic memory.[113] Memory, for the Empiricist sect, refers to the accumulation of data, the raw experiential data on which all true medical knowledge should be based. But in a world in which medical experimentation on live subjects was unknown and the dissection of dead human subjects largely frowned upon, that effectively meant the mental accumulation of experiential case histories in an attempt to build up a significant body of ἱστορία.[114] The faculty of memory was valued simply because it was the only way to build up a personal databank and the only way to make the connections that might result in a scientific insight. What this effectively means is that students trained in the Empiricist tradition were encouraged to cultivate the skills of observation (τήρησις) and memory of a cumulative anecdotal tradition of case histories going back to Hippocrates.[115] In this they are contrasted with the Dogmatic sect, which taught its students to rely more on the power of reasoning by analogy in order to determine the underlying causes of medical conditions.

Among the philosophers, the school of Epicurus assigned an unusually significant role to memory in the instruction of the disciple. Unlike Plato, who "regarded memorization as the antithesis of philosophical enquiry," Epicurus placed memorization at the heart of his system of philosophical investigation:

> The student reenacts the discoveries made previously by going through a similar process of reasoning. Memorization becomes in this way a rational exercise. Subsequently she keeps reiterating these truths in such a way that they are constantly to hand, ready to produce the correct response to anything that may happen. Thoroughly appropriated, the principles dictate the correct attitude and conduct.[116]

Crucial to this process were the Κύριαι Δόξαι or *Authoritative Opinions*, forty key sayings encapsulating the essential doctrines of Epicureanism and designed for ease of memorization: these were learnt at the initiatory level, then unpacked in successively deeper levels of complexity as the student advanced through the school.[117] Even shorter was the "four-fold remedy" based on the first four *Opinions* on God, death, the good, and pain: "By memorizing the remedy and keeping it constantly in mind, the student might cure himself of anxiety and achieve mental health."[118] Protreptic texts like the *Letter to Menoecus* are also designed to be memorized: Epicurus exhorts the reader to "practice" (μελετᾶν) or "rehearse" this material day and night, a process of verbal reiteration which, along with practical application, is the key to "living like a god":

> When memorizing the text, the student internalizes Epicurus' imperatives as directives addressed by herself to herself. She appropriates the doctrines in this way as a personal creed or catechism. Just as though she were reenacting a dramatic scene, she tells herself, as well as her companion, that she must believe what Epicurus has propounded. She is part of a chorus of believers, all of whom appropriate Epicurus' doctrines as a personal standard of conduct.[119]

This process of memorization and reiteration, designed to "imprint" pupils with the models and values of the culture, is a universal feature in ancient education, and as we have seen, it is far from being a static process of data retrieval.[120] Epicurus' call to "rehearse" his teachings (μελετᾶν) recalls Diogenes the Cynic "rehearsing" his *chreia* (μεμελετηκώς), ready to humiliate the unfortunate Aristotle. The one refers to a process of free composition, the other to inherited wisdom handed down from a revered teacher: what they have in common is the mental process by which the *chreia* is manipulated, rolled around the mind, formalized, internalized.[121] μελετᾶν is not simply a passive process of committing to memory but an active process of internalizing—a totalizing process of cultural formation reinforced by its performative context. What Epicurus is proposing is not a new system of education so much as a new set of core values. His system of philosophical education (and he liked to start it as young as possible) was based on the simple but audacious step of replacing the core values of the traditional *paideia*, encoded in mythology and fable, with the core values of Epicurean rationalism.[122]

This attention to memory went far beyond the memorizing of abstract principles. Despite its rationalistic foundation, the Epicurean school quickly developed a cultic framework for the performance of memory.[123] Monthly feast days in honor of the founder were built into the life of the Epicurean community from the start and extended into a process of memorializing the heroes of the sect in word and ritual. The library of Philodemus in Herculaneum preserves fragments of numerous Epicurean "memorials," commemorative volumes of Epicurus' disciples and family, some of them going back to Epicurus himself. Many of these commemorative writings focus on the subject's final illness and death, seen as a paradigm of the philosophic life: they are part of an elaborate system of communal commemoration of the dead in which "Memory took the place of lamentation: ἀντὶ γόου μνήμη."[124]

> Imitation and emulation were ingrained in the Epicurean concept of the philosophical life. We know from Seneca how Epicurus and Metrodorus were rivals in the frugality of their lives (*Ep.* 18.9). The memorial literature of the first generation of the Epicurean community is perhaps the clearest expression of a tendency to offer the individual life as a model (or δεῖγμα) of the philosophical life.[125]

The school of Epicurus developed the common currency of the cultural hero, enshrined in the whole concept of *apomnemoneumata*, and took it to heights few outsiders were prepared to follow. Yet the comments of perplexed observers provide valuable testimony to the survival within the school not only of memorial texts but of a cultic framework for the performance of memory more than three centuries after the death of Epicurus.[126]

This preliminary survey shows that there is abundant testimony to the importance of memory in the Hellenistic schools: it is assumed across the curriculum at the lower levels and emphasized in particular ways in individual schools at the tertiary level. What is less clear is the role of personal testimony in all this. To what extent did the schools value the preservation of a personal link with their founders through the reminiscences of their disciples? Where the memory belongs to the first generation, the link with personal testimony is relatively straightforward. Lucian's *Life of Demonax* claims to be based on the author's own memory of his teacher; his object in writing is to perpetuate that memory in future generations:

> Both of these men I saw myself (εἶδον αὐτός), and saw with wonderment; and under one of them, Demonax, I was long a student. . . . It is now fitting to tell of Demonax for two reasons—that he may be retained in memory (διὰ μνήμης) by men of culture as far as I can bring it about, and that young men of good instincts who aspire to philosophy may not have to shape themselves by ancient precedents (παραδειγμάτων) alone, but may be able to set themselves a pattern (κανόνα) from our modern world and to copy (ζηλοῦν) that man, the best of all the philosophers whom I know about. (Lucian, *Demonax* 1–2, LCL)

The connection with personal testimony takes us right back to the *Apomnemoneumata* of Xenophon, for whom memory is important as the chief means of preserving the beneficial effects of being in Socrates' company even in his absence: "The very recollection of him in absence (τὸ ἐκείνου μεμνῆσθαι μὴ παρόντος) brought no small good to his constant companions and followers; for even in his light moods they gained no less from his society than when he was serious" (*Mem.* 4.1).[127]

Some at least of Xenophon's Socratic memoirs claim to be based on personal reminiscence: "In order to support my opinion that he benefited his companions, alike by actions that revealed his own character and by his conversations, I will set down what I recollect of these" (*Mem.* 1.3.1). Given the forensic setting of his work, we would expect personal testimony to play a significant role in Xenophon's work.[128] Diogenes Laertius believes Xenophon's work to be based on notes taken by Xenophon as a pupil (ἀκροατής) of Socrates: "He was the first to take notes of (ὑποσημειωσάμενος), and to give to the world the conversation of Socrates, under the title of *Apomnemoneumata*" (D.L. 2.48).[129] Yet Xenophon does not claim to give an exact record of Socrates' conversations so much as a common pattern of Socratic discourse: "Such views frequently found expression in his conversations with different persons; I recollect the substance of one that he had with Hippias of Elis concerning Justice."[130]

Despite the strongly personal nature of Xenophon's reminiscences, however, the ἀπομνημονεύματα tradition overall is not structured in such a way as to give undue weight to the personal testimony of the tradents.[131] For Lucian, the memory (μνήμη) of Demonax has an objective value quite distinct from its origins: what is important is the μνήμη of Demonax, memory kept alive through verbal recall across successive generations. Where the memory comes from is not important. Ἀπομνημονεύματα are generally handed on as autonomous and anonymous items of tradition; verbs tend to take the impersonal form "it is said" (λέγεται, ἀναφέρεται) rather than attribution to a named tradent in the familiar rabbinic form. Even in Diogenes Laertius, named written sources are the exception rather than the rule. The verb ἀπομνημονεύω is used sparingly, and its focus is more on the performance of the tradition (oral or written) than on its origins (cf. Lucian, *Demonax* 67). If we were to look for the Greek equivalent of the chain of tradition in *Pirke Abot* 1:1, we should have to look to the Διαδοχαί or Successions literature, which provides a genealogy of philosophical ideas by tracing the links between one school or teacher and another, or to the prefaces of individual writers, which often take pains to specify the writer's fidelity to a particular teacher.[132] What is at issue here is not so much the reliability of personal memories as the faithful and critical "following" of a particular teaching tradition: once again, the emphasis is on authentic performance in the present rather on a static process of passing on data.[133] Galen supplies plentiful evidence that the schools were concerned to pass down the authentic memory of their teachers (a concern echoed in Papias' "living voice" tag).[134] But few of the schools, apart perhaps from the Epicureans, would have assigned as much importance to αὐτοψία as Papias appears to do. Galen, like Justin, shows the utmost respect for an authoritative διαδοχή, chain of tradition, but it can be passed down by followers (παρηκολουθηκότες) just as well as by eyewitnesses. Personal testimony does not in itself provide the logical demonstration required by a philosophical audience; for Justin, the key "proofs" of the gospel message are supplied by the prophets, not the "eyewitnesses."[135]

Memory and Tradition in the Collegium of the Apostles

This brief survey, I believe, allows us to endorse Gerhardsson's hunch that the Hellenistic school tradition has as much to offer as the rabbinic tradition to the student of the Gospels. It is important to stress that the Jewish and Hellenistic traditions are not to be seen as rival models, certainly not as mutually exclusive; neither are we seeking to establish "borrowing" or "influence" in one direction or the other. Rather, we need to see the rabbinic tradition itself as a particular instantiation of the broader formational patterns that can be observed right across the ancient Mediterranean world. And as we broaden our lens, it becomes clear that many of the features identified by Gerhardsson as typical of the rabbinic academies are in fact characteristic of the wider formational patterns of the ancient Mediterranean world of which the rabbis formed a part.[136] This does not preclude the recognition of distinctive flavors and emphases across the tradition. The Hellenistic schools are not a uniform system but a complex and many-faceted phenomenon with many shades of local differentiation. There are significant differences in both praxis and terminology between rhetoric and philosophy, between medicine and other technical schools—and, as we have seen, between individual schools of philosophy or medicine. Nevertheless, I believe that there is a sufficient degree of commonality to make it worthwhile to consider the phenomenon generically, while recognizing that its very diversity makes it easier for contemporary observers to approximate "the followers of Moses and Christ" (as Galen calls contemporary Jews and Christians) to one kind of school rather than another.[137]

In essence, then, this study is a contribution to what Gerhardsson calls the phenomenology of memory and tradition within the Hellenistic schools.[138] It affirms the fundamental importance of Gerhardsson's key insight, which is to take seriously the early Christian designation of Jesus as a teacher and his followers as μαθηταί, "disciples" or, more simply, "students." This immediately gives us a durable social context for the passing on and processing of tradition: we are not talking about random memories or village gossip, but about the operations of memory and the construction of tradition within a very specific social matrix. Within this matrix, the anecdotal tradition embodies the whole complex of mental and verbal processes that we associate with the generation of tradition, from personal memory via oral reminiscence to written memoir. The origins of this process will necessarily remain inaccessible to us, since the eyes that saw and the minds that framed their oral reminiscences have long disappeared into the dust, but the ἀπομνημονεύματα provide a window into the more visible parts of the process. In this final section I shall not attempt to develop the parallel at length, but will draw together briefly what seem to me to be the most significant ways in which a comparison with the Hellenistic schools may advance our understanding of the operations of memory and tradition in the Jesus tradition.

Memory and the Oral Tradition

The interplay between memory and form goes back right to the origins of the ἀπομνημονεύματα tradition. Even within one generation, as we can see from Xenophon and Lynceus, personal memory is already molded by the literary forms and expectations of the larger society. At the heart of this process is the formalized oral activity of ἀπομνημόνευσις, "recounting" or "commemoration," in which personal memories are shaped and processed (μελετᾶν) into ἀπομνημονεύματα, "reminiscences." Sometimes the process can be traced back to the originator of the saying or witticism (as with Diogenes), sometimes to a first-generation auditor (like Lucian). Ἀπομνημονεύματα thus exemplify the process described by anthropologist Jan Vansina, whereby "news" is shaped into "reminiscences."[139] These are the basic building blocks of oral tradition, which can become relatively stable within a short time and can then survive transmission across many generations. What is transmitted, however, is not a verbally exact repetition but the "gist" of a story. In fact we might say that Hellenistic educational practice, in training students to tell and retell the same story in different words, positively discouraged verbal exactitude: the *chreia*, with its characteristic narrative shape, was designed to make it easy to retain plot essentials while varying the story's verbal expression. The ἀπομνημονεύματα thus exhibit a combination of stability and fluidity similar to what Kenneth Bailey observed in the village storytelling of the Middle East, and can be cited as an ancient example of "controlled informal" traditioning.[140] The parallel with the Jesus tradition, at least for Justin, was obvious. If we are to take Justin's paradigm seriously as a means to further our understanding of the gospel tradition, we need to triangulate the ἀπομνημονεύματα in relation to three fixed points: form, function, and vehicle or performative context.

Form

The Hellenistic anecdote is a compressed narrative genre which conveys the wisdom of a named sage in the form of a saying ("X used to say . . ."), a response to a question ("On being asked . . . , X replied . . ."), a response to a situation ("On seeing . . . , X responded . . . "), or a didactic action ("On seeing . . . , X did . . ."). Marion Moeser's detailed analysis of gospel anecdotes in comparison with the Greek and rabbinic anecdotal traditions confirms that, as we might expect, there are both similarities and differences at the surface level: each cultural tradition has its own individual flavor and should initially be studied and appreciated on its own terms.¹⁴¹ Nevertheless, as gospel scholarship has recognized for some time, the anecdote is a sufficiently stable form to allow for cross-cultural comparison.¹⁴² Much of the confusion over the formal identification of anecdotes in gospel studies goes back to the over-refinement of generic types perpetuated by the form critics in a mistaken deference to the definitions of Greek rhetoric. As we have seen, it is virtually impossible to insist on strict definitions in this field: the rhetors are evidently struggling to impose a stable terminology on a linguistic usage that is inherently fluid. Thus while relatively few gospel anecdotes match the extreme syntactical compression of the Hellenistic *chreia*, the underlying narrative structure of the classic gospel pericope can be accommodated without difficulty to the Hellenistic anecdotal tradition, with its focus on encounter and riposte.¹⁴³ As John Kloppenborg recognizes,¹⁴⁴ it is in fact dangerous and artificial to draw a hard and fast distinction between gnomic and biographical material in the Hellenistic school tradition: ἀπομνημονεύματα transcend the distinction by conveying chunks of wisdom in narrative form. Equally, there is no support in the Hellenistic tradition for the widespread assumption in gospel studies that "sayings tradition" automatically predates "biographical anecdotes": gnomic and anecdotal forms run side by side throughout the tradition. It is equally unsafe to be dogmatic about the relative length and complexity of the χρεία and the ἀπομνημόνευμα. The rhetors are unanimous that the ἀπομνημόνευμα tends to be longer than the χρεία, and that the χρεία normally follows the highly compressed, single-period form popular in the classes of the grammarians: in this sense, Justin is correct to describe the Gospels as ἀπομνημονεύματα rather than χρεῖαι. But the Hellenistic school tradition offers no warrant for the common assumption that the more compressed anecdotes of the *Gospel of Thomas* are intrinsically earlier than the longer pericopes found in the synoptic tradition: on the contrary, the pressures within the school system would seem to produce more compression over time rather than less, and the papyri demonstrate that longer narrative ἀπομνημονεύματα were in circulation at an earlier date than the highly compressed forms we find in the *Progymnasmata* or Diogenes Laertius.¹⁴⁵

Function

As we have seen, the preservation of biographical information about a particular teacher is one, but only one, of the functions of this variegated tradition, which can serve the needs of polemic, protreptic, and ethical instruction and of simple frivolous curiosity. Yet behind the variegated surface it is not difficult to discern the common underlying function of identity formation. "Conversion to philosophy" stories have a clear protreptic function, which could be readily paralleled in the Gospels and Acts.[146] Polemic serves the needs of boundary definition, whether in relation to rival sects or over against the unenlightened other. In rabbinic anecdotes, Martin Jaffee notes, "Gentiles, undisciplined Jews, and their women symbolize the negation of the very thing that makes the disciple what he is—or rather, what he strives to become."[147] Teresa Morgan makes a similar point about the portrayal of the undisciplined other in the Diogenes *chreia*:

> It is clear from Diogenes' sentiments what the listener or reader should be like—the opposite of all the objects of his disdain, which is to say, powerful, male and Greek. The *chreiai* communicate, "If you can read this, you are one of us, unlike any of these characters."[148]

Even the more frivolous anecdotes play their part in the broader formational role of Greek *paideia*, in codifying and transmitting a body of wit and wisdom attached to the cultural heroes of *hellenismos*: nothing is more powerful in cultural bonding than a shared joke.[149]

Underneath all this is a clear understanding of the core function of anecdotes and apophthegms as psychological capsules, clues to a person's soul. The sayings and deeds of the sages are the fundamental building blocks in the construction of a paraenetic discourse centered on mimesis: they provide the exemplary types (παραδείγματα) presented for emulation at every stage of ancient education. This identity-forming function was well understood—and readily subverted—by the philosophers. Just as Epicurus used the traditional techniques of Hellenistic education to inculcate the core values of his own philosophy, so the Christian tradition embodied in the Gospels and Acts supplies its own databank of cultural heroes—primarily Jesus, but the apostles also play their role—to act as countercultural exemplars in the construction of a Christian *paideia*.[150] Alongside the Jewish Scriptures, the *Apomnemoneumata of the Apostles* provide the raw material for this program of reeducation, the σπέρματα or "seeds" that hold not just information about the past but the key to a whole way of life.

Vehicle

The essential third component of any account of oral tradition is its vehicle or performative context. Inevitably, the social frameworks of the Hellenistic ἀπομνημονεύματα will encompass the variety of the anecdotal tradition itself: the gossip of the Macedonian court, the symposia of the elite, the street life of the Greek city. But the prime context for the maintenance and performance of these anecdotes has to be the schools. In the highly compressed form of the *chreia*, these anecdotes became the staple building blocks of Greek *paideia*, worked and reworked at all levels of the educational system. And at the more specialized level of the philosophical schools, we can glimpse in the writings of Philodemus or Seneca how the biographical anecdotes of the sages, repeated and passed on in polemic and paraenesis, formed an essential tool in the definition of the philosophic βίος and thus in the formation of the philosopher. We should therefore be looking to the educational practice of the ancient world to gain some understanding of the mechanics of this tradition. The rhetorical label χρεία is a double-edged one. It signals that the anecdote is "useful for life" (βιωφελής), but also (and I suspect primarily) useful in teaching: these biographical mini-pods are designed both for ease of memory and for constant practice. Repetition is fundamental to ancient education—not just rote repetition but internalization by constant retelling and reworking, a process designed to "imprint" core cultural values on the hearer's soul:

> This image of imprinting, also used throughout antiquity to express the effect of perception and the persistence of memory, implies that the student is indelibly marked by what he is exposed to. He is physically distinct from those who have not undergone this education.[151]

Given the prevalence of this model of cultural formation across the ancient world, we should expect to find an analogous performative context for the ἀπομνημονεύματα τῶν ἀποστόλων in early Christianity, and this is in fact what the sources reveal. For Justin the "school" in which they are deployed is not his own rather specialized academy but the regular weekly Christian assembly: these anecdotes (now re-oralized from a written text, and read alongside the prophets) form part of the regular instruction of all Christians. Luke implies a similar pattern when he states that his gospel provides written confirmation (ἀσφάλεια) of the oral instruction Theophilus has already received (κατηχήθης)—a term from the medical schools that was already gaining currency for Christian instruction.[152] Peter's instruction in Rome, according to Papias, takes the basic form of ἀπομνημόνευσις, a pattern of teaching based on oral reminiscences of "the Lord's sayings and doings" (τὰ ὑπὸ τοῦ κυρίου ἢ λεχθέντα ἢ πραχθέντα), and shaped πρὸς τὰς χρείας—a phrase that irresistibly reminds us of the rhetorical term χρεία.

These notices often are dismissed because of their obvious apologetic function, but they would not work even as apologetic if they did not present a plausible picture to ancient auditors. And what they present is a vivid and quite specific picture of early Christian *paideia* at work. Peter, like most ancient teachers, gathers a disciple circle around him and teaches them in public by passing on to them his own reminiscences of the words and deeds of his teacher. Listening to this once is not enough: Peter's hearers want to be able to "commit it to memory" and expect Mark, as a member of the inner disciple circle, to be able to produce a written version from memory.[153] This oral performance tradition is still a live one in the mid-second century: Papias expects to be able to quiz the followers of the Lord's disciples in order to access the "living voice" of apostolic tradition—a preference he shares with Galen and his contemporaries in the Hellenistic schools.[154] Papias himself belongs to a parallel disciple circle based on the dominical traditions taught by "the elders" in Asia and claims to base his writings on "what I learned well and remembered well" (καλῶς ἔμαθον καὶ καλῶς ἐμνημόνευσα) from his teachers (Eusebius, *Hist. eccl.* 3.39.1–3). Polycarp, so Irenaeus tells us, belonged to the same disciple circle, and both pass on traditions about their own teacher John.[155] Irenaeus gives us a vivid and affectionate portrait of Polycarp's school in later life, the disciple circle based in the teacher's house, the public lectures and disputations:

> For while I was still a boy I knew you in lower Asia in Polycarp's house when you were a man of rank in the royal hall and endeavouring to stand well with him. I remember (διαμνημονεύω) the events of those days more clearly than those which happened recently, for what we learn as children grows up with the soul and is united to it, so that I can speak even of the place in which the blessed Polycarp sat and disputed (διελέγετο), how he came in and went out, the character of his life, the appearance of his body, the discourses (διαλέξεις) which he made to the people, how he used to tell us about (ἀπήγγελλεν) his discipleship (συναναστροφήν) with John and with the others who had seen the Lord, and how he used to recount (ἀπεμνημόνευεν) their words; and what he had heard from them about the Lord, and about his miracles, and about [his] teaching, all this Polycarp used to tell us as tradition received (ὡς παρειληφώς) direct from the eyewitnesses of the word of life, completely consistent with the Scriptures. (Eusebius, *Hist. eccl.* 5.20.5–7, citing Irenaeus, *Letter to Florinus*)[156]

This is ἀπομνημονεύματα in the making: Irenaeus remembers not only his teacher's words but the whole character of his life (τὸν χαρακτῆρα τοῦ βίου), that is, the impression his life made on his pupils. Polycarp in his turn is passing on the ἀπομνημονεύματα of his own teacher, John: not just his own reminiscences of John, but the reminiscences of John and the other apostles about the teachings and miracles of Jesus. Irenaeus also gives us a valuable glimpse into the learning strategies that undergird this oral *paideia*: childhood apprenticeship (cf. John Mark), eager listening, committing to memory, and "chewing the cud" (ἀναμαρυκῶμαι).[157] This last metaphor appears already in Philo and the *Letter of Aristeas* as a symbol for the private processes of mental assimilation that ensure teaching is retained:

> For as the animal that chews the cud renders digestible the food taken in . . . , so the soul of the keen learner, when it has by listening taken in this and that proposition, does not hand them over to forgetfulness, but in stillness all alone goes over them one by one quite quietly, and so succeeds in recalling them all to memory. (Philo, *Agr.* 132)[158]

Essential to the rumination process are the "constant exercises" (συνεχέσι μελέταις) which act as a kind of mental glue (κόλλα νοημάτων) to "stamp a firm impression on the soul" (Philo, *Spec.* 4.107)—a marvelous mixed metaphor which vividly evokes the language of the Hellenistic schools.

Memory and the Written Tradition

The ambivalent relationship between memory and text in ancient understanding is captured nicely in a floating apophthegm attributed to Diocles of Carystus: "Someone once told Diocles the doctor that he would not need any more teaching because he had bought a medical book. Diocles responded: 'For those who have studied, books are reminders, but for the unlearned, they are tombs.'"[159] Within the matrix of the school, such a text provides useful "notes" or "reminders" (ὑπομνήματα) of the teaching; outside that context, it becomes a dead end, a fossilized "memorial" (μνῆμα) cut off from the "living voice" of tradition. This duality is endemic to the school tradition. The initial rendition of oral teaching to writing need not mark any major rupture in the dynamics of tradition. A ὑπομνῆμα, "reminder," is precisely how Clement describes Mark's written version of Peter's ἀπομνημονεύματα, and the *equites* who begged Mark to provide it desired it not as a substitute for memory but in order to support it (*ut possent quae dicebantur memoriae commendare*).[160] But the transfer to writing, once made, is irreversible, and as many ancient writers reflected, it could mark the beginning of a very different relationship between memory and text.

The transition from oral ἀπομνημόνευμα to written anecdote collection can be mapped as a two-stage progression—though with full awareness of the dangers of creating a too-tidy model. Once memory has achieved the relatively stable form of anecdote ("reminiscence"), the initial transfer to writing can be managed with relative ease. Textualization here is not the end of a one-way process, the culmination of a linear evolution, but a nodal point in the complex multidirectional operations of social memory, in which reminiscences of the past are constantly being collected, organized, and recombined in elastic formats that open up new possibilities of access and re-oralization. So the written text serves a mediary role in a fluid and creative performance tradition, capturing a fleeting moment between performance and re-oralization,[161] and memory remains the key to accessing this material, both before and after it is written down. The initial transfer to writing can happen within a single generation (as with Xenophon or Lucian) or can tap into the oral tradition several generations later (Diogenes Laertius). Written collections of sayings and anecdotes (γνῶμαι, ἀποφθέγματα, ἀπομνημονεύματα) of varying degrees of literary complexity are attested from the fourth century B.C.E. onwards and form the backbone of the biographical tradition in the Hellenistic schools. The "biographical" papyri provide valuable physical evidence of how such a collection might have looked: a bare, unsequenced collection of disconnected anecdotes, with no framing narrative.[162] The burgeoning classicism of the second century C.E. sees a secondary phase of textualization, in a renewed frenzy of scholastic activity seeking to identify and codify the oral traditions that define the essence of *hellenismos* in a colonial world dominated by Rome. This "scholastic" phase, exemplified by Athenaeus and Diogenes Laertius, draws both on earlier written collections and on the continuing oral tradition to record the anecdotal tradition in a variety of new combinations and literary reconfigurations.

A similar two-stage progression can be seen in early Christianity. Both Papias and Justin in different ways testify to a parallel "scholastic" phase in the second century: both draw on written and oral tradition to reconfigure and reconstitute gospel traditions into new literary formats, but both presuppose and build on a preexisting gospel tradition which is already in writing and has an identifiable social location in the worship of Christian assemblies.[163] In that sense, as Justin's title implies, we should assign the Gospels themselves to the prior, initial phase of the transfer to writing of the raw anecdotal tradition. These texts already have a regular place in Christian liturgy—something that suggests an incipient canonic function. Yet they are written only to be re-oralized in a cultic context, and they may well have functioned as a graphic databank for Christian preachers and teachers, a collection of dominical anecdotes to be quarried and recombined (alongside scriptural *testimonia*) in live performance of *apologia* or paraenesis). This is how the Hellenistic anecdote collections seem to have functioned, as databanks ("notebooks," *volumina*) of raw material to be quarried for the construction of paraenetic or rhetorical discourse.[164] Something similar can be discerned in the rabbinic schools, where (so Martin Jaffee argues) "the so-called Oral Torah may have lived out a long shadow-life as a loosely-arranged, textually polymorphous collection of written sources with no discernible iconic significance."[165] These texts were studied in the schools and could be used as *aides-mémoire* for the oral transmission of rabbinic tradition ("from memory"), but remained ideologically distinct from the Written Torah.[166]

Formally speaking, of course, the canonical Gospels are clearly more complex literary creations than the disconnected anecdote collections that we see in the papyri, with a much stronger narrative connection. In that sense the *Gospel of Thomas* provides a closer analogy, with its more loosely connected sequence of dominical sayings and anecdotes. Even the rudimentary narrative sequencing provided by Mark ("And immediately"; "And on the next day") displays a greater narrative connectivity and focus than we find in the Hellenistic ἀπομνημονεύματα. In fact, as I have argued elsewhere, although there are many parallels at the anecdotal level, it is surprisingly difficult to find a convincing parallel for the narrative focus and complexity of the Gospels in the Greek biographical tradition.[167] In this sense, the Greek biographical tradition raises the same "profound enigma" (though in a less acute form) as the rabbinic. Philip Alexander poses the question, "Why no rabbinic biography?" and suggests that the difference lies in the status of Jesus: "The obvious answer is that neither Eliezer nor any other sage held in rabbinic Judaism the central position that Jesus held in early Christianity."[168] In the Hellenistic tradition, we might compare the status of the two nonwriting sages, Socrates and Diogenes. Both inspired a rich anecdotal tradition and both played a crucial formative role in the tradition as paradigms of the philosophic life, but neither became the subject of a narrative biography (outside the collective format of Diogenes Laertius) as such. The overall shape of the gospel tradition, with its unusually tight focus on the words and deeds of a single teacher (already deeply embedded in the transitivity patterns of individual pericopes),[169] should not be seen as a natural or inevitable progression from the anecdotal tradition, but has to be considered as a creative outworking of the ideology of the Jesus movement in its own right, and may owe as much to the Bible as to Greek biography.

There is no reason to assume that the existence of written texts brings to an end either the oral performance of the anecdotal tradition or its written reformulation. The "intermediary" nature of these collections, poised between use and reuse, orality and re-oralization, throws light on the whole question of stability and fluidity across the proliferating gospel tradition of the second century. Helmut Koester points out that gospel texts in the second century were not considered to be inviolable: "On the contrary, their texts could be reused freely in new forms of writing, be expanded by new materials, and be shaped otherwise according to the demands of the community."[170] Within the matrix of the Hellenistic anecdotal tradition, none of this should occasion any surprise. By their very nature, ἀπομνημονεύματα lend themselves to continual reconfiguration and recombination in an infinite variety of spoken and written formats: it is a tradition in which there is no such thing as a "final form." The prolific use of the *chreia* as a staple of Greek education encourages this constant process of retelling as a mark of cultural skill. But it is a mistake to conclude, as Koester does, from this relative fluidity that the texts so freely reused are not authoritative. On the contrary, within the framework of the Hellenistic school tradition, it is precisely because of their iconic status that certain texts and traditions are accorded the honor of constant reshaping and reperformance. In a performative culture, it is the texts of central importance that are selected (i.e., become part of the "canon," which in this context means primarily the school curriculum) for continual paraphrase, intertextual allusion, and creative rewriting. Paradoxically, canonic status encourages new forms of mimesis. The crucial moment in the process of canonization is not the initial reduction to writing but a gradual shift from "performance" to "philology," a slow process in which "canonic" texts are gradually ring-fenced as texts and the locus of "performative" updating shifts from the text itself to the margins, to the multifarious activities of glossing and exegesis. This shift can be documented clearly across the medical schools of late antiquity and can be paralleled in the rabbinic academies and in the Hellenistic schools; it is hardly surprising that the same dynamics should be working themselves out in the gospel tradition throughout the second and third centuries.[171]

Apomnemoneumata *and History*

Finally, and much more briefly: what is the role of historical memory in all this? Ἀπομνημονεύματα, as we have noted, exactly fit Jan Vansina's category of "reminiscences." But Vansina also notes that it is impossible for the historian to get behind the reminiscence to the raw, unprocessed "news" of eyewitness reports.[172] The anecdotal tradition is one of the prime carriers of social memory for the Hellenistic schools and bears within itself all the ambiguities, the tension between past and present, of such traditions.[173] On the one hand, it is clear that the anecdotes themselves were designed and shaped for ease of memorization and transmission. Yet the fact that this is a memory of "gist" rather than exact wording does not preclude the possibility that some anecdotes may preserve authentic personal recollection and can be treated as potentially valuable historical material: "Selectivity [in oral tradition] implies discarding certain information one has about the past and from that pool of information keeping only what is still significant in the present. However, the information that is retained, still comes from the past."[174] In this respect the role of biographical tradition in early Christianity is no different from much of the Greek biographical tradition and of the anecdotal tradition that lies behind it. The fact that stories are shaped for present needs does not mean they are no use to the historian: the historicality of the material itself has to be assessed on other grounds.[175]

What is clear is that the schools themselves formed a communal vehicle—more, a motivating matrix—for the formation and preservation of biographical anecdotes about the sages and (more selectively) about their disciples, especially where the person of the sage came to be regarded as the embodiment of the teaching of the school. So Luke's picture of the "*collegium* of the apostles," focused on the task of shaping the Jesus story and interpreting its significance in the light of the Jewish Scriptures, is exactly what we should expect in the light of Hellenistic school tradition. The task of memorializing and codifying the school's inner tradition was too important to be left to the chances of memory: it was an essential bearer of identity, and to see its preservation as part of the task of the teacher's disciples—a communal task—is entirely plausible.[176] For Luke and his successors, it is Jesus' disciples who are accorded the status of "eyewitnesses" (Luke 1:2), rather than (as Bauckham suggests) the participants in individual episodes.[177] It is the apostles, the members of the disciple circle, who are appointed to shape and transmit the Jesus tradition and who therefore control access to it—a picture endorsed indirectly by Paul.[178] Whether or not Luke's picture is historically accurate is outside the scope of this paper, but we can say that it is consistent with the general patterns of memorializing that we have observed across the school systems of antiquity and that it is borne out by the grammatical structure of the anecdotal tradition itself. In ἀπομνημονεύματα (unlike γνῶμαι) the sage does not speak in his own voice. The narrative structure presupposes a narrator, a recording mind, an observer who is neither the sage nor the persons who encounter the sage along the way, be they questioners or the objects of his gaze. Teresa Morgan's structural analysis of a series of Diogenes χρεῖαι brings this structural aspect out clearly:

> The first thing to note is the relative position of the protagonists. Diogenes is probably to be imagined talking to a group of admirers or students, and the reader or listener is as if part of the group, laughing appreciatively at the master's wit. The objects of his observations are all at a distance and on a par, both spatially and grammatically, separated from the group by the word *idon*, seeing, which begins each sentence. This word serves to distance the object from the seeing subject.[179]

In other words, the disciple circle plays an invisible but essential role in the dramatic structure of the ἀπομνημόνευμα, the invisible third party to whom the sage speaks, for whose benefit he performs didactic actions, and (implicitly) by whom his wisdom is recorded and committed to memory. The grammatical structure of the *chreia* serves both to distance the reader/auditor from the scene being described and to draw him or her into "complicity" (Morgan's word) with the disciple circle. Diogenes, as grammatical subject, dominates and controls the hearer's viewpoint—but as subject of a third-person narrative, is himself the object of the hearer's mimetic gaze. The controlling perspective of the disciple-circle serves simultaneously to authenticate the narrative as observation and, by enticing its auditors into complicity, to create new disciples. It would be hard to think of a better definition of the form and function of the gospel tradition.

Chapter 6

Memory

Alan Kirk

It was because Birger Gerhardsson was concerned for a history of the gospel tradition grounded in historically attested cultural practices that he came to assign to memory the crucial operational role in the origins and transmission of tradition. In so doing, moreover, he anticipated important contemporary developments in the humanities and social sciences, where memory has become a dominant research paradigm.[1] This is all the more remarkable given that *Memory and Manuscript* appeared at a time when gospel scholarship, dominated by form criticism, was devoid of interest in memory.

Gerhardsson indicted the form critics and their followers, sometimes to the point of exasperation, for their failure to ground their history of the gospel tradition adequately in historical and cultural realities.[2] In fact, the form critics' lack of interest in positioning their model for tradition plausibly in ancient milieus and the peculiar absence of memory from their model for the tradition were closely connected. Opposing eschatological to historical consciousness, Rudolf Bultmann held that orientation to the past arose in the early Christian communities only secondarily, as a consequence of the exhaustion of eschatological enthusiasm. Therefore, he argued, this reorientation and with it conscious traditioning activities were not significant factors in the formative period of the gospel traditions.[3] Given this scenario, Bultmann and many of his contemporaries could be persuaded that the gospel tradition was largely the reflection of the present, enthusiastic life of the eschatological communities. They could assume, moreover, that the *Umwelt* could not offer many points of contact with early Christian traditioning activities and that the gospel tradition had to be approached as virtually *sui generis*, as *Kleinliteratur*, by definition lacking significant analogies in ancient cultural practices. This helps account not just for the striking absence of the factor of memory from their theorizing on the formation of the tradition, but also for the curious insouciance in the face of challenges like Gerhardsson's to give historical and cultural justification for their views.[4]

Gerhardsson's recognition that memory, that is, orientation to a normative past, and correspondingly the cultivation of tradition are constitutive of viable communities is now axiomatic in studies on the social and cultural aspects of memory. By the same token, Gerhardsson's original working conception of memory may itself be critically reassessed in the light of contemporary advances in research. In what follows we will work through Gerhardsson's understanding of the operations of memory and identify its limitations but show how memory in its cultural, social, and cognitive dimensions is indeed the crucial factor in the formation and transmission of tradition. We will give particular attention to what has been a primary focus of Gerhardsson's work, namely, the nexus of memory with the origins of tradition.

Rethinking the Framework: Memory in Ancient Education

Gerhardsson conceives the factor of memory in tradition in terms of memorization of more or less fixed texts through repetition, with faithful repetition also being the mechanism of transmission.[5] This is reminiscent of the replication of fixed texts associated with the written medium, and Gerhardsson in fact will defend taking the model of written fixation as his major point of reference. Though the focus of his discussion is rabbinic practices, Gerhardsson argues that similar techniques may be predicated more generally of Jewish Palestine in the Second Temple period.

Contrary to the way his work has sometimes been caricatured, Gerhardsson develops a reasoned justification for this latter claim, namely, in locating rabbinic techniques in their essentials in the wider context of ancient educational practices:

> [T]he learning by heart of basic texts; the principle that "learning comes before understanding"; the attempt to memorize the teacher's *ipsissima verba*; the condensation of material into short, pregnant texts; the use of mnemonic technique . . . the frequent repetition of memorized material . . . [I]n almost every case the basis is provided by . . . popular educational practice.[6]

In other words, rabbinic memory practice is a plausible analogy for Jesus' own practice and early Christian cultivation of tradition because it was an expression of educational techniques widespread in the ancient world. Drilled memorization of written works with classic status and their recitation from memory was the major pedagogical feature of Hellenistic education from the elementary level to the advanced rhetorical level.[7] Moreover, Gerhardsson argues, there is little evidence of any alternative model for tradition; these were "*the* ancient forms of oral instruction and oral transmission."[8] Hellenistic education, he further assumes, was widely diffused, with schools attested for Palestine "centuries before Christ."[9] This parallel and "highly organised school system" of Jewish schools developed in Palestine from the time of the Maccabees.[10] Though attendance was not universal, "we may be quite sure that at the time of the fall of the Temple there were private elementary schools in all the Jewish towns of Palestine."[11] These schools mirrored the Hellenistic curriculum, with less qualified *soferim*, the counterparts of the Hellenistic *grammatici*, providing elementary education based on Torah memorization to children in synagogue congregations in the *bet sofer*, with higher rabbinic education in the *bet hammidrash* corresponding to the advanced Hellenistic rhetorical education.[12] Though most evidence for this, Gerhardsson acknowledges, is from the rabbinic sources themselves, he argues that the widespread existence of schools and literacy that they depict in the period of the Second Temple is nonetheless probable.[13]

As noted, the postulated existence of this wider educational milieu with its characteristic practices supplies Gerhardsson with the crucial premise for generalizing rabbinic memorization techniques to Jesus and primitive Christianity. Jesus in his role as teacher would have had his disciples memorize his teachings by repetition, which once fixed in memory might become objects for interpretation. His disciples would have perpetuated his practice, constituting with their "service in the word" a collegium in the early church analogous to the "persistent occupation with the study of Torah" of the rabbinic associations.[14]

Though Gerhardsson's argument cogently reflects scholarship on education and literacy in the ancient world current until even quite recently, it is now vulnerable on both those points, and with the weakening of this premise is weakened the justification for extrapolating from rabbinic to early Christian traditioning practices.[15] It is becoming increasingly clear that access to Hellenistic education and the cultural literacy it inculcated was largely limited to elite circles and their retainers.[16] Few even of these progressed beyond the elementary to the secondary level and even fewer to rhetorical training, the level at which the ability to use the repertoire of memorized cultural texts in interpretative, creative ways was acquired.[17] Corresponding to this were the quite low overall literacy rates. In his study of ancient literacy William Harris estimates overall illiteracy at ninety percent, with somewhat lower rates for the cities.[18] Teresa Morgan states of Egypt, "Since those who acquired any form of literacy were already a small proportion of the population as a whole, grammar [secondary education] was the preserve of a very small minority indeed."[19] Raymond Starr points out that books for the most part circulated among friends in literate social networks and that bookshops catered mostly to these groups.[20] To be sure, literacy was diffused outside elite circles across a broad range of applications but in steep gradations of competence. Many might have possessed signature literacy, that is, the ability to sign one's name; others phonetic literacy, the ability to sound out the syllables of, say, an inscription; others a rudimentary "craft literacy" adequate for carrying on one's trade.[21] For the illiterate majority, access to the written word was brokered by the "relatively small number of functional literates."[22]

Restricted access to education and literacy was even more the case for Jewish Palestine, with its predominantly rural character.[23] Catherine Hezser in her recent analysis rejects the widespread existence of schools in Jewish Palestine in the Second Temple period as a retrojection of Amoraic ideals and developments: "[L]ater Talmudic texts . . . are not only anachronistic in associating the educational institutions of the Amoraic period with pre-70 times, but also vastly exaggerate with regard to the number of education establishments likely to have existed at either time."[24] Moreover, "although some Pharisees as well as other Jewish leaders before 70 C.E. may well have recommended a basic Torah education for children, they never enforced this view by actually establishing schools."[25] Literate education was the preserve of elites, and as was the case in Hellenistic education few would have advanced beyond basic and intermediate levels to the high level of cultural expertise in Torah characteristic of the rabbis and their disciples.[26] The fact that Palestinian Judaism was a Torah-centered religion is not incongruous with this scenario. Written Torah would have been appropriated by the nonliterate population orally and aurally.[27]

It is difficult, therefore, to follow Gerhardsson in taking a general educational *Sitz* as bridging from rabbinic to early Christian traditioning practices. More to the point, the fixed-text memorization model, belonging as it does to the highly literate, elite educational *Sitz*, cannot act plausibly as the model for memory in the cultivation and transmission of early Christian oral tradition, though it must certainly become pertinent when the gospel tradition moves into the written medium of the Gospels and under the control of scribal tradents. And yet Gerhardsson is surely right that an indissoluble relationship of some sort exists between memory and tradition. The key, accordingly, lies in grasping the dynamics of memory and tradition in contexts of pervasive orality.

Memory, Tradition, and the Problem of Medium

In developing his phenomenology of tradition, Gerhardsson, as noted, is influenced by the rabbinic context, the most pertinent cultural permutation of the wider educational setting. Hence he takes practices attaching to Oral Torah, specifically, the oral cultivation of the memorized text of the Mishnah as well as other rabbinic works, as prototypical.[28] This accounts for his construal of early Christian oral tradition and its transmission in terms of the textual fixation and vocalized memorization practices characteristic of the written medium.[29] "In reality," he observes, "there was hardly a great difference between memorized written texts and memorized oral texts of the same type."[30] This analogue with written texts makes itself felt in Gerhardsson's tendency to distinguish interpretation and commentary cleanly from the tradition artifact itself, its memorization, and its transmission.[31]

In developing this view of early Christian oral tradition Gerhardsson is influenced not just by the cultivation of the Mishnah but the corollary assumption that in a society of pervasive literacy and literate education such as he believes Jewish Palestine to have been, the written medium becomes normative for oral traditioning and the cognate memory practices.[32] Consequently, he generally does not concede the relevance of contemporary research on orality in predominantly oral societies. In fact, Gerhardsson tends to understand unalloyed orality as characterized by extreme fluidity, as weak in stabilizing forces and hence marked by an uncontrolled, shapeless variability, as standing, in other words, in virtually categorical opposition to the fixity characteristic of writing. Any sign of genre-mediated stability in the tradition, therefore, is for Gerhardsson indexical of the fixating effects of the written medium and of memorization-based and at times even writing-assisted transmission. Gospel genres such as the *mashal* are "texts," or more precisely, memorized texts.[33] This is to say that Gerhardsson does not have a strong working conception of oral genres, of variable yet stable speech forms adapted to the exigencies of oral communication and transmission. In his view, variable oral retellings would eventually have produced a homogenized body of tradition lacking genre distinctions, in other words, a complete leveling of "the *different text types* within the gospel tradition."[34]

It is the case that applications of oral theory in gospel scholarship not infrequently have been guilty of exaggerating the fluidity of oral tradition and also of egregious overreach, even to the point at times of dissolving the written gospels almost completely into oral dynamics. Doubtless Gerhardsson is at least in part reacting against these extremes. A phenomenology of memory and tradition centered upon multiple oral genres is, however, not just requisite but easily reconcilable with important aspects of his work, for as we shall see in detail later in this essay, oral genres are grounded in memory dynamics.[35] Joseph Russo analyzes the proverb (*paroimia*), maxim (*gnome*), and the *apothegma*, Greek counterparts of the gospel *mashal* and pronouncement story, as oral wisdom genres. Their utterance was "essentially emergent and responsive to specific contexts," and they might be transmitted orally and anecdotally "for centuries before attaining formal documentation in the highly literate postclassical era."[36] Traditional societies, Elizabeth Tonkin observes, preside over a repertoire of oral genres whose formal features are calibrated for oral communication settings as well as memorability for oral transmission.[37] Collectively they incorporate a community's moral norms (instructional genres) and its foundational stories (narrative genres), constituting what Jan Assmann terms a community's "cultural memory."[38]

The formal features of such genres ensure stability and thus continuity across many oral enactments. However, through their equally core property of variability, or better, multiformity, the tradition is brought to expression in ways responsive to the different social and historical contexts in which it is enacted.[39] Oral genres, in other words, though stable are not fixed in the sense that the written medium fixes a text. To fix them would be to impair their capacity for oral (as opposed to written) transmission, for loss of adaptability to different social and historical settings entails erosion of relevance and hence survivability. Oral genres thus both limit variation and allow it expression, though it is important to emphasize that they fall on a spectrum running from quite marked stability, that is, minimal change from enactment to enactment (proverbs for example), to extempore freedom in retelling (some narrative genres).

Medium, therefore, is indeed a pertinent factor in the operations of memory and tradition. Interpretation occurs in oral tradition by virtue of its multiformity, and accordingly, "*textintern*."[40] In other words, interpretation and transmission, rather than being distinct, are "untrennbar miteinander verknüpft."[41] Shifting the tradition into writing—its transformation into manuscript tradition—marks a major change in the dynamics of transmission. By virtue of its material and visual properties, writing more securely stabilizes wording. As a result, interpretation becomes increasingly extrinsic to the tradition itself, eventually taking the form of citation and commentary.[42]

This places rabbinic memory practices with respect to Oral Torah, practices that Gerhardsson so clearly delineated, in a different light. The salient point is Oral Torah's close association with the written medium. Unlike primitive Christian tradition or oral tradition conceived more generally, Oral Torah existed in symbiosis with Written Torah. Mishnah tractates stood in different sorts of direct or indirect relationships to Scripture and Midrash collections in an explicit commentary relationship.[43] In other words, "both the midrashic and in large part the halakhic tradition . . . are . . . supported by a base text."[44] In rabbinic circles cultivation of Oral and Written Torah moved in tandem: "The performative study of the Oral Torah," writes Steven Fraade, "intertwined as it is with the ritual recitation of the Written Torah, is a reenactment and extension of the originary [aural] revelation at Sinai."[45] As Martin Jaffee similarly points out, Oral Torah "guaranteed the continuity of rabbinic knowledge and authority with the founding revelations recorded in the Hebrew scriptures."[46]

More to the point, however, is the fact that through intricate mnemonics Oral Torah received a level of fixation such that it emulated the properties of the written medium. Rabbinic mnemonics in the Mishnah were intended to facilitate its memorization and accordingly its recitation from memory as a text made up of lengthy and composite blocks of material. It is important to note that in antiquity complex mnemonic techniques of this sort were typical of highly literate settings. Jocelyn Penny Small characterizes them as "very much an art of literacy for the highly literate."⁴⁷ "They are devised to deal *with written texts*," David Olson explains. "[M]emory arts are not devices for remembering just what someone says but primarily for preserving written documents in memory."⁴⁸ In the scholarly discussion the question of the origins of the Mishnah is in fact usually framed in terms of its "redaction and publication," and its official memorizers, the *tannaim*, are characterized in both the rabbinic literature and scholarship as "living books" or "living editions."⁴⁹ It may indeed be possible to view the Mishnah, as well as other works in the rabbinic corpus, in terms of a cultural project consisting in a consolidation of rabbinic tradition comparable to a written consolidation.⁵⁰

Whatever the case may be, the orality of Oral Torah was prescribed, strategic, and ideological. While present inchoately in the Tannaitic period, the concept of Oral Torah as the rubric for rabbinic tradition emerged only after the redaction of the Mishnah. Its orality was prescriptive, the effect of the stipulation that in the study circles it was to be held in and recited from memory, not like Written Torah from a scroll.⁵¹ Strategically and ideologically Oral Torah's orality secured Israel's claim against usurpers of its written scripture (the Christians) to exclusive possession of God's covenant revelation.⁵² As Jaffee further points out, this strategy also served to distinguish the rabbis as an elite circle within Israel.⁵³ The doctrine of Oral Torah thus may be seen as a permutation of the elitist scribal ethos that had its basis in the memory competence scribes exercised in the cultural texts of their respective societies.⁵⁴

This effectively calls into question the direct applicability of rabbinic memory practices to early Christian traditioning. Nevertheless Gerhardsson has put his finger on a critical aspect of ancient memory practice. Rabbinic mastery of Oral Torah through memorization is a case of manuscript memory, a defining feature of what Armin Sweeny terms "oral manuscript culture."⁵⁵ Jaffee states that "*what rabbinic disciples encountered as oral tradition was the performative embodiment of memorized rabbinic manuscript*."⁵⁶ In antiquity and the medieval world, manuscript was adjunct to memory. The manuscript version of a cultural text was largely ancillary to a work's operative and more authentic existence as a memory artifact.⁵⁷ At one level this was simply pragmatic: the formidable difficulties the scroll format presented for random access made memory control of a text requisite for its actual utilization. This is certainly the case for Oral Torah; in their debates rabbis could not be constantly flipping and scrolling to locate pertinent passages.⁵⁸ However, memory also functioned as the major support for the oral enactment of a written work that constituted the primary mode of the latter's cultural existence.[59]

Oral Torah, accordingly, may be a case of the typical marginality of manuscript relative to memory pushed programmatically to its extreme. In rabbinic practice and ideology its manuscript embodiment recedes, virtually to a vanishing point, in favor of the prominence of the memory artifact. It may not even be necessary to postulate the presence of manuscript at its redaction (scholars tend to leave this question open), for in antiquity memory was also the primary faculty for literary composition.[60] Because the mnemonic formalization of the Mishnah was quite methodical and its memorization and recitation the focused concern of the rabbinic discipleship circles, there may have been little need for accessory written versions to support its transmission.[61]

We have been able to clarify that Gerhardsson's working concept of memory and tradition is modeled on literate, manuscript memory. There is in fact some reason to believe that prior to the redaction of the Mishnah, rabbinic tradition was at least to some extent cultivated in oral-traditional multiformity and not fixed-text memorization. Elizabeth Shanks Alexander and Martin Jaffee undertake to demonstrate this by isolating predocumentary clusters of rabbinic oral tradition in the Tannaitic collections. A comparison of parallel units, they argue, reveals the emblematic multiformity of oral tradition: stability and flexibility in equilibrium and meaning generated not through external commentary but by reconfigurations of the tradition artifact itself.[62] Whatever the case may be, fixed-text memorization cannot be taken as normative for the formation and transmission of oral tradition prior to the latter's programmatic embodiment in writing.[63]

GERHARDSSON ON MEMORY AND THE ORIGINS OF TRADITION

The precise nature of the relationship of memory and tradition in primitive Christianity therefore remains a crux problem. As we noted at the outset, the form critics largely eliminated the factor of memory from their phenomenology of tradition. They conceived of memory narrowly on the model of individual recollections by eyewitnesses, which manifestly did not match the profile of the gospel tradition. Dennis Nineham, writing just prior to the publication of *Memory and Manuscript*, gives articulate expression to this view. For Nineham it is just obvious that memory and tradition are distinct, even incommensurable, entities. Memory is phenomenologically equivalent to personal eyewitness testimony such as might be elicited in court; it is marked by "knowledge of the particular, inclusion of the merely memorable, as opposed to the edifying, exact biographical and topographical precision and the like."[64] These traits are notable for their absence from the synoptic tradition, which is formal, stereotyped, restrained in descriptive detail, and hence, he states, clearly the product not of memory but "the impersonal needs and forces of the community."[65] To be sure, Nineham acknowledges, some very early interface with eyewitness memory was likely; such would account for the residual presence in the tradition of authentic recollections of Jesus. Since this "initial stage," however, the tradition obviously has followed an independent course of development, for otherwise individual eyewitness testimony would have come to be visible within it as foreign matter: "[I]f the Gospel material derives from *two very different types of source* we should expect it to show signs of its double origin."[66] Thus while memories were ingredient in some undertheorized manner in the "initial" formation of the tradition, they were residues, inert with respect to subsequent developments in the tradition. Memory so conceived was of such inconsequence that the form critics were markedly uncurious even about the nature of its postulated initial contact with the tradition.

This had all the force of a cognitive paradigm and so in retrospect it is not surprising that Gerhardsson's program for a thorough convergence of memory dynamics with tradition was received with incomprehension. Gerhardsson challenged the form critics on a number of issues. Against the notion of its immanence in the social dynamics of various ecclesiastical *Sitze*, he argued that from its origins the gospel tradition was a distinct, in his word "isolated," entity and correspondingly that its cultivation was itself a *Sitz* autonomous from its uses in preaching and exhortation. Likewise, the forms of the tradition were conventional genres circulating in the cultural environment which though differing from one another in pragmatic function were capable of utilization across different social settings.[67] Research on the phenomenology of tradition supports Gerhardsson on these points. Tradition is "marked," or dedicated, speech with the shift from ordinary discourse into tradition enactment typically signaled by linguistic cues and formulas of various sorts.[68] "The speaker," Russo states, "momentarily ceases to use a personal voice in the here and now and instead uses the voice of the shared cultural tradition."[69] Likewise, tradition genres are cultural entities distinguishable from the social structure and dynamics of the groups that make use of them.[70]

The most important problem that Gerhardsson faced, however, was to give an account of how memory might be implicated in the formation of tradition, an account reconcilable, moreover, with the observable traits of the synoptic tradition. Gerhardsson pointed out, quite plausibly, that much of the sayings and parabolic material would have originated in Jesus' own practice as a teacher of memorable meshalim in the framework of the master-disciple relationship, a historically grounded *Sitz* for the cultivation and transmission of tradition in sapiential and prophetic circles.[71] That various narrative elements (not formulated by Jesus) should come to exist in the tradition is not surprising, Gerhardsson further argued, for in antiquity the *bios* of the master was as crucial as his *logos*. The quest of the communities of his followers for comprehensive sets of norms was doubtless the major impetus for efforts at remembering Jesus. This is evident in the strong normative charge carried by the narrative gospel genres, the pronouncement stories in particular.[72] As mentioned, however, Gerhardsson had to address the problem of how this memory work issued in the artifactual forms of the tradition. Notably, he argued that the raw material of eyewitness memories was fashioned into tradition by an apostolic collegium in Jerusalem dedicated to this activity as its "work with the word." All members of the community were active in remembering Jesus, but it was the collegium, comprised of the Twelve and hence the most authoritative eyewitnesses, that did the specialized work of collecting remembrances and converting them into, or as Gerhardsson puts it "fixing" them in, the transmissible forms of the tradition.[73]

Viewed in light of our earlier discussion, the difficulty that emerges in this account is not its close coordination of memory with tradition but its construal of the memory factor as memorization of fixed texts, or stated differently, its overdetermination by the properties of the written medium. Gerhardsson's apostolic collegium in its work on the Scriptures and its creation of collections of traditions has a pronounced scribal complexion, analogous in its activities to the Qumran scribal community and of course to rabbinic circles.[74] Gerhardsson describes tradition formation in the collegium in terms redolent of literary operations: the collegium's members are like individual authors (sometimes depicted at desks), crafting, editing, and revising their work in consultation with others. Adverting to the literary model entails, moreover, that in a manner incongruous with the actual dynamics of oral tradition Gerhardsson separates the formation of a tradition artifact almost categorically from its subsequent usage in various social settings.[75] If the form critics exaggerated the ontological convergence of tradition with social contexts of its enactment, Gerhardsson is led by his literary assumptions to overdraw the extent of its autonomy from those contexts. Tradition artifacts, in his view, are first formulated as fixed texts that are then memorized for subsequent transmission, recitation, and commentary in various social settings.[76]

Memory and the Formation of Tradition

The appropriate response, however, is not skepticism with regard to Gerhardsson's essential point—memory as the key agent in the formation and cultivation of tradition—but to describe that relationship even more comprehensively in terms of the cognitive, social, and cultural dynamics of memory. Tradition emerges from such an analysis as no less than an artifact of memory.

The conversion of memory into tradition has an important cognitive dimension. Research on the cognitive operations of memory indicates that memory is not so much a passive faculty of storage and recall as it is an active artificer that condenses and schematizes raw perceptual input from experiences, creating efficient memory scripts that give cognitive orientation to the world.[77] More to the point, these artificing operations of memory correspond closely to observable features and functions of the gospel tradition. Memory economizes and condenses, selecting from the undifferentiated flux of experience what is most salient. Though frequently construed negatively as memory's major limitation, this large-scale "forgetting" of particulars is in fact an expression of memory's efficiency, its capacity to distill out the essential from the nonessential, to generalize and analyze, and by the same token to avoid the cognitive overload that would result from total recall. Larry Squire and Eric Kandel write:

> We are best at generalizing, abstracting, and assembling general knowledge, not at retaining a literal record of particular events. We forget the particulars, and by our forgetfulness gain the possibility of abstracting and retaining the main points. Normal memory is not overwhelmed by the individual and separate details that fill each moment of experience. We can forget the details, and we can therefore form concepts and gradually absorb knowledge by adding up the lessons from different kinds of experiences.[78]

To these ends, memory blurs distinctions among memories of similar events, compounding them into generic memories with representational, emblematic functions.[79] A corollary cognitive operation is the rapid conforming of memories to generic types, schemata, and conventional narrative patterns. In addition to giving the resulting memory artifacts durability and mnemonic properties, these function to make sense of memories, that is, to give them coherence and to foreground their existential, or more precisely their normative, significance for the remembering subjects.[80]

In these schematizing operations, memory's agency in the formation of tradition comes into especially sharp relief. Cognitive memory work draws upon the existing cultural repertoire of genres, symbols, and narrative schemata to mediate memory formation, a charged convergence of memory and culture that Robin Wagner-Pacifici describes as "the cultural realities of modes of generic encodings."[81] The schematic types, the cultural genres to which memories are conformed, mediate between memory and publicly available tradition, particularly in virtue of their core function to render memories coherent and communicable. Memory, Jerome Bruner and Carol Fleischer Feldman state, becomes public "by being based on narrative properties like genre and plot type that are widely shared within a culture, shared in a way that permits others to construe meaning as the narrator has. In this way private experiences . . . are constituted meaningfully into a public and communicable form."[82] The past, moreover, will come to be "represent[ed] in a variety of genres," and "different genres will render and amplify different aspects of the 'same' events."[83]

Communication as the necessary condition of memory formation underscores that memory is a social and cultural phenomenon. Maurice Halbwachs, a principal founder of modern memory studies, showed that it is in the context of the social realities and communicative practices of communities that the memories of the individuals belonging to those groups receive substance, coherence, and durability.[84] Communities for their part fashion and cultivate their foundational memories collaboratively, in face-to-face communication, processes not wholly insulated, moreover, from impinging social realities.[85]

This enterprise has a number of features that distinguish it from the "individual eye-witness recollection" model for memory that dominates discussion of the topic in gospel scholarship. Studies show that such collaboratively formed memories are "more richly recollected" than those constructed by individuals alone.[86] Community members prompt and monitor one another's recollections of past events and contribute collectively to bestowing coherence upon the emerging memory artifacts. These shared memories bring to expression, moreover, the community's foundational norms, and conversely, individual remembering in such contexts is guided by the shared norms of the community.[87] As Mary Susan Weldon and Krystal Bellinger observe, the persons involved in these processes increasingly tend to conform their individual memories to, and therefore to share, the memories that are collaboratively shaped. Most pertinently for the emergence of tradition, memories forged within the communicative dynamics of a community receive collectively held, formal representations that render them more stable over time than individual memories.[88] Liisa Malkki takes note of this phenomenon in camps in Tanzania for Hutu refugees escaping from the 1972 genocide in Burundi. "Accounts of key events," she states, "very quickly circulated among the refugees and, often in a matter of days, acquired what can be characterized as 'standard versions' in the telling and retelling."[89] This description neatly captures the real-time formation and cultivation of durable tradition artifacts at the intersection of social context, communication, and memory.

This sort of memory work is a normative enterprise, which is to say essential to constituting the commemorating group as a moral community.[90] A community marks and commemorates certain elements of its past as being of fundamental significance to its identity, typically events and persons foundational to its origins and embodying its values. "Memory work," says Barry Schwartz, "like a lens, filters extraneous materials the better *for us* to see the kind of recollecting relevant to our purposes . . . [M]emory work is a limiting concept against which real situations are scanned for cultural significance."[91] These elements are configured in commemorative narratives and instructional genres which distill the norms perceived to be explicitly or implicitly immanent in the events. In the ritual rehearsal of this tradition the community relates itself to its cultural identity and the cognate norms in ever-changing historical circumstances. "Es handelt sich," states Assmann, "um die Transformation von Vergangenheit in fundierende Geschichte."[92] As with any commemorative symbol, the forms of the tradition into which memory material is transmuted render the community's norms "visible, permanent, and transmittable."[93] Critical to this semiotic intensification is the internal keying and tuning of the tradition to archetypal narratives, persons, and motifs of the epic past, that is, to established bodies of authoritative cultural tradition.[94] In short, the foundational memory material of a group coalesces in culturally available genres and narrative patterns that ground its identity deeply in the past, constitute it as a moral community, and enable transmission of cultural identity across time. In this manner tradition comes to transcend the limitations of unreflective and notoriously unstable eyewitness memories and their fragmentary, individualistic perspectives.[95]

It is possible, therefore, to account not just for the forms but the pronounced normative complexion of the gospel tradition, particularly its density in dominical sayings and pronouncement stories. In the tradition the diffuse actualities of foundational events have been converted into transmissible linguistic artifacts that bear the axiomatic meanings and norms of the Jesus communities. This also explains the tradition's uniformity, that is, the absence of the idiosyncrasies of eyewitness recollection that Nineham and other form critics mistakenly took as indicating the incommensurability of memory and tradition.[96]

Not least, it accounts for what perhaps most impressed the form critics, namely, the tradition's striking autonomy with respect to the empirical past, its taking on a life of its own in remarkably kinetic and protean histories of development within historically contingent tradent communities. Memory, it has been seen, is a constructive, artificing faculty that compounds memory artifacts out of the flux of pertinent experience. Its condensing, blending, schematizing, and morally signifying operations entail significant differentiation and distancing from the empirical realities. Aptly termed by Edward Casey the "thick autonomy of memory," this is itself a mnemonic strategy crucial to the efficient operation of memory as an active cognitive function.[97] The point here though is that the memory work of groups produces finely wrought, autonomous representations, or stated differently refinements, of the past, symbolically and normatively concentrated, that receive artefactual form in various communicative genres. As with any cultural object, these tradition artifacts lead a cultural life of their own as they constantly and reciprocally react with the social and historical contingencies of their tradent communities.[98]

"Autonomy" therefore denotes not a sundered but an essentially representational relationship of tradition to the past that Casey characterizes as "intensified remembering."[99] It is only through the transmutation of formative events into transmissible tradition artifacts that the past is preserved at all. Paradoxically, it is the tradition's autonomy that enables the tradent community to "remember" the normative past, in other words, to mobilize the tradition in effective ways in ever-changing frameworks of reception. Likewise, the autonomy of the tradition comes to expression—as Gerhardsson argued—largely in terms of the internal resources and symbolic potential of the tradition itself.[100]

Memory and the Variability of Tradition

Finally, it is possible in light of these realities to grasp the variability that is such a conspicuous feature of the gospel tradition also as a memory phenomenon. Tradition is the artifact of memory, and as David Rubin argues in his wide-ranging study of oral tradition, oral-traditional genres are mnemonic strategies for transmission of tradition and its effective reenactment in pervasively oral communication environments.[101] "A formalized utterance," Assmann states, "is a carrier of memory, a mnemonic mark in being both an element of tradition (which is in itself a form of memory) and memorable for future recourse."[102] Memory's artificing of material into oral genres has the mnemonic effect of shedding the surfeits of detail that human memory is so notoriously inefficient at retaining and thereby radically reducing the quantity of content actually to be held in memory. For their part the recurrent formal features of oral genres strongly enhance the memorability—the capacity for recollection—of the tradition they encode.

However, despite the fact that frequently they enable close replication from utterance to utterance, oral genres are not calibrated for verbatim memorization, which is a transmission strategy predicated on the fixity of written texts.[103] Rather, oral genres operate as "systems of multiple constraints" that cue memory in a nonrote manner and constrain variation by limiting its possible range.[104] Memory as a factor in the transmission of oral tradition, accordingly, does not signify verbatim mastery and recitation but accurate recall through competence in a system of constraints and cues that eliminate the burden of carrying a verbatim version of a tradition in one's head as a condition for reproducing it from occasion to occasion.[105] Multiformity is the emblematic feature of oral tradition because genre-embodied configurations of constraints and cues permit a range of possible realizations of a given tradition.[106] Multiformity is consequently itself a mnemonic strategy indispensable for remembering the tradition, its transmission in enactment to enactment, for tradition that is inflexibly unresponsive to the changing social realities of the tradent community falls into oblivion. In the multiformity of the gospel tradition, in other words, mnemonic and normative concerns converge.

In this connection it is possible to see with greater clarity why the patterns of variation and agreement in the synoptic tradition have often been viewed as raising difficulties for Gerhardsson's model for tradition. Gerhardsson in fact takes full cognizance of the phenomenon of variation, but, consistent with his approach, his tendency is to account for it in terms of scribal modifications of texts or how fixed texts might vary in a system of memorization.[107] Jesus, he suggests, may have had his disciples memorize more than one version of a given saying, while other variants may have arisen from imperfect memorization of an original.[108] Some may be translation variants and others may have been introduced in Matthew and Luke's redaction of Mark.[109] Gerhardsson conceives much tradition variation in the pre-Gospels period similarly in terms of editorial alterations of fixed texts by teacher-tradents whose authorship of the tradition extends to its continued interpretation, their interpretive work in effect producing new fixed editions of the traditions to be committed to memory alongside the other versions.[110] Along similar lines he posits the "flexible interpretation" of "fixed texts" of the tradition, a binary predicated upon the categorical distinction between scriptural text and commentary as with *miqra-targum*.[111]

While Gerhardsson is right to insist on the moderate scale of variation, his model entails that he approach it as a difficulty to be explained and marginalized rather than embraced as a core property of the gospel tradition. Accordingly, his explanations strain to adequately encompass the phenomenon. It is difficult, for example, to square the evangelists' frequently wide-ranging transformations of their sources with an ethos of fixed-text transmission, in other words to countenance for the evangelists, tradents in their own right, a free hand with the tradition programmatically ruled out from its oral transmission. Likewise, the "fixed text, flexible interpretation" rubric, fitting as it is for commentary practices with respect to established written texts, is hard to square with the phenomenology of the gospel tradition where it is the base traditions themselves that are subject to variation. As Gerhardsson acknowledges in the case of the *targum* analogy, the base text *miqra*, "the fixed and uncompromising holy word of Scripture," remains impermeable.[112] In fact Gerhardsson often observes that the traditions have in numerous cases undergone adaptation and reformulation.[113] While he is correct that such largely occurs within the stable linguistic configuration of the tradition, this form of transmission (likewise for the parallel haggadic tradition) is not strictly commensurable with a fixed-text, memorization model. This difficulty is visible in Gerhardsson's marginalization of variation in such cases by ascribing greater importance to the "firm elements" of such traditions and in his more qualified assertion that such were "in principle memorized."[114]

We have argued for affirming variation as a core property of the gospel tradition while at the same time integrating memory dynamics into its formation and transmission perhaps even more thoroughly than Gerhardsson envisioned. For Gerhardsson, memorization functioned to maintain a closeness of correspondence between the gospel tradition and memories of Jesus.[115] We have explored the likelihood of an even fuller convergence of memory with the phenomenology of tradition. This would include, moreover, the shift to the written gospel medium, where the dynamics of manuscript memory become particularly important for grasping the continued history of the gospel tradition.

Conclusion

The Work of Birger Gerhardsson in Perspective

Werner H. Kelber

> I do not believe that there is any *simple* answer to the question concerning the origins of the gospel tradition.
> Birger Gerhardsson, *The Reliability of the Gospel Tradition*

> ... the greater part of the ancient literature is intended for the ears as much as, if not more than, the eyes.
> Birger Gerhardsson, *Memory and Manuscript*

> The study of the Torah is, according to a typical rabbinic mode of expression, "a work of the mouth."
> Birger Gerhardsson, *Memory and Manuscript*

Half a century after Birger Gerhardsson wrote his signature piece, *Memory and Manuscript*, the contributors to this volume, along with the editors, are offering a reassessment of his scholarly accomplishments. No doubt the status of New Testament studies at the outset of the twenty-first century is impressively different from what it was in the late 1950s and early 1960s. However, humanistic scholarship, including biblical studies, is not a history merely of steady growth and systematic advance in knowledge which would allow us to simply slough off the past as dead matter. To say that biblical scholarship manifests itself in complex interfaces of present with past states of learning is to acknowledge that with genuine advances come transformations of ostensibly assured knowledge and rediscoveries of what we thought we had known for sure. This hermeneutical insight applies with special relevance to the work of Gerhardsson. Individually and collectively, the essays gathered in this volume treat areas that have been the focus of Gerhardsson's scholarly attention or have been suggested by him as subject for further inquiry. Building on recent advances in orality, scribality, memory, and rabbinic studies, as well as in our understanding of communications and education in Hellenistic culture, prompted us to revisit and to reacquaint ourselves with principal aspects of Gerhardsson's work. Taken together these essays offer a vast array of topics and issues pertaining to the early Christian, rabbinic, and Hellenistic tradition processes, which in this variety and combination are not available anywhere else. They are testimony both to Gerhardsson's wide range of interests and to the productive intellectual impulses that have issued forth from his work.

Of the many issues that Gerhardsson's *Memory and Manuscript* has raised, none has drawn greater attention than the assumed backdating of rabbinic techniques of transmission into the Second Temple period and their application to the early Jesus tradition. Ever since Morton Smith made this the central point,[1] reviews have revisited this topic again and again, defining it frequently as the sole criterion by which to judge the author's theses. By now the issue has been explicated by Gerhardsson[2] and clarified by Samuel Byrskog in the introduction to this volume, while the criticism itself has been revoked by Jacob Neusner in his foreword[3] to the reprint of *Memory and Manuscript*. One can, therefore, proceed from the premise that Gerhardsson's rabbinic model is just that, "an example, a model, a possibility,"[4] a cultural pattern, in other words, which was meant to facilitate comparative thinking in relation to the rabbinic and the early Jesus tradition. While the study of the latter in the context of Second Temple scribalism and post-70 rabbinism remains a fruitful undertaking, as will be shown below, any further discussion of the specific topic of a backdating of rabbinic techniques has become pointless, all the more so since the heavy focus on this issue has had the effect of eclipsing other more significant features of Gerhardsson's work.

Form Criticism

More important at this stage is the observation that in its totality Gerhardsson's work was meant to propose an alternative to the form-critical paradigm of the gospel origins. As is well known, he developed his paradigm of tradition and gospel in the face of what Byrskog has called "the most influential scholarly agenda at the time" and what for the longest part of the twentieth century was the reigning methodology in large parts of gospel studies. Christopher Tuckett is, therefore, quite correct in calling Gerhardsson's magnum opus "highly courageous" and indeed "seminal in opening up and generating debate and discussion in important areas." Not surprisingly, form critics were among the most vociferous critics of *Memory and Manuscript*, often seizing upon Gerhardsson's rabbinic thesis and thereby deflecting his objections to their own form-critical project. Gerhardsson himself never articulated his position vis-à-vis form criticism systematically in a single piece. The closest he came to a methodical articulation of his critical appraisal was an enumeration of ten critical points in "The Path of the Gospel Tradition."[5]

Tuckett has registered some of Gerhardsson's major objections and added a fair number of his own. I have systematically treated the conceptual and linguistic flaws of form criticism in a recent publication.[6] In view of this growing discontent not only in Anglo-American scholarship, but on the continent as well,[7] Gerhardsson's position vis-à-vis form criticism today appears far more relevant than the form critics were willing to concede half a century ago. The value of his own alternative model quite apart, it needs to be acknowledged that in light of the current discussion and from the vantage point of retrospectivity many of his observations and reservations concerning form criticism are well taken and often to the point.

To do justice to Gerhardsson's concept of the so-called synoptic tradition, four interconnected features need to be taken into consideration. There is, firstly, his contribution to a conceptualization of the origin and mechanisms of the early Jesus tradition. It is a subject which, not unlike his rabbinic studies, has met with much criticism, overshadowing highly commendable aspects of his work. To begin with, conveniently ignored is Gerhardsson's rather adroit treatment of the issue of origin: how does one capture and conceive of the commencement of the Jesus tradition in the context of history? It may come somewhat as a surprise to read that it is "not possible historically to understand the origins of [the] early Christian tradition by beginning with the *preaching* of the primitive Church."[8] Even more astonishing, however, is his follow-up statement: "Nor is it possible to begin with Jesus."[9] And there is, finally, the assertion that Jesus sayings "have been used for many different purposes" and appear "in different contexts" so that it is "often extremely difficult to decide the 'original' meaning of a saying of Jesus which has become separated from its situation."[10] One needs to compare this with form criticism's basic objective as programmatically formulated by Rudolf Bultmann:

> The aim of form-criticism is to determine the original form of a piece of narrative, a dominical saying or a parable. In the process we learn to distinguish secondary additions and forms, and these in turn lead to important results for the history of the tradition.[11]

It bears remembering that form criticism's primary objective is "the original form" (*die ursprüngliche Form*), which is claimed to be accessible through a process of elimination of secondary features. By contrast, current orality-scribality studies have emphatically parted with the concept of "the original form." In oral performance, the argument goes, each rendering represents a freshly communicated speech event.[12] Gerhardsson's skepticism concerning the retrievability of the "original" meaning, although not consciously arising from orality studies and not systematically developed, nonetheless reflects appropriate insights into the variable employment of Jesus sayings in the tradition. Not only are his sayings and stories inescapably "'remembered', repeated, expounded and applied"[13] in different historical settings, but his message was from the start bound up with what Gerhardsson calls the "Torah tradition,"[14] broadly understood as Judaism's oral and scribal legacy. On this specific issue of "the original form" and "the original meaning," then, two rather different models of thought are apparent. There is, on the one hand, the form-critical search for the narrow and pure base from which to trace secondary developments of the tradition and on the other hand Gerhardsson's situational concept, which is far less concerned with "the original form" or meaning of a saying, emphasizing instead a saying's interfacing with an already existing tradition.

There is, secondly, Gerhardsson's firm grasp of the oral property and forces of tradition. I have expressed my appreciation for Gerhardsson's exquisitely sensitive study of the oral dynamics and mechanisms that empowered the tradition.[15] Whether his explorations pertained to the auditory function of much of ancient literature, the concept of language as sound, the oral principle of arranging materials by association, the practice of recitation, repetition, and memorization, the significance of imitation in the relation between teacher and pupil—these and other aspects have all contributed to a communications model that is largely in keeping with what today we know about the verbal arts in the ancient world. As far as oral sensibilities are concerned, Gerhardsson has taken the early Jesus tradition out of the scholarly web of intertextuality by developing features that form criticism should have displayed but unaccountably failed to do so. In short, on the matter of the oral property and forces of the tradition, form criticism could have greatly benefited from his work.

Gerhardsson has thirdly advanced an explanatory model that was suited to demonstrate the historical concreteness of the traditioning processes and the actual techniques that were operative in the transmission and reception of the tradition. This is once again an area where form criticism appeared to be rather reticent, exhibiting little curiosity about the physical nature of manuscripts, copying processes, learning mechanisms, reading and recitation, and next to no interest in memory. Minimal interest in the material and technical aspects, Gerhardsson rightly observed, was a contributing factor to form criticism's lack of historical specificity as far as its concept of tradition was concerned. In placing emphasis on what he called the "material tradition"[16] and what today is known as the materiality of communication, he has fostered sensibilities that have long been a central topic in Scandinavian biblical scholarship and that stand at the center of current media and communications studies.

Fourthly, Gerhardsson articulated a concept of tradition that was "both oral and written," taking account of the fact that "for several decades the tradition concerning Christ appears to have been carried orally" while at the same time a beginning was made "within the Church to write down parts of the tradition."[17] Even more to the point, what was distinctive about the relation of oral versus written words was that the latter "were hardly more than an aid to oral presentation, declamations."[18] What was written down, in other words, functioned less as self-standing, silent text than as "a vocal word."[19] This applies to the copying process as well: "Even the copyists used to read vocally when they copied."[20] And scripted words were vocal not only in the sense of being subject to recitation, but in the sense as well of standing in need of oral support and explication. What typifies tradition, therefore, appears to be essentially a rather complex interplay of oral and written communication.[21] In sum, Gerhardsson projected the mechanisms of the tradition in ways that have next to nothing in common with the still pervasive form-critical notion of a linear, indeed evolutionary, progression of smaller units into larger entities. Nor are the Gospel authors, as form criticism suggested, correctly identified as mere collectors or editors. Mark, Gerhardsson states, "certainly was a pioneer."[22] Even though he qualifies his statement by adding in italicized font that *"his [Mark's] achievement was hardly very creative*,"²³ a distinction, however nuanced, from Bultmann's view is evident. The latter would not call Mark "a pioneer," because in his view the Gospel arose largely out of developmental drives immanent in the tradition. Last but not least, Gerhardsson posited that up to the middle of the second century the Gospels "function to all appearances mainly orally,"²⁴ a view, daring no doubt at the time of writing his magnum opus, that is, however, widely shared today by performance criticism. In sum, it needs to be acknowledged that on a number of rather substantive points Gerhardsson's model of the origin and mechanisms of the early Jesus tradition serves not merely as a corrective to the form-critical paradigm, but as a superior alternative to it.

The Synoptic Jesus Tradition

As current scholarship extricates itself from form-critical premises and seeks to develop a more adequate grasp of the ways speech operates and generates meaning, it presents new and formidable challenges to our manner of conceptualizing the so-called synoptic tradition. There is, for example, the issue of oral-scribal dynamics in the tradition. Martin Jaffee[25] and David Carr,[26] among others, have recently made a powerful case for the oral-scribal model of tradition prevalent in the ancient Near Eastern, Mediterranean, Judaic, and Hellenistic world of communications. In *Torah of the Mouth* Jaffee sketched a wide-ranging scenario of what he called the oral-performative tradition of Second Temple and early Jewish scribal culture. His interactive model is predicated on the notion of relatively open borders between scribal products and performative activities. Jaffee delineated an ancient Jewish and rabbinic cultural context where "oral communication was the primary medium of textual knowledge,"[27] and "the characteristic organs of literary life were the mouth and the ears and its main textual reservoir was the memory."[28] Understandably, most texts drew upon habits of speech and rhetoric. But not only were scripts shaped by oral, rhetorical features to secure their public delivery and audition, but oral renditions of scripts in turn impacted their rewriting. "Scribal orality,"[29] as Jaffee designated this phenomenon, therefore entailed not merely oral-scribal interdependence but mutual media reabsorptions. We will have occasion to revisit Jaffee's model in connection with the discussion of Gerhardsson's contribution to rabbinic scholarship. But the paradigm of media interactivity suggests that, on the whole, notions of pure orality versus pure scribality fail to capture the communications dynamics of Second Temple and early Jewish history.

In his exceedingly ambitious *Writing on the Tablet of the Heart* Carr discussed ways in which ancient Near Eastern and Mediterranean cultures produced and lived with texts and, more specifically, the manner in which writing and literature functioned orally, scribally, and memorially in ancient communication contexts. Writing and literacy, he suggested, have to be understood as core constituents of the educational project. From Mesopotamia to Egypt and from Israel to Greece and into the Hellenistic period, scribalism and education were closely interconnected phenomena. Central to what Carr has designated as the "enculturation transmission process"[30] was the internalization of texts on people's hearts and minds, and scribes were the principal agents in that cultural, educational enterprise. But the role of scribes, Carr explained, is insufficiently described in terms merely of writing and copying. Many were proficient in oral, scribal, and memorial skills, embodying the multimedia culture in their professional activities. No doubt, scribes were engaged in consulting, comparing, and copying scrolls. But the notion of scribes juggling multiple written sources that were physically present to them is for the most part not a fitting model for media dynamics in the ancient world. Rather, scribes who were very often literate in the cultural core curriculum carried the texts as mental templates, repeating or recasting them in the process of writing. Having mentally ingested the tradition that could have consisted of one or more than one text, they were able to carry the tradition forward without any need for textual sources. Rewriting texts that had been ingested memorially was a hallmark of enculturation process. According to Carr's enculturational model, scribal, oral, and memorial forces are intertwined. "The writing metaphor is used to conceptualize a process that is also oral, all of which is focused on the sort of word-for-word internalization of a text that is characteristic of oral written, rather than strictly oral, cultures."[31] Carr has opened before our eyes a grand vision of ancient texts, scribes, and a profoundly memorial, performative culture—a world vastly different from ours and, we must admit, from much of modern biblical scholarship and its treatment of texts.

Gerhardsson has repeatedly expressed skepticism with regard to comparative models that are historically distanced and presumably different from what we find in the first century C.E. We must respect the fact, he writes, that Jesus and his earliest followers "were active as Jews in Hellenistic times in Palestine."[32] Concerned about historically inappropriate analogies, he has specifically questioned the suitability of Albert Lord's Serbo-Croatian materials for understanding the early Jesus tradition:

> It is not clear to me, for instance, why we should elevate the type which A. B. Lord investigated in Yugoslavia to the status of standard model for "orality," "oral tradition," "oral composition," "oral literature," or the like, when after all the world is full of alternatives.[33]

On one level, Gerhardsson's statement points to multiple manifestations of orality, an observation with which one is bound to agree. That orality is a plural phenomenon is a feature John Foley has recently emphasized in his remarkable book *How to Read an Oral Poem*:

> Variation in oral poetry is not an inconvenience or a symptom of imperfect composition or transmission, nor is it something to be avoided whenever possible. It is the necessary condition of oral poetry, the very heart of the matter.[34]

What holds true of oral poetry applies *pari passu* to the phenomenon of orality. Globally, we have to reckon with a myriad of oral genres, cultural contexts, and ethnic groups. Moreover, similar or identical genres can serve different needs. The form-critical premise regarding a single correspondence between speech forms and social context remains puzzling; it is not a theorem known in current orality-scribality studies. Moreover, people bring different experiences, varying attitudes, and unequal skills to given performances and receptions. "Oral-poetry *is a very plural noun*,"[35] and so is orality generally. Given orality's plural manifestation, what justifies my selection of Lord's Yugoslavian fieldwork for an illumination of the Jesus tradition? As a matter of clarification, I did not "elevate" Lord's work "to the status of standard model for 'orality,'"[36] but I selected one concept that I thought was pertinent to oral performance virtually anywhere: plural originality in the place of the conventional single originality. When Lord observed that "each performance is 'an' original, if not 'the' original,"[37] he was in effect making the case for a plurality of originals. I was (and still am) of the opinion that he discovered a principle that is as relevant to the Serbo-Croatian tradition as it was to the early Jesus tradition. While conscious of the haste by which we tend to universalize what lies before us, I still hold the view that Lord's insight has near-global applicability in dominantly oral cultures.

On a broader level, Gerhardsson's statement raises the issue of the historical appropriateness and limits of comparative thinking, a topic that warrants a far more extensive treatment than can be accorded here. On this, the reader is referred to Terence Mournet's excursus, "The Value of Comparative Methodology," in his contribution to this volume. However, a general rationale for a comparative outreach, I trust, should be readily acknowledged. As an academic discipline, biblical scholarship is laden with centuries of received manners and mannerisms. Not infrequently it has operated in a state of culturally conditioned and/or institutionally enforced isolation. More to the point, many of its historical methods and assumptions about the functioning of biblical texts originated in perennial working relations with print versions—typographic constructs of modernity. Plainly, New Testament (and biblical) studies stand in need of a rethinking of the communications environment in which the early Jesus tradition participated. When, therefore, we strive to enlarge our view of the ancient art of verbalization, we are not merely searching for direct correspondences with and apt historical analogues to the early Jesus tradition. A broadening of the frame of reference and the map of communications can sharpen our sense of optics and allow us to perceive our data in ways not viewed or heard before. Jaffee's scribal orality model and Carr's enculturation model, for example, have projected an ancient communications landscape within which the early Jesus tradition can be expected to have functioned—unless one views the latter as a phenomenon *sui generis*, which is an imprudent historical proposition. Partially overlapping and partially different as Jaffee's and Carr's models are in terms of historical scope and cultural specificities, they both give us a clear sense of media interactivity that was essential to the verbal arts in ancient Near Eastern, Second Temple, and early Judaism. In view of the narrowly confined angle conventionally pursued in biblical scholarship, it may well be beneficial to let a more broadly conceived compass of orientation appear the subject matter in a new configuration.

As far as the synoptic tradition is concerned, the search is on for a conceptual paradigm that can take the place formerly held by form criticism. Mournet has contrasted Gerhardsson's "rabbinic model"—which I prefer to call "didactic model"[38]—with the current "orality model,"[39] paying particular attention to recent studies by Kenneth Bailey[40] and James Dunn.[41] The comparison, while narrow in scope, has the advantage of illuminating principal issues current scholarship is facing. A recapitulation of the representational features of the didactic versus the orality model will let us see what is at stake in our choice of the available conceptual options.

To begin with Gerhardsson's didactic model, it distances itself from form criticism by stipulating that individuals are indispensable carriers of the tradition. In the initial stage, Jesus himself was the principal authority and the Twelve the leading traditionists in the chain of transmission. The apostles were initiated into the role of carriers of the tradition by observing Jesus' mode of living and by listening to, repeating, and memorizing his words. In adopting the principle of imitation, they practiced a lifestyle that had been appropriated by other followers of Jewish and Hellenistic teachers. There is a high degree of historical plausibility that the apostles "presented their preaching and teaching in the form of an eyewitness account."[42] As far as Jesus' speech was concerned, it was comprised of aphoristic and narrative meshalim that were conspicuous by "*their laconicism and brevity.*"[43] Lacking the kind of verbosity that "is characteristic of much popular narration,"[44] his diction suggests that it originated and was carried forward in deliberate and programmatic teaching situations. In different words, we must think of transmission as a "conscious, technical act of instruction."[45] Memory in the form of mechanical memorization was central to Jesus' mode of teaching and that of his followers. Transmission was transacted for the sake of preservation so that what was being preserved was marked by relatively stable verbal properties. One is, moreover, dealing with an "institutional" and "intraecclesiastical"[46] tradition that proceeded from and was largely controlled by "the leading *collegium* in the Jerusalem church."[47] There was "an obvious unity, constancy, and continuity in the Jesus tradition."[48] Changes undoubtedly did take place in the course of transmission, but they were more in the nature of "*interpretive adaptations.*"[49] Communal needs colored the tradition but did not create it. As far as the Gospels are concerned, they can generally be understood as the written editions of Jesus' teachings and of eyewitness reports that exist in organic unity with tradition. Last but not least, Gerhardsson interpreted the fact that the Jesus tradition was permeated with words and motifs from the Hebrew Bible in the sense that "Jesus and his disciples did not live within an oral society."[50] Centuries of intense relations with sacred texts had left a deep imprint on Jewish life and culture.

What characterizes the orality model is a focused reflection on the performance[51] circumstances that are assumed to have characterized the early Jesus tradition. Performance as well as memory is central to the oral concept of tradition. As far as Jesus' speech was concerned, the orality model, just like the didactic model, is exquisitely conscious of the degree to which his sayings and stories have kept faith with a rhetorically patterned diction. Entirely in keeping with current mnemonic requisites and sensibilities, Jesus' formalized verbalization served the dictates of oral needs and conventions, and may thus not necessarily be evidence of an institutional, didactic transmission. Clearly designed as an aid to memory, his language facilitated mental retention and commemorative processes, but not necessarily mechanical memorization in the literal, verbatim sense. Orally delivered, each rendering of Jesus' words constituted a fresh and authentic act of communication. Strictly speaking, therefore, there is no such thing as a singular *ipsissimum verbum* any more than there are variants, since there is no single original to be varied.[52] As long as Jesus' words were transacted orally—by himself or by others—they existed without exception in human, existential settings. Social contexts were integral to the delivery of his message and in fact codetermined its meaning. Jesus' spoken words, as all oral verbalizations, involved more than purely linguistic elements and can, therefore, never be fully abstracted as language. They were always more than just verbal phenomena.[53] This forces the conclusion that there cannot be such a thing as detachable, context-free speech. Performance was transacted not merely for purposes of preservation, but also very much for reasons of persuasion. What was being communicated, therefore, was not merely marked by mnemonic stability but subject to social adaptability as well. While the tradition was launched in a dominantly oral society, parts of it were early on transposed into writing (see, e.g., Q), thereby complexifying the tradition, causing multiple oral-scribal interfaces and mutual feedbacks. As Kirk has described it in his contribution to this volume, one is dealing with a tradition that is characterized by variability, while retaining stable, mnemonic markers as facilitators of remembering. Communication in the early period thrived in a social world where teachers and apostles sped up the process of verbal and geographical proliferation, and where prophets, authorized by the Spirit, prompted a rapid if irregular dissemination of the message. The Gospels, finally, rather than absorbing a single stream of eyewitness accounts, drew on diverse traditions, eyewitness accounts included, which they subjected to processes of rememorization.

These two notable models open up a range of options and queries and they make us aware of how much there is that has remained unsettled. Gerhardsson himself has no illusions about the numerous unresolved issues that still lie ahead of us. Far from considering the case closed, he has kept the discussion open by raising a series of stimulating questions.[54] In that spirit, I shall conclude this section on the synoptic tradition with questions that are addressed to both the didactic and the orality models and also extend beyond them.

If it is granted that individuals played a role as carriers of the tradition, do the Gospel narratives attest to collected materials in terms, for example, of a Petrine tradition? Can one invoke "the evidence of reliable eyewitnesses" without consideration of the cognitive implications of memory? In other words, should we not think of eyewitness reports as ultimately the work of memorial processes? How can we match the narrative causalities of the Gospels with the notion that these narratives are the result of and basically structured by apostolic preaching? In different words: can narrative critics and proponents of a strongly developed eyewitness theory ever find common ground? To what extent do Gerhardsson's concessions to changes in the Jesus tradition, to revisionist activities on the Gospel narrative level, and to textual variants,[55] as well as his acknowledgment that Luke "obviously provides a highly simplified, tendentious, and stylized picture of a complicated historical process,"[56] soften or undercut his model of a formalized, didactic teaching mechanism? How can we sort out oral from scribal components inscribed in the Gospel narratives? For example, are the densely constructed miracle and pronouncement stories the result of oral, memorial economizing or of a literary tightening of a living oral tradition? Have the advocates of the orality model come to terms with performance as a key feature of tradition or are they still captive to the notion of transmission as a process of handing down and passing on words from person to person? Has the orality model taken seriously the inseparability of memory from tradition and has it integrated "the wide range of memorializing activities practiced within viable communities"[57] into its mode of thinking? How do recent claims that Mark is a thoroughly oral text,[58] designed to facilitate recitation and memorization, square with the idea of a pre-Gospel, oral, oral-scribal tradition? In different words, does the view of Mark as oral composition still require the notion of Mark as product of a history of oral, oral-scribal tradition? (On this see also below Neusner's understanding of the oral form of the Mishnah and the issue of a pre-Mishnaic oral tradition.) Gerhardsson's basic question remains a valid one: "How do we imagine that Mark, Matthew, Luke, John—let me call them so—actually proceeded, when they produced their famous books?"[59]

In the end, one should not underestimate the degree to which prevalent needs and one's cultural horizon can exercise influence on nearly every aspect of historical inquiry, including the preference for one model over the other. Does the model of relative stability aspire to escape from the corrosive effects of time, seeking quasi-religious transcendence beyond the reach of temporality? Or, is the model of relative adaptability conceived under the impact of modernity's fast-paced communications world and its predilection for change?

THE JESUS TRADITION IN PAUL

The issue of Paul and orality entails two different, but not entirely unrelated, features. One part comprises the broad area of the oral composition and delivery of the apostle's letters, the rhetorical style and diction of his message, the oral mediation of his teaching, and the appeal to oral authorities in the Pauline churches.[60] The other part relates to Paul's transmission or reactivation, as we shall see, of the Jesus tradition. The scholarship reviewed by David Aune in his contribution to this volume leans heavily in the direction toward the second issue. Since Gerhardsson's work on Paul is also centered on the Jesus tradition in the apostolic letters, my attention will in great measure be devoted to that issue.

Gerhardsson's paradigm suggests that Paul relied on a twofold source of revelation: the Jewish Scriptures and tradition. As far as the latter, the tradition (*paradosis/paradoseis*) in the Pauline letters consisted in "a body of authoritative material,"[61] the core of which was provided by "sayings of, and about, Christ."[62] Gerhardsson refers to it as "the gospel tradition."[63] It formed "a foundation and a focus"[64] for the apostle and it, rather than abstract principles, informed a good deal of his teaching. In Gerhardsson's view, Paul had received this "gospel tradition" from "the college of Apostles in Jerusalem,"[65] or, to be more precise, from Jesus via the college of the apostles. Among Gerhardsson's arguments for the apostolic Jerusalem origin of "the gospel tradition," two merit attention. One, in the case of Paul's fifteen-day visit with Peter in Jerusalem, Gerhardsson translates the rationale for the trip, ἱστορῆσαι Κηφᾶν, in the sense of "to get information from Kephas" (Gal 1:18).[66] Two, in the case of the confessional formulae referring to Christ's death and resurrection, classically defined as a tradition (1 Cor 15:3ff.), Gerhardsson proposes that each line functions as a succinct formula representing a passage in the gospel narrative: the passion story (which views events κατὰ τὰς γραφάς), the burial, the resurrection on the third day, the appearance of the risen Lord to Peter, the appearance to the Twelve and to the others in chronological order.[67] There is "good reason to suppose that he [Paul] derived this tradition . . . from the college of Apostles in Jerusalem."[68]

In the larger context of scholarship, Gerhardsson's Pauline thesis will have to be understood as an antithesis to an influential segment of the *religionsgeschichtliche Schule*,[69] which drove a wedge between Jesus and what it considered to be the Hellenistic Paul. Whether Gerhardsson was conscious of his position vis-à-vis the *religionsgeschichtliche Schule* (and its influence on Bultmann) or not, he clearly endeavored to (re)confirm continuity between Paul and Jesus, "the Apostle's doctrinal authority."[70] No doubt Gerhardsson is correct in affirming that the apostle has access to a tradition of Jesus' words and confessional formulae (1 Cor 11:23-26; 15:3-5). As for the historical starting point of these traditions, it has to be said that tracing the precise point of origin for oral traditions is fraught with difficulties and often impossible.

Since it is in Paul's epistolary literature that we encounter Jesus sayings for the first time in writing, the precise circumstances of their occurrence deserve close scrutiny. In 1 Thessalonians 4:15 the apostle cited a dominical saying (ἐν λόγῳ κυρίου) about the fate of the dead and the living in relation to the coming of the Lord. All other dominical sayings occur in 1 Corinthians. In that epistle, 7:10-11 communicates a command of the Lord (ὁ κύριος) on the issue of divorce, 9:14 conveys the Lord's instruction (οὕτως καὶ ὁ κύριος διέταξεν) on remuneration of apostles, and 11:23-26 submits a formulation of the Lord's Supper as a tradition received from the Lord (ἀπὸ τοῦ κυρίου). Moreover, in 1 Corinthians 7:25 Paul made the point that concerning the virgins he was not in possession of a dominical saying (ἐπιταγὴν τοῦ κυρίου οὐκ ἔχω).

As has often been observed, Paul consistently introduced the Jesus material, including his statement about the unavailability of a dominical saying, by appeal to the authority of the Lord (ὁ κύριος). It would seem to be a reasonable assumption to view the association of the Jesus tradition with the Lord as intentional. A key to understanding the significance of this use of κύριος lies in Paul's framing of the institution of the Lord's Supper (1 Cor 11:23-26). In this ritual tradition he drew a subtle distinction between "the Lord Jesus" (ὁ κύριος Ἰησοῦς) and "the Lord" (ὁ κύριος). The person who initiated the breaking of the bread and the drinking of the cup "in the night when he was betrayed" is identified as "the Lord Jesus." He is the earthly Jesus who presided over the last meal at the end of his life and maintains his presence as Lord in continuing eucharistic celebrations. In the ritual, therefore, he functions as "the Lord Jesus" who embodies his past and present authority. But as far as the tradition of the Last Supper is concerned, Paul has "received it from the Lord" (παρέλαβον ἀπὸ τοῦ κυρίου). This carefully drawn differentiation between Jesus and the Lord suggests that the Jesus tradition, far from being bound to the earthly Jesus, let alone the historical Jesus, is being legitimated by the Lord who continues to exercise his authority in the present. Or, more precisely, the tradition is sanctioned by Jesus only insofar as he has assumed the authority of the living Lord. Based on very similar observations, Jens Schröter has drawn significant consequences for an understanding of the operation of the Jesus tradition in Paul:

> When Paul, in these passages, always refers to the Lord (κύριος) but never speaks of the "word of Jesus," it shows that he understands the "words of the Lord" to be a teaching legitimated by the Risen and Exalted One that is made concrete in various situations through the apostles and prophets. His intention is thus not to hand on, word for word, what was spoken by the earthly Jesus but to connect to a tradition grounded in the authority of the Lord as the basis for Christian teaching.[71]

Schröter's understanding here is that the exclusive authority the κύριος has assumed over the Jesus sayings points in the direction not toward a "word for word" rendering, but toward what he calls "a free and living tradition."[72]

Gerhardsson is not, of course, unaware of the signal importance of the κύριος, and he is sensitive to the differentiated relation between Jesus and the Lord in Paul's letters. However, his evaluation of the evidence does not arrive at the concept of a living tradition. Once again we discern two separate models drawing rather different pictures for the nature and function of the Jesus tradition. When Gerhardsson stated that the "earthly Jesus, too, was Paul's Lord," he meant to say that "Paul did not consider that what the earthly Jesus had said and done had been cancelled out by the cross and resurrection."[73] The emphasis remains on the earthly Jesus so as to make sure that the correct transmission of his sayings is in no way eclipsed by the authority of the Lord. Schröter reads the evidence differently. "In instances," he writes, "involving words that originated with the earthly Jesus, Paul is interested in the fact they are Jesus' words only insofar as the earthly Jesus is also the one raised and exalted by God."[74] The emphasis here is on the present Lord so as to make sure that it is he, and not solely the earthly Jesus, who continues to legitimate the living tradition.

If we ask precisely how the living tradition worked, Paul's own dealing with the Jesus sayings offers a clue. In 1 Thessalonians 4:15 he explicated the word of the Lord about the dead and the living by following up with a detailed apocalyptic scenario about the Lord's coming (1 Thess

4:16-18). In 1 Corinthians 7:10-11, after citing a command on divorce, issued not by him but by the Lord (v. 10: οὐκ ἐγὼ ἀλλὰ ὁ κύριος), he added a rather differentiated amendment (1 Cor 7:12-16), issued not by the Lord but by him (v. 12: λέγω ἐγώ, οὐκ ὁ κύριος), explicating the command in the case of marital relations between believers and unbelievers. In 1 Corinthians 9:14 Paul expounded a command of the Lord that pertained to apostolic remuneration only to dissociate himself as far as his own apostolic lifestyle was concerned (1 Cor 9:15-18). Gerhardsson readily acknowledges the significance of Paul's decision on this matter: "Paul thus relinquished the right, bestowed by the Lord himself, 'to live off the gospel.'"[75] Instead of "relinquishing the right," could one perhaps suggest that Paul here overruled what he himself perceived to be a command of the Lord (1 Cor 9:14: ὁ κύριος διέταξεν)? Moreover, the apostle did not seem to have a problem offering in one and the same epistle a version of the Lord's Supper (1 Cor 10:16) that is at variance with the very one he had received from the Lord (1 Cor 11:23-25). This is nothing short of astonishing since it is fair to assume that ritualized verbalization generally inclined toward greater fixity. It seems that in the few cases where Paul introduced Jesus materials, he explicated and amended sayings, set his authority apart from that of the Lord, and in fact overruled a command of the Lord. Do we not have evidence here of Paul operating in the spirit and context of a living tradition? Again, Gerhardsson fully recognized that Paul's employment of both the Jewish Scripture and the Jesus tradition "take[s] account of both solid and fluid elements," and he had no doubt that "we must reckon with material having a more powerfully accentuated normative standing, and material giving less emphatic authority (according to Paul himself)."[76] That Gerhardsson is prepared to deal with both fixity and fluidity in the tradition is duly noted by Aune. Yet in the end Gerhardsson's summary assessment is that "Paul subjects himself to the tradition from the Lord, and regards what Jesus bound as being bound indeed."[77] But does the evidence encourage this very conclusion? Could one not interpret the evidence in the sense that Paul remembered Jesus' sayings and traditions not for their own sakes but for the purpose of reactivating them in current situations? It would seem that in his case the Jesus tradition was not canonically fixed. Far from being canonical, it appears to have operated as a living tradition.

The operation of the Jesus tradition aside, there remains the "perennial issue" (Aune) of the paucity of sayings in Paul's epistolary literature. Why is it that he did not seem to have felt a greater urgency to resort to Jesus material so as to ground his message in what Gerhardsson has termed "the Apostle's doctrinal authority"? As Aune has explained the case, two closely interrelated features are frequently invoked to solve the problem. One is the widely held thesis that Paul could assume prior knowledge of the words of Jesus among his addressees. Gerhardsson himself subscribed to the thesis: "[Paul] always expressly assumes in his epistles that the basic authoritative tradition has already been passed *on at an earlier stage* himself, when the congregations in question were founded."[78] And secondly, this argument from silence is sometimes buttressed with reference to the numerous allusions to Jesus sayings in Paul. Aune correctly observed: "The view that Paul alludes to Jesus traditions almost unconsciously is one of the major solutions to the problem of the apparent neglect of Jesus traditions in Paul." These allusions, I suggest, deserve careful scrutiny, less for what they reveal about Paul's knowledge of Jesus sayings, but more for the valuable insight they offer us, once again, into the workings of the tradition. The more obvious allusions and their matching sayings in the synoptic traditions are as follows:

- The saying on mountain-moving faith (1 Cor 13:2) appears in Mark 11:22-23 and Matthew 17:20.
- The call to be at peace (1 Thess 5:13) is used in Mark 9:50 and Matthew 5:9.
- The blessing of the persecutors (Rom 12:14) has an analogy in Matthew 5:44.
- The statement regarding uncleanness (Rom 14:14) is similar to Matthew 15:11.
- The council regarding the sudden coming to the Lord (1 Thess 5:2, 4) is echoed in Matthew 24:43.
- The saying about kindness to the enemies (Rom 12:20), a citation from Proverbs 25:21, figures in Matthew 5:44 and Luke 6:27, 35 as the commandment to love one's enemies.

What merits attention is that none of the Pauline allusions is identified as a Jesus saying. Their analogy to Jesus sayings is obvious to us only because we can identify them in the Gospels. But as far as we know, narrative Gospels were not available to Paul and his communities. While Paul undeniably had access to Jesus traditions, it is far from certain whether he was alluding consciously to Jesus sayings and/or whether the hearers of his letters were able to recognize the voice of Jesus in these allusions. Or, to be more precise, we cannot be sure that in the Pauline communities this material was meant to be and in fact recognized as (allusions to) Jesus sayings. What we can say with certainty is that a number of topics that in the synoptic tradition came to be identified as Jesus sayings already existed in the Pauline sphere, although not as Jesus sayings. Once we formulate the evidence in this manner, it does not, however, contribute to the issue of the paucity of Jesus sayings in Paul. Instead, what the evidence seems to suggest is the implementation of a living tradition. Not only was the tradition of Jesus sayings subject to reactivation and revision, but the boundaries of the Jesus tradition were still pliable and as yet not unalterably fixed. Schröter, once again, has seen this very clearly:

> [T]here was a sphere of tradition made up of words of Jesus, early Christian teaching authorized by the Lord, *topoi* from Jewish-Hellenistic ethics, and citations from scripture. Within this sphere . . . the distinction between "genuine" words of Jesus and other traditions played no part at all.[79]

We must not, therefore, operate with too firmly established a concept of the early Jesus tradition to the extent that we think of it as a fully formed entity. In the Pauline purview at least, the scope and identity of the tradition was as yet not fully determined and in a sense still in the making.[80] This could suggest that the so-called allusions in Paul contribute next to nothing to the problem of the scarcity of Jesus saying in Paul because they appear to be allusions only in hindsight.

In turn this forces attention more than ever to the well-known preponderant occurrence of Jesus sayings in 1 Corinthians. To James M. Robinson goes the honor of having first developed the thesis of an existent tradition of Jesus sayings in the Corinthian community among those who challenged the Pauline version of the gospel.[81] The thesis was confirmed by Helmut Koester[82] and substantially elaborated by Heinz-Wolfgang Kuhn.[83] One need not agree with Robinson's crosscultural trajectory of a *Gattung* of wisdom sayings ranging from Second Temple Judaism to Hellenistic Gnosticism, but the emergence of *sophia* and Paul's challenge to it in 1 Corinthians is certainly noteworthy. Could it be that Paul's polemically articulated reconceptualization of wisdom via a theology of the cross, his extension of resurrection hope toward the dead and the living, to cite only two distinct features of the epistle, were directed toward those who employed Jesus sayings in proclaiming wisdom made perfect in the present arrival of the kingdom and the realization of personal resurrection? This would also explain Paul's peculiarly defensive posture that in certain cases he was not in possession of a saying of the Lord (1 Cor 7:12, 25). If in fact knowledge of Jesus sayings had been communicated to the Corinthian community without the mediation of Paul, we will have to imagine a model of greater diversification for the operation of the Jesus tradition. In that case, there was not simply a sayings trajectory from Jesus through the apostles to Paul, but diverse channels of communication. Nor was there simply an assured process of the transmission of Jesus sayings, but the latter may have been implicated in the inevitable conflict of interpretation.

The Rabbinic Tradition

One of Gerhardsson's abiding achievements remains his detailed attention he has paid to rabbinic Judaism in conjunction with his work on the early Jesus tradition. His rabbinic scholarship merits commendation both for its high academic quality and for its comparative breadth. The dating question aside, the comparison of rabbinic processes of transmission with those of the early Jesus tradition was as relevant a project fifty years ago as it is today. Indeed, it was one of the unfortunate byproducts of the receptionist history of *Memory and Manuscript* that form criticism chose to pay very little, if any, attention to the rabbinic tradition. Challenging Gerhardsson on the dating of the rabbinic tradition, form criticism felt reassured to disregard rabbinics in its conceptualization of the early Jesus tradition. As a result, the discipline tended to develop a culturally rather isolated model of the tradition. Often overlooked by Gerhardsson's critics is the fact that his work on the role of oral learning and memorial techniques in the formation and transmission of rabbinic tradition has by and large received a favorable reception in rabbinic scholarship. Jaffee, for example, has expressed his deep appreciation for Gerhardsson's pioneering work in rabbinics. As will be shown below, recent scholarship in rabbinics, including Jaffee's own innovative contribution, has illuminated dynamics and mechanisms in the rabbinic tradition that ought to engage the close attention of New Testament scholars. Whatever the specific interpretations of both the early Jesus and the rabbinic tradition, it needs to be acknowledged that in principle Gerhardsson's academic engagement of rabbinics merits applause rather than criticism.

The most significant value of Gerhardsson's study of rabbinic Judaism in the Tannaitic and Amoraic periods has to be seen in his erudite and sensitive elaboration of the oral, scribal, memorial operations of the tradition. The first part of *Memory and Manuscript* treats the Written and the Oral Torah in the broadest sense, encompassing both Scripture and what was carried forward orally on the Mishnaic and talmudic levels. The so-called Oral Torah, initially advocated by the Pharisees,[84] was "formulated in quite a fixed way,"[85] aspiring to the virtues of verbal brevity and conciseness. Though predominantly verbalized in compliance with oral principles, the Oral Torah operated in close affiliation with Scripture interpretation and was in the beginning processed midrashically, in interaction with the Written Torah, until at a later period it developed independently. Because the rabbinic material was both orally fixed and subject to interpretation, both scripturally related and recited memorially, it must by and large "be classified as oral text material."[86] In principle, therefore, it can be reasonably affirmed that Gerhardsson envisioned rabbinic Judaism in its Mishnaic and talmudic manifestation not as a purely literary phenomenon any more than as a purely oral performance culture, but as literature empowered both by oral and textual dynamics. In whatever form the oral-textual dynamics are specifically conceptualized, the premise of oral-textual interfacing enjoys the full support of current orality-literacy studies and large parts of rabbinic scholarship.

Gerhardsson's model has not always been appreciated, let alone recognized, for the claims it has and has not made. It is often asserted that he solely advocated the preservative instincts of the tradition. Yet while preservation for him is a key feature of transmission, it does by no means, in his thinking, define the tradition on all counts. In their entirety, Gerhardsson suggested, the traditional texts of the Oral Torah were characterized both by conservation of the authentic wording and by a general mobility of the tradition. On the one hand, the oral texts were recited again and again by skilled professional traditionists, repeated by their pupils, and corrected once more by teachers until the wording was learned by heart. In these processes, the chief concern was the faithful and flawless preservation of the "*condensed memory-texts.*"[87] On the other hand, repeated and memorized as the rabbinic traditions were, they were also accompanied by expository processes, whereby "continual interpretation gives rise to newly concentrated text material."[88] In this fashion, the sacred texts, while fixed and memorized, were also subject to augmentation by interpretation and growth until the body of collections was systematized and given final form in the Mishnah—that body of traditions which the Tannaim came to know by heart. While envisioning processes of growth, Gerhardsson did not force tradition into a linear, let alone evolutionary, pattern. For him tradition consistently remained contextualized in situations of recitation and memorization. Basically, he advocated an educational, not an evolutionary, theory. Thus, far from defining the tradition wholly in terms of strictly verbatim retention and transmission, Gerhardsson's model is empowered by repetition and interpretation, memorization and augmentation. In whatever form stability and flexibility are nuanced and specifically conceptualized, the premise of both preservative and dynamic trends in the tradition is well established in his work.

Among the models of tradition that have been advanced since *Memory and Manuscript,* Neusner's documentary hypothesis ranks at the top in terms of sheer volume and magnitude of detailed analyses.[89] His thesis proceeds from the premise that each of the principal books of rabbinic Judaism—Mishnah, Tosefta, and the Talmudim Yerushalmi and Bavli—is characterized by an inner integrity that gives voice to coherent points of view. Hence, every single rabbinic document has to be studied as an entity unto itself "essentially out of all relationship to the other documents of the larger canon of authoritative and holy books of Judaism."[90] When thus examined on its own terms, the Mishnah consistently exhibits stylized formulations, fixed and identifiable commonplace patterns both in its smallest component parts and in its intermediate divisions that are largely made up of conglomerates of the individual units. Additionally, the Mishnah displays literary and ideational traits that evidence redactional activities, shaping the mass of separate materials into a logical and syllogistic whole.

The kind of mnemonic characteristics that are observable with regard to the Mishnah—and not the Tosefta and the Talmudim—confirm that "Mishnah is Oral Torah,"[91] a designation that requires careful explication. To begin with, it signifies that the Mishnah undoubtedly carries materials, even ancient traditions, from earlier generations, that exhibit precise and striking mnemonic patterning. Clearly, that material and the Mishnah in its final form were designed to facilitate oral transmission, recitation, and memorization. But the claim that the Mishnah is a profoundly oral document does not (necessarily) force the conclusion that it is the product of an (identifiable) history of oral tradition. Here Neusner proposes that the oral composition, or reshaping, of the Mishnaic materials presents itself as an integral whole that has been accomplished in writing by the authors of the final version: "the bulk of the [Mishnaic] document has been formulated all at once, and not in an incremental, linear process extending into the remote past."[92] In the context of questioning a pre-Mishnaic oral tradition, Neusner also challenged the widely assumed thesis concerning the Pharisees as possessors and curators of oral traditions apart from Scripture. When guided by

Josephus and the Gospels, he suggested, one should not have assumed Pharisaic cultivation of an expressly oral tradition.[93] In the absence of a demonstrable oral tradition, therefore, the Mishnah itself is Oral Torah as far as its composition is concerned, but it cannot, in its final form, be understood as (the product of) oral tradition.

In the course of problematizing the notion of an oral, pre-Mishnaic tradition, Neusner also expressed disapproval of Gerhardsson's concept of tradition. The latter, he explained, has made "the most extreme claim" about "originally orally composed and orally transmitted materials" of the rabbinic tradition.[94] But in view of our analysis of Gerhardsson's model of tradition, it is an open question whether Neusner has grasped it in its entirety. What can be affirmed with certitude is that Neusner's model is more heavily weighted toward a literary analysis, and Gerhardsson's more toward oral performance culture.

A rather different approach to rabbinic literature has been proposed by Peter Schäfer. If Gerhardsson advocated an oral, pedagogical model, and Neusner a literary, synchronic one, it was Schäfer's insight that textual criticism, albeit a critically revised form of it, provided a key to appreciating the nature and dynamics of the rabbinic tradition. Intensive studies of the Hekhalot[95] literature took him to the center of questions that, while by no means unacknowledged in rabbinic scholarship, had, in his view, not been given adequate consideration. Recognition of the enormous fluctuation and complexities of the status of Hekhalot manuscripts convinced Schäfer that one was dealing with a genre of literature that "proves to be astonishingly unstable."[96] Hence his reasoning that the convention of operating on the basis of a critical edition, the so-called *textus receptus* accompanied by an apparatus of variants, was incommensurate with the manuscript evidence that had been reassembled over lengthy periods of time in ever new literary configurations. Among the principal conclusions Schäfer has drawn with regard to the Hekhalot tradition, the following two seem to be of special significance:

> Divergent settings of a tradition are therefore not to be reduced to assumed "original" forms but have to be respected as autonomous stages of the development . . . Any edition of texts of Hekhalot literature has to take into consideration that the *one* text is an illusion.[97]

In different words, if the Hekhalot manuscripts reached the stage of standardization "very late or not at all,"[98] then the text-critically sanctioned procedure of building interpretation solely on the so-called *textus receptus* was running the risk of overlooking, suppressing even, the realities of the tradition as manifested by the manuscript evidence.

Textual criticism perceived in this fashion, Schäfer proposed, is applicable to rabbinic literature as a whole.[99] As long as one treats Mishnah, Tosefta, Midrashim, and the Talmudim Yerushalmi and Bavli as stable entities, one has failed to take account of the bulk of manuscript traditions that has sustained rabbinic life and piety over the centuries. Instead of placing the major rabbinic works in a closed frame of reference one ought to reach behind the final redactions and familiarize oneself with the "open text-continuum"[100] of rabbinic literature. This, however, will require that text criticism "must rid itself of the odium of the whimsical scholar constantly in quest of the 'better' reading and finally buried under his collection of variants."[101] For what should truly matter in text criticism is not the identification and marginalization of variants of the assumed static text, but rather "the documentation and description of a dynamic manuscript tradition."[102] It, and it alone, can be the presupposition for a historically more realistic assessment of the nature of the rabbinic tradition. One senses in the work of Schäfer the makings of a profoundly mobile paradigm of rabbinic literature, one that is in tension with the synchronic model, yet deeply sensitive to the actual life of the tradition.[103]

While Schäfer has set his gaze on textual traditions that lie behind the final redaction, Steven Fraade looks forward to the text's receptionist implications and to students' engagement in interpretation. His principal book, *From Tradition to Commentary*,[104] conducted an inquiry into the oldest extant, midrashic commentary on Deuteronomy. Three features characterize the directions into which he is taking rabbinic scholarship: a hermeneutical appreciation of the "formal and substantive heterogeneity"[105] of the commentary tradition, an explication of the commentary as a "performative medium,"[106] and the commentary's function as "transformative work."[107] On the first point, Fraade has raised the heterogeneous and sometimes discordant copiousness of midrashic meanings and perspectives to a level of heightened hermeneutical consciousness. Discursive and fragmentary as the interpretations are, they are woven "on the loom of Scripture itself,"[108] so that the fixed text of Deuteronomy still can be assumed "to have been a commonly held cultural possession."[109] As "performative medium" the commentary aspired not simply to transmit correct information, but to engage the students in the unfinished process of interpretation. Poring over and absorbing the multiple midrashic versions, the Torah students were engaged "in the reconstructive and redemptive work of its interpretation,"[110] advancing though never fully completing it. And thirdly, the internalization and actualization of the midrashic network of interpretations was understood to generate transformative effects upon the rabbinic sages and their students. "In a sense, as they work through the commentary the commentary works through them."[111] Fraade has moved rabbinics a long way toward the recognition of an oral, performative aesthetics. Certainly, Oral Torah and oral tradition, recitation and repetition, have long been central issues in rabbinic scholarship. But it is Fraade's achievement to have skillfully integrated the resources of current hermeneutical, literary, and communicative theory into a compelling thesis about the *Sifre*: this commentary, and the rabbinic commentary tradition in general, operates dialogically and interactively as an "oral circulatory system of study and teaching"[112] and in "the multivocality of a received yet restless tradition."[113] Historical criticism's elevation of the text as a cultural icon with a fixed, uniform, and autosemantic integrity is thereby severely challenged.

Ten years after Fraade's *From Tradition to Commentary* and forty years after Gerhardsson's *Memory and Manuscript*, Jaffee's *Torah in the Mouth* succeeded in conceptualizing a coherent and comprehensive theory of the oral, performative nature of Jewish scribalism in late antiquity. Ranging widely from the last centuries of the Second Temple period to the compilations of Mishnah and Tosefta, and amply benefiting from current orality-scribality studies, Jaffee set before us a "model of interpenetration or interdependence of oral and written textual formations."[114] Briefly, the model suggests that texts "enjoyed an essentially oral cultural life"[115] by being continuously re-oralized, while the recitation in turn derived from and was shaped by scribal skills. It is difficult, therefore, "to posit a rabbinic tradition of 'pure' orally transmitted discourse prior to the Mishnah,"[116] and more reasonable to think of "the continuous loop of manuscript and performance [which] had no 'ground zero' at which we can isolate . . . an oral text or tradition as fundamental."[117] Like Neusner, Jaffee disavowed any specifically Pharisaic claim on the Oral Torah. The most one can say is that the Pharisees, like most other Jewish communities in the Second Temple period, participated in the prevalent oral-performative transaction of texts. Negatively, Jaffee's model of oral-scribal penetration stated that pure, oral tradition, unaffected by scribality, is as much in doubt as direct intertextuality devoid of oral-performative mediation. Positively, the model highlighted the oral dimension of scribal literacy, the interpretive intervention of scribes and reciters alike, and the genuine open-endedness of tradition.

In his contribution to this volume Jaffee undertakes a re-oralization of the rabbinic text about Honi the Circler, sampled from the Bavli. In keeping with his model of an oral-scribal interfacing, Jaffee postulates a history of reperforming and rewriting the text whereby earlier renditions are not (necessarily) being sloughed off. For this reason, the text can be viewed, or rather listened to, as a depository of literary stages, or rather performance phases, identifiable as strata, or rather voices, representative of the work of Tannaitic memorizers, Amoraic expounders, and Stammaitic editors. In this way, Jaffee seeks to let us hear the voices which the text has neutralized while it has simultaneously secured the condition for their recovery. His is a highly innovative approach. Unlike form criticism that sought to isolate assumed oral units and different from Neusner's synchronic analysis of separate text units, Jaffee attempts to retrieve the diachronic performance history in and from the final text.

When recent rabbinic scholarship is thus aligned and surveyed in this manner, Gerhardsson's accomplishment shows up rather well. No doubt, since the writing and publications of his masterful *Memory and Manuscript*, knowledge in Second Temple scribalism and in the oral-scribal literature and dynamics of Mishnah, Tosefta, and the Talmudim has been advanced in ways that extend, correct, and at times supplant his model. Inevitably, his work has been winnowed by ongoing rabbinic scholarship and outpaced by time itself. What is, however, remarkable is the extent to which his fundamental premise of the oral, memorial dynamics as root condition of rabbinic Judaism has stood the test of time. Jaffee, in his contribution, agrees: "To Gerhardsson goes the lion's share of the credit for placing the oral-performative dimension of rabbinic literature at the center of the study of this literary corpus." This represents an appreciative understanding of Gerhardsson's achievement in rabbinics that has been all but absent in New Testament studies.

THE HELLENISTIC SCHOOL TRADITION

While Gerhardsson's work is closely allied with rabbinic scholarship, his intellectual curiosity reached far beyond rabbinics and the early Jesus tradition. Throughout his incisive and wide-ranging examination of rabbinics, he adverted to relations between Jewish and Hellenistic school traditions, wondered about the role of reading, writing, recitation, and repetition in cultic and noncultic contexts among Jews, Greeks, and Romans, and posed questions about methods of teaching and transmission of knowledge in philosophical schools. On the important matter of memory, he specifically inquired to what extent Judaism had been influenced by

Hellenism and broadly concluded that memory's significance extended beyond Judaism across all of classical antiquity. He clearly recognized that the rabbinic techniques of memorization were to be located and understood in the broader context of ancient educational practices.[118]

In her contribution to this volume, Loveday Alexander has followed up Gerhardsson's hints to examine features of the philosophical and rhetorical school traditions in order to ascertain to what extent the Hellenistic cultural context can illuminate the rise of the gospel tradition. Her principal attention is focused on the genre of the *apomnemoneumata*, the biographical anecdotes which serve as vehicles for sayings deemed to be significant. These are, of course, materials well established in the Synoptic Gospels and in the *Gospel of Thomas* as well, a fact which heightens the comparative relevance of Alexander's explorations. In the area of the anecdotal genre, she is primarily concerned with the "phenomenology of memory and tradition," much in the sense as Gerhardsson had elaborated it in relation to the rabbinic and early Jesus traditions. In different words, hers is a study less of the ideational aspects of the *apomnemoneumata*, and more of their oral-rhetorical performance character.

Trained as most of us are in the hard and fast categories of form criticism, it may be difficult to appreciate the vast and varied repertoire of the anecdotal compositions and the degree of generic fluidity that, according to Alexander, can mutate into a wider range of generic formations and serve multiple purposes. Both the narrative settings and the maxims, as well as the combination of the two, are subject to a great deal of variation. For all practical purposes, the *apomnemoneumata* tradition is not appropriately categorized as a single genre. Like many rhetorical genres, the anecdotal tradition retains an inherent generic fluidity that renders it resistant to the strict definitions of the rhetors. From this perspective, the objective of rhetoric and the rhetorical handbooks appears to have been to tame the uncontrolled state of language, to impose definitional discipline upon speech and scribal activities, to standardize communication, and, in a word, to categorize orality. The question this raises for gospel scholarship is whether the form-critical categories (biographical apophthegms, scholastic dialogues, controversy dialogues, prophetic sayings, apocalyptic sayings, apocalyptic predictions, etc.), which have been subject to ever more subtle rhetorical refinements, have not overdetermined the synoptic information to the point where it threatens to extinguish the lifeblood of the tradition.

In view of the variegated nature of the anecdotal tradition, it is not surprising that it serves a wide spectrum of different purposes.

One obvious incentive for the citation of anecdotes is the preservation of biographical information. But, Alexander writes, one must not think of the *apomnemoneumata* functioning exclusively in the interest and aspirations of the cultural elite. Entertainment, gossip, polemics, and sheer curiosity were often a desirable objective. In the area of speech and communication, orators relied on the anecdotes as resources for their speeches, schools used them as learning samples, and pupils found them useful for writing and reading practices. The question the multipurpose anecdotal tradition raises for gospel form criticism is whether the conventionally assumed one-to-one correspondence between oral form and a distinct setting in life is a viable proposition. What is emphasized in current orality-scribality studies is that "context matters."[119] But context is understood not only as a historically definable social context, but also in the broader sense of register.[120] When addressing an audience, the speaker not only operates within a social context, but he or she connects with and plays on the so-called register, for example, the encoded *lingua franca* which is more than a social phenomenon and includes values and symbols, memories and experiences shared by speaker and hearers alike. These issues that are currently being raised by orality-scribality studies are a world apart from the kind of correspondences that form criticism assumed to have existed between oral and social life. Granted the coexistence, indeed interaction, of orally communicated speech and social setting (including the register), the form-critical premise regarding predictable relations between characteristic speech forms and specific social contexts remains puzzling. There is no theorem like it known in orality studies. Alexander's review of the Hellenistic multipurpose and multisetting of the anecdotal tradition once more underscores the problematic nature of this form-critical premise.

The prime context of the *apomnemoneumata* tradition is education. Their composition, and above all their sheer endless re-oralization, serves as a key instrument in the processes of the Hellenistic *paideia*. The anecdotes and their more compressed form, the *chreia*, writes Alexander, are being "worked and reworked at all levels of the educational system." On one level, they are simply deemed useful for living. But there is more to it. Recounting the sayings and deeds of the philosophers brings their lives before the ears of the audience, elevating them to accessible *Erinnerungsfiguren*[121] who embody the wit and the values, the ethics and the customs of their culture. In this sense the anecdotal tradition is a contributing factor to cultural memory that encourages hearers to identify themselves as a people with common values. There are remarkable affinities between Alexander's explication of the educational function of the *apomnemoneumata* and Carr's enculturation model that I touched on earlier. Both models share an almost identical understanding of the function and purpose of ancient texts, and both delineate very similar communication processes. For Carr, as for Alexander, scribalism, recitation, and memorization were intertwined features of the educational process, and the primary aim of education was the internalization of texts in people's minds and hearts. Instead of resorting to concepts of "borrowing" or "influence" in one direction or the other, they both interpret the oral-scribal-memorial commonalities in ancient Near Eastern, Jewish, Christian, Hellenistic, and rabbinic traditions as manifestations of broader communications patterns that run across the ancient Mediterranean world.

While the *apomnemoneumata* can gravitate toward a documentary philological status, they never ceased to function as primary vehicles for oral delivery. Explicating the anecdotal tradition in a "performance context," Alexander has set herself apart from earlier generations of classical scholarship that were inclined to approach the material from a dominantly literary perspective. Working not with a model of textuality focused exclusively on written and mostly printed materials, but with an oral-scribal-memorial model, she takes great pains to clarify the oral design and purpose of the genre. As the anecdotes are being ceaselessly involved in processes of writing and rewriting, re-oralization, memorization, and internalization, the borders between scripted and oral versions appear to be remarkably porous. In Alexander's felicitous phrase, the anecdotes are "perched on the cusp between orality and writing." And then, there is always memory. In a culture where remembering is the foundation of knowledge, memory is a key factor in accessing, organizing, inculcating, and reciting the anecdotes. Even in their written status, they served for the most part as scripts for purposes of memorization and recitation. As texts the anecdotes are therefore to be viewed as potentialities who would reach their actual fulfillment in performance and in people's minds. This is once again hard to comprehend for our text-focused hermeneutics that is in the habit of turning potentialities into actualities. It is one of Alexander's genuine achievements to have reoriented the sensibilities of those of us who are inclined to treat texts as end products with a sense of verbal finality, and encouraged us to grasp the chirographic *apomnemoneumata* not as products as much as process.

The implications Alexander has drawn for gospel and tradition are illuminating and not without surprises. If the vast and variegated history of the *apomnemoneumata* has anything to tell us about the synoptic tradition, it is that the latter does not lend itself to hard and fast rules and predictable patterns. For example, there is no indication in the anecdotal tradition that sayings must predate the biographical elements, as is sometimes implied in gospel studies. Nor are the more compressed anecdotal forms in the *Gospel of Thomas* necessarily evidence of their chronological priority over the more elaborate forms in the Synoptic Gospels. To the contrary, the papyrological evidence points in the other direction: the longer format of the *apomnemoneumata* was in circulation earlier than the shorter ones. The presence of biographical elements in Q, moreover, is entirely within the realm of the Hellenistic *apomnemoneumata* tradition. The teacher-disciple model as one specific social context for Jesus' teachings finds ample confirmation in the Hellenistic school tradition. More surprisingly perhaps, the anecdotal tradition offers no encouragement that the individual stories had to collect into a sequential life story as if by a law of nature. Indeed, as Alexander observed, "there were a thousand and one other things you could do with anecdotes, and weaving them together into a connected narrative was by no means the most obvious." Form criticism's premise of a quasi-evolutionary flow into the narrative Gospel is thus once more powerfully disconfirmed. In fact, the formation of the *bios* genre enjoyed a rather low priority in the *apomnemoneumata* tradition. Last but by no means least, Alexander finds it difficult to arrive at a biographical narrative model that matches the generally more complex Gospel narratives. This could suggest, she reasons, that the Gospels will have to be viewed as "a creative outworking of the ideology of the Jesus movement in its own right." Little wonder that our numerous comparative efforts to define the genre of Mark have generally remained inconclusive.

Memory

Among the numerous features that distinguish Gerhardsson's work, one achievement looms larger than all others: his boldness in making memory a centerpiece of both the rabbinic and the early Jesus tradition. Byrskog has rightly extolled the powers enjoyed by and the virtues attributed to *Mnemosyne*, first among the Muses, goddess and fountain of life, mother of all civilized activities. Gerhardsson's insistence on the inseparability of memory and tradition thus enjoys strong historical backing. Yet the significance of his elevation of memory to a principal category for conceptualizing the tradition is not fully appreciated unless one is mindful of the virtual absence of memory in much of twentieth-century studies of gospel and tradition. His was a lonely voice while the form critics, who appeared to signal the way of the future, failed in taking his memory work to heart. This is a serious matter. "The disappearance of memory as an analytical category in biblical studies," write Alan Kirk and Tom Thatcher in a recent programmatic essay on memory, "may be attributed to a number of factors, most significantly the effects of form criticism."[122] It is indeed the case that the work of Bultmann and of those who employ form-critical methodology to this day displays next to no sustained reflection on the role of memory. The reason, one suspects, is that form criticism never succeeded in devising a conceptual apparatus commensurate with oral, spoken words. Its principal focus was, and continues to be, on securing the original form of a saying or story, and not on the rhetorical, performative, memorial aspects of speech. Whereas form criticism operated, in Byrskog's words, with the effect to "dissolve the ancient relationship between memory and tradition," Gerhardsson was working toward the historically entirely appropriate project of probing the relations between memory and tradition. To be sure, the actual mechanics of memory are certainly debatable, but it needs to be acknowledged that Gerhardsson's work exhibits a keen perception of memory, without which any concept of tradition in the ancient world remains entirely unrealistic.

While from a strictly disciplinary perspective the virtual absence of memory can thus closely be allied with form criticism, the roots of the demise are sunk more deeply in Western intellectual history. It is helpful to remember that memory has a history, extending far into the past, a fact to which Byrskog has alerted us in his introduction. If we catch a sense of this history, in however sketchy a fashion, we can locate memory's demise, and biblical scholarship's implication in it, in a broader cultural context. Widely viewed as the centralizing authority of civilized life in ancient and to some extent medieval culture, memory was traditionally assigned a formal role in rhetoric, until it was gradually deprived of its primary status, taking on auxiliary functions in the ethical, metaphysical, and eventually historical disciplines. In medieval culture, memory became integrated into prayer, meditation, and moral philosophy, until early modernism and modernity itself increasingly privileged logic—typographically grounded logic—over against memory and rhetoric.

Divested of its honorable position as *fons et origo* of civilization, memory was thus steadily denigrated to a peripheral position. Modern biblical scholarship's prevalent disregard of memory can thus well be understood as being fully in keeping with Western intellectual history and its progressive marginalization of memory. By and large our discipline has been operating in an intellectual culture where memory had become unnecessary, if not an obstacle. Put differently, when the academic discipline of biblical studies sided with modernity in the form of historical criticism it did so by eagerly embracing the documentary revolution in which tradition was synonymous with texts (mostly printed texts) and the texts of tradition were deemed intelligible without recourse to memory.

All contributors to this volume, including Alan Kirk, who wrote the piece on memory, have acknowledged Gerhardsson's signal achievement in elevating memory to central position and making it the mainstay of tradition. While giving full credit to Gerhardsson's work on memory, Kirk suggests that the latter's model is marked by an "overdetermination by the properties of the written medium." Kirk himself views memory largely as a constructive force. He envisions memory taking on a life of its own, condensing, schematizing, and framing history, and constructing a place for empirical reality that cannot in its full sense be retrieved into the present. The past, he is convinced, cannot be re-presented without transformative strategies. Ultimately, Kirk is interested in integrating memory even more closely with tradition than even Gerhardsson may have anticipated it.

It is now incumbent upon us to take up Gerhardsson's insights about memory and tradition and bring them to fuller intellectual fruition. The difficulty of the project cannot be overrated. For it needs to be restated: with the possible exception of rhetorical criticism, memory has no place in the modern biblical curriculum. And even in rhetorical criticism, it has more often than not been assigned a marginal slot. Everywhere memorial sensibilities run up against the limits of historical criticism's analytical categories. Memory in the practice of biblical scholarship is by and large nobody's business.

In taking tentative steps toward rehabilitating memory, I shall conclude this piece with a brief meditation on four ways in which memory can be viewed as a force in the early Jesus tradition.

To begin with, there exists a dual nexus of memory with Jesus' words of teaching. In conceptualizing the synoptic tradition we are often inclined to think of Jesus as its solitary starting point. It is a notion that the quest for the historical Jesus continues to reinforce in its Herculean efforts to reconstruct the *ipsissima verba* as the basis of the synoptic tradition. As I pointed out above, Gerhardsson did not share this concept of the ground zero origin of the tradition. To borrow his phrase, cited before, Jesus teachings were bound up with "The Torah tradition," that is, they were flowing from and engaged in the oral and scribal legacy of Judaism. Although cast in his own diction and in response to current affairs, Jesus' stories, maxims, and teachings nonetheless drew from and responded to "The Torah tradition." If, therefore, we keep cultural contextuality in mind—as we must in all oral-performative settings—we may say that he was feeding from and living in the memories of his tradition, not necessarily as he had read and studied them, but more likely as he had heard, pondered, and recited them. In other words, one will have to imagine Jesus enmeshed in the memories of his people.

Secondly, memory is a force in Jesus' very own teaching activities. When he reactivated some of his earlier messages, he was confronted with an interval that had elapsed between his prior delivery and his present re-actualization. We cannot think of this situation without the role of memory because whenever time elapses there is bound to be memory. But the mnemonic mode in that case was not that of an active search for items buried in the past, nor of items present in the tradition, but rather an affective remembering, in however conscious or unconscious a manner, of what was already present in his mind.

A third nexus exists between memory and the oral-scribal Jesus tradition. If we part company with the form-critical model of a linear, indeed evolutionary, model of the tradition, what is one going to put in its place? To approach the early Jesus tradition in a novel way, it may be salutary to turn our attention to recent advances in textual criticism, pioneered above all by David Parker and Eldon Epp. They have chosen to abandon, or at least partially abandon, text criticism's privileging of "the original text," this one assumed fixed point in the tradition. Instead they have selected to take each scribal variation seriously on its own terms. In refocusing the discipline away from the so-called original text toward the papyrological evidence, Parker and Epp have succeeded in facilitating new access to the early Jesus tradition. What must be regarded as one of their key insights into the early papyrological Jesus tradition is its considerable fluidity. This raises questions that the text critics themselves have as yet barely raised. How is the relatively fluid, oral-scribal tradition accomplished? How do we imagine the processes of copying? What are the media mechanics of this early Jesus tradition, and what is the role of memory in it?

It is not inconceivable that our conventional view of iconographical depictions of scribes bent over their reading desks in the process of copying texts has fed our imagination about ancient scribal practices. Earlier we adverted to Carr's reconceptualization of the role and function of scribes in the ancient Near Eastern and Mediterranean culture.[123] This is an important matter that requires expansion with a view toward the early Jesus tradition. Scribes in the ancient world were often high profile figures, who functioned as professional counselors and administrators and possessed the requisite skills concerning politics and communication. As scribal experts and in command of scribal learning, they were the guardians of the cultural repertoire. In the case of scribes working with the Jesus sayings, knowledge of that tradition would have to be assumed. "The training and professional practice of scribes was devoted to learning and cultivating in memory the various texts of the cultural tradition."[124] That is to say that scribes were not so much copying the Jesus sayings with their eyes in a distinctly literary environment, but rehearsing them in their minds so as to configure, or reconfigure, them as they were writing for their own time and place. One could well speak of the performance character of their labors, as long as it is understood that scribal activity is not perceived separate from memorial activities. Memory was located between writing and re-oralization, or to be more precise, memory, on this view, was the presiding force in the early Jesus tradition.

There is fourthly the nexus between memory and Jesus' death. No event is less likely to have been communicated in its raw facticity than Jesus' crucifixion. Hearers no more than readers can directly be confronted with it. What is required in the case of extreme trauma is a mediating agent, and memory provides precisely such mediation. To make the trauma accessible, memory avails itself of mnemonic frames and tradition-honored patterns to bring the unimaginable in accord with familiar, normative patterns and in that sense "normalizes" the death of Jesus. But how does memory work in the case of Mark's Passion Narrative?

In 1972 and 1973 Lothar Ruppert[125] published several studies on what to date is still the most exhaustive examination of the motif of the "Offended, Attacked, Persecuted, and Suffering Just One" in the Hebrew Bible, Qumran, and apocalypticism, covering almost a millennium of ancient Jewish and Hellenistic Jewish scribal productivity on that theme. In 1980 George Nickelsburg[126] demonstrated that Mark's Passion Narrative was structured around the ancient Jewish theme of the "Persecution and Vindication of the Innocent One." There can be little doubt that the theme of the *passio justi*, the suffering of the just one, was a widespread and tradition-honored one, and many of its basic elements can without doubt be ascertained in Mark's Passion Narrative. It was, however, Arthur Dewey[127] who, freeing himself from source and redaction critical logic, recognized the memorial potential of the theme of the "Suffering Just One." He deserves full credit for having associated the Markan *passio justi* theme with memory. Writing the passion story, Dewey correctly observed, was not simply a matter of recalling the death of Jesus. "The basic task was to 'invent' a *locus* for his death."[128] The choice of the well-known *passio justi* theme was eminently suitable to serve as a memory place for Jesus' death. Memory place, understood in this context not as a topographical location as much as a mental place, has been one of the oldest mnemonic devices in the ancient Greek and Roman art of memory.[129] From the perspective of memory place, therefore, Mark is locating the indescribable events in a familiar place on which the trauma could be constructed, and suffering made accessible, aesthetically and religiously.

Epilogue

This volume strikes pathways through a vast area of subjects and opens rich fields of research. What impact do the editors wish that these essays may have on their readers? Given the numerous disciplines and topics that are being discussed, our fondest wish is that the book will succeed in initiating dialogue between the various academic positions and subdisciplines: narrative criticism with the eyewitness theory, rhetoric with orality, form criticism with orality-scribality studies, the new textual criticism with current media studies, comparative studies on the early Christian, Hellenistic, and rabbinic traditions, and always the role of memory in every one of these disciplinary approaches. That would be the most fitting tribute to Birger Gerhardsson, whose keen sense of the voiced nature of ancient texts has pointed a clear way for the future in biblical studies.

Notes

Introduction

1. Günther Zuntz, *Persephone: Three Essays on Religion and Thought in Magna Graecia* (Oxford: Clarendon, 1971), 378–81.
2. New editions appeared in 1964 (slightly corrected) and 1998 (rpt of the 1964 ed.), the latter one including another publication from 1964 and a foreword by Jacob Neusner. See Birger Gerhardsson, *Memory and Manuscript: Oral Tradition and Written Transmission in Rabbinic Judaism and Early Christianity, with Tradition and Transmission in Early Christianity* (Grand Rapids: Eerdmans, 1998).
3. Gerhardsson describes his relationship to Fridrichsen and Fridrichsen's career in his book *Fridrichsen, Odeberg, Aulén, Nygren: Fyra teologer* (Lund: Novapress, 1994), 9–83.
4. Their publications are listed in Gerhardsson, *Memory and Manuscript*.
5. Krister Stendahl, *The School of St. Matthew and Its Use of the Old Testament* (ASNU 20; 2d ed.; Lund: Gleerup, 1968).
6. Harald Riesenfeld argued that the disciples memorized and recited certain episodes as holy words. See his "The Gospel Tradition and Its Beginnings," *SE* 1 (TU 73) (1959): 43–65. Gerhardsson regrets that this view has often been confused with his own more elaborate and differentiated view.
7. Gerhardsson, *Memory and Manuscript*, 123.
8. For a list of reviews, see Gerhardsson, *Memory and Manuscript*, xxiii.
9. Birger Gerhardsson, *Tradition and Transmission in Early Christianity* (ConNT 20; Lund: Gleerup, 1964); idem, "Innan evangelierna skrevs," *SEÅ* 69 (2004): 167–89; idem, "The Secret of the Transmission of the Unwritten Jesus Tradition," *NTS* 51 (2005): 1–18.

10 Birger Gerhardsson, "Die Boten Gottes und die Apostel Christi," *SEÅ* 27 (1962): 89–131. The article criticizes especially the newly (1961) published work on the twelve apostles (Hans Klein) and the Christian apostolate (Walter Schmithals).

11 Birger Gerhardsson, *The Testing of God's Son (Matt 4:1-11 & Par): An Analysis of an Early Christian Midrash* (ConBNT 2.1; Lund: Gleerup, 1966). The volume contains four of the projected eleven chapters. For the substance of the most significant unpublished chapters of the book, see idem, "Gottes Sohn as Diener Gottes," *ST* 27 (1973): 73–106.

12 This aspect of Gerhardsson's contribution to the study of the Jesus tradition has, to his regret, been almost entirely neglected. He has collected seventeen of these studies in *The Shema in the New Testament: Deut 6:4-5 in Significant Passages* (Lund: Novapress, 1996).

13 His presidential address at the SNTS meeting in 1990 dealt with the parables. See Birger Gerhardsson, "If We Do Not Cut the Parables Out of Their Frames," *NTS* 37 (1991): 321–35. His further extensive publications on the parables are listed in idem, *Jesu liknelser* (Lund: Novapress, 1999), which also includes two previously unpublished papers. It is further noteworthy that he published a work on the Good Samaritan already in his youth. See Birger Gerhardsson, *The Good Samaritan—The Good Shepherd?* (ConNT 16; Lund: Gleerup, 1958). For the mighty acts, see idem, *The Mighty Acts of Jesus According to Matthew* (Scripta Minora 1978–1979: 5; Lund: Gleerup, 1979). This publication has been translated into Swedish and expanded. See idem, *Jesu Maktgärningar i Matteusevangeliet* (Lund: Novapress, 1991).

14 See for instance his contribution to New Testament ethics in Birger Gerhardsson, *The Ethos of the Bible* (Philadelphia: Fortress, 1981); to the confession of the church in Gerhardsson and Per Erik Persson, *Kyrkans bekännelsefråga* (Malmö: Liber, 1984); to the resurrection of Jesus in Gerhardsson, *Kristi uppståndelse* (Lund: Novapress, 2001); to the Lord's Prayer in idem, *Fader vår i Nya testamentet* (Lund: Novapress, 2003). The books mentioned here contain references to his further publications on the same subjects.

15 Peabody, Mass.: Hendrickson, 2001. The volume contains a preface by Gerhardsson and a foreword by Donald Hagner.

16 Originally published as *Die Anfänge der Evangelientradition* (Glauben und Denken 919; Wuppertal: Brockhaus, 1977). It was translated into several languages.

17 One of the students was Rainer Riesner, who later published his Tübingen dissertation *Jesus als Lehrer: Eine Untersuchung zum Ursprung der Evangelien-Überlieferung* (WUNT 2.7; 3d ed.; Tübingen: Mohr Siebeck, 1988).

18 The symposium volume was published as *Das Evangelium und die Evangelien: Vorträge vom Tübinger Symposium 1982* (ed. Peter Stuhlmacher; WUNT 28; Tübingen: Mohr Siebeck, 1983). Gerhardsson's contribution is entitled "Der Weg der Evangelientradition." The volume was translated into English, *The Gospel and the Gospels* (ed. Peter Stuhlmacher; Grand Rapids: Eerdmans, 1991). Gerhardsson prefers the German version of his article.

19 The symposium volume was published as *The Interrelations of the Gospels* (ed. David L. Dungan; BETL 95; Leuven: Leuven University Press and Peeters, 1990). Gerhardsson published his contribution also in a separate volume, *The Gospel Tradition* (ConBNT 15; Lund: Gleerup, 1986).

20 Werner H. Kelber, *The Oral and the Written Gospel: The Hermeneutics of Speaking and Writing in the Synoptic Tradition, Mark, Paul, and Q* (with a new introduction by the author; Voices in Performance and Text; Bloomington: Indiana Uni-

versity Press, 1997). The first edition of the book was published in 1983 and had just appeared when Gerhardsson gave his lecture.

21 See for instance Peter H. Davids, "The Gospels and Jewish Tradition: Twenty Years after Gerhardsson," in *Gospel Perspectives: Studies of History and Tradition in the Four Gospels* (ed. Richard T. France and David Wenham; Sheffield: JSOT Press, 1980), 75–99; Ben F. Meyer, "Some Consequences of Birger Gerhardsson's Account of the Origins of the Gospel Tradition," in *Jesus and the Oral Gospel Tradition* (ed. Henry Wansbrough; JSNTSup 64; Sheffield: JSOT Press, 1991), 424–40.

Chapter 1

1 At the time, I myself was Secretary of the Society and it was a great joy to be able to work with Birger Gerhardsson and to get to know him at the personal level. This essay is offered as a token, however inadequate, of my own deep appreciation and thanks for Birger Gerhardsson's scholarly contributions which have done so much to invigorate and inform the subject of this essay, and also for his personal friendship and kindness over many years.

2 Gerhardsson, *Memory and Manuscript*.

3 Gerhardsson, *Tradition and Transmission*; this responds especially to the essay of Morton Smith, "A Comparison of Early Christian and Early Rabbinic Tradition," *JBL* 82 (1963): 169–76, which was in effect a sharp critique/review of Gerhardsson's *Memory and Manuscript*. See also Gerhardsson, *Reliability of the Gospel Tradition* (Peabody, Mass.: Hendrickson, 2001) (this book contains three important separate earlier studies of Gerhardsson's, all of which deal variously with aspects of form criticism: "The Origins of the Gospel Tradition," "The Path of the Gospel Tradition," and "The Gospel Tradition"; citations here are from the *Reliability* book). Moreover, see Gerhardsson's "Illuminating the Kingdom: Narrative Meshalim in the Synoptic Gospels," in *Jesus and the Oral Gospel Tradition*, ed. Wansbrough, 266–309; and idem, "The Secret of the Unwritten Jesus Tradition," *NTS* 51 (2005): 1–18.

4 The very first sentence of the introduction (*Memory and Manuscript*, 9) refers to "a particularly fruitful epoch for gospel research" dawning with the works of Dibelius and Bultmann in the early twentieth century, even if the rest of the introduction (*Memory and Manuscript*, 9–15) raises important questions marks against some aspects of their work.

5 In this essay, I focus primarily on form criticism as applied to the Jesus tradition, mostly in the Synoptic Gospels. Form-critical approaches have certainly been applied to materials in the Fourth Gospel, in the New Testament Epistles and elsewhere. It is however in relation to the synoptic tradition that form criticism has made its most distinctive mark in the history of scholarship and it is here that many discussions of form criticism have tended to focus.

6 See Karl Ludwig Schmidt, *Der Rahmen der Geschichte Jesu: Literarkritische Untersuchungen zur ältesten Jesusüberlieferung* (Berlin: Trowitzsch, 1919); Martin Dibelius, *From Tradition to Gospel* (London: Ivor Nicholson and Watson, 1934; German 1st ed. 1919); Bultmann, *The History of the Synoptic Tradition* (New York: Harper & Row, 1963). Form criticism as such was by no means new in the 1920s and in many respects scholars such as Dibelius and Bultmann were following in the footsteps of Hermann Gunkel and others in their work on the Old Testament and its traditions. Nevertheless, form-critical approaches took

a distinctive turn when applied to the gospel traditions, especially when raising issues about the development of traditions including claims about historicity and the reliability of the gospel tradition.

7   Cf. Bultmann, *History*, 4 (citing Dibelius approvingly): the aim of form criticism is "to recover the origin and history of the particular units and thereby to throw some light on the history of the tradition before it took written form."
8   On the changing use of the term over the course of time, see Samuel Byrskog, "A Century with the *Sitz im Leben*: From Form-Critical Setting to Gospel Community and Beyond," *ZNW* 98 (2007): 1–27.
9   See Gerhardsson, *Reliability*, 23, 41.
10 Gerhardsson, *Reliability*, 62. For Acts, the exception is Acts 20:35, but that is not a saying ascribed to Jesus in Luke's own Gospel (or indeed in any Christian Gospel).
11 Borrowing the term of Gerhard Kittel, *Die Probleme des palästinischen Spätjudentums und das Urchristentum* (Stuttgart: Kohlhammer, 1926), 69: see Gerhardsson, *Reliability*, 59–63, 64; cf. too *Memory and Manuscript*, 332; *Tradition and Transmission*, 42. The claim of Kittel is also cited by Bultmann (*History*, 369), though, e.g., Samuel Byrskog, review of Rudolf Bultmann, *The History of the Synoptic Tradition*, in *JBL* 122 (2003): 549–55 (553), claims that the full implications of Kittel's comment were not appreciated by Bultmann. Gerhardsson, *Reliability*, 63, also notes that the "isolation" of the Jesus tradition can be taken in different ways: e.g., it can refer to the fact that the tradition is isolated in literary terms (i.e., it does not appear in other literary texts) and also to the way in which the Gospels ascribe all the traditions to Jesus as a single individual, not (as, e.g., in rabbinic literature) to a range of different teachers. The issue here is the first of these (Byrskog's comment, noted earlier, relates more to the second issue).
12 Gerhardsson, *Reliability*, 65: "Our knowledge of the forms of early Christian activity—the typical situations and modes of conduct—is limited: the sources yield only meager. But what we do know we know from Acts, the letters, and Revelation, and there we find . . . no concrete Jesus traditions at all, neither in a finished form nor in the making."
13 Gerhardsson, *Reliability*, 23. Cf. too *Memory and Manuscript*, 335, distinguishing clearly between the *transmission* of a tradition and its *use*.
14 Gerhardsson, *Memory and Manuscript*, 330–35; *Tradition and Transmission*, 43. Cf. too "Illuminating the Kingdom," 289–90 (on "actualization").
15 See James D. G. Dunn, "Jesus Traditions in Paul," in *Studying the Historical Jesus* (ed. Bruce Chilton and Craig A. Evans; Leiden: Brill, 1994), 155–78.
16 In *Memory and Manuscript*, 324, Gerhardsson explicitly acknowledges that his work at that stage has not discussed in any detail the evidence from the Synoptic Gospels themselves, primarily for reasons of space ("This would require an independent monograph"). However, in his more recent writings (cf. n. 3 above), he has discussed the Gospel material in more detail.
17 Cf. Gerhardsson's reference in *Memory and Manuscript*, 14, to the early form critics' ideas as presupposing "a non-literary, anonymous crowd."
18 One should of course note that "aim" and "result" may not always coincide!
19 As well as the (many) reviews of his books, see, e.g., E. P. Sanders and Margret Davies, *Studying the Synoptic Gospels* (London: SCM Press, 1989), esp. 128–37; Kelber, *Oral and Written Gospel*, 8–14; Davids, "The Gospels and Jewish Tradition," 75–99; Meyer, "Some Consequences," 424–40.
20 Smith, "Comparison," 169–76.
21 The intemperateness of Smith's article is acknowledged by Jacob Neusner in his

foreword to the 1998 reprint of Gerhardsson's *Memory and Manuscript* book, where Neusner now sharply disassociates himself from Smith's earlier criticisms and fully acknowledges the positive value in Gerhardsson's use of Jewish materials and evidence in this discussion.

22   Cf. Sanders and Davies, *Studying the Synoptic Gospels*, 130; Kelber, *Oral and Written Gospel*, 14, and others.

23   Cf. Gerhardsson, *Reliability*, 63: "Jesus' followers have influenced his words in various ways," and this is emphasized even more strongly in the preface to the 1998 reprint of his *Memory and Manuscript*: see, e.g., xiv–xv, xix, referring to *Memory and Manuscript*, 79–83, 324–35; *Tradition and Transmission*, 35–47, for the recognition that in both the rabbinic and the Christian traditions, there is always a combination of fixed and flexible elements. Cf. too *Reliability*, 117–18.

24   Gerhardssson, *Reliability*, 53; also *Tradition and Transmission*, 45.

25   Gerhardssson, *Reliability*, 49; also p. 79, arguing that especially the sayings of Jesus and the parables "were transmitted in fixed wording and with minimal editing"; note too the title chosen (*Reliability*) for this collection! Also "Illuminating the Kingdom," 290: the "narrative meshalim" were "actualized," "but the alterations of the texts do not seem to have been very great"; also his conclusion: "Is it reasonable to believe that the evangelists can give us a fairly reliable picture of the way in which Jesus himself taught, granted that elements of it are secondary? I think so" (305). Cf. too Kelber's summary: "the underlying, nagging question in all his [Gerhardsson's] explorations is that of the 'historical credibility of the Gospels'" (*Oral and Written Gospel*, 8, with reference to Gerhardsson, *Memory and Manuscript*, 194, and *Origins*, 90 [= *Reliability*, 57]).

26   Cf. Gerhardsson's more recent work on the temptation narratives, *Testing of God's Son*, arguing that these traditions are the product of early Christian exegetical, creative activity, rather than anything that can easily be traced back to Jesus himself. (Cf. too Gerhardsson's own summary [*Reliability*, 56], which refers to the Christian tradition here as being "remarkably free and creative in character.") See too his extensive work on the parables and the comments of Samuel Byrskog in the introduction to this volume. There is perhaps something of a tension in Gerhardsson's writings where, on the one hand, he fully accepts that early Christians did introduce changes at times into the tradition, at times freely and creatively, and on the other hand, he stresses the general reliability of the tradition, claiming that any such activity by Christians is relatively small-scale and not significant in substance.

27   One need only note here the many studies, especially in the early years of so-called redaction criticism of the Gospels, which focused on the (many) changes which the later evangelists have made to their earlier traditions (e.g., Matthew and Luke using Mark) and which at times produce a significant change in the meaning of the earlier tradition (e.g., in Matthew's redaction of Mark in passages relating to the Jewish Law).

28   The classic example, often quoted, is the tradition about fasting in Mark 2:18-20, where the saying in v. 20, apparently allowing a reintroduction of fasting after the "bridegroom" (= Jesus?) has gone away, seems to be a secondary addition to an earlier tradition reflected in vv. 18-19, where Jesus says that fasting is inappropriate in the new situation (by implication that of his own ministry).

29   Sanders and Davies, *Studying the Synoptic Gospels*, 131, take the examples of the sayings about marriage and divorce, and the Last Supper traditions, where there is not only the evidence from the Gospels themselves but also from Paul's letters.

30 For example, Gerhardsson accepts readily the Lukan picture whereby Paul appears to acknowledge and accept the authority of the Jerusalem apostles as the ultimate arbiters and decision makers in key areas; but more recent studies of Paul have suggested a much more critical attitude on the part of Paul to the Jerusalem apostles. See, e.g., Bengt Holmberg, *Paul and Power: The Structure of Authority in the Primitive Church as Reflected in the Pauline Epistles* (Philadelphia: Fortress, 1980); Nicholas H. Taylor, *Paul, Antioch and Jerusalem: A Study in Relationships and Authority in Earliest Christianity* (JSNTSup 66; Sheffield: JSOT Press, 1992).

31 See (with varying degrees of criticism), in addition to the works of Gerhardsson already mentioned, Erich Fascher, *Die formgeschichtliche Methode: Eine Darstellung und Kritik. Zugleich ein Beitrag zur Geschichte des synoptischen Problems* (Giessen: Alfred Töpelmann, 1924); B. S. Easton, *The Gospel before the Gospels* (London: Allen & Unwin, 1928); Edgar V. McKnight, *What Is Form Criticism?* (Philadelphia: Fortress, 1969); Graham N. Stanton, "Form Criticism Revisited," in *What about the New Testament? Essays in Honour of Christopher Evans* (ed. Morna Hooker and Colin Hickling; London: SCM Press, 1975), 13–27; Erhardt Güttgemanns, *Candid Questions Concerning Gospel Form Criticism: A Methodological Sketch of the Fundamental Problematics of Form and Redaction Criticism* (The Pittsburgh Theological Monograph Series 26; Pittsburgh: Pickwick Press, 1979); Reiner Blank, *Analyse und Kritik der formgeschichtlichen Arbeiten von Martin Dibelius und Rudolf Bultmann* (Basel: Friedrich Reinhardt Kommissionsverlag, 1981); Sanders and Davies, *Studying the Synoptic Gospels*; Stephen H. Travis, "Form Criticism," in *New Testament Interpretation* (ed. I. Howard Marshall; Exeter: Paternoster, 1977), 153–64; Walter Schmithals, "Kritik der Formkritik," *ZTK* 77 (1980): 149–85; Vernon K. Robbins, "Form Criticism: New Testament," *ABD* 2:841–43; Byrskog, review of Bultmann, 549–55; Richard Bauckham, *Jesus and the Eyewitnesses: The Gospels as Eyewitness Testimony* (Grand Rapids: Eerdmans, 2006).

32 See n. 7 above and the citation of Bultmann there, claiming that form criticism was concerned to recover both the "history" and the "origin" of individual traditions.

33 As we have seen, part of Gerhardsson's critique relates to this broad issue of the "reliability" of the material in the Gospels. It should however be noted that both Bultmann and Dibelius elsewhere produced significant studies of the historical Jesus on the basis that substantial parts of the tradition were indeed historical and authentic.

34 Cf. the often quoted comment of T. W. Manson, "The Quest of the Historical Jesus—Continued," in *Studies in the Gospels and Epistles* (Manchester: Manchester University Press, 1962), 5: "We can list these stories in the Gospels. We can label them . . . But a paragraph of Mark is not a penny the better or the worse as historical evidence for being labelled, 'Apophthegm' or 'Pronouncement Story' or 'Paradigm.'" Similarly Easton, *Gospel before the Gospels*, 80–81. Some strong reactions in the past may be due to a rather literal reading of the English term "form criticism," claiming that the discipline should focus simply on the classification of the different forms. (This is reflected too in the attempts by some to distinguish "form criticism" [narrowly conceived in this way] from study of the history of the tradition [e.g., Easton: "historical criticism"; Travis: "tradition history"].) However, the discipline of *Formgeschichte* as developed by German form critics has always regarded it as an integral part of its work to analyze the history of the tradition, not just to classify the different forms. See explicitly Bultmann, *History*, 4. The point above is that the two issues—the *use* of a tradition and its

origin—may be related, and are important, but they are (logically) separable. See too Gerhardsson, *Tradition and Transmission*, 43.

35 See, e.g., Stanton, "Form Criticism Revisited," 14, who refers to this as "an assured result of form-critical studies." Also Sanders and Davies, *Studying the Synoptic Gospels*, 123–24; Bauckham, *Jesus and the Eyewitnesses*, 243.

36 In the Markan tradition, sections such as Mark 2:1-3:6 or Mark 4:1-34 are always mentioned in this context. For a full discussion of the issue of pre-Markan traditions, see William R. Telford, "The Pre-Markan Tradition in Recent Research (1980–1990)," in *The Four Gospels 1992: Festschrift Frans Neirynck* (ed. F. Van Segbroek et al.; BETL 100; 3 vols.; Leuven: Leuven University Press and Peeters, 1992), 2:693–723. The Q tradition in Matthew and Luke might also constitute another major exception to this "rule," with many arguing that Q existed as a written text prior to the writing of Matthew and Luke: see John S. Kloppenborg, *Excavating Q: The History and Setting of the Sayings Gospel* (Minneapolis: Fortress, 2000), esp. 56–60.

37 See too Gerd Theissen, *The Gospels in Context: Social and Political History in the Synoptic Tradition* (Edinburgh: Clark, 1992), 4: the point is not that the individual pericopes were necessarily handed down in isolation, but that they "could be separated and reappear in new contexts."

38 Also, if they clearly belong integrally to an account of the passion, it is hard to see them ever existing as independent, self-contained pericopes.

39 See, e.g., C. H. Dodd, "The Framework of the Gospel Narratives," in *New Testament Studies* (Manchester: Manchester University Press, 1953), 1–11, with the reply by Dennis E. Nineham, "The Order of Event in St. Mark's Gospel—An Examination of Dr. Dodd's Hypothesis," in *Studies in the Gospels: Essays in Memory of R. H. Lightfoot* (ed. Nineham; Oxford: Blackwell, 1955), 223–39. More recently, the work of Stephen Hultgren, *Narrative Elements in the Double Tradition: A Study of Their Place within the Framework of the Gospel Narrative* (BZNW 113; Berlin: de Gruyter, 2002), has also sought to establish the existence of a traditional "outline" of the ministry of Jesus in Christian tradition (on the basis of a wider range of materials than Dodd, though see my review in *JTS* 54 [2003]: 691–94).

40 This is not to say that all narrative elements (or narrativizing features) in the tradition are secondary. See, for example, below on *chreia*. What is said above applies only to the ordered narratives of our present Gospels taken as wholes.

41 Cf. Dibelius, *From Tradition to Gospel*, 2; Bultmann, *History*, 6.

42 Cf. Bultmann's heavily stylized view of the development of the Christian movement, and of early Christian thought, whereby the tradition moves out from its "Palestinian" roots into the "Hellenistic" world.

43 The "paradigms" as isolated by Dibelius were very similar (broadly) to the "apophthegms" as isolated by Bultmann or the "pronouncement stories" (of many English-speaking critics): these were the short stories culminating in a saying of Jesus. (For descriptions of the different categories, see the standard descriptive treatments of form criticism.) For Bultmann, the essence of the apophthegm was really the (climactic) saying alone: apophthegms were "sayings of Jesus set in a brief context" (*History*, 11) and any narrative features were often taken as secondary additions. On this, see below on *chreia*.

44 For Dibelius, they were *Novellen* ("Tales"), for Bultmann "miracle stories": stories told with a wealth of detail and seeking to further heighten the claims of the miracle worker (perhaps against rivals).

45 For the general model presumed by Bultmann as essentially one of growth, with elements constantly being added (rather than subtracted), see Kelber, *Oral and Written Gospel*, 4.

46 See, e.g., Gerhardsson, *Reliability*, 82–83.

47 See the (by now classic) study of Martin Hengel, *Judaism and Hellenism: Studies in Their Encounter in Palestine during the Early Hellenistic Period* (2 vols.; London: SCM Press, 1974).

48 In fact, secular "folk" literature is referred to surprisingly little by the early form critics.

49 See Sanders and Davies, *Studying the Synoptic Gospels*, 137. For *chreia*, see Ronald F. Hock and Edward O'Neil, *The Chreia in Ancient Rhetoric*. Vol. 1: *The Progymnasmata* (SBLTT 27; Atlanta: Scholars Press, 1986).; Burton Mack and Vernon K. Robbins, *Patterns of Persuasion in the Gospels* (Sonoma: Polebridge, 1989), and especially the essay of Robbins there: "*Chreia* and Pronouncement Story in Synoptic Studies" (pp. 1–29). Dibelius, *From Tradition to Gospel*, 152–64 (only in the 2d edition of the German), had noted the *chreia* and their similarity in form to the Gospel paradigms, but had discounted the parallel because of allegedly widely differing contents (cf. p. 157), though this may have been due to his focusing rather narrowly on Cynic *chreia*.

50 In turn, this might cast considerable doubt on the tendency by Bultmann to focus on the sayings in these stories alone: the narrative element may be just as integral to the nature of a *chreia*. See Robbins in Mack and Robbins, *Patterns of Persuasion*, 1–29. The tendency of Bultmann to focus on "sayings" to the detriment of any "narrative" is also criticised by Byrskog, review of Bultmann, 552–54; see too Gerhardsson, *Reliability*, 80–82, 84. The parallels between the Gospel (and indeed New Testament) traditions and *Gattungen* in "Hellenistic" literature are exhaustively set out in the work of Klaus Berger, *Formgeschichte des Neuen Testaments* (Heidelberg: Quelle & Mayer, 1984); see pp. 80–93 on *chreia*.

51 So the ET for Dibelius. Bultmann refers to "Historical Stories and Legends."

52 Dibelius, *From Tradition to Gospel*, 104. One example is the story of Jesus in the temple in Luke 2:41-49.

53 Dibelius, *From Tradition to Gospel*, 178–217.

54 In fact it may well do: see, e.g., the programmatic essay of George W. E. Nickelsburg, "The Genre and Function of the Markan Passion Narrative," *HTR* 73 (1980): 153–84; but this was not the claim of the early form critics.

55 See Easton, *Gospel before the Gospels*, 74: "What *formal* difference is there between the 'logion'—Whosoever exalteth himself shall be humbled—the 'apocalyptic word'—Whosoever shall be ashamed of me, the Son of Man shall be ashamed of him—and the 'Church rule'—Whosoever putteth away his wife and marrieth another committeth adultery?" (emphasis in original); see also pp. 61–62.

56 There is the question of whether the whole of the tradition prior to the writing of Mark was indeed oral. Quite apart from the question of Q, some have argued that written traditions may have been in existence from a very early, if not the earliest, period in the history of the Christian movement, with some even suggesting that Jesus' disciples took written notes of his teaching in the pre-Easter period. See E. Earle Ellis, "New Directions in Form Criticism," in Ellis, *Prophecy and Hermeneutic in Early Christianity: New Testament Essays* (WUNT 18; Tübingen: Mohr, 1978), 237–53, esp. 242–47. Gerhardsson, *Reliability*, 135–36, appears to rule this out, arguing that traditions were only written down later when collections of Jesus traditions became "more extensive than in the earliest period."

57 This is developed particularly in the work of Kelber, *Oral and Written Gospel*; also Güttgemanns, *Candid Questions*.
58 See Sanders and Davies, *Studying the Synoptic Gospels*, 129; Ellis, "New Directions," 244; Bauckham, *Jesus and the Eyewitnesses*, 247. Cf. too Gerhardsson, *Reliability*, 40.
59 See especially Byrskog, review of Bultmann, 550–51.
60 Bultmann, *History*, 4
61 Byrskog, review of Bultmann, 551. On this broader question, see also below.
62 So explicitly Bultmann, *History*, 6.
63 E. P. Sanders, *The Tendencies of the Synoptic Tradition* (SNTSMS 9; Cambridge: Cambridge University Press, 1969).
64 Cf. his summary (Sanders, *Tendencies*, 272): "There are no hard and fast laws of the development of the Synoptic tradition. On all counts the tradition developed in opposite directions. It became both longer and shorter, both more and less detailed, and both more and less Semitic." Hence: "Dogmatic statements that a certain characteristic proves a certain passage to be earlier than another are never justified."
65 Cf. Sanders, *Tendencies*, 8: "the tendencies of the one are presumably the tendencies of the other." See the comments of Kelber, *Oral and Written Gospel*, 7. For other criticisms of the application of a literary model to oral tradition, see Robbins, "Form Criticism," 842; Bauckham, *Jesus and the Eyewitnesses*, 248. The same comment might also apply to some of Gerhardsson's work: e.g., his claims about the (relative) lack of variability in the wording of the parables/meshalim in the Jesus tradition (cf. his "Illuminating the Kingdom," passim) is based (inevitably—there is no other evidence!) on the differences in wording between the *written* synoptic versions in the extant Gospels.
66 See n. 45 above.
67 It is rarely found! For example, Dibelius gave a number of examples which he claimed were "pure" paradigms in Mark, including, e.g., Mark 2:1-12; 2:18-22; 2:23-28 (*From Tradition to Gospel*, 43). However, many would now claim that certainly these stories in their present form have been secondarily expanded. It is also possible to argue, as, e.g., Vincent Taylor did, that the tradition developed toward a "pure" form, rather than away from it: hence "jumbled" forms of the tradition, with extraneous details, etc., were more likely to be original and to be purged as the tradition developed through time: see Vincent Taylor, *The Formation of the Gospel Tradition* (London: Macmillan, 1933). (Hence the extraneous details, taken by Bultmann and others as evidence of later additions to the tradition, were taken by Taylor as evidence of the very early form of the tradition, perhaps based on eyewitness accounts.) See the discussion in Sanders and Davies, *Studying the Synoptic Gospels*, 127. For criticisms of appeals to a "pure" form, see Blank, *Analyse und Kritik*, 201; Gerhardsson, *Reliability*, 83; Theissen, *Gospels in Context*, 6; Bauckham, *Jesus and the Eyewitnesses*, 246.
68 See James D. G. Dunn, *Jesus Remembered* (Grand Rapids: Eeerdmans, 2003); Terence C. Mournet, *Oral Tradition and Literary Dependency: Variability and Stability in the Synoptic Tradition and Q* (WUNT 2.195; Tübingen: Mohr Siebeck, 2005); also Werner H. Kelber, "The Case of the Gospels: Memory's Desire and the Limits of Historical Criticism," *Oral Tradition* 17 (2002): 55–86 (64). But see also Gerhardsson, "Secret of the Transmission," for a strong statement against the model of Dunn who posits a (somewhat amorphous) group of "teachers" or storytellers in Christian communities, re-presenting the Jesus tradition with some freedom; in similar vein too, *Reliability*, 113–13 (on Kelber).

69 Cf. too Gerhardsson, "Secret of the Transmission," 16.
70 Cf. n. 28 above.
71 Samuel Byrskog, "A New Perspective on the Jesus Tradition: Reflections on James D. G. Dunn's *Jesus Remembered*," *JSNT* 26 (2004): 459-71 (esp. 468-69). See also idem, *History as Story: The Gospel Tradition in the Context of Ancient Oral History* (WUNT 123; Tübingen: Mohr Siebeck, 2002), 131-33; and Bauckham, *Jesus and the Eyewitnesses*, 246, 271-74. Both refer to the work of Jan Vansina. See, e.g., Jan Vansina, *Oral Tradition as History* (Madison: University of Wisconsin Press, 1985).
72 Byrskog, *History as Story*, 131-32, referring to the work of Jack Goody and Ian Watt, "The Consequences of Literacy," in *Literacy in Traditional Societies* (ed. Jack Goody; Cambridge: Cambridge University Press, 1968): 27-68.
73 This contrasted with Dibelius' approach of starting with (fairly general) ideas of possible *Sitze im Leben* in early Christianity (e.g., "preaching"), derived from elsewhere, and seeking to map the gospel traditions onto these categories.
74 For example, the Sabbath controversy stories in the Gospels are taken by Bultmann as reflecting attempts by Christians to justify their own practices (*History*, 12, 16). But, as far as we know, there is very little evidence that the issue of Sabbath observance (or at least of working on the Sabbath) was ever really a controversial one in the life of early Christians. See my "Jesus and the Sabbath," in *Jesus in Continuum* (ed. Tom Holmén; Tübingen: Mohr Siebeck, forthcoming).
75 Cf. Gerhardsson, *Memory and Manuscript*, 10: "a circle of this kind is unavoidable in all historical research, but the inevitable dangers must be recognized and limited."
76 Cf. the similar point made by Byrskog, "Century with the *Sitz im Leben*," 16, with reference to Bengt Holmberg, *Sociology and the New Testament: An Appraisal* (Minneapolis: Fortress, 1990), 119-25, on what he calls a "one-dimensional, functional and homeostatic correlation between a tradition/text and a group" (in the work of Gerd Theissen). The point also relates to the issue of whether traditions emanate from (amorphous) communities as wholes or from particular people within communities: see further (briefly) below.
77 See, e.g., Dibelius, *From Tradition to Gospel*, 205; Bultmann, *History*, 265.
78 See Gerd Theissen and Anette Merz, *The Historical Jesus* (London: SCM Press, 1998), 109. For the general point, see too Stanton, "Form Criticism Revisited," 23; also Bauckham, *Jesus and the Eyewitnesses*, 246, citing Vansina, *Oral Tradition*, 101: oral traditions "often serve multiple purposes and uses."
79 See especially Gerhardsson, *Reliability*, 66.
80 A number of his important studies in relation to the Gospels are collected together in his *Gospels in Context*.
81 See especially Theissen, *Gospels in Context*, ch. 1; also the comments at the start of his famous "Wanderradikalismus" article: ET in Gerd Theissen, "The Wandering Radicals," in Theissen, *Social Reality and the Early Christians: Theology, Ethics, and the World of the New Testament* (Edinburgh: Clark, 1992), 33-59 (33-34) (German original 1973).
82 See Byrskog, "Century with the *Sitz im Leben*," 15.
83 See Byrskog, "Century with the *Sitz im Leben*," passim, esp. 5, 8, 20.
84 See, e.g., Gerhardsson, *Memory and Manuscript*, 12; Byrskog, review of Bultmann, 551-52. The model is also rather different from that proposed by Gunkel in relation to Old Testament traditions: see Byrskog, "Century with the *Sitz im Leben*," esp. 4-5 (on Gunkel, Dibelius, and Bultmann).

85 Most recently, Bauckham, *Jesus and the Eyewitnesses*, has stressed the role of possible eyewitnesses in early Christian communities as fulfilling this role, as well as buttressing Gerhardsson's views about the role of the Twelve and/or the Jerusalem church. (The importance of eyewitness testimony is emphasized by Byrskog, especially in his *Story as History*, though without making quite as far-reaching claims about the actual presence of specific eyewitnesses.) There is no space to discuss this in detail here; however, Bauckham's claims about the existence of such people, and about the role of the Jerusalem church, rely at times on quite an optimistic reading of the Gospel (and other) evidence. See my review in *RBL* 2008: 380–85.

86 Cf. Byrskog, review of Bultmann, 554: "Groups consist of individuals, and individuals do not always think and act in an entirely predictable way." Cf. also earlier on doubts now raised about any such "laws" or "tendencies" in the tradition as having universal validity.

87 See above on difficulties felt by many in relation to Gerhardsson's suggestions about the role of the Twelve in this respect.

88 Perhaps unfairly, this is the impression which might be given to a reader of Bauckham, *Jesus and the Eyewitnesses*.

89 It is also one that is fully endorsed by Gerhardsson himself.

90 Cf. the work of Theissen, considered earlier.

91 See, e.g., Meyer, "Some Consequences," 424–40.

Chapter 2

1 See Gerhardsson, *Memory and Manuscript*.

2 As Richard Burridge has noted, both terms were adopted from the earlier work of Karl Ludwig Schmidt ("Die Stellung der Evangelien in der allgemeinen Literaturgeschichte," in ΕΥΧΑΡΙΣΤΗΡΙΟΝ: *Studien zur Religion und Literatur des Alten und Neuen Testaments* [vol. 2; Göttingen: Vandenhoeck und Ruprecht, 1923], 50–134 [76]). See further Richard A. Burridge, *What Are the Gospels? A Comparison with Graeco-Roman Biography* (2d ed.; Grand Rapids: Eerdmans, 2004), 8–11, for more on Schmidt's work and how the use of both terms was adopted by Bultmann.

3 See Mournet, *Oral Tradition and Literary Dependency*, 55–63, for a more detailed exposition of these unvoiced and unjustified assumptions; cf. Kelber, *Oral and Written Gospel*, 2–8.

4 The modern use of the term "Ockham's Razor" derives from the work of the medieval philosopher William of Ockham (alt. "Occam" ca. 1280–1349 C.E.). The maxim is based upon the premise *pluralitas non est ponenda sine neccesitate*.

5 Joanna Dewey, "Oral Methods of Structuring Narrative in Mark," *Int* 43 (1989): 32–44, proposes that "[f]inally, or perhaps first of all, we must develop a media model for the Gospel of Mark and early Christianity in general. We need a better understanding of how oral and written media work both together and in opposition to each other in the early Christian mixed media situation" (44).

6 Thomas Bergemann, *Q auf dem Prüfstand: Die Zuordnung des Mt/Lk-Stoffes zu Q am Beispiel der Bergpredigt* (FRLANT 158; Göttingen: Vandenhoeck & Ruprecht, 1993), 56.

7 Robert Morgenthaler, *Statistische Synopse* (Zurich: Gotthelf-Verlag, 1971), 261.

8 Theodore Rosché, "The Words of Jesus and the Future of the 'Q' Hypothesis," *JBL* 79 (1960): 210–20 (217–18).

9   See Mournet, *Oral Tradition*, ch. 6.
10 See James D. G. Dunn, "Altering the Default Setting: Re-envisaging the Early Transmission of the Jesus Tradition," *NTS* 49 (2003): 139–75, for a more extended critique of what he has labeled as the "literary paradigm." See also Mournet, *Oral Tradition*, 13–53.
11 See Marshall McLuhan, *The Gutenberg Galaxy: The Making of Typographic Man* (Toronto: University of Toronto Press, 1962); Elizabeth L. Eisenstein, *The Printing Press as an Agent of Change: Communications and Cultural Transformations in Early-Modern Europe* (New York: Cambridge University Press, 1979).
12 See Isidore Okpewho, *African Oral Literature* (Indianapolis: Indiana University Press, 1992), 7–8, 168, on this perspective and for how this "evolutionary" view of tradition development impacted the Grimm brothers and those who subsequently appropriated their work.
13 In particular, Bultmann, who wrote, "[i]f we are able to detect any such laws [regarding the process of tradition transmission], we can infer back to an earlier stage of the tradition than appears in our sources. Moreover it is at this point a matter of indifference whether the tradition were oral or written, because on account of the unliterary character of the material one of the chief differences between oral and written traditions is lacking" (*History*, 6).
14 See Sanders, *Tendencies*, passim, for his systematic refutation of the claims that there are any universal "tendencies" (i.e., "laws of transmission") operating within the synoptic tradition.
15 Mournet, *Oral Tradition*, 62–63.
16 Barry W. Henaut, *Oral Tradition and the Gospels: The Problem of Mark 4* (JSNTSup 82; Sheffield: JSOT Press, 1993), passim.
17 It is necessary to remind the reader that the so-called orality model does allow for, and indeed affirm, the existence of written sources, including a written Q.
18 This is among the points of emphasis in Donald A. Hagner's recent preface to Gerhardsson's *Reliability*, vii–xvi. Also see Christopher Tuckett's chapter on form criticism in this volume.
19 E.g., John Dominic Crossan, *The Historical Jesus: The Life of a Mediterranean Jewish Peasant* (San Francisco: HarperSanFrancisco, 1991), xxvii–xxxiv.
20 Gerhardsson, *Memory and Manuscript*, 14–15, enphasis in original.
21 Gerhardsson, *Memory and Manuscript*, 85.
22 Gerhardsson, *Memory and Manuscript*, 105, 157–63.
23 Gerhardsson, *Memory and Manuscript*, 130–31.
24 See esp. Morton Smith's review of Gerhardsson, *Memory and Manuscript*, *JBL* 82 (1963): 169–76.
25 See Jacob Neusner's summary of the historical and scholastic setting which colored the reception of Gerhardsson's work. Neusner's summary appears in the new edition of Gerhardsson, *Memory and Manuscript*, xxv–xlvi.
26 Eric A. Havelock, *The Literate Revolution in Greece and Its Cultural Consequences* (Princeton: Princeton University Press, 1982), 9.
27 See Neusner's foreword to the new edition of Gerhardsson's *Memory and Manuscript*.
28 Mournet, *Oral Tradition*.
29 Milman Parry, "Studies in the Epic Technique of Oral Verse-Making. I: Homer and Homeric Style," *HSCP* 41 (1930): 73–147; idem, "Whole Formulaic Verses in Greek and Southslavic Heroic Song," *TAPA* 64 (1933): 179–97.

30　Albert Lord, *Singer of Tales* (Harvard Studies in Comparative Literature 24; 2d ed.; Cambridge, Mass.: Harvard University Press, 2000).
31　Lord, *Singer of Tales*, 26–28.
32　Albert B. Lord, "The Gospels as Oral Traditional Literature," in *The Relationships Among the Gospels: An Interdisciplinary Dialogue* (ed. William O. Walker Jr.; San Antonio: Trinity University Press, 1978), 33–91; also Thomas P. Haverly, "Oral Traditional Literature and the Composition of Mark" (Ph.D. diss., University of Edinburgh, 1983).
33　See John Miles Foley, *The Theory of Oral Composition: History and Methodology* (Bloomington: Indiana University Press, 1988); idem, *How to Read an Oral Poem* (Urbana: University of Illinois Press, 2002).
34　Ong contributed the preface to Kelber's highly influential *The Oral and the Written Gospel*. In many respects, Kelber's work represents a creative reading and appropriation of Ong's thesis with reference to the Gospel of Mark.
35　Walter J. Ong, *Orality and Literacy: The Technologizing of the Word* (2d ed.; London: Routledge, 2002).
36　Ong, *Orality and Literacy*, 31–77.
37　Ruth Finnegan, "How Oral is Oral Literature?," *BSOAS* 37 (1974): 52–64 (59); Havelock, *Literate Revolution*, 10. Shemaryahu Talmon, "Oral Tradition and Written Transmission, or the Heard and the Seen Word in Judaism of the Second Temple Period," in Wansbrough, *Jesus and the Oral Gospel Tradition*, 121–58, writes ". . . the real opposition was not *oral versus written*, but rather *voiced versus silent*. Orality and textuality were both deemed handmaidens of aurality" (150, emphasis in original). More recently, see Holly Hearon, "Implications of Orality for Studies of the Biblical Text," in *Performing the Gospel: Orality, Memory, and Mark* (ed. Richard A. Horsley, Jonathan A. Draper, and John Miles Foley; Minneapolis: Fortress, 2006): 3–20, who writes "in 'rhetorical culture' the oral and the written text are bound together in a dynamic relationship. The impact of this insight . . . is profound. It disrupts any notion of a clear distinction between an 'oral phase' and a 'written phase' and points to the reality that both oral and written versions of the same text may have been in circulation at the same time" (9). In regard to the *Gospel of Thomas*, see Risto Uro, "*Thomas* and Oral Gospel Tradition," in *Thomas at the Crossroads: Essays on the Gospel of Thomas* (ed. Uro; Edinburgh: Clark, 1998), 8–32 (15).
38　Øivind Anderson, "Oral Tradition," in Wansbrough, *Jesus and the Oral Gospel Tradition*, 17–58 (50).
39　The recent work of David M. Carr, *Writing on the Tablet of the Heart: Origins of Scripture and Literature* (Oxford: Oxford University Press, 2005), sheds light upon many of the issues related to the role of texts in antiquity, and in particular, the interface between written texts and oral tradition.
40　It is clear that the early Christians did participate to a certain extent in a "manuscript culture" with regard to LXX and other sacred writings of the period. For example, a cursory examination of Paul's letters reveals a significant level of indebtedness to a textual tradition. However, there remains uncertainty as to the extent to which Paul was citing a fixed manuscript of the LXX/MT or recalling the tradition from his memory. From media perspectives, the history of the early church reflects the transition that began to take place from a predominately oral culture to one where increasing emphasis was placed on written texts. A complex confluence of factors following the destruction of the temple led to the situation where the text would become, over time, an authoritative and fixed tradition

which would have prominence over an ongoing oral tradition. David E. Aune, "Oral Tradition and the Aphorisms of Jesus," in Wansbrough, *Jesus and the Oral Gospel Tradition*, 211–65, writes that "in early Christianity, it is probable that texts became relatively fixed and unchanging only by attributing sacred status to them, and by the increasing role which Christian scholars educated in Greco-Roman schools played in the writing and transmission of the intellectual tradition of early Christianity" (240).

41 In particular see Michael B. Thompson, "The Holy Internet: Communication Between Churches in the First Christian Generation," in *The Gospels for All Christians: Rethinking the Gospel Audiences* (ed. Richard Bauckham; Grand Rapids: Eerdmans, 1998), 49–70, on the interconnected nature of the early Christian congregations.

42 William V. Harris, *Ancient Literacy* (Cambridge, Mass.: Harvard University Press, 1989), 114.

43 Harris, *Ancient Literacy*, 328.

44 In particular, see Alan R. Millard, *Reading and Writing in the Time of Jesus* (New York: New York University Press, 2000), 157–84. Loveday Alexander, "Ancient Book Production and the Circulation of the Gospels," in *The Gospels for All Christians: Rethinking the Gospel Audiences* (ed. Richard Bauckham; Grand Rapids: Eerdmans, 1998), 71–111, describes a "commercial booktrade" (87) whereby copyists and booksellers earned income from the production and sale of texts.

45 Hezser concludes that Jewish literacy was *lower* than that of their peers during the first centuries C.E. See Catherine Hezser, *Jewish Literacy in Roman Palestine* (TSAJ 81; Tübingen: Mohr Siebeck, 2001), 496–504. See also Meir Bar-Ilan, "Illiteracy in the Land of Israel in the First Centuries C.E.," in *Essays in the Social Scientific Study of Judaism and Jewish Society* (ed. Simcha Fishbane, Stuart Schoenfeld, and Alain Godschlaeger; New York: KTAV 1992): 46–61. Bar-Ilan correlates the rate of literacy with the extent to which a society is agrarian-based and thus argues that Jewish literacy would have been lower than that within the Greco-Roman world. Richard Horsley, along the same lines, points out that despite the low estimations of literacy levels, scholars "continue to trust generalizations about high rates of Judean or diaspora Jewish literacy that preceded recent critical studies of literacy in antiquity" (Richard A. Horsley and Jonathan A. Draper, *Whoever Hears You Hears Me: Prophets, Performance, and Tradition in Q* [Harrisburg: Trinity Press International, 1999], 127). Also see Richard A. Horsley, *Hearing the Whole Story: The Politics of Plot in Mark's Gospel* (Louisville, Ky.: Westminster John Knox, 2001), 53–55. Lastly, Karel Van Der Toorn, *Scribal Culture and the Making of the Hebrew Bible* (Cambridge, Mass.: Harvard University Press, 2007), 9–26, provides a helpful summary of literacy in the world in which the Hebrew Bible was inscribed.

46 Harris, *Ancient Literacy*, 250.

47 Loveday Alexander, "The Living Voice: Scepticism Towards the Written Word in Early Christian and in Greco-Roman Texts," in *The Bible in Three Dimensions: Essays in Celebration of Forty Years of Biblical Studies in the University of Sheffield* (ed. David J. A. Clines, Stephen E. Fowl, and Stanley E. Porter; JSOTSup 87; Sheffield: Sheffield Academic Press, 1990), 220–47 (esp. 244). This view towards the "living voice" is not confined to the Greco-Roman world but is affirmed across the wide spectrum of cultures at the time of Jesus, including that of the Hebrew Bible itself. See also Mournet, *Oral Tradition*, ch. 4.

48 Luke 1:1-4; *Let. Aris.* 1; and Philo, *Mos.* 1.1.4 all claim to have been aware of the existence of both oral and written sources concerning their subject matter, and all

three authors claim to have incorporated oral tradition in their respective narratives. See also Herodotus, *Hist.* 3.55.2; 4.76.6; 9.16.1; Thucydides, *Hist.* 1.138.6, 2.5.5–6; 2.48.2; 2.88.3; 6.2.2.

49   For the *Didache*, see Willy Rordorf, "Does the Didache Contain Jesus Tradition Independently of the Synoptic Gospels?," in Wansbrough, *Jesus and the Oral Gospel Tradition*, 394–423 (422); Ian Henderson, "Didache and Orality in Synoptic Comparison," *JBL* 111 (1992): 283–306 (esp. 297, 305); Huub van de Sandt and David Flusser, *The Didache: Its Jewish Sources and Its Place in Early Judaism and Christianity* (CRINT 5; Assen: Van Gorcum, 2002), who write in regard to the *Didache* version of the Lord's Prayer: ". . . there is no need to assume that the Didache is dependent on the gospel of Matthew, for it is most unlikely that the (Christian) editor of this unit in the Didache would have needed Matthew's text in order to reproduce the prayer. On the contrary, it makes more sense to assume that he is citing the liturgical, that is, the oral form of public prayer" (294–95). For the *Acts of Paul*, see Dennis R. MacDonald, "From Audita to Legenda: Oral and Written Miracle Stories," *Forum* 2:4 (1986): 15–26 (16–17). For Q, see Horsley and Draper, *Whoever Hears You Hears Me*. For the Apostolic Fathers, see Helmut Koester, *Synoptische Überlieferung bei den apostolischen Vätern* (TUGAL 65; Berlin: Akademie-Verlag, 1957).

50   Paul J. Achtemeier, "*Omne Verbum Sonat*: The New Testament and the Oral Environment of Late Western Antiquity," *JBL* 109 (1990): 3–27, and the response by Frank D. Gilliard, "More Silent Reading in Antiquity: *Non Omne Verbum Sonabat*," *JBL* 112 (1993): 689–94, who, despite his critique of Achtemeier, concludes that there is abundant evidence to suggest that the culture of late Western antiquity is one of "high residual orality."

51   Mournet, *Oral Tradition*, ch. 4.

52   Kenneth E. Bailey, "Informal Controlled Oral Tradition and the Synoptic Gospels," *AJT* 5:1 (1991): 34–54; idem, "Informal Controlled Oral Tradition and the Synoptic Tradition," *Themelios* 20:2 (1995): 4–11.

53   N. T. Wright, *Jesus and the Victory of God* (Christian Origins and the Question of God 2; Minneapolis: Fortress, 1996), 136.

54   Dunn, *Jesus Remembered*; Mournet, *Oral Tradition*.

55   Bailey, "Informal Controlled Oral Tradition and the Synoptic Gospels," 40.

56   Bailey, "Informal Controlled Oral Tradition and the Synoptic Gospels," 44.

57   Bailey, "Informal Controlled Oral Tradition and the Synoptic Gospels," 42, emphasis in original.

58   Bailey, "Informal Controlled Oral Tradition and the Synoptic Gospels," 42–44. See also Ernest L. Abel, "The Psychology of Memory and Rumor Transmission and Their Bearing on Theories of Oral Transmission in Early Christianity," *JR* 51 (1971): 270–81.

59   Dunn, *Jesus Remembered*, 154–55, uses the terms "fixity and flexibility," "variation within the same," "stability and diversity." I use the terms "variability" and "stability" (Mournet, *Oral Tradition*, 179–91).

60   Michael F. Bird, "The Formation of the Gospels in the Setting of Early Christianity: The Jesus Tradition as Corporate Memory," *WTJ* 67 (2005): 113–34 (128–30), points out five specific strengths of the Bailey model and then proceeds to outline what he describes as "a new paradigm" based on the recent work of Dunn which Bird labels "Jesus in corporate memory." Despite Bird's affirmation of Dunn's model, "Jesus in corporate memory" is not the best description of Dunn's thesis as the latter does not offer a well-developed model of corporate/social memory in his *Jesus Remembered*. For a critique on just such grounds, see

Byrskog, "A New Perspective," 459–71, and Dunn's response, "On History, Memory and Eyewitnesses: In Response to Bengt Holmberg and Samuel Byrskog," *JSNT* 26 (2004): 473–87.

61 Gerhardsson has responded to Kelber's earlier characterization of the rabbinical model as "a model of passive transmission." Gerhardsson writes: ". . . in *Memory and Manuscript* I do not depict the Jewish tradition as simply a heritage to be preserved but as extraordinarily rich and living, variegated and variable, and freshly creative . . . even the rabbis could rework their traditions, change formulations, cancel elements, and insert additions and new layers" (*Memory and Manuscript*, xix). See also Gerhardsson, "Illuminating the Kingdom," 266–309, ". . . I think, that early Christianity has felt itself entitled to rework some of the Master's texts and even formulate new narrative meshalim created in the spirit and style of Jesus, and also to put them in the mouth of Jesus . . . the freedom of re-working (sometimes creating) seems to have been considerable. This especially applies to the Lukan tradition" (296–97).

62 Reiterated by Gerhardsson in his recent response to the work of Dunn. See Gerhardsson, "Secret of the Transmission," 1–18.

63 There are instances where Gerhardsson does suggest that the *ipsissima verba* were retained when he writes that throughout this process of tradition transmission the "reverence and care for the *ipsissima verba* of each authority remains unaltered" (*Memory and Manuscript*, 130–31). The pertinent question here is this: to what extent did Jewish teachers of Jesus' day, and those early, influential rabbis of nascent rabbinic Judaism, utilize verbatim memorization as means for teaching? For further details on nature of rabbinic memorization, see Jaffee's chapter in this volume.

64 Here I readily admit that I too have erred on the side of oversimplification and caricature when assessing Gerhardsson's contribution (see Mournet, *Oral Tradition*, 63–67). Were I to revisit the topic again, I would likely be more careful in articulating my critique.

65 Gerhardsson, "Secret of the Transmission," 6.

66 See the oft-cited early critiques of Jacob Neusner and Morton Smith.

67 See Mournet, *Oral Tradition*, 160–64, for a more detailed exposition on this topic.

68 Mournet, *Oral Tradition*, 161, emphasis in original.

69 Mournet, *Oral Tradition*, 162, emphasis in original.

70 Mournet, *Oral Tradition*, 163.

71 I use this term rather than "Judaism" or "Roman Palestine," etc., because, given my own perspective on the phenomena of "orality" and "oral performance," the greater context of the Mediterranean is inclusive enough to describe the greater communicative processes of the day.

72 Mournet, *Oral Tradition*, passim.

73 Here I am not using the term "homeostatic" to argue for the position of nondifferentiation between the present and past which is how the term was initially used (Goody and Watt, "Consequences of Literacy," 31–34). As Jan Vansina has demonstrated in *Oral Tradition as History*, 120–23, this view on homeostasis is overstated. Rather, I use the term in reference to the fact that traditional cultures are slow to change and change typically occurs gradually, over extended periods of time.

74 Ong, *Orality and Literacy*, 32.

75 Gerhardsson, "Secret of the Transmission," 7.

76   Gerhardsson, "Secret of the Transmission," 7.
77   Gerhardsson, "Secret of the Transmission," 3.
78   Gerhardsson, "Secret of the Transmission," 7.
79   The relatively new interest in "orality" has led to an awakening regarding this likelihood. The type of well-crafted teachings of Jesus—full of mnemonic "hooks" and rhetorical devices—would have surely been utilized on more than one occasion and in different contexts. The notion that, for example, the so-called Lord's Prayer can be best understood as the intentional departure from an original, exemplar source text (i.e., Q) is simply without merit once one is willing to appreciate how oral performers utilized a repertoire of material in varying contexts and in front of different audiences (Dunn, "Default Setting," 129–75; idem, *Jesus Remembered*, 226–28). Given the type of tradition represented in the Lord's Prayer, we should at least be willing to entertain the possibility that some of the variation between the canonical versions of the prayer reflect the varying performances of Jesus himself. See also Mournet, *Oral Tradition*, 221–26.
80   Gerhardsson, "Secret of the Transmission," 7, emphasis in original.
81   John Miles Foley, *Immanent Art: From Structure to Meaning in Traditional Oral Epic* (Bloomington: Indiana University Press, 1991), 7. Foley's work on "metonymic referencing" was appropriated by Horsley and Draper in their work on Q and the Q community (Horsley and Draper, *Whoever Hears You Hears Me*, 160–61).
82   For an extensive treatment of memory in Gerhardsson's work, see Alan Kirk's chapter in this volume.
83   See Gerhardsson, "Illuminating the Kingdom," 306: "I still believe that there also existed a more programmatic form of transmission: somebody actually 'handed over' a Jesus-text to another who received it in an appropriate way, whether a single text or a collection. This could be one either orally or in writing, or in both ways."
84   See esp. Samuel Byrskog, *Story as History*, 146–75, passim, who emphasizes the importance of *autopsy* in the Greco-Roman context; and Bauckham, *Jesus and the Eyewitnesses*.

Chapter 3

1   Gerhardsson, *Memory and Manuscript*. A second edition of this monograph, with minor corrections, appeared in 1964. A third edition appeared in 1998, with a new introduction by Jacob Neusner and the addition of *Tradition and Transmission in Early Christianity*.
2   Gerhardsson, *Memory and Manuscript*, 335, 328–29.
3   Gerhardsson, *Memory and Manuscript*, 221 n. 2, 230, 321.
4   Gerhardsson, *Memory and Manuscript*, 9–15.
5   W. D. Davies, "Reflections on a Scandinavian Approach to 'the Gospel Tradition,'" in *Neotestamentica et Patristica: Freundesgabe Oscar Cullmann* (NovTSup 6; Leiden: Brill, 1962), 14–34. Reprinted with some alterations in W. D. Davies, *The Setting of the Sermon on the Mount* (Cambridge: Cambridge University Press, 1964), 464–80; Smith, "A Comparison," 169–76; Jacob Neusner, "The Rabbinic Traditions about the Pharisees before 70 A.D.: The Problem of Oral Tradition," *Kairos* 14 (1972): 57–70; Norman Perrin, *Rediscovering the Teaching of Jesus* (New York: Harper & Row, 1967), 30–32; Kelber, *Oral and Written Gospel*, 8–14; idem,

"The Works of Memory: Christian Origins as Mnemo-History—A Response," in Kirk and Thatcher, *Memory, Tradition, and Text*, 221–48 (231–35).
6   Joseph A. Fitzmyer, "Memory and Manuscript: The Origins and Transmission of the Gospel Tradition," *TS* 23 (1961): 442–47.
7   Bauckham, *Jesus and the Eyewitnesses*, 249–52.
8   He has compiled a helpful list of the early reviews of *Memory and Manuscript*. See Gerhardsson, *Memory and Manuscript*, preface to the 1998 edition, xxiii.
9   Gerhardsson responds to the views of Werner Kelber in *Gospel Tradition*, 32–57 and passim.
10 This is a major objection of Smith, "Comparison," 169–76; Neusner, "Rabbinic Traditions," 57–70 (he later retracted this criticism); Kelber, *Oral and Written Gospel*, 14. Gerhardsson essentially rejects this criticism as an incorrect understanding of his views (see *Memory and Manuscript*, preface to the 1998 edition, xiii).
11 Jacob Neusner, "Gerhardsson's *Memory and Manuscript* Revisited: Introduction to a New Edition," *Approaches to Ancient Judaism* NS 12 (1997): 171–94 (the denunciation of Smith is on pp. 172–75).
12 Neusner, "Gerhardsson's *Memory and Manuscript* Revisited," 176.
13 Neusner, "Gerhardsson's *Memory and Manuscript* Revisited," 178–90. Along the same lines, Bauckham considers the pedagogy of rabbinic Judaism as an "illuminating parallel despite being later than the New Testament period" (*Jesus and the Eyewitnesses*, 250).
14 Martin Jaffee, *Torah in the Mouth: Writing and Oral radition in Palestinian Judaism, 200 BCE–400 CE* (Oxford: Oxford University Press, 2001, on the Pharisees see pp. 39–61, and on Oral Torah see pp. 65–83. Avery-Peck dates the first evidence for the concept of Oral Torah to the opening lines of *m. Abot*, which dates to the early third century C.E. (Alan J. Avery-Peck, "Oral Tradition [Judaism]," *ABD* 5:36).
15 Jaffee, *Torah in the Mouth*, 146–52.
16 For example, Gerhardsson, *Memory and Manuscript*, 274–75, 311 and passim.
17 Jaffee, *Torah in the Mouth*, 43.
18 Kelber, *Oral and Written Gospel*, 13.
19 Kelber, "Works of Memory," 232.
20 Gerhardsson, *Memory and Manuscript*, preface to the 1998 edition, xi–xii; see also Jaffee, *Torah in the Mouth*, 162–63 n. 13.
21 Perrin, *Rediscovering the Teaching of Jesus*, 30.
22 Jacob Neusner, *Oral Tradition in Judaism: The Case of the Mishnah* (New York: Garland, 1987), 93. See also Jacob Neusner, *The Memorized Torah: The Mnemonic System of the Mishnah* (BJS 96; Chico, Calif.: Scholars Press, 1985).
23 Neusner, *Memorized Torah*, 28.
24 Philip S. Alexander, "Orality in Pharisaic-Rabbinic Judaism at the Turn of the Eras," in Wansbrough, *Jesus and the Oral Gospel Tradition*, 159–84 (175).
25 Philip S. Alexander, "Orality," 175–76.
26 Philip S. Alexander, "Orality," 181–82.
27 Randolph E. Richards, *The Secretary in the Letters of Paul* (WUNT 2.42; Tübingen: Mohr Siebeck, 1991); idem, *Paul and First-Century Letter Writing: Secretaries, Composition, Collection* (Downers Grove, Ill.: InterVarsity, 2004). A major question, with which Richards deals, is the extent to which secretaries influenced the formulation of letters.
28 On the creativity of scribes, see Kim Haines-Eitzen, *Guardians of Letters: Literacy,*

Power, and the Transmitters of Early Christian Literature (Oxford: Oxford University Press, 2000).

29   A "critical text" of the *Testament of Solomon* was produced in 1922 by C. C. McCown (Leipzig: J. C. Hinrichs), yet the incredible number of variants listed by McCown, some extremely extensive, made it apparent that McCown had not really succeeded in constructing an original text of the document so much as a search for the common denominator of the dozen or so extant manuscripts.

30   Kelber, *Oral and Written Gospel*; Traugott Holtz, "Paul and the Oral Gospel Tradition," in Wansbrough, *Jesus and the Oral Gospel Tradition*, 380–93; John D. Harvey, *Listening to the Text: Oral Patterning in Paul's Letters* (Grand Rapids: Baker Books, 1998).

31   Gerhardsson, *Memory and Manuscript*, 262–323.

32   Gerhardsson, *Memory and Manuscript*, 291 (entire quotation italicized in the original).

33   Gerhardsson, *Memory and Manuscript*, 295.

34   Gerhardsson, *Memory and Manuscript*, 295, emphasis in original. A similar statement is made on p. 301.

35   Gerhardsson, *Memory and Manuscript*, 299–300.

36   Gerhardsson, *Memory and Manuscript*, 153–56; Philip Alexander, "Orality," 170–71.

37   Gerhardsson, *Memory and Manuscript*, 300.

38   Gerhardsson, *Memory and Manuscript*, 301.

39   Gerhardsson, *Memory and Manuscript*, 302.

40   Gerhardsson, *Memory and Manuscript*, 79–84, 94–98, 171–81.

41   Gerhardsson, *Memory and Manuscript*, 311–21.

42   Kelber, *Oral and Written Gospel*, 140–83.

43   In the preface, he claims that he does not wish to "romanticize orality at the expense of writing, but I describe writing as it appears to an oral mentality" (Kelber, *Oral and Written Gospel*, xvi).

44   Robert W. Funk, "The Apostolic Parousia: Form and Significance," in *Christian History and Interpretation: Studies Presented to John Knox* (ed. William R. Farmer, C. F. D. Moule, and R. R. Niebuhr; Cambridge: Cambridge University Press, 1967), 249–68.

45   Kelber, *Oral and Written Gospel*, 141.

46   Kelber, *Oral and Written Gospel*, 146.

47   Kelber, *Oral and Written Gospel*, 148.

48   Kelber, *Oral and Written Gospel*, 153.

49   This view, which goes back at least to F. C. Baur, finds a convincing modern proponent in Daniel Boyarin, *A Radical Jew: Paul and the Politics of Identity* (Berkeley: University of California Press, 1994), and in the representatives of the new perspective on Paul, E. P. Sanders, T. Wright, and J. D. G. Dunn.

50   Kelber, *Oral and Written Gospel*, 157–58.

51   William A. Graham, "Scripture as Spoken Word," in *Rethinking Scripture: Essays from a Comparative Perspective* (ed. Miriam Levering; Albany: State University of New York Press, 1989), 129–69.

52   Graham, "Scripture as Spoken Word," 135.

53   Graham, "Scripture as Spoken Word," 163.

54   Kelber, *Oral and Written Gospel*, 167.

55   Kelber, *Oral and Written Gospel*, 169.

56   Kelber, *Oral and Written Gospel*, 172–73.

57 Kelber, *Oral and Written Gospel*, 174.
58 Kelber, *Oral and Written Gospel*, 177.
59 Holtz, "Paul," 380–93.
60 Gerhardsson argued for the presence of both fixed and flexible elements; Jesus delivered the first type of material with the intention that it be memorized, while the flexible material, largely in the form of exposition, he did not regard as memory texts (*Memory and Manuscript*, 328–29). This binary approach to the material is apparently based on the rabbinic distinction between text and interpretation, with an analogous arrangement of fixed oral texts in Oral Torah together with more fluid interpretations (*Memory and Manuscript*, 79–83). There are several models for conceptualizing early Christian forms of communication. He also suggests that most of the Gospel material is haggadic, and that haggadic material was transmitted in a more fluid form than sayings material (*Memory and Manuscript*, 335). Analogously, Dodd speaks of two distinct channels of tradition in early Christianity, the catechetical pattern and the Passion Narrative (C. H. Dodd, "The 'Primitive Catechism' and the Sayings of Jesus," in *More New Testament Studies* [Grand Rapids: Eerdmans, 1968], 11–29 [21]). James MacDonald rejects the earlier binary model *kerygma* ("preaching") and *didache* ("teaching'), for a more complex model of early Christian communication consisting of *propheteia, paraclesis, paraenesis,* and *paradosis* (James I. H. MacDonald, *Kerygma and Didache: The Articulation and Structure of the Earliest Christian Message* [Cambridge: Cambridge University Press, 1980]).
61 Holtz, "Paul," 382–83.
62 Holtz, "Paul," 389–90.
63 Holtz, "Paul," 390–92.
64 Holtz, "Paul," 393.
65 Holtz, "Paul," 393.
66 Harvey, *Listening to the Text*, 61–96.
67 Harvey, *Listening to the Text*, 97–118.
68 Harvey, *Listening to the Text*, 119–282.
69 For a brief survey of the present state of the Parry Collection of Moslem oral epic, see John Miles Foley, "Editing and Translating Traditional Oral Epic: The South Slavic Songs and Homer," in *Epea and Grammata: Oral and Written Communication in Ancient Greece* (ed. Ian Worthington and John Miles Foley; Supplements to Mnemosyne 230; Leiden: Brill, 2002), 3–27.
70 Harvey, *Listening to the Text*, 287, 289, 291.
71 Harvey, *Listening to the Text*, 289–90.
72 Ian Worthington, "Greek Oratory and the Oral/Literate Division," in *Voice into Text: Orality and Literacy in Ancient Greece* (ed. Ian Worthington; Leiden: Brill, 1996), 165–77.
73 Leonhard Goppelt, *Theology of the New Testament* (2 vols.; Grand Rapids: Eerdmans, 1982), 2.45.
74 Both Christopher Tuckett and Dale Allison argue that there is no evidence that Paul was acquainted with Q. See Tuckett, "Paul and the Synoptic Mission Discourse?," *ETL* 60 (1984): 376–81 (380 n. 19); Allison, "The Pauline Epistles and the Synoptic Gospels: The Pattern of the Parallels," *NTS* 28 (1982): 1–32.
75 Alfred Resch, *Der Paulinismus und die Logia Jesu in ihrem gegenwärtigen Verhältnis untersucht* (Texte und Untersuchungen zur Geschichte der altchristlichen Literatur, NF 12; Leipzig: Hinrichs, 1904).

76 W. D. Davies, *Paul and Rabbinic Judaism: Some Rabbinic Elements in Pauline Theology* (rev. ed.; New York: Harper & Row, 1955), 140.
77 W. D. Davies, "Paul and the Law: Reflections on Pitfalls in Interpretation," in *Jewish and Pauline Studies* (Philadelphia: Fortress, 1984), 112–15; idem, "The Moral Teaching of the Early Church," in *Jewish and Pauline Studies*, 284–87; idem, *Paul and Rabbinic Judaism*, 136–43.
78 Allison, "Pauline Epistles," 1–32.
79 Nikolaus Walter, "Paulus und die urchristliche Jesustradition," *NTS* 31 (1985): 498–522.
80 Franz Neirynck, "Paul and the Sayings of Jesus," in *L'Apôtre Paul: Personnalité, style et conception du ministère* (ed. Albert Vanhoye and Jean-Noël Aletti; BETL 73; Leuven: Leuven University Press and Peeters, 1986), 267–321.
81 Neirynck, "Paul," 268–81.
82 Neirynck, "Paul," 320.
83 David Wenham, *Paul: Follower of Jesus or Founder of Christianity?* (Grand Rapids: Eerdmans, 1995).
84 Wenham, *Paul*, 3.
85 Wenham, *Paul*, 377.
86 James D. G. Dunn, *The Theology of Paul the Apostle* (Grand Rapids: Eerdmans, 1998), 189–95, 649–58.
87 Dunn, *Theology of Paul*, 652.
88 Dunn, *Theology of Paul*, 195.
89 Dunn, *Theology of Paul*, 650–51.
90 Detlef Häusser, *Christusbekenntnis und Jesusüberlieferung bei Paulus* (WUNT 2.210; Tübingen: Mohr Siebeck, 2006).
91 Häusser, *Christusbekenntnis*, 351.
92 Häusser, *Christusbekenntnis*, 72–73, 149–50. Cf. Gerhardsson, *Memory and Manuscript*, 299–300.
93 Häusser, *Christusbekenntnis*, 61–158.
94 Häusser, *Christusbekenntnis*, 351–52.
95 Häusser, *Christusbekenntnis*, 352.
96 Häusser, *Christusbekenntnis*, 354.
97 Häusser, *Christusbekenntnis*, 356–58.
98 *Les Lieux de mémoire* (ed. Pierre Nora; 3 vols. in 7; Paris: Gallimard, 1984–1992); abbreviated English translation: *Realms of Memory: Rethinking the French Past* (ed. Pierre Nora; 3 vols.; New York: Columbia University Press, 1996–1998).
99 Frances A. Yates, *The Art of Memory* (Chicago: University of Chicago Press, 1966).
100 Maurice Halbwachs, *The Collective Memory* (New York: Harper & Row, 1980).
101 Pierre Nora, "From *Lieu de mémoire* to Realms of Memory," in *Conflicts and Divisions* (vol. 1 of *Realms of Memory*), xvii.
102 Pierre Nora, "General Introduction: Between Memory and History," in *Conflicts and Divisions* (vol. 1 of *Realms of Memory*), 1–20.
103 Nora, "General Introduction," 20.
104 Aspects of this problem are discussed by Lukas Bormann, "Autobiographische Fiktionalität bei Paulus," in *Biographie und Persönlichkeit des Paulus* (ed. Eve-Marie Becker and Peter Pilhofer; WUNT 187; Tübingen: Mohr Siebeck, 2005), 106–24. See also the earlier monograph of George Lyons, *Pauline Autobiography: Toward a New Understanding* (SBLDS 73; Atlanta: Scholars Press, 1985).

105 Based on J. Harold Greenlee, *A New Testament Greek Morpheme Lexicon* (Grand Rapids: Zondervan, 1983).
106 Johannes P. Louw and Eugene A. Nida, *Greek-English Lexicon of the New Testament Based on Semantic Domains* (2 vols.; New York: United Bible Societies, 1988), 1.§29.1–18.
107 Louw and Nida, *Greek-English Lexicon of the New Testament*, 1.§28.1.
108 Emphasis added in all six verse quotations.
109 The list of pseudo-Pauline letters typically includes 2 Thessalonians, Colossians, Ephesians, 1 and 2 Timothy, and Titus. The first two letters on the list are less certainly assigned to Pauline pseudepigraphy by critical scholars.
110 The wide variety and even the apparent contradictions between the various eschatological scenarios found in the Pauline letters should be noted; see David E. Aune, "The Judgment Seat of Christ (2 Cor. 5:10)," in *Pauline Conversations in Context: Essays in Honor of Calvin J. Roetzel* (ed. Janice Capel Anderson, Philip Sellew, and Claudia Setzer; JSNTSup 221; Sheffield: Sheffield University Press, 2002), 68–86.
111 In an earlier book, I argued that in 1 Thess 4:15-17, Paul is rehearsing a saying of Jesus mediated by an early Christian prophet: David E. Aune, *Prophecy in Early Christianity and the Ancient Mediterranean World* (Grand Rapids: Eerdmans, 1983), 253–56.
112 One of the more recent discussions of this issue is found in Craig Allert, *A High View of Scripture? The Authority of the Bible and the Formation of the New Testament Canon* (Grand Rapids: Baker Academic, 2007), 109–12.
113 On the potential value of the sayings tradition in the *Gospel of Thomas*, see David E. Aune, "Assessing the Historical Value of the Apocryphal Jesus Traditions: A Critique of Conflicting Methodologies," in *Der historische Jesus: Tendenzen und Perspektiven der gegenwärtigen Forschung* (ed. Jens Schröter and Ralph Brucker; BZNW 114; Berlin: de Gruyter, 2002), 243–72. For a competent (though incomplete) collection of *agrapha*, see William D. Stroker, *Extracanonical Sayings of Jesus* (SBLRBS 18; Atlanta: Scholars Press, 1989).
114 Nora, "General Introduction," 1.
115 For a convincing theory of the stages in the collection of the Pauline corpus, see David Trobisch, *Die Entstehung der Paulusbriefsammlung: Studien zu den Anfängen christlicher Publizistik* (NTOA 10; Freiburg: Universitätsverlag, 1989).
116 Gerhard Lohfink, "Die Vermittlung des Paulinismus zu den Pastoralbriefen," *BZ* 32 (1988): 169–88.

Chapter 4

1 See Jacob Neusner, "Oral Torah and Oral Tradition: Defining the Problematic," in *Method and Meaning in Ancient Judaism* (Chico, Calif.: Scholars Press, 1979), 59–75. Neusner's programmatic essay remains as important today as it was when it was published. Following Neusner's lead, I have elsewhere explored the soteriological dimension of rabbinic oral performance of memorized tradition by viewing it as a "sacramental" activity: Martin S. Jaffee, "Oral Transmission of Knowledge as a Rabbinic Sacrament," in *Study and Knowledge in Jewish Thought* (ed. Howard Kreisel; Beer Sheva: Ben-Gurion University of the Negev Press, 2006), 65–79.
2 This issue occupies one of this generation's major theorists of oral tradition and oral literature, John Miles Foley, in *The Singer of Tales in Performance* (Bloomington: Indiana University Press, 1995). For the problem in relation to texts cultur-

ally, chronologically, and geographically contiguous with the rabbinic literature, see, for example, David Aune, "Prolegomena to the Study of Oral Tradition in the Hellenistic World," in Wansbrough, *Jesus and the Oral Gospel Tradition*, 59–105.

3   *The Anthology in Jewish Literature* (ed. David Stern; Oxford: Oxford University Press, 2004) offers an excellent set of essays clustered around the anthological nature of rabbinic compilations. See the essays by Yaakov Elman (53–80), Eliezer Segal (81–107), and David Stern (108–39).

4   See Robert Brody, *The Geonim of Babylonia and the Shaping of Medieval Jewish Culture* (New Haven: Yale University Press, 1998), 158–59. Hebrew readers will benefit from Yaakov Spiegel, *Chapters in the History of the Jewish Book: Scholars and Their Annotations* (Heb.) (Ramat Gan: Bar-Ilan University Press, 1996), 57–62.

5   The earliest known partial manuscript of rabbinic literature, found in Cambridge University's collection of texts from the Cairo Genizah, is a fragment of *Avot de-Rabbi Natan*, version A, from about the ninth century. See Marc Bregman, "An Early Fragment of Avot de Rabbi Nathan from a Scroll (Heb.)," *Tarbiz* 52 (1982–83): 201–22. In the same collection, Bregman also reports finding several fragmentary texts of the Babylonian Talmud corresponding to *b. Hul.* 101a–105a; *b. B. Bat.* 4a–5b, 29a–b. All of these appear to have been written on scrolls and would seem to predate the eighth century, when Jews in the Islamic world began to accept the codex rather than the scroll for the preservation of canonical literature. Bregman summarizes the codicological aspects of these fragments in an unpublished paper, "Non-Biblical Scrolls: The State of the Question," from 2005. I am grateful to Bregman for sharing a printout of this discussion with me.

On the basis of the Hullin fragment, Yaakov Elman estimates that the manuscript of the entire Babylonian Talmud could have filled ten and one half scrolls of 245 columns each. He concludes: "All in all, it must be admitted, copying the entire Babylonian Talmud onto scrolls seems not to have been a feat beyond the capability of the scribal art of the time. But it would not have been easy" ("Orality and the Redaction of the Babylonian Talmud," *Oral Tradition* 14 [1999]: 52–99 [75]. Cf. Yaakov Elman, "The Small Scale of Things: The World Before the Geniza," *PAAJR* 63 [2001]: 72–73).

Helpful summaries of the various extant manuscripts of the Bavli are available in H. L. Strack and Günter Stemberger, *Introduction to the Talmud and Midrash* (2d ed.; Minneapolis: Fortress, 1996), 210–11, and Michael Krupp's contribution to *The Literature of the Sages* (ed. Samuel Safrai; Assen/Maastricht: Van Gorcum, 1987), 351–63. The bulk of the surviving manuscripts were produced in Ashkenazic lands, among them MS Munich 95, which represents the only nearly complete manuscript of the Bavli. But other important manuscripts of this Talmud were produced in Spain, Italy, North Africa, and Yemen up till the fifteenth century.

6   See Birger Gerhardsson, *Memory and Manuscript*, 93–170. Cf. Samuel Byrskog, *Jesus the Only Teacher: Didactic Authority and Transmission in Ancient Israel, Ancient Judaism and the Matthean Community* (ConBNT 24; Stockholm: Almquist & Wiksell, 1994), 156–96. The most important recent studies of Palestinian rabbinic culture as discipleship communities are Catherine Hezser, *The Social Structure of the Rabbinic Movement in Palestine* (TSAJ 66; Tübingen: Mohr Siebeck, 1997), and Stuart S. Miller, *Sages and Commoners in Late Antique 'Erez Israel: A Philological Inquiry into Local Traditions in Talmud Yerushalmi* (Tübingen: Mohr Siebeck, 2006). For late Sasanian rabbinism, see now Jeffrey

Rubenstein, *The Culture of the Babylonian Talmud* (Baltimore: The Johns Hopkins University Press, 2003).

7   On the mnemonic technology that undergirds the Mishnah in particular, see the monumental form-critical study of Jacob Neusner, *The Redaction and Formulation of the Order of Purities in the Mishnah and Tosefta* (vol. 21 of *A History of the Mishnaic Law of Purities*; Leiden: Brill, 1977). More recent works exploring the mnemonics of rabbinic texts include Dov Zlotnick, *The Iron Pillar Mishnah: Redaction, Form, and Intent* (Jerusalem: Bialik Institute, 1988), 42–106; Martin S. Jaffee, "What Difference Does the Orality of Rabbinic Writing Make for the Interpretation of Rabbinic Writings?," in *How Should Rabbinic Literature Be Read in the Modern World?* (ed. Matthew A. Kraus; Piscataway, N.J.: Gorgias Press, 2006), 11–33; W. David Nelson, "Oral Orthography: Oral and Written Transmission of Parallel Midrashic Tradition in the *Mekhilta of Rabbi Simon b. Yohai* and the *Mekhilta of Rabbi Ishmael*," *AJS Review* 29 (2005): 1–32; Elizabeth Shanks Alexander, *Transmitting Mishnah: The Shaping Influence of Oral Tradition* (Cambridge: Cambridge University Press, 2006), 18–24.

The most important recent contribution to understanding the mnemonic methods of the classical rabbinic sages in the comparative context of broader Late Antique intellectual circles is the essay of Shlomo Naeh, "The Art of Memory: Structures of Memory and the Construction of Texts in Rabbinic Literature (Heb.)," in *Mehqerei Talmud: Talmudic Studies Dedicated to the Memory of Professor Ephraim E. Urbach* (ed. Yaakov Zussman and David Rozental; Jerusalem: Magnes Press, 2005), 2:543–90. Naeh points out that the rabbinic cultivation of capacious mnemonic skills need not entail the absence of written versions of Tannaitic texts, insofar as the same memorization skills were applied in the mastery of scriptural texts as well, which were, of course, readily available (556–57 n. 64). See following note.

8   This Aramaic term means "external traditions" and refers to rabbinic traditions of the Tannaitic period (ca. 70–200 C.E.) that were not compiled into the collections know as the Mishnah, the Tosefta, or the various midrashic collections. Nevertheless, as Tannaitic traditions, they are accorded an authority approaching those canonized in the collections above. A common problem in both Talmuds is to reconcile apparent contradictions between material compiled in the Mishnah and those that circulate as *baraitot*. See also n. 13.

9   The most encyclopedic presentation of the sources is now that of Yaakov Zussman, "Oral Torah Means Just What It Says (Heb.)," in Zussman and Rozental, *Mehqerei Talmud*,1:209–384. He argues that certainly the Mishnah, and probably most other halakhic works of Tannaitic venue were transmitted by exclusively oral means and were entirely unwritten until perhaps the sixth- through eighth-century "dark ages" of rabbinic literary history.

Zussman's main argument for the view that no written version of the Mishnah existed between the early third century C.E. and, say, the early sixth, is that no one—in the entire known literature of the rabbis—is ever depicted as consulting a written copy of the Mishnah to settle one of the thousands of cases in which doubt is cast upon the received version of this or that Mishnaic passage. By contrast, rabbinic sages are repeatedly shown consulting scriptural writings, reading scriptural books, and otherwise behaving in relationship to scriptural books precisely as we would expect *literati* to handle them—by reading them and explaining them. For Zussman, the total lack of such representation of rabbinic readers with Mishnaic texts can be explained in only one way—rabbis read no Mishnaic texts because there were none to be read.

The decisive refutation of such an argument *ex silentio w*ould be a discovery of a vast rabbinic library of texts corresponding more or less to the current versions of the Mishnah, the Tosefta, etc., and datable prior to the sixth century C.E. But, barring the discovery of such a rabbinic treasure of "oral torah scrolls," there is still something to be said for the argument that writing is certainly among the modes of composition and transmission of early rabbinic texts, although hardly the preferred or "canonical" method of textual production. Gerhardsson himself, committed as he was to an exclusively "oralist" model of rabbinic textual production, recognized that, as Saul Lieberman had already pointed out a decade earlier, talmudic sources mentioned informal written notes that served rabbinic disciples in their preparations for oral-performative exercises. More importantly, Yaakov Elman, basing himself in part on the various stages of Middle Hebrew discernable in the Mishnah, Tosefta, and Toseftan parallels in the Bavli, has proposed the hypothesis that the Mishnah and Tosefta in particular were committed to writing in the late second and early third centuries, but were transmitted by oral means alone in the Babylonian academies (*Authority and Tradition: Toseftan Baraitot in Talmudic Babylonia* [Hoboken, N.J.: KTAV, 1994], 71–111, esp. 73–75; cf. n. 13 below). Oddly enough, Zussman's exhaustively researched essay mentioned above makes no mention of Elman's important model, proposed over a decade ago. More recently, Elman has also offered a strong case that the Bavli was edited largely without the aid of writing. See Elman, "Orality and the Redaction," 52–99, a contribution also ignored in Zussman's essay.

See Strack and Stemberger, *Introduction*, 31–44, for a balanced discussion of the role of written texts in the formation of rabbinic tradition. My own attempt to formulate a model of oral-written "interpenetration" for the transmission of early rabbinic tradition in Palestine is available in Jaffee, *Torah in the Mouth*, 100–25. Catherine Hezser ("The Mishnah and Ancient Book Production," in *The Mishnah in Contemporary Perspective. Part One* [ed. Alan J. Avery-Peck and Jacob Neusner; Leiden: Brill, 2002], 182–87) offers yet another model for a mixed-media process of oral and written tradition in the creation of the extant text of the Mishnah in particular.

10   Thus the advice offered in *b. Hor.* 12a:
"Said Rav Mesharshia to his son:
When you wish to display your learning
before your Master,
rehearse the tradition
and then go to your Master.
And when you sit before him,
gaze at his mouth . . . ;
and when you review [after leaving the Master],
review near a stream of water,
for as the water flows,
so flows your rendering of the tradition."

11   As indicated in such introductory formulae as "The disciples were explaining the matter before Rabbi X" (e.g., *b. Pesah.* 32b and frequently). For other formulae and studies of their social significance, cf. David Goodblatt, *Rabbinic Instruction in Sasanian Babylonia* (Leiden: Brill, 1975), 199–259, and Miller, *Sages and Commoners*, 211–97.

12 For example, references to disciples who, as study partners, "sharpen" each other's mastery of halakhic tradition (*b. Shab.* 63a; *b. Taan.* 7a).

13 Here arises a potential source of confusion. In this paper, by "Tannaim" and "Tannaitic" I refer to rabbinic authorities deemed by later talmudic sages to be the earliest named receivers and transmitters of Oral Torah. The term means "repeaters of tradition" and refers to figures who thrived from roughly the late Second Temple period through the early third century C.E.

The same term, "Tannaim," is also applied throughout the Talmud to contemporaries of the third- to sixth-century sages who served as professional text-memorizers in the Amoraic academies of Palestine and Babylonia. Unless otherwise stated, my usage in this paper refers to the former rather than the latter. A classic account of the role of the Tanna-memorizer as a "living book" is offered in Saul Lieberman, *Hellenism in Jewish Palestine: Studies in the Literary Transmission, Beliefs, and Manners of Palestine in the I Century B.C.E.–IV Century C.E.* (New York: The Jewish Theological Seminary of America, 1950), 88–90. Gerhardsson builds on Lieberman's depiction in *Memory and Manuscript*, 93–96. Cf. Naeh, "Art of Memory," 552 n. 45.

A common trope is that a certain disciple or Tanna repeated his text "forty times until it was arranged in his mouth" (*b. Taan.* 8a; *b. Meg.* 27a) or "until it was in his pocket" (*b. Meg.* 7b). The famous *baraita'* at *b. Erub.* 54b that asks "how the oral tradition was arranged" recommends a minimum of four repetitions (cf. *Mekhilta de Rabbi Yishmael*, par. *Mishpatim*). There follows a story about the disciple of Rabbi Pereda who required no less than four hundred repetitions.

A thorough discussion of the various types of audiences for the oral-performative renditions of rabbinic sages in Amoraic Palestine is now available in Miller, *Sages and Commoners*, 387–466.

14 I make no effort to locate this "earliest" textualizing activity in any specific time or place, but I am impressed by the cogency of Yaakov Elman's suggestion that "both the Mishnah and the Tosefta were reduced to writing during the era of *mhe¹* [Middle Hebrew¹, viz., second to third century: MJ] but transmitted orally during the subsequent period" (*Authority and Tradition*, 74; and, more amply, regarding the Tosefta, Elman, "Babylonian Baraitot in the Tosefta and the 'Dialectology' of Middle Hebrew," *AJS Review* 16 [1991]: 17–20). Thus, perhaps, the scenario I imagine might have taken place in the upper Galilee around 200 C.E. See also n. 9.

15 For explorations of this point in recent scholarship on rabbinic literature, see Elizabeth Shanks Alexander, *Transmitting Mishnah*; Nelson, "Oral Orthography," 1–32.

16 I never tire of pointing out that Steven Fraade has produced the most important theoretical model of this process of performative rabbinic textual production in his influential study *From Tradition to Commentary: Torah and Its Interpretation in the Midrash Sifre to Deuteronomy* (Albany: State University of New York, 1991), e.g., 17–20. I find Fraade's thinking about rabbinic textuality nearly as fruitful as Gerhardsson's.

17 The fact that the fuller text may appear *as* a commentary on a briefer parallel does not automatically mean that anyone composed the fuller text as a conscious comment on an earlier, less fulsome, version. I explore this matter in relation to the vexed question of the relationship of the Mishnah and Tosefta in Jaffee, *Torah in the Mouth*, 111–25, 135–40. Cf. the critical response of Judith Hauptman,

Rereading the Mishnah: A New Approach to Ancient Jewish Texts (Tübingen: Mohr Siebeck, 2005), 28–29, and the briefer, but theoretically more articulate, discussion of Shamma Friedman, "Uncovering Literary Dependencies in the Talmudic Corpus," in *The Synoptic Problem in Rabbinic Literature* (ed. Shaye J. D. Cohen; BJS 326; Providence: Brown Judaic Studies, 2000), 35–57. Avraham Walfish, in his comments on Hauptman's work, admirably resists the temptation to impose a chronological interpretation upon the relationship between ample and spare versions of Mishnaic-Toseftan inter-texts ("Approaching the Text and Approaching God: The Redaction of Mishnah and Tosefta Berakhot," *Jewish Studies* 43 [2005–2006]: 22–25).

18   *Babylonian Talmud Codex Munich 95: A Limited Facsimile Edition of 400 Copies* (vol. 1; Jerusalem: Sefer Publishing, 1971), 252–53. This and all other translations are provided by the author.

19   Honi is also often known as the "Circle-Drawer" (*hame`agel*), based upon his practice of enclosing himself in a circle to pray for rain. But, as Jeffrey Rubenstein points out (*Rabbinic Stories* [New York: Paulist Press, 2002], 279), the Hebrew *me`agel* is used in *m. Mak.* 2:1 in reference to a worker who rolls pitch or plaster on roofs to protect them from rain. So Honi probably should be called "Honi the Roofer." This solves a perplexing problem. We might expect that Honi's nickname should be etymologically linked to the narration of his circle drawing. But the root `-g-l does not figure in the story's description of Honi's prayer method. Rather, there the crucial root is `-w-g (`ag `ugah, "circled a circle").

For the most part, wonder-working figures placed in Second Temple times are nameless, normally identified as "a certain pious man" (*hasid ehad*): e.g., *t. Taan.* 2/3:13, *t. Peah* 3:8, or collectively as "pietists and men of deeds" (*hasidim ve-anshei ma`aseh*): e.g., *m. Suk.* 5:4, *t. Suk.* 4:2.

The classic study of these and other charismatic figures recalled in rabbinic tradition is much in need of updating: Adolph Buechler, *Types of Jewish-Palestinian Piety from 70 BCE to 70 CE* (1922; repr. New York: KTAV, 1968).

20   I follow the enumeration of the Mishnah text's chapters and paragraphs offered in the edition of Hanoch Albeck, *The Six Orders of the Mishnah: Order Mo`ed* (Jerusalem: Bialik and Dvir, 1973), 339–40. Manuscripts and editions of the Mishnah often diverge widely in their enumeration of paragraph divisions within chapters. Albeck's edition follows the Kaufman manuscript, widely regarded as the best of the medieval manuscripts of the Mishnah.

21   MS Munich—the sole extant manuscript copy of the entire Bavli—is relatively reader-friendly, by medieval standards, in that it includes along its inner margins a version of the Mishnah-text to which the Babylonian Gemara corresponds. But MS Munich's Mishnah-text is identical neither to that preserved in other manuscripts of the Mishnah nor to that which seems to lie before the editors of the Bavli. For the present purpose, therefore, we need not address the specific problem of this manuscript's Mishnah-text.

22   While MS Munich's text is the fundamental background of this translation, I have taken certain liberties by including variations found especially in the more familiar Vilna edition. Where these changes materially affect my interpretation of the texts, I signal this in footnotes.

23   Adar falls in early spring, just before Passover. The point is that the community has been praying and fasting for rain since late autumn without success. Thus Honi is the last resort for a desperate people.

24 Munich's scribe includes a space of about three letters at this point. This is too brief to constitute evidence that the scribe discerned a distinction between the two passages. See nn. 25, 27, and 28 below for such usage.
25 Munich's scribe includes a space of about ten letters, indicating a new literary unit.
26 Vilna reads: "Our masters transmitted a tradition," a common formula for citing Tannaitic materials. Rav Nahman b. Rav Hisda, however, is a Babylonian sage of the fourth century. Munich's attribution is attested in other manuscripts and early editions of midrashic epitomes (see Raphael Rabbinovicz, *Diqduqei Sofrim* [repr. New York: MP Press, 1976], *ad loc.*, note *nun*).
27 Munich's scribe includes a space of about five letters, indicating a new literary unit.
28 Munich's scribe introduces a space that distinguishes the end of this passage from the next passage of Gemara.
29 On textual practices in medieval Ashkenazi talmudic academies, see Ephraim Kanarfogel, *Jewish Education and Society in the High Middle Ages* (Detroit: Wayne State University Press, 1992), 66–85. Kanarfogel pinpoints the twelfth century as a crucial point of transition distinguishing early Ashkenazic talmudism, focused upon "reading and mastering as much earlier material as possible without creative attempts at reconciling differences between the sources," from the classic focus on dialectical analysis characteristic of the Tosafists (71). For the role of textual memorization in contemporary Christian monastic culture, see Mary J. Carruthers, *The Book of Memory: A Study of Memory in Medieval Culture* (Cambridge Studies in Medieval Literature 10; Cambridge: Cambridge University Press, 1990).
30 The theoretical basis of this depiction has been worked out by Foley, *Singer of Tales*, 60–98, in his distinction between "performances" and "librettos." See in particular p. 65: ". . . the scenario assumes an audience who can rhetorically simulate the performance arena—in the absence of the actual enabling event of performance itself—on the basis of textualized cues that engage the enabling referent of tradition. . . . At a second level of complication, which emerges when we take into active account the possibility or near-certainty that some texts are not simply oral dictations but also at least partly the result of composition-in-writing, it will again be the performance register and its signals that demand interpretation through . . . an understanding of how the performance is keyed."
31 My colleague, Elizabeth Shanks Alexander, encourages me to "prove" this point, or at least supply a footnote to work that has proven it (phone conversation of 8/13/07). I am, in fact, unaware of any scholarship that has addressed the issue of the "rabbinic oral-literary breath." Readers who control rabbinic languages will ultimately have to judge if my renderings match the claims made for them. But if rabbinic literature is grounded in an oral-performative *Sitz im Leben*, as virtually all scholars claim, one wonders how the measure of a human breath can be anything *but* the basic measure of the rabbinic literary phrase. See also n. 33 below.
32 Jacob Neusner has made the definitive contribution to studying the mnemonic foundations of the Mishnaic literary forms in particular. See his *Oral Tradition in Judaism* and *Form-Analysis and Exegesis: A Fresh Approach to the Interpretation of the Mishnah* (Minneapolis: University of Minnesota Press, 1980). Both of these are based upon his pioneering study in vol. 21 of *Purities*. See n. 7.
33 The work of Lord, *The Singer of Tales*, remains fundamental to my understanding of the oral-performative character of the rabbinic texts. See especially his discussion of "the formula" on pp. 30–67.

34 The Mishnah at this point continues as follows: "He said to them: Go out and bring in your Passover ovens so they don't melt!"

35 Whether they were also preserved (at least in part) in writing remains under dispute among contemporary scholars. See n. 9.

36 "Amoraim" are rabbinic sages of both Palestine and Babylonia who received and transmitted the Tannaitic textual tradition, augmenting it through commentary. Chronologically, their activity extends from the early third century C.E. until the early fifth century in Palestine and the middle sixth century in Babylonia. The bulk of both the Palestinian and Babylonian Talmuds are composed of Tannaitic traditions, Amoraic discussions, and the editorial interventions of a later group, to be discussed momentarily, known as the "anonymous ones" (Stammaim). See n. 38.

37 See Baruch Bokser, *Samuel's Commentary on the Mishnah. Part One: Mishnayot in the Order of Zera`im* (Leiden: Brill, 1976); idem, *Post-Mishnaic Judaism in Transition: Samuel on Berakhot and the Beginning of the Gemara* (Chico, Calif.: Scholars Press, 1980).

38 Literally, "the anonymous ones." Over the past generation the term "stammaitic" has come to incorporate and replace what earlier scholars called the "savoraic" ("discursive" or "ratiocinative") contribution to the shaping of the Talmud. A helpful thumbnail history of the discovery and interpretation of this anonymous layer of post-Amoraic talmudic tradition is offered in David Goodblatt, "The Babylonian Talmud," in *The Study of Ancient Judaism. Vol. 2: The Palestinian and Babylonian Talmuds* (ed. Jacob Neusner; New York: KTAV, 1981), 154–60. This is updated in Strack and Stemberger, *Introduction*, 202–9. Perhaps the major contemporary figure in isolating the extent and significance of the Stammaitic material is David Weiss-Halivni. See his programmatic discussion in *Midrash, Mishnah, and Gemara: The Jewish Predilection for Justified Law* (Cambridge, Mass.: Harvard University Press, 1986), 76–115. Various current models for the redaction of the Babylonian Talmud are compared with helpful visual diagrams in Richard Kalmin, *The Redaction of the Babylonian Talmud: Amoraic or Saboraic?* (HUCM 12; Cincinnati: Hebrew Union College Press, 1989), xvii–xviii. Jeffrey Rubenstein offers an illuminating discussion of the role of the Stammaim in shaping the ideological, theological, and sociological perspectives of the Talmud as a whole (*Culture of the Babylonian Talmud*, 143–62). For an attempt to characterize and trace the development of patterns of conceptual reasoning from the Tannaitic stratum to that of the Stammaitic editors of the Babylonian Talmud in particular, see Leib Moscovitz, *Talmudic Reasoning: From Casuistics to Conceptualization* (Tübingen: Mohr Siebeck, 2002).

39 Some obvious examples that appear ubiquitously in the Talmud: *peshita'* ("this is obvious"); *qashya'* ("this is a problem"); *ma'i nafqa' minah* ("what's the practical distinction between these opinions?"); *tanna' heyka' ka'i* ("what is this tannaitic passage taking for granted?"); *'i ba`it 'ayma'* ("if you want, I can argue as follows"); *vetisbera'* ("is that what you really think?"). For in-depth discussion, see Rubenstein, *Culture of the Babylonian Talmud*, 39–58.

40 See Elizabeth Shanks Alexander, *Transmitting Mishnah*, 77–116, and the works cited in nn. 7, 9.

41 In isolating these units, I follow the judgment of MS Munich's scribe, who separated the units with gaps of about ten letters apiece (see nn. 25, 27, 28).

42 The Mishnah's text up till this point is rather different. See the discussion below.

43 The Mishnah at this point continues as follows: "He said to them: Go out and bring in your Passover ovens so they don't melt!"
44 This material is unknown to the Mishnah and the Yerushalmi.
45 This formal title for a teacher of disciples does not appear in the Mishnah or the Yerushalmi account. The scribe of Munich abbreviates the title with a single *resh* (= R.), as if he were assuming for Honi the title of "R. Honi."
46 This material is unknown to the Mishnah and the Yerushalmi and poorly attested in the mss. See Rabbinovicz, *Diqduqei Sofrim, ad loc.*, nn. *tof* and *aleph*, and the proposed emendation of R. Yoel Sirkis (*BaH*) at *b. Taan.* 23a.
47 This phrase appears in MS Munich, other mss, and early editions and parallels, but not in the Vilna edition. See Rabbinovicz, *Diqduqei Sofrim, ad loc.*, n. *aleph*.
48 These two lines are absent from the Mishnah. The Yerushalmi records in their place a comment by the early third century Babylonian *amora*, Shmuel, who notes a Tannaitic tradition that the drops were as large as the mouth of a wineskin. Thus I assign this passage to the Amoraic stratum.
49 This time the title is omitted in MS Munich. See n. 45.
50 This passage does not appear in the Mishnah or the Yerushalmi.
51 See n. 47.
52 See n. 45.
53 The Mishnah and its parallel in the Yerushalmi continues with:
    "He said to them: Go see if the Claimant's stone has melted.
    Shimon b. Shetah said to him. . . . "
54 This passage does not appear in the Mishnah or the Yerushalmi.
55 The entire passage up to "Shimon b. Shetah said to him . . ." is closely paralleled in the Yerushalmi's version but makes no appearance in the Mishnah.
56 This explanatory language is closely paralleled in the Yerushalmi's version.
57 William Scott Green, "Palestinian Holy Men: Charismatic Leadership and Rabbinic Tradition," *ANRW* II.19 (1978): 619–47; Rubenstein, *Culture of the Babylonian Talmud*, 27–28, 51–52.
58 That the sages controlled the priesthood's conduct of the Second Temple cult is a fundamental assumption of the Tannaitic tradition (e.g., *m. Yoma* 1:3–7/*t. Kippurim* 1:8; *m. Suk.* 4:9/*t. Suk.* 3:16; *m. Parah* 3:1–11/*t. Parah* 3:1–14).
59 See Green, "Palestinian Holy Men," 644.
60 While both Green and Rubenstein remark on the "rabbinizing" motivations of these texts, neither points out the role of the Stammaim in this "rabbinization."
61 Compare in this regard, the efforts of Israel, escaping Egypt, to have God part the sea in various convenient patterns before they design to take advantage of Moses' summons to cross over (*Abot R. Nat.* A:33):
    When our ancestors stood by the sea
    Moshe said to them: Arise and cross!
    They replied: We'll not cross
    Until the sea is transformed into tunnels!
    Moshe took his staff and struck the sea
    And it was transformed into little tunnels . . .
    Then Moshe said to them: Arise and cross!
    They replied: We'll not cross
    Until the sea is transformed into valleys!
    Moshe took his staff and struck the sea
    And it was transformed into valleys . . .
    Then Moshe said: Arise and cross!

They replied: We'll not cross
Until the sea is transformed into tiny strips!
Moshe took his staff and struck the sea
And it was transformed into tiny strips . . .

This pattern is repeated several times with ever new requests until the passage concludes:

And the clouds of glory
Hovered above them,
So that the sun wouldn't overcome them
And Israel passed over in this way
So that they should not be inconvenienced.

Apparently Israel, the "first born" of God, is, like Honi, a "member of the divine household" and entitled to act the brat if it yields a good family story!

62 Acording to Rashi, *ad loc.*, the "desecration of the Name" involves the use of the tetragrammaton in swearing a vain oath.

63 Significantly, both *y. Taan.* 67a and *b. Taan.* 23a go on to stress this point by supplementing their Honi narratives with further examples of *zaddiqim* who prevail upon God to change his decrees.

64 Cf. *t. Taan.* 2/3:13, which makes a similar point in its description of an anonymous rain-making *hasid* with suspicious similarities to the Mishnah's Honi. The Yerushalmi, *ad loc.*, works a version of the Toseftan passage into its account of Honi's success at stopping the rains, ascribing the teaching to the first-century *tanna*, R. Eliezer. The Bavli records no knowledge of this Toseftan source.

65 See n. 26. The citation formula found in the Vilna edition would indicate that the cited text is Tannaitic. But this reading is not well-attested in the mss. Moreover, *y. Taan.* 67a (MS Leiden; followed by ed. Vilna) agrees that Rav Hisda (Babylonia, late third to early fourth century) is the proximate source of the exegesis, linking it to him through a chain of Palestinian and Babylonian Amoraim: "R. Berakhyah, Rav Abba b. Kahana, R. Zeira, in the name of Rav Yehudah; and some say in the name of Rav Hisda." Thus an Amoraic venue for this text is probable.

66 Rav Nahman b. Rav Hisda is a Babylonian Amora of the early to mid-fourth century.

67 A Palestinian Amora of the mid-third century.

68 Cf. *b. Ketub.* 62b, where the same phrase emerges from the mouth of the Tanna, Haninah b. Hakhinai, who infers from an overheard conversation that a certain young lady is his daughter, whom he has not seen in the twelve years that he has spent in the *be midrasha*. The entire narrative is in Aramaic and certainly stems from the late Amoraic or Stammaitic circles who have cobbled together our Honi materials.

69 I follow here the *novellae* of R. Shmuel Idels (the *MeHaRSHa*) *ad loc.* in standard editions of the Babylonian Talmud.

70 Readers of this volume need hardly be reminded that upon this basic observation Werner Kelber built his extraordinary contrast of the christologies of the oral tradition of Q and the written occlusion of that tradition constituted by the Gospel of Mark (*Oral and the Written Gospel*). A careful study of the *implications* of the chirographic rendering of rabbinic literature for both the antecedent rabbinic oral tradition as well as for the ensuing "written-oral tradition," along the lines pioneered by Kelber, has yet to be attempted.

71 I am indebted to Yaakov Elman, David Nelson, and Elizabeth Shanks Alexander for their careful reading of earlier versions of this essay and for their honest and

Chapter 5

1. Gerhardsson, *Memory and Manuscript*, 193.
2. Walter C. Sellars and Robert J. Yeatman, *1066 and All That: A Memorable History of England, Comprising All the Parts You Can Remember Including One Hundred and Three Good Things, Five Bad Kings and Two Genuine Dates* (Methuen: London, 1930).
3. *Memory, Tradition, and Text: Uses of the Past in Early Christianity* (ed. Alan Kirk and Tom Thatcher; SemeiaSt 52; Atlanta: Society of Biblical Literature, 2005) is a useful introduction. Cf. also Jan Assmann, "Form as a Mnemonic Device: Cultural Texts and Cultural Memory," in *Performing the Gospel: Orality, Memory, and Mark* (ed. Richard A. Horsley, Jonathan Draper, and John Miles Foley; Minneapolis: Fortress, 2006), 67–82; Rafael Rodriguez, "Jesus and His Traditions: Memory, Performance, History" (Ph.D. diss., Sheffield, 2008).
4. Gerhardsson, *Memory and Manuscript*, 245 (emphasis added).
5. Gerhardsson, *Memory and Manuscript*, 234–44. I have developed this analysis further in "Community and Canon: Reflections on the Ecclesiology of Acts," in *Einheit der Kirche im Neuen Testament* (ed. Anatoly A. Alexeev, Christos Karakolis, and Ulrich Luz; WUNT 218; Tübingen: Mohr Siebeck, 2008), 45–78.
6. Gerhardsson, *Memory and Manuscript*, 214–20.
7. "Teaching" (διδαχή/διδάσκειν): Acts 1:1 (of Jesus, as frequently in the Gospel); 2:42; 4:2, 18; 5:21, 28, 42. The same verb is used of Saul and Barnabas (11:26; 13:12; 15:35), of Apollos (18:25), and of Paul (17:19; 18:11; 20:20; 21:21, 28; 28:31). "Teacher" (διδάσκαλος), however, though commonly used of Jesus in the Gospel, occurs in Acts only at 13:1 and is never used of the apostles. "Witness" (μάρτυς/μαρτυρέω/μαρτύριον) is used of the apostles at Luke 24:48; Acts 1:8, 22; 2:32; 3:15; 4:33; 5:32; 10:39, 41; of Stephen at 22:20; and of Paul at 14:3; 22:15; 23:11; 26:16. It is also used of the testimony of Scripture at 10:43; 13:22.
8. As, e.g., in the *Egbert Codex*, Stadtbibliothek Trier.
9. Believers as "disciples" (μαθητής): Acts 6:1, 2, 7; 9:1, 10, 19, 25, 26 *bis*, 38; 11:26, 29; 13:52; 14:20, 22, 28; 15:10; 16:1; 18:23, 27; 19:1, 9, 30; 20:1, 30; 21:4, 16 *bis*. Cf. also the unique feminine form μαθήτρια at 9:36. The corresponding verb μανθάνειν is not however used: the activity that characterizes a disciple is not "learning" but "believing" (πιστεύειν): Acts 2:44; 4:4, 32; 5:14; 8:12, 13, [37]; 9:42; 10:43; 11:17, 21; 13:12, 39, 48; 14:1, 23; 15:5, 7; 16:31, 34; 17:12, 34; 18:8 *bis*, 27; 19:2, 4, 18; 21:20, 25; 22:19. The object of that faith is not the apostles but Christ.
10. Gerhardsson, *Memory and Manuscript*, 223; idem, *The Origins of the Gospel Traditions* (Philadelphia: Fortress, 1979), 47–49. Cf. Byrskog, *Jesus the Only Teacher*.
11. Gerhardsson, *Memory and Manuscript*, 193, citing i.a. Elias Bikerman, "La chaîne de la tradition pharisienne," *RB* 59 (1952): 44–54. Cf. also Gerhardsson, *Origins*, 23.
12. Gerhardsson, *Memory and Manuscript*, 124–26, citing esp. Henri-Irenée Marrou's classic *History of Education* (New York: Sheed & Ward, 1956).
13. Cf. especially the two indispensable studies of the educational papyri: Raffaela Cribiore, *Gymnastics of the Mind: Greek Education in Hellenistic and Roman Egypt*

(Princeton: Princeton University Press, 2001); Teresa Morgan, *Literate Education in the Hellenistic and Roman Worlds* (Cambridge: Cambridge University Press, 1998); together with the essays in *Education in Greek and Roman Antiquity* (ed. Yun Lee Too; Leiden: Brill, 2001). Tor Vegge, *Paulus und das antike Schulwesen: Schule und Bildung bei Paulus* (BZNW 134; Berlin: de Gruyter, 2006), provides a valuable survey of the literature. For a schematic survey, see Loveday Alexander, "Schools, Hellenistic," *ABD* 5:1005–11; Loveday Alexander and Philip Alexander, *The School of Moses and the School of Christ: Essays in Early Jewish and Christian Scholasticism* (Tübingen: Mohr Siebeck, forthcoming).

14   Justin's references to the *Apomnemoneumata of the Apostles* are conveniently listed by R. G. Heard, "The APOMNHMONEUMATA in Papias, Justin, and Irenaeus," *NTS* 1 (1954–55): 122–29. Cf. also Helmut Koester, *Ancient Christian Gospels: Their History and Development* (London: SCM Press, 1990), §1.7.5:37–40; idem, "From the Kerygma-Gospel to Written Gospels," *NTS* 35 (1989): 36–81; Luise Abramowski, "Die 'Erinnerungen der Apostel' bei Justin," in *Das Evangelium und die Evangelien: Vorträge vom Tübinger Symposium 1982* (ed. Peter Stuhlmacher; WUNT 28; Tübingen: Mohr Siebeck, 1983), 341–53; Klaus Berger, "Hellenistische Gattungen im Neuen Testament," *ANRW* II.25.2 (1984): 1245–47; Gabriella Aragione, "Justin, 'Philosophe' chrétien et les '*Mémoires des Apôtres* qui sont appelés *Évangiles*,'" *Apocrypha* 15 (2004): 41–55.

15   For reading, cf. *Dial.* 18.1. Justin also speaks of the apostles' "writing" (*Dial.* 88.3) and uses the citation-formula "as it is written" (γέγραπται): *Dial.* 100.1; 101.3; 103.6, 8; 104.1; 105.6; 106.1, 3, 4; 107.1. Cf. also γεγραμμένον in 100.4.

16   So Heard, "APOMNHMONEUMATA," 125. Koester takes this as a reference to Mark, the only one of the canonical Gospels to include the name Boanerges, which would provide a link with the Papias tradition ("Gospels and Gospel Traditions in the Second Century," in *Trajectories through the New Testament and the Apostolic Fathers* [ed. Andrew Gregory and Christopher Tuckett; Oxford: Oxford University Press, 2005], 27–44 [30 n. 12]).

17   Heard, "APOMNHMONEUMATA," 122–29; Koester, *Ancient Christian Gospels*, 360–402. See now further Koester, "Gospels and Gospel Traditions," 27–44. There are no identifiable quotations from noncanonical Gospels in Justin's *Apomnemoneumata*.

18   Loveday Alexander, *The Preface to Luke's Gospel: Literary Convention and Social Context in Luke 1.1-4 and Acts 1.1* (SNTSMS 78; Cambridge: Cambridge University Press, 1993), 76–78.

19   Bauckham, *Jesus and the Eyewitnesses*, 211–12, accepts Peter as subject, but lays more stress on the "memory" aspect of the verb.

20   H. G. Liddell, R. Scott, and H. S. Jones, eds., *A Greek-English Lexicon* (9th rev. ed.; Oxford: Clarendon, 1940), 1139.

21   Cf. Josephus, *C. Ap.* 1.5: "I shall further endeavour to set out the various reasons which explain why our nation is mentioned by only a few of the Greek historians (ἐν ταῖς ἱστορίαις ... ἐμνημονεύκασιν)."

22   For the verb (with citations mainly from Plato), LSJ records "relate from memory," "remember, call to mind," "keep in mind," and "bear in mind." Later usage clearly embraces "mentioning" in writing: cf. Lucian, *Demonax* 67.

23   The search for a middle ground goes back to Karl Ludwig Schmidt's classic 1923 study "Die Stellung der Evangelien in der allgemeinen Literaturgeschichte," reprinted in English translation as *The Place of the Gospels in the General History of Literature* (Columbia: University of South Carolina Press, 2002).

24　See now Dunn, *Jesus Remembered*, 192–210, esp. 205–10; Kenneth Bailey, "Middle Eastern Oral Tradition and the Synoptic Gospels," *ExpT* 106 (1995): 363–67; Hearon, "Implications," 3–20, esp. 16–17.
25　Byrskog, *Story as History*.
26　Bauckham, *Jesus and the Eyewitnesses*, esp. 290–318.
27　Schmidt, *Place of the Gospels*, 6–8.
28　Heard, "APOMNHMONEUMATA," 125.
29　On the title, see Koester, *Ancient Christian Gospels*, 38–39; and E. C. Marchant's introduction to the Loeb edition of Xenophon, *Memorabilia* (Cambridge, Mass.: Harvard University Press, 1923), vii. This title is echoed in Aulus Gellius, *Libri quos dictorum et factorum Socratis commentarios composuit: Noct. Att.* 14.3.
30　Aragione, "Justin," 47–48, citing Harpocration, *Lexeis* Δ 85; E 123; Θ 25; Φ 1; Theon, *Progymnasmata* 66.15; 126.34.
31　Andrew Dalby, "Lynceus and the Anecdotists," in *Athenaeus and His World: Reading Greek Culture in the Roman Empire* (ed. David Braund and John Wilkins; Exeter: University of Exeter Press, 2000), 372–94.
32　Dalby, "Lynceus," 377.
33　Dalby, "Lynceus," 378.
34　Dalby, "Lynceus," 380.
35　Dalby, "Lynceus," 382.
36　Dalby, "Lynceus," 382–83. The emergence of prefatory letters to technical manuals can be seen as a response to similar pressures. Cf. Loveday Alexander, *Preface*, 18–22, 42–66.
37　Jan Fredrik Kindstrand, "Diogenes Laertius and the *Chreia* Tradition," *Elenchos: Rivista di studi sul pensiero antico* 7 (1986): 219–43.
38　Kindstrand, "Diogenes Laertius," 226–29. Aragione, "Justin," cites also Athenaeus, *Deipnosophistae* 4.162; 9.9; 11.116; Moiragenes, *Apomnemoneumata* of Apollonius of Tyana, as cited by Origen, *Cels*. 6.41; Arrian, *Discourses of Epictetus*, also sometimes known as *Apomnemoneumata*.
39　On Diogenes' sources, see esp. Jørgen Mejer, *Diogenes Laertius and His Hellenistic Background* (Hermes Einzelschriften 40; Wiesbaden: Steiner, 1978); Bernadette Anne Desbordes, "Introduction à Diogène Laërce: Exposition de l'Altertumswissenschaft servant de préliminaries critiques à une lecture de l'œuvre" (Ph.D. diss.; Utrecht: Onderwijs Media Instituut, 1990), vols. 1 and 2. On Favorinus, see Eckart Mensching, *Favorin von Arelate, Memorabilien und Omnigena Historia* (Texte und Kommentare 3; Berlin: de Gruyter, 1963).
40　Loveday Alexander, "Acts and Ancient Intellectual Biography," in *Acts in Its Ancient Literary Context: A Classicist Looks at the Acts of the Apostles* (Library of New Testament Studies 289; London: Clark, 2006), 43–68 (57); see also Ingemar Düring, *Aristotle in the Ancient Biographical Tradition* (Studia Graeca et Latina Gothoburgensia 5; Göteborg: Elanders, 1957), 469.
41　On Diogenes' composition techniques, see Loveday Alexander, "Ancient Intellectual Biography," 50–60; Michael G. Stollenberger, "The Lives of the Peripatetics: An Analysis of the Contents and Structure of Diogenes Laertius' 'Vitae philosophorum' Book 5," *ANRW* II 36:6 (1992): 3793–3879 (and other essays in the same volume).
42　Stollenberger, "Lives," 3832–42.
43　Italo Gallo, *Frammenti Biografici da Papiri*. Vol. 2: *La biografia dei filosofi* (Roma: Edizioni dell' Ateneo & Bizzarri, 1980). Cf. *P.Hibeh* 182 col. 2 with D.L. 2.34 (280/250 B.C.E.: Gallo, *Frammenti Biografici da Papiri* 2, 185); *P.Vindob.G.*

29946 col. 2 with D.L. 6.55 (3d–2d century B.C.E.: Gallo, *Frammenti Biografici da Papiri* 2, 267); *P.Vindob.G.* 19766 with D.L. 6.51 (Gallo, *Frammenti Biografici da Papiri* 2, 345); *P.Sorbonne* 826 with D.L. 6.40 (3d–4th century C.E.: Gallo, *Frammenti Biografici da Papiri* 2, 383).

44 Kindstrand, "Diogenes Laertius," 230–31; Fritz Wehrli, "Gnome, Anekdote und Biographie," *Museum Helveticum* 30 (1973): 193–208. For an example of this type of text, cf. Leo Sternbach, *Gnomologium Vaticanum e Codice Vaticano Graeco 743* (Berlin: de Gruyter, 1963); Kindstrand, "Diogenes Laertius," 234–37. For the sayings of the Seven Sages, see also *Die Fragmente der Vorsokratiker* (ed. Hermann Diels and Walther Kranz; 9th ed.; Berlin: Weidmann, 1964), vol. 1, §10: 61–66.

45 On Epicurus' *Kuriai Doxai*, see Norman W. DeWitt, *Epicurus and His Philosophy* (Minneapolis: University of Minnesota Press, 1954), 106–20; Elizabeth Asmis, "Basic Education in Epicureanism," in Too, *Education in Greek and Roman Antiquity*, 209–39 (218–19).

46 John Barns suggests that "The purpose of this collection of anecdotes and sayings of Diogenes was perhaps much the same—to provide the student with material for use in composition" ("A New *Gnomologium*: With Some Remarks on Gnomic Anthologies: II," *CQ* 1 [1951]: 1–19 [14]). Gallo, *Frammenti Biografici*, 261, disagrees.

47 Frederick E. Brenk, "Setting a Good Exemplum: Case Studies in the Moralia, the Lives as Case Studies," in *With Unperfumed Voice: Studies in Plutarch, in Greek Literature, Religion and Philosophy, and in the New Testament Background* (Potsdamer altertumswissenschaftliche Beiträge 21; Stuttgart: Franz Steiner Verlag, 2007), 195–215 (201).

48 Donald L. Clark, *Rhetoric in Greco-Roman Education* (New York: Columbia University Press, 1957), 125. Cf. Plutarch's collections of ἀποφθέγματα collected under generic categories: *Sayings of Spartans, Sayings of Kings and Generals, Sayings of Lacaenae* (*Mor.* 172–242, LCL vol. 3).

49 Clive Skidmore, *Practical Ethics for Roman Gentlemen: The Work of Valerius Maximus* (Exeter: University of Exeter Press, 1996), xi–xvii, argues that the collection also has a more immediate moral function. Cf. also W. Martin Bloomer, *Valerius Maximus and the Rhetoric of the New Nobility* (London: Duckworth, 1992); Teresa Morgan, *Popular Morality in the Early Roman Empire* (Cambridge: Cambridge University Press, 2007), ch. 5.

50 Loveday Alexander, "Ancient Intellectual Biography," 60.

51 Mejer, *Diogenes Laertius*, 61.

52 Mejer, *Diogenes Laertius*, 62–75.

53 Mejer, *Diogenes Laertius*, 75–81; Heinrich von Staden, "Hairesis and Heresy: The Case of the *haireseis iatrikai*," in *Jewish and Christian Self-Definition 3: Self-Definition in the Graeco-Roman World* (ed. Ben F. Meyer and E. P. Sanders; London: SCM Press, 1982), 76–100.

54 Mejer, *Diogenes Laertius*, 82–89; Jaap Mansfeld, *Studies in the Historiography of Greek Philosophy* (Assen: van Gorcum, 1990), 22–70. For doxographic use of anecdotal material, cf. Aristotle, *De an.* 405a19–21 (= Thales A22, Diels and Kranz, *Die Vorsokratiker*, 79; Mansfeld, *Studies*, 40); Plato, *Soph.* 217c / *Parm.* 127a–c (Mansfeld, *Studies*, 64–68).

55 Loveday Alexander, "Ancient Intellectual Biography," 60. For biography as part of an annotated bibliography, cf. Düring, *Aristotle* (Loveday Alexander, "Ancient Intellectual Biography," 61 n. 69).

56 Mejer, *Diogenes Laertius*, 90–93; Arnaldo Momigliano, *The Development of Greek Biography* (expanded ed.; Cambridge, Mass.: Harvard University Press, 1993), 68–82. I have examined the evidence more fully in "Ancient Intellectual Biography," 43–68 (with further literature).

57 On the immensely influential Socratic tradition, see esp. Klaus Döring, *Exemplum Socratis: Studien zur Sokratesnachwirkung in der kynisch-stoischen Popularphilosophie der frühen Kaiserzeit und im frühen Christentum* (Hermes Einzelschriften 42; Wiesbaden: Steiner, 1979). On Diogenes, see Derek Krueger, "The Bawdy and Society: The Shamelessness of Diogenes in Roman Imperial Culture," in *The Cynics: The Cynic Movement in Antiquity and Its Legacy* (ed. R. Bracht Branham and Marie-Odile Goulet-Cazé; Berkeley: University of California Press, 1996), 222–39.

58 Aristotle, *Eth. eud.* 7.12, 1245b20. Cf. *Eth. nic.* 9.10.6, 1171a15–17.

59 D.L. 5.34: πολλὰ γὰρ καὶ ἄλλα εἰς αὐτον ἀναφέρεται συγγράμματα· αὐτοῦ καὶ ἀποφθέγματα, ἀγράφου φωνῆς εὐστοχήματα. Cf. also 5.17–21; 4.47. See further Kindstrand, "Diogenes Laertius," esp. 240; Stollenberger, "Lives," 3832–42.

60 Diogenes' commonest term for this anecdotal material is ἀποφθέγματα (cf. 5.34). He tends to reserve the term ἀπομνημονεύματα for written collections (Kindstrand, "Diogenes Laertius," 225). Ἀποφθέγματα do not figure in the rhetorical definitions, and the distinction is one of perspective rather than of form. Cf. Kindstrand, 222 n. 16: "According to Diodorus Siculus fr. 7.7 libri 33 the terms can be used for the same item, viewed from different aspects: τὸ δὲ ἀφελείᾳ λόγου βραχέως καὶ ἀπερίττως ῥηθὲν τοῦ μὲν εἰπόντος ἀπόφθεγμα γίνεται, τοῦ δὲ ἀκούσαντος ἀπομνημόνευμα."

61 *Sayings* pref., Plutarch, *Mor.* 172c: τὴν χρείαν ἀπόδεξαι τῶν ἀπομνημοευμάτων.

62 On the *Progymnasmata*, see Hock and O'Neil, *Chreia*; George A. Kennedy, *Progymnasmata: Greek Textbooks of Prose Composition and Rhetoric* (Leiden: Brill, 2003); Ruth Webb, "The Progymnasmata as Practice," in Too, *Education in Greek and Roman Antiquity*, 289–316; Morgan, *Literate Education*, esp. ch. 6; Cribiore, *Gymnastics of the Mind*, esp. ch. 8.

63 Kennedy, *Progymnasmata*, 15. I follow Kennedy's translation but have retained the Greek words for clarity. See also Hock and O'Neil, *Chreia*, 63–112; Morgan, *Literate Education*, 185–88. Ps.-Hermogenes first defines the *chreia* as "a recollection (ἀπομνημόνευμα) of a saying or action or both," then differentiates the ἀπομνημόνευμα as longer than the *chreia* (Kennedy, *Progymnasmata*, 76–77). For Nicolaus the Sophist, the ἀπομνημόνευμα "differs from the maxim in almost all the ways the *chreia* does, and from the *chreia* in the length of its statements; for a *chreia* is expressed in a few words, while an ἀπομνημόνευμα uses more" (citing Xenophon's *Apomnemoneumata*). See Kennedy, *Progymnasmata*, 143.

64 Why the *chreia* in particular attracted this name, the ancients knew no better than we do: cf. Theon, *Progymnasmata* 97 (Kennedy, *Progymnasmata*, 15; Hock and O'Neil, *Chreia*, 82–83); Nikolaus, *Progymnasmata* 20 (Kennedy, *Progymnasmata*, 140; Hock and O'Neil, *Chreia*, 254–55).

65 Theon, *Progymnasmata* 97, distinguishes four varieties of "responsive *chreias*" (Kennedy, *Progymnasmata*, 16; Hock and O'Neil, *Chreia*, 86–87). For examples, cf. D.L. 5.18; 20.

66 Diogenes and Alexander: Theon, *Progymnasmata* 98 (Kennedy, *Progymnasmata*, 17; Hock and O'Neil, *Chreia*, 87). On stock types, see esp. Morgan, *Literate Education*, ch. 4.

67 Theon, *Progymnasmata* 101–2 (Kennedy, *Progymnasmata*, 19–21; Hock and O'Neil, *Chreia*, 94–99).
68 Theon, *Progymnasmata* 101 (Kennedy, *Progymnasmata*, 19; Hock and O'Neil, *Chreia*, 94–95).
69 Hermogenes, *Progymnasmata* 3 (Kennedy, *Progymnasmata*, 77; Hock and O'Neil, *Chreia*, 176–77). So Priscian, *De usu* 30–35 (Hock and O'Neil, *Chreia*, 194–95).
70 Hermogenes is more dubious: *Progymnasmata* 3.1 (Kennedy, *Progymnasmata*, 76; Hock and O'Neil, *Chreia*, 174–75). Cf. Kindstrand, "Diogenes Laertius," 223. I suspect that the rhetors' anxiety to prove the moral usefulness of the *chreia* is a post-eventum justification for a name that primarily indicates its all-encompassing usefulness as a school exercise.
71 Plutarch, *Sayings* pref., *Mor.* 172c; cf. Plato, *Prot.* 342–43, esp. 343a8–b2.
72 Isocrates cited in Hermogenes, *Progymnasmata* 3 (Kennedy, *Progymnasmata*, 77; Hock and O'Neil, *Chreia*, 176–77). The saying is also attributed to Aristotle in D.L. 5.18.
73 Theon, *Progymnasmata* 98–99 (Kennedy, *Progymnasmata*, 17; Hock and O'Neil, *Chreia*, 88–89).
74 *Sententiae quoque et chriae et ethologiae subiectis dictorum rationibus apud grammaticos scribantur, quia initium ex lectione ducunt; quorum omnium similis est ratio, forma diversa, quia sententia universalis est vox, ethologia personis continetur*. Quintilian, *Inst.* 1.9.3. But see the long discussion in Hock and O'Neil, *Chreia*, 122–28.
75 Galen, *On the Passions and Errors of the Soul*, trans. Paul W. Harkins (Columbus: Ohio State University Press, 1963), 38–39; Brenk, "Exemplum," 195–215. For a more detailed study of this material, see now Morgan, *Popular Morality*, esp. ch. 5.
76 Translation by Robin Campbell, *Seneca: Letters from a Stoic* (Harmondsworth: Penguin, 1969), 190.
77 Cf. Plutarch, *Sayings* pref.: "Their pronouncements and unpremeditated utterance in connection with what they did or experienced or chanced upon afford an opportunity to observe, as in so many mirrors, the workings of the mind of each man" (*Mor.* 172d; cf. 172e). Plutarch makes a similar distinction (and underlines the foundational nature of anecdotes for biography) in the prefaces to the *Lives* of Nicias and Alexander. See further Loveday Alexander, "Ancient Intellectual Biography," 43–68.
78 In Theon, *Progymnasmata* 96, 99. Theon admits that "sometimes the *chreia* is a pleasantry not useful for life" (Kennedy, *Progymnasmata*, 15, 17–18; Hock and O'Neil, *Chreia*, 82–83, 88–91).
79 Mejer, *Diogenes Laertius*, 93. The fundamental study is still Momigliano, *Development of Greek Biography*, esp. 119–20. Cf. Janet Fairweather, "Fiction in the Biographies of Ancient Writers," *Ancient Society* 4 (1974): 231–75.
80 Mary Lefkowitz, *The Lives of the Greek Poets* (London: Duckworth, 1981), 88.
81 Werner Jaeger, *Aristotle: Fundamentals of the History of His Development* (2d ed.; Oxford: Clarendon, 1948), appendix 2, 426–61.
82 Düring, *Aristotle*, 299–311. This passage draws on a long-established Epicurean critique of Aristotle, but the anecdote itself seems to be independent: cf. D.L. 5.3, where the same saying appears with a different antagonist (Xenocrates) and a different point (aetiology of the name "Peripatetic").
83 Philodemus, *Rhetorica* II 50, col. 36; cited from Harry M. Hubbell, *The Rhetorica of Philodemus* (Transactions of the Connecticut Academy of Arts and Sciences 23; New Haven: Yale University Press, 1920), 329.

84   Philodemus, *Rhetorica* II 55 col. 40 (Hubbell, *Rhetorica*, 330).
85   Düring, *Aristotle*, 306.
86   Kennedy, *Progymnasmata*, 20; Hock and O'Neil, *Chreia*, 96–97.
87   Cf. Theon, *Progymnasmata* 64.29–30: "We begin, first, with the *chreia*, for this is short and easily remembered" (Kennedy, *Progymnasmata*, 8).
88   Κατεῖχον δὲ οἱ παῖδες πολλὰ ποιητῶν καὶ συγγραφέων καὶ τῶν αὐτοῦ Διογένους, πᾶσαν τ' ἔφοδον σύντομον πρὸς τὸ εὐμνημόνευτον ἐπήσκει.
89   Morgan, *Literate Education*, 246, 250.
90   Cribiore, *Gymnastics of the Mind*, 166. For a full account of ancient mnemonics, see Jocelyn Penny Small, *Wax Tablets of the Mind: Cognitive Studies of Memory and Literacy in Classical Antiquity* (London: Routledge, 1997); Herwig Blum, *Die Antike Mnemotechnik* (Hildesheim: Olms, 1969). Whitney Shiner gives a useful account of this material in "Memory Technology and the Composition of Mark," in Horsley, Draper, and Foley, *Performing the Gospel*, 147–65.
91   Morgan, *Literate Education*, ch. 4.
92   Cribiore, *Gymnastics of the Mind*, 224.
93   Morgan, *Literate Education*, 223.
94   Morgan, *Literate Education*, 224.
95   Morgan, *Literate Education*, 224.
96   Morgan, *Literate Education*, ch. 4.
97   Loveday Alexander, "Canon and Exegesis in the Medical Schools of Antiquity," in *The Canon of Scripture in Jewish and Roman Tradition* (ed. Philip S. Alexander and Jean-Daniel Kaestli; PIRSB 4; Lausanne: du Zèbre, 2007), 115–53.
98   Morgan, *Literate Education*, 224.
99   Gregory Nagy, *Homeric Questions* (Austin: University of Texas Press, 1996), 3–4.
100 Morgan, *Literate Education*, chs. 1–2, 7; Joy Connolly, "The Problems of the Past in Imperial Greek Education," in Too, *Education in Greek and Roman Antiquity*, 339–72; Raffaella Cribiore, "The Grammarians' Choice: Euripides' *Phoenissae* in Hellenistic and Roman Education," in Too, *Education in Greek and Roman Antiquity*, 241–59. On Athenaeus, see Braund and Wilkins, *Athenaeus and His World: Reading Greek Culture in the Roman Empire*, and for Hellenism in the Roman period, Simon Swain, *Hellenism and Empire: Language, Classicism and Power in the Greek World, A.D. 50–250* (Oxford: Clarendon, 1996).
101 Webb, "Progymnasmata as Practice," 302.
102 Webb, "Progymnasmata as Practice," 302–3, 309–10.
103 Yun Lee Too, "The Walking Library: The Performance of Cultural Memories," in Braund and Wilkins, *Athenaeus and His World: Reading Greek Culture in the Roman Empire*, 111–23. Cf. Christian Jacob, "Athenaeus the Librarian," in Braund and Wilkins, *Athenaeus and His World: Reading Greek Culture in the Roman Empire*, 85–110 (108): "Eunapius describes the sophist Longinus as a sort of living library and walking museum (βιβλιοθήκη τις ἦν ἔμψυχος καὶ περιπατοῦν μουσεῖον)."
104 Dalby, "Lynceus," 377–79.
105 Small, *Wax Tablets*, 192–93.
106 E.g., Theon, *Progymnasmata* 102 (Kennedy, *Progymnasmata*, 20).
107 Cf. Quintilian, *Inst.* 11.2 *de memoria* (Small, *Wax Tablets*, chaps. 7–9).
108 Small, *Wax Tablets*, 71, emphasis in original.
109 Jacob, "Athenaeus the Librarian," 109.

110 Jacob, "Athenaeus the Librarian," 105.
111 Ease of memorization (εὐμνημόνευτος): Loveday Alexander, *Preface*, 96. Fidelity to tradition: Loveday Alexander, *Preface*, 82–87.
112 Cf. LSJ s.v. μνημονευτικός: "They are accustomed to call the empirical sect τηρητικήν τε καὶ μνημονευτικήν": Galen, *De Sectis* 1 (SM 3.2.3–11).
113 Though the life of Hippocrates played an important role in medical training; cf. Jody Rubin Pinault, *Hippocratic Lives and Legends* (Studies in Ancient Medicine 4; Leiden: Brill, 1992).
114 Cf. Galen, *De Sectis* 2 (SM 3.3.9–20): Empiricist theory is based on repeated observations of the same event. This accumulation, Galen says, is called αὐτοψία, which is "a kind of memory (μνήμη) of things seen many times in exactly the same way."
115 Cf. Galen, *De Sectis* 4, SM 3.7.6 τὴν ὑπόμνησιν τῆς τηρησέως 3.8.20–21 τῶν διὰ τῆς πείρας φανέντων μεμνημένοι. For the role of Hippocrates in inter-sect polemic, cf. *De Sectis* 8 (SM 3.20.8–17).
116 Asmis, "Basic Education," 216–17.
117 Asmis, "Basic Education," 218–19. Cf. DeWitt, *Epicurus and His Philosophy*, 106–20, esp. 111–12. On the *Kuriai Doxai*, see also Diskin Clay, *Paradosis and Survival: Three Chapters in the History of Epicurean Philosophy* (Ann Arbor: University of Michigan Press, 1998), 32–39.
118 Asmis, "Basic Education," 219, esp. n. 41.
119 Asmis, "Basic Education," 220.
120 Cf. John Miles Foley, "Memory in Oral Tradition," in Horsley, Draper, and Foley, *Performing the Gospel*, 83–96 (84): "Memory in oral tradition is emphatically not a static retrieval mechanism for data. It is very often a kinetic, emergent, creative activity . . . linked to performance, without which it has no meaning."
121 Cf. Quintilian's simple but effective recipe for memory: *Si quis tamen unam maximamque a me artem memoriae quearat: exercitatio est et labor; multa ediscere, multa cogitare, et si fieri potest cotidie, potentissimum est* (*Inst.* 11.2.40). ("But if anyone should ask me the single and most important art of memory, I would say practice and hard work; learn a lot, think it over a lot, and if you can do it every day, this is the most effective way.")
122 Asmis, "Basic Education," 222.
123 Cf. Clay, *Paradosis and Survival*, 75–102.
124 Clay, *Paradosis and Survival*, 64. Clay underlines the "memorial character" of these Epicurean festivals and argues that "memorial pamphlets such as Epicurus' *Metrodorus* and *Neocles* and Karneiskos' *Philistas* were read during these festivals" (87).
125 Clay, *Paradosis and Survival*, 66.
126 Clay, *Paradosis and Survival*, 78. Cf. Cicero, *Fin.* 2.31.101: *ut et sui et Metrodori memoria colatur*; Plutarch, *Live Unknown* 3: "What is the meaning of your common meals? What of the gatherings of your associates and of the fine people who join them? And what of the countless lines devoted to Metrodorus, Aristoboulos, and Chairedemos, laboriously composed and collected to preserve their memory even in death?" (*Mor.* 1129a, cited from Clay, *Paradosis and Survival*, 88–95).
127 Cf. also *Mem.* 4.2 on the "ability to remember (μνημονεύειν) what they learned" as the mark of an excellent soul.
128 Cf. *Mem.* 1.2.31; 1.2.62; 1.4.2; 2.4.1; 2.5.1; 4.7.1. In 4.8.1 Xenophon promises to "repeat what Hermogenes, the son of Hipponicus, told me about him."

129 Diogenes attributes a similar though less ambitious role to Simon the Shoemaker, a cobbler who used strips of leather to write down "what he remembered" (ὧν ἐμνημόνευσεν) of the conversations Socrates held in his shop, and was allegedly "the first who introduced the Socratic dialogues as form of conversation" (D.L. 2.122, 123).

130 τοιάδε διαλέχθεντα 4.5.2. Cf. 4.6.1: "To go through all his definitions would be an arduous task. I will say only enough to indicate his method of analysis. His analysis of Piety was more or less as follows (ὧδε πῶς ἐσκόπει)."

131 Even Xenophon seems to rely as much on the evidential value of his arguments as on the probative value of personal testimony per se: cf. 1.2.17ff.; 62–63; and cf. 1.2.21, where μαρτυρῶ refers to the author's independent moral judgment, not to personal testimony.

132 The classic study remains Bikerman's "La chaîne de la tradition pharisienne," 44–54. But cf. now also Amram Tropper, *Wisdom, Politics, and Historiography: Tractate Avot in the Context of the Graeco-Roman Near East* (Oxford: Oxford University Press, 2004), 158–72. On fidelity to tradition in Greek prefaces, cf. Loveday Alexander, *Preface*, 82–85.

133 Loveday Alexander, "Canon and Exegesis," 115–53.

134 Loveday Alexander, "The Living Voice," 220–47.

135 Cf. Justin, 1 *Apol.* 30; Koester, *Ancient Christian Gospels*, 377: "What is *demonstrated* to be true is the Christian kerygma, not the story of the gospels. The reports contained in the gospels are used to show that the facts about Christ which the kerygma proclaims happened in complete agreement with the prophecy that announced them" (emphasis added).

136 Gerhardsson, *Memory and Manuscript*, 122–70; idem, *Origins*, 19–24.

137 This thesis is developed more fully in Alexander and Alexander, *The School of Moses*.

138 Gerhardsson, *Gospel Tradition*.

139 Vansina, *Oral Tradition*, 8–9, 17–18.

140 Bailey, "Middle Eastern Oral Tradition," 364; Hearon, "Implications of Orality," 16.

141 Marion Moeser, *The Anecdote in Mark, the Classical World and the Rabbis* (JSNT-Sup 227; Sheffield: Sheffield Academic Press, 2002), 188–242.

142 For earlier discussion, cf. Moeser, *The Anecdote*, 150–87; John Kloppenborg, *The Formation of Q: Trajectories in Ancient Wisdom Collections* (Philadelphia: Fortress, 1987, and Harrisburg: Trinity Press International, 1999), 263–328. Cf. also the extensive collection in *Ancient Quotes and Anecdotes* (ed. Vernon K. Robbins; Sonoma: Polebridge Press, 1989).

143 Even in the *Gospel of Thomas*, many individual sayings have an internal narrative context in the form of a question or an observation by Jesus or others (disciples' question: *Gos. Thom.* 6, 12, 13, 18, 20, 21, 24, 37, 43, 51, 52, 53, 91, 99, 104, 113, 114; outsiders' question: 72, 79; observation: 22, 60, 100). These would be classed as χρεῖαι or ἀπομνημονεύματα rather than γνῶμαι by the Hellenistic rhetors.

144 Kloppenborg, *Formation of Q*, 292.

145 Cf. Gerhardsson, *Memory and Manuscript*, 173–74, on the "condensing tendency" in rabbinic anecdotes, and Vansina, *Oral Tradition*, 20–21, on oral tradition in general. On this evidence, the relative compression of Matthew's gospel anecdotes over against their Markan counterparts would tend to support the traditional view of the priority of Mark over Matthew.

146 Wehrli, "Gnome," 194.
147 Martin Jaffee, "Gender and Otherness in Rabbinic Oral Culture: On Gentiles, Undisciplined Jews, and Their Women," in Horsley, Draper, and Foley, *Performing the Gospel*, 21–43 (24).
148 *P.Bouriant 1*: Morgan, *Literate Education*, 185–88.
149 Cf. Morgan, *Literate Education*, 137, 187 n. 117.
150 Frances Young notes the importance of maxims and exemplars in the construction of Christian identity in the second century. See Frances M. Young, "Christian Teaching," in *The Cambridge History of Early Christian Literature* (ed. Frances M. Young, Lewis Ayres, and Andrew Louth; Cambridge: Cambridge University Press, 2004), 91–104.
151 Webb, "Progymnasmata as Practice," 302–3; cf. 309–10.
152 Cf. Gal 6:6; further, Loveday Alexander, *Preface*, 136–42.
153 Clement (who also uses the word διδασκαλία) adds a little more circumstantial detail: Peter was preaching δημοσίᾳ, "publicly," in Rome, and it was "certain *equites* of Caesar's household" who asked Mark to give them a written copy of Peter's preaching "so that they could commit it to memory" (*Hypotyposeis* 6 *ap*. Eusebius, *Hist. eccl.* 2.15.1–2, 6.14.5–7. See Kurt Aland, *Synopsis Quattuor Evangeliorum* (5th ed.; Stuttgart: Bible Societies, 1967), 539.
154 Loveday Alexander, "Living Voice," 220–47.
155 Papias: Eusebius, *Hist. eccl.* 3.39.1, 7; Polycarp: Eusebius, *Hist. Eccl.* 3.28.6 = *Hist. eccl.* 4.14.6. Irrespective of whether this John is the same as the apostle John or (as Eusebius argues) a different "elder," Papias cites him as a source of dominical traditions.
156 The translation is my own. LCL has "remembered" for ἀπεμνημόνευεν (on which see above) and "their miracles" for τῶν δυνάμεων αὐτοῦ (which is a straight mistake). Gerhardsson, who rightly recognizes the significance of this passage for understanding early Christian paideia, translates "How he told of his intercourse with John and with the others who had seen the Lord, how he remembered their words and what he had heard from them about the Lord, about his miracles, and about his teaching" (*Memory and Manuscript*, 204).
157 "I listened eagerly to these things through the mercy of God which was given me, and made notes of them (ὑπομνηματιζόμενος), not on paper but in my heart, and ever by the grace of God I do truly ruminate on them." Irenaeus here follows a biblical (and Egyptian) conception of the anatomy of learning rather than a Greek one. Cf. Small, *Wax Tablets*, passim and esp. 131–36.
158 Cf. *Spec.* 4.107; *Let. Aris.* 154.
159 Διοκλῆς ὁ ἰατρὸς λέγοντος αὐτῷ τινος βιβλίον ἠγορακέναι ἰατρικὸν καὶ μὴ προσδεῖσθαι διδασκαλίας εἶπε· τὰ βιβλία τῶν μεμαθηκότων ὑπομνήματα εἰσι, τῶν δὲ ἀμαθῶν μνήματα. Max Wellmann, "Zu Diokles," *Hermes* 47 (1912): 160.
160 Clement of Alexandria, *Adumbrationes ad 1 Pet.* 5.13 (Aland, *Synopsis*, 539).
161 Cf. Jaffee, *Torah in the Mouth*, 132: "The written record of a text was itself a version, whose literary purpose was fulfilled in the oral variations played upon it by the orator."
162 Though there are signs of thematic "clustering" in these collections. See Kloppenborg, *Formation of Q*, 306–11.
163 Compare Justin's reference (1 *Apol.* 26) to his own Σύνταγμα πρὸς πάντας τὰς αἱρέσεις, which clearly echoes the concerns for codification and differentiation within the *Haireseis*-literature of the contemporary philosophical and

medical schools. Cf. also Papias' typically scholastic concern to evaluate critically (ἀνέκρινον) the oral tradition of his own teachers with those from other disciple circles (Eusebius, *Hist. eccl.* 3.39.4).

164 Gerhardsson, *Origins*, 23. For the paraenetic use of rabbinic anecdotes, cf. Philip S. Alexander, "Rabbinic Biography and the Biography of Jesus: A Survey of the Evidence," in *Synoptic Studies: The Ampleforth Conferences of 1982 and 1983* (ed. Christopher M. Tuckett; JSNTSup 7; Sheffield: JSOT Press, 1984), 19–50 (38).

165 Martin S. Jaffee, "A Rabbinic Ontology of the Written and Spoken Word: On Discipleship, Transformative Knowledge, and the Living Texts of Oral Torah," *JAAR* 65 (1997): 525–49 (536). See further, Jaffee, *Torah in the Mouth*, esp. 126–52.

166 Hezser, *Jewish Literacy*, 202.

167 Loveday Alexander, "Ancient Intellectual Biography," 43–68.

168 Philip Alexander, "Rabbinic Biography," 40–41.

169 Cf. Todd Klutz, *The Exorcism Stories in Luke-Acts: A Sociostylistic Reading* (SNTSMS 129; Cambridge: Cambridge University Press, 2004), 102–7, 168–71.

170 Koester, "Gospels and Gospel Traditions," 43.

171 Loveday Alexander, "Canon and Exegesis," 115–53.

172 Vansina, *Oral Tradition*, 17.

173 Small, *Wax Tablets*, 193.

174 Vansina, *Oral Tradition*, 191.

175 A point made strongly by Vansina, *Oral Tradition*, 27–32, 186–201.

176 For memorializing as a communal task in the rabbinic schools, cf. Jaffee, "Gender and Otherness," n. 14. Cf. also the role of communal memorials in the Epicurean schools (above).

177 *Pace* Bauckham, *Jesus and the Eyewitnesses*. Papias does however show some interest in the participants in Jesus' miracles, according to Philippus Sidetes (Aland, *Synopsis*, 531).

178 1 Cor 15:3-7; Gal 1:18; 2:6-9. Note that Paul's phrase ἱστορῆσαι Κῆφαν would follow Galen's definition of ἱστορία as "learning what has been observed by others," sc. from those with αὐτοψία.

179 Morgan, *Literate Education*, 186.

Chapter 6

1 Kelber, "Works of Memory," 221–48 (222).

2 Gerhardsson, *Tradition and Transmission*, 6–7, 47; idem, *Origins*, 8–9.

3 Bultmann, *History and Eschatology*, 37–39.

4 Morton Smith's review of *Memory and Manuscript* is a case in point. After criticizing Gerhardsson's reasoned analogy with rabbinic traditioning practices, Smith, oblivious to the irony, posits "the sermon" as the origins of the tradition without any attempt to describe in concrete historical and cultural terms precisely how tradition as a tangible entity might have coalesced out of preaching. See Smith, "Comparison," 169–76 (174).

5 Gerhardsson, *Memory and Manuscript*, 81, 144.

6 Gerhardsson, *Tradition and Transmission*, 17. Cf. also idem, *Memory and Manuscript*, 76, 100. This is likely the basis for his claim that similar techniques are probable for the Pharisees and their Oral Torah and that Pharisaic practices were "representative of the methods common among Palestinian teachers" (*Tradition and Transmission*, 21). He concedes though the probability "that written

transmission played a more prominent role in these groups [Sadducees, Essenes, Apocalyptic circles] than in Rabbinic Judaism" (*Memory and Manuscript*, 30).

7   Gerhardsson, *Memory and Manuscript*, 125; idem, *Origins*, 21.
8   Birger Gerhardsson, "The Path of the Gospel Tradition," in *The Gospel and the Gospels* (ed. Peter Stuhlmacher; Grand Rapids: Eerdmans, 1991), 75–96 (81), emphasis added.
9   Gerhardsson, *Tradition and Transmission*, 16.
10 Gerhardsson, *Memory and Manuscript*, 25. Cf. also idem, *Origins*, 15.
11 Gerhardsson, *Memory and Manuscript*, 59.
12 Gerhardsson, *Memory and Manuscript*, 50–51, 63–65, 74–75, 83.
13 Gerhardsson, *Memory and Manuscript*, 58–59; idem, *Gospel Tradition*, 32–33. Gerhardsson's most recent statements on the extent of literacy in Jewish Palestine are considerably more qualified. See "Secret of the Transmission," 1–18 (13–14).
14 Gerhardsson, *Memory and Manuscript*, 240–44, 334; idem, *Tradition and Transmission*, 22; idem, *Gospel Tradition*, 32–33.
15 See Werner H. Kelber, "The Generative Force of Memory: Early Christian Tradition as a Process of Remembering," *BTB* 36 (2006): 15–22 (16–17).
16 Morgan, *Literate Education*, 23–33, 45–46, 162–63; idem, "Literate Education in Classical Athens," *CQ* 49 (1999): 46–61 (60); Cribiore, *Gymnastics of the Mind*, 3, 53–56, 75–76, 249. Both Morgan and Cribiore work extensively from the papyrus evidence of school exercises and note the elite orientation of the educational handbooks and treatises.
17 Morgan, *Literate Education*, 56–57, 72; Cribiore, *Gymnastics of the Mind*, 187, 205.
18 Harris, *Ancient Literacy*, 22.
19 Morgan, *Literate Education*, 163.
20 Raymond Starr, "The Circulation of Literary Texts in the Roman World," *CQ* 37 (1987): 213–23.
21 Morgan, *Literate Education*, 16; Cribiore, *Gymnastics of the Mind*, 168.
22 Morgan, *Literate Education*, 2; also Cribiore, *Gymnastics of the Mind*, 60–61.
23 Hezser, *Jewish Literacy*, 496; Meir Bar-Ilan, "Scribes and Books in the Late Second Commonwealth and Rabbinic Period," in *Mikra: Text, Translation, Reading and Interpretation of the Hebrew Bible in Ancient Judaism and Early Christianity* (ed. Martin Jan Mulder; Peabody, Mass.: Hendrickson, 2004), 21–38 (33–34); idem, "Illiteracy," 46–61 (54–56); Carr, *Writing*, 115–16.
24 Hezser, *Jewish Literacy*, 39.
25 Hezser, *Jewish Literacy*, 69.
26 Hezser, *Jewish Literacy*, 95; Carr, *Writing*, 204–8. Carr notes that Josephus' claim for universal Jewish literacy does not reflect reality (247).
27 Bar-Ilan ("Illiteracy," 47) points out that Egypt and Turkey, both Qur'an-centered societies, in the first half of the twentieth century had illiteracy rates of 88 percent and 92 percent respectively. On oral and aural reception of the Bible in many contemporary African churches, see Philip Jenkins, *The New Faces of Christianity: Believing the Bible in the Global South* (Oxford: Oxford University Press, 2006), 26.
28 Gerhardsson, *Memory and Manuscript*, 76, 159–60, 333. In later writings Gerhardsson gravitates towards taking the transmission of rabbinic haggadah as normative for understanding the dynamics of the gospel tradition.

29 Gerhardsson, *Memory and Manuscript*, 100; idem, *Origins*, 21, 68, 86. Gerhardsson frequently uses the modifiers "fixed" or "relatively fixed" in reference to tradition; cf., e.g., *Tradition and Transmission*, 44. See Kelber, *Oral and Written Gospel*, 9–10.

30 Birger Gerhardsson, "Illuminating the Kingdom: Narrative Meshalim in the Synoptic Gospels," in Wansbrough, *Jesus and the Oral Gospel Tradition*, 266–309 (307–8).

31 Gerhardsson, *Memory and Manuscript*, 94–99, 110–11, 124–26; idem, *Origins*, 20.

32 Gerhardsson, *Origins*, 37–38; idem, *Gospel Tradition*, 12–13; idem, "Illuminating the Kingdom," 307–8. In his most recent essay Gerhardsson has begun to reconsider this stance. See "Secret of the Transmission," 13–14.

33 Gerhardsson, "Illuminating the Kingdom," 298–99; idem, *Origins*, 86; idem, *Gospel Tradition*, 36; idem, "Secret of the Transmission," 7–8, 12. We note that Gerhardsson views his memorization-based approach as itself a model of oral transmission.

34 Gerhardsson, "Secret of the Transmission," 18, emphasis in original. Cf. also idem, *Gospel Tradition*, 30–37; idem, "Illuminating the Kingdom," 303; idem, "Path of the Gospel Tradition," 94–95.

35 Without a model for memory dynamics in oral tradition, Gerhardsson's writing-oriented model runs into the sort of dilemma that emerges in his most recent essay, where his recognition of the reality of limited literacy and widespread orality in Palestine forces him to identify early Christian traditionists with scribes who might in all likelihood have joined the community ("Secret of the Transmission," 14). An unintended consequence of this scenario, as well as of strict application of the rabbinic model (see Jaffee, "Gender and Otherness," 21–43 [42]), would be that early Christian tradition becomes largely an enterprise of a restricted circle of literate males.

36 Joseph Russo, "Prose Genres for Performance of Traditional Wisdom in Ancient Greece: Proverb, Maxim, Apothegm," in *Poet, Public, and Performance in Ancient Greece* (ed. Lowell Edmunds and Robert W. Wallace; Baltimore: The Johns Hopkins University Press, 1997), 49–64 (50, 57).

37 Elizabeth Tonkin, *Narrating Our Pasts: The Social Construction of Oral History* (Cambridge Studies in Oral and Literate Culture 22; Cambridge: Cambridge University Press, 1992), 3, 53.

38 Jan Assmann, *Das kulturelle Gedächtnis: Schrift, Erinnerung und politische Identität in frühen Hochkulturen* (Munich: Beck, 1992).

39 Ruth Finnegan, *Oral Poetry: Its Nature, Significance, and Social Context* (Bloomington: Indiana University Press, 1977), 140–41; idem, *Literacy and Orality: Studies in the Technology of Communication* (Oxford: Blackwell, 1988), 88; Jack Goody, *The Power of the Written Tradition* (Washington: Smithsonian Institution Press, 2000), 126; A. N. Doane, "Oral Texts, Intertexts, and Intratexts: Editing Old English," in *Influence and Intertextuality in Literary History* (ed. Jay Clayton and Eric Rothstein; Madison: University of Wisconsin Press, 1991), 75–113 (103).

40 Assmann, *Das kulturelle Gedächtnis*, 295.

41 Assmann, *Das kulturelle Gedächtnis*, 175.

42 Assmann, *Das kulturelle Gedächtnis*, 295; idem, *Religion und kulturelles Gedächtnis: Zehn Studien* (Munich: Beck, 2000), 59.

43 Strack and Stemberger, *Introduction*, 128–29. Cf. also Gerhardsson, *Memory and Manuscript*, 90.

44   Strack and Stemberger, *Introduction*, 38.
45   Steven D. Fraade, "Literary Composition and Oral Performance in Early Midrashim," *Oral Tradition* 14 (1999): 33–51 (45).
46   Jaffee, "Gender and Otherness," 21.
47   Jocelyn Penny Small, *Wax Tablets*, 100. Cf. also Goody, *Power of the Written Tradition*, 43; Mary J. Carruthers, *Book of Memory*, 9–12, 83–85, 111–21.
48   David Olson, *The World on Paper: The Conceptual and Cognitive Implications of Writing and Reading* (Cambridge: Cambridge University Press, 1994), 63, emphasis in original.
49   Strack and Stemberger, *Introduction*, 138.
50   See Strack and Stemberger, *Introduction*, 138–39; Martin S. Jaffee, "Writing and Rabbinic Oral Tradition: On Mishnaic Narrative, Lists and Mnemonics," *Journal of Jewish Thought and Philosophy* 4 (1994): 123–46; Elizabeth Shanks Alexander, "The Fixing of Oral Mishnah and the Displacement of Meaning," *Oral Tradition* 14 (1999): 100–39; Assmann, *Das kulturelle Gedächtnis*, 32–38, 50–56, 218–21.
51   Fraade, "Literary Composition," 35–36; Martin S. Jaffee, "Oral Tradition in the Writings of Rabbinic Oral Torah: On Theorizing Rabbinic Orality," *Oral Tradition* 14 (1999): 3–32 (9).
52   Jaffee, "Gender and Otherness," 26. Cf. also Strack and Stemberger, *Introduction*, 37.
53   Jaffee, "Gender and Otherness," 27, 42.
54   See Carr, *Writing*, 82–104.
55   Armin Sweeny, *A Full Hearing: Orality and Literacy in the Malay World* (Berkeley: University of California Press, 1987), 73.
56   Jaffee, "Writing," 144, emphasis in original.
57   Jaffee, "Oral Tradition," 9; idem, *Torah in the Mouth*, 16–17; Assmann, *Religion*, 136; Carr, *Writing*, 9; Carruthers, *Book of Memory*, 101, 156; Small, *Wax Tablets*, 154, 220; Rosalind Thomas, *Literacy and Orality in Ancient Greece* (Cambridge: Cambridge University Press, 1992), 91–92; Gerhardsson, *Memory and Manuscript*, 149.
58   Jaffee, "Writing," 126.
59   Carruthers, *Book of Memory*, 122; Fraade, "Literary Composition," 46; Jaffee, "Writing," 125–26, 145–46.
60   Small, *Wax Tablets*, 71; Carruthers, *Book of Memory*, 194. Cf. also Whitney Shiner, "Memory Technology," 147–65.
61   See Strack and Stemberger, *Introduction*, 38; Eliezer Segal, "Anthological Dimensions," 81–107 (82).
62   Elizabeth Shanks Alexander, "Fixing of Oral Mishnah," 107–24; Jaffee, "Oral Tradition," 12–15.
63   It is increasingly recognized that manuscript tradition itself is not characterized by textual fixation, as with print, but displays in some measure the dynamic properties usually associated with oral tradition. John Dagenais refers to this as manuscript *mouvance* (*The Ethics of Reading in Manuscript Culture: Glossing the* Libro de buen Amor [Princeton: Princeton University Press, 1994], 130). *Mouvance* has been observed in the transmission of works in the rabbinic corpus, including the Mishnah. See Peter Schäfer, "Research into Rabbinic Literature: An Attempt to Define the Status Quaestionis," *JJS* 37 (1986): 139–52; idem, "Once Again the Status Quaestionis of Research in Rabbinic Literature: An Answer to Chaim Milikowsky," *JJS* 40 (1989): 89–94; Elman, *Authority and Tradition*; Paul Mandel, "Between Byzantium and Islam: The Transmission of a Jewish Book in the

Byzantine and Early Islamic Periods," in *Transmitting Jewish Traditions: Orality, Textuality, and Cultural Diffusion* (ed. Yaakov Elman and Israel Gershoni; New Haven: Yale University Press, 2000), 74–106; Segal, "Anthological Dimensions," 83.

64 Dennis Nineham, "Eyewitness Testimony and the Gospel Tradition," *JTS* n.s. 9 (1958): 13–25, 243–52; *JTS* n.s. 11 (1960): 253–64 (13).
65 Nineham, "Eyewitness Testimony," 13.
66 Nineham, "Eyewitness Testimony," 17; emphases added. Robert McIver and Marie Carroll's interpretation of the characteristic patterns of variation and agreement in the synoptic tradition in terms of cognitive dynamics of eyewitness memory runs the risk of correcting to the other extreme ("Experiments to Develop Criteria for Determining the Existence of Written Sources, and Their Potential Implications for the Synoptic Problem," *JBL* 121 [2002]: 667–87).
67 Gerhardsson, *Memory and Manuscript*, 332–33; idem, *Origins*, 38–39, 67–68; idem, "Illuminating the Kingdom," 266; idem, "Path of the Gospel Tradition," 78–84, 93.
68 John Miles Foley, "Memory in Oral Tradition," 83–96 (87–90); Carol Fleisher Feldman, "Oral Metalanguage," in *Literacy and Orality* (ed. David R. Olson and Nancy Torrance; Cambridge: Cambridge University Press, 1991), 47–65 (50–51); Paul Zumthor, *Oral Poetry: An Introduction* (Theory and History of Literature 70; Minneapolis: University of Minnesota Press, 1990), 102–103; Tonkin, *Narrating Our Pasts*, 53.
69 Russo, "Prose Genres," 53.
70 Tonkin, *Narrating Our Pasts*, 15, 37.
71 Gerhardsson, *Memory and Manuscript*, 326–29; idem, *Origins*, 70; idem, "Illuminating the Kingdom," 303; idem, "Path of the Gospel Tradition," 87–89.
72 Gerhardsson, *Memory and Manuscript*, 184–88, 328; idem, *Origins*, 73–74; idem, "Path of the Gospel Tradition," 91.
73 Gerhardsson, *Memory and Manuscript*, 12–13, 282–83, 296–97, 330–31. Cf. also idem, *Tradition and Transmission*, 40; idem, *Gospel Tradition*, 25–29. A key piece of evidence for Gerhardsson is 1 Cor 15:3-7, a tradition artifact that prominently features the motif of eyewitness testimony. Richard Bauckham (*Jesus and the Eyewitnesses*) appeals to the cognitive schematizing activity of human memory to argue that the forms of tradition emerge with some immediacy from individual eyewitness memory, the result being an almost seamless identification of "eyewitness testimony" with tradition. Apart from the difficulty of his claim that named individuals in the Gospels are the eyewitness sources of the evangelists (an attempt to construe those passages in terms of eyewitness-source claims of the sort conventional in ancient historiography), Bauckham, in an overreaction to form criticism, does not give sufficient weight to the social and cultural dynamics of memory.
74 Gerhardsson, *Memory and Manuscript*, 330; idem, *Tradition and Transmission*, 40.
75 Gerhardsson, *Memory and Manuscript*, 142, 335; idem, *Gospel Tradition*, 43–44; idem, "Path of the Gospel Tradition," 80, 91–93.
76 Gerhardsson, *Memory and Manuscript*, 328; idem, *Gospel Tradition*, 43–44; idem, "Illuminating the Kingdom," 303.
77 Frederic C. Bartlett, *Remembering: A Study in Experimental and Social Psychology* (Cambridge: Cambridge University Press, 1995), 44–45, 200–225; George Bonanno, "Remembering and Psychotherapy," *Psychotherapy* 27 (1990): 175–86

(175–77); Jeffrey Prager, *Presenting the Past: Psychoanalysis and the Sociology of Misremembering* (Cambridge, Mass.: Harvard University Press, 1998), 207.

78 Larry R. Squire and Eric R. Kandel, *Memory: From Mind to Molecules* (New York: Scientific American Library, 1999), 206. Cf. also Alan D. Baddeley, *Essentials of Human Memory* (East Sussex: Psychology Press, 1999), 191; Bartlett, *Remembering*, 126–27; Martin A. Conway, "Autobiographical Knowledge and Autobiographical Memories," in *Remembering Our Past: Studies in Autobiographical Memory* (ed. David C. Rubin; Cambridge: Cambridge University Press, 1996), 67–93 (88).

79 William F. Brewer, "What Is Recollective Memory?," in Rubin, *Remembering Our Past*, 19–66 (51–60); Squire and Kandel, *Memory*, 46; David C. Rubin, *Memory in Oral Traditions: The Cognitive Psychology of Epic, Ballads, and Counting-out Rhymes* (Oxford: Oxford University Press, 1995), 111; Bonanno, "Remembering and Psychotherapy," 177.

80 Jerome Bruner and Carol Fleisher Feldman, "Group Narrative as a Cultural Context of Autobiography," in Rubin, *Remembering Our Past*, 291–317 (291–93); Craig R. Barclay, "Autobiographical Remembering: Narrative Constraints on Objectified Selves," in Rubin, *Remembering Our Past*, 94–125 (95–97); Squire and Kandel, *Memory*, 78.

81 Robin Wagner-Pacifici, "Memories in the Making: The Shape of Things that Went," *QS* 19 (1996): 301–21 (308).

82 Bruner and Feldman, "Group Narrative," 293.

83 Tonkin, *Narrating Our Pasts*, 60, 133. Compare tendencies in contemporary gospel scholarship, in a variation on the form-critical association of the individual forms of the gospel tradition narrowly with specific *Sitze*, to make different genres of the gospel tradition correspond to distinct Jesus communities (e.g., Burton Mack, *A Myth of Innocence: Mark and Christian Origins* [Philadelphia: Fortress, 1988]).

84 Maurice Halbwachs, *On Collective Memory* (ed. Lewis A. Coser; Chicago: University of Chicago Press, 1992); idem, *The Collective Memory*.

85 Gérard Namer, *Mémoire et société* (Paris: Méridiens Lincksieck, 1987), 140–57; Roy Rosenzweig and David Thelen, *The Presence of the Past: Popular Uses of History in American Life* (New York: Columbia University Press, 1998), 196.

86 William Hirst and David Manier, "Remembering as Communication: A Family Recounts Its Past," in Rubin, *Remembering Our Past*, 271–90 (273). Cf. also Mary Susan Weldon and Krystal D. Bellinger, "Collective Memory: Collaborative and Individual Processes in Remembering," *Journal of Experimental Psychology: Learning, Memory, and Cognition* 23 (1997): 1160–75 (1161, 1167).

87 Tonkin, *Narrating Our Pasts*, 27; Bruner and Feldman, "Group Narrative," 302; Weldon and Bellinger, "Collective Memory," 1161; Hirst and Manier, "Remembering as Communication," 276.

88 Weldon and Bellinger, "Collective Memory," 1167, 1173.

89 Liisa H. Malkki, *Purity and Exile: Violence, Memory, and National Cosmology among Hutu Refugees in Tanzania* (Chicago: University of Chicago Press, 1995), 106.

90 Halbwachs, *On Collective Memory*, 59; Assmann, *Das kulturelle Gedächtnis*, 16–17, 76–80, 141–42; Barry Schwartz, *Abraham Lincoln and the Forge of National Memory* (Chicago: University of Chicago Press, 2000), xi; Malkki, *Purity and Exile*, 54–56, 140.

91 Barry Schwartz, "Jesus in First-Century Memory—A Response," in Kirk and Thatcher, *Memory, Tradition, and Text*, 249–61 (251), emphasis in original.

92   Assmann, *Das kulturelle Gedächtnis*, 77. Cf. also Assmann, *Religion*, 55; Barry Schwartz, "The Social Context of Commemoration: A Study in Collective Memory," *Social Forces* 61 (1982): 374–402 (377); Yael Zerubavel, *Recovered Roots: Collective Memory and the Making of Israeli National Tradition* (Chicago: University of Chicago Press, 1997), 4–7; Jeffrey K. Olick, "Collective Memory: The Two Cultures," *ST* 17 (1999): 333–48 (342).
93   Jan Assmann, "Form as a Mnemonic Device," 67–82 (70).
94   Barry Schwartz, "Frame Image: Towards a Semiotics of Collective Memory," *Semiotica* 121 (1998): 1–38; Foley, "Memory," 88. Notably, μνημονεύειν in two prominent occurrences in the Gospel of John, with the disciples as subjects, denotes the connection of episodes in Jesus' life (John 2:22, temple cleansing; John 12:16, triumphal entry) to Scripture in light, moreover, of Jesus' passion and resurrection. See Tom Thatcher, *Why John Wrote A Gospel: Jesus—Memory— History* (Louisville, Ky.: Westminster John Knox, 2006), 24–28.
95   Kelber, *Oral and Written Gospel*, 56; Bruner and Feldman, "Group Narrative," 295; Tonkin, *Narrating Our Pasts*, 44, 60, 112; Squire and Kandel, *Memory*, 76–78; Assmann, *Das kulturelle Gedächtnis*, 58–59, 139–40; Malkki, *Purity and Exile*, 96.
96   Gerhardsson in taking this as indicating that the tradition was given shape centrally, in the Jerusalem collegium ("Secret of the Transmission," 17), was closer to the mark, since its uniformity is the consequence of the communicative formation of shared memory artifacts in publicly available genres.
97   Edward S. Casey, *Remembering: A Phenomenological Study* (Bloomington: Indiana University Press, 1987), 286.
98   See Assmann, "Form as a Mnemonic Device," 69; George Kubler, *The Shape of Time: Remarks on the History of Things* (New Haven: Yale University Press, 1962).
99   Casey, *Remembering*, 280. Cf. also David Lowenthal, *The Past Is a Foreign Country* (New York: Cambridge University Press, 1985), 204.
100 Gerhardsson, *Origins*, 57–58; idem, "Illuminating the Kingdom," 290–97; idem, "Path of the Gospel Tradition," 89. Cf. also Michael Fishbane, *Biblical Interpretation in Ancient Israel* (Oxford: Clarendon, 1985), 86–87.
101 Rubin, *Memory in Oral Traditions*.
102 Assmann, "Form as a Mnemonic Device," 72. Cf. also Kelber, "Generative Force of Memory," 17; Ward Parks, "Orality and Poetics: Synchrony, Diachrony, and the Axes of Narrative Transmission," in *Comparative Research on Oral Traditions: A Memorial for Milman Parry* (ed. John Miles Foley; Columbus, Ohio: Slavica, 1987), 511–32 (522).
103 Ian M. L. Hunter, "Lengthy Verbatim Recall: The Role of Text," in *Progress in the Psychology of Language* (vol. 1; ed. Andrew W. Ellis; London: Erlbaum, 1985), 207–34 (207).
104 Rubin, *Memory in Oral Traditions*, 119, 300.
105 Rubin, *Memory in Oral Traditions*, 90, 101, 143, 293. Cf. also Foley, *Theory*, 51–52; Kelber, *Oral and Written Gospel*, 26–27, 51–54; idem, "Generative Force of Memory," 16–19; Weldon and Bellinger, "Collective Memory," 1170; Parks, "Orality and Poetics," 524–25.
106 Rubin, *Memory in Oral Traditions*, 300.
107 Gerhardsson, *Gospel Tradition*, 45.
108 Gerhardsson, *Memory and Manuscript*, 335.
109 Gerhardsson, *Origins*, 82; idem, "Illuminating the Kingdom," 293–94.

110 Gerhardsson, *Memory and Manuscript*, 98; idem, *Origins*, 85–86; idem, *Gospel Tradition*, 41; idem, "Illuminating the Kingdom," 289–93; idem, "Path of the Gospel Tradition," 84–96; idem, "Secret of the Transmission," 15–16.
111 Gerhardsson, *Memory and Manuscript*, 65–66, 82, 113, 329; idem, *Origins*, 82; idem, *Gospel Tradition*, 36–37.
112 Gerhardsson, *Memory and Manuscript*, 70.
113 Gerhardsson, *Tradition and Transmission*, 44–45; idem, *Origins*, 48; idem, "Illuminating the Kingdom," 292–98; idem, "Path of the Gospel Tradition," 89–90; idem, "Secret of the Transmission," 6.
114 Gerhardsson, *Gospel Tradition*, 40. Cf. also idem, "Secret of the Transmission," 18.
115 Gerhardsson, *Tradition and Transmission*, 43. For example, Gerhardsson sometimes associates variants in Jesus sayings with "errors in memory" ("Path of the Gospel Tradition," 90).

Conclusion

1 Smith, "Comparison," 169–76.
2 See esp. the three essays collected in *Reliability*; idem, "Illuminating the Kingdom," 266–309; and idem, "Secret of the Transmission," 1–18.
3 Jacob Neusner, "Foreword," in Gerhardsson, *Memory and Manuscript*.
4 Jacob Neusner, "Foreword," xxv–xlvi.
5 Gerhardsson, "Path of the Gospel Tradition," in *Reliability*, 82–86; the article was originally published as "Der Weg der Evangelientradition," in *Das Evangelium und die Evangelien: Vorträge vom Tübinger Symposium 1982* (ed. Peter Stuhlmacher; WUNT 28; Tübingen: Mohr Siebeck, 1983), 79–102.
6 Werner H. Kelber, "The Oral-Scribal-Memorial Arts of Communication in Early Christianity," in *Jesus, the Voice, and the Text* (ed. Thomas Thatcher; Waco, Tex.: Baylor University Press, 2008, 235–62; see also, idem, "The Work of Walter Ong and Biblical Scholarship," in *Language, Culture, and Identity: The Legacy of Walter Ong, S.J.* (eds. Sara van den Berg and Thomas M. Walsh; Creskill, N.J.: Hampton Press, forthcoming; and idem, "Rethinking the Oral-Scribal Transmission/Performance of the Jesus Tradition" (Grand Rapids: Eerdmans, forthcoming).
7 One of the earliest and most trenchant critics of form criticism was Erhard Güttgemanns, *Candid Questions*.
8 Gerhardsson, *Memory and Manuscript*, 324.
9 Gerhardsson, *Memory and Manuscript*, 324.
10 Gerhardsson, *Memory and Manuscript*, 332.
11 Bultmann, *History*, 6.
12 See above all Lord, *Singer of Tales*, 101.
13 Gerhardsson, *Memory and Manuscript*, 332.
14 Gerhardsson, *Memory and Manuscript*, 324.
15 Kelber, *Oral and Written Gospel*, 13.
16 Gerhardsson, *Reliability*, 104. See also idem, *Memory and Manuscript*, 14.
17 Gerhardsson, *Memory and Manuscript*, 202.
18 Gerhardsson, *Reliability*, 119.
19 Gerhardsson, *Reliability*, 113.
20 Gerhardsson, *Reliability*, 113.
21 In my earlier review of Gerhardsson's work (*Oral and Written Gospel*, 8–14), I made critical reference to his "blurring of oral and written dynamics" (10). His

objection to my criticism (*Reliability*, 116–17, passim) is fully justified. With others I have come to recognize that the interface of oral and written dynamics was a hallmark not merely of Second Temple and early Judaism, and of the early Jesus tradition, but of the ancient Near Eastern and ancient Mediterranean communications world by and large. I quite agree with Gerhardsson's statement: "The verbal Jesus tradition was at no stage pure 'orality' in the sense theorists of orality give the term" (*Reliability*, 116).

22 Gerhardsson, *Reliability*, 134.
23 Gerhardsson, *Reliability*, 134.
24 Gerhardsson, *Memory and Manuscript*, 202.
25 Jaffee, *Torah in the Mouth*.
26 Carr, *Writing*.
27 Jaffee, *Torah in the Mouth*, 61.
28 Jaffee, *Torah in the Mouth*, 18.
29 Jaffee, *Torah in the Mouth*, 15–27.
30 Carr, *Writing*, 150.
31 Carr, *Writing*, 128.
32 Gerhardsson, "Secret of the Transmission," 6.
33 Gerhardsson, *Reliability*, 85, n. 56.
34 Foley, *How to Read*, 140.
35 Foley, *How to Read*, 215, emphasis in original.
36 Gerhardsson, *Reliability*, 85, n. 56.
37 Lord, *Singer of Tales*, 101.
38 In view of the controversy surrounding Gerhardsson's assumed retrojection of rabbinic techniques—now a moot point in the discussion—I prefer to call his the "didactic model" because, in his view, "the synoptic material has functioned basically as teaching material" ("Secret of the Transmission," 18). Mournet himself uses terms such as "didactic intentionality," "didactic activity," and "formalized Jewish didactic context."
39 Gerhardsson ("Secret of the Transmission") has tended to associate the "orality model" with folklore studies. He refers to it as "the folkloristic orality model" (5) because it "takes its inspiration from folkloristic research (and additionally from folkloristic textual theory)" (3). I feel uncomfortable with this designation. Mournet is quite right in calling it "a composite model derived from the contributions of scholars from various disciplines within the humanities."
40 Kenneth E. Bailey, *Poet and Peasant: A Literary-Cultural Approach to the Parables in Luke* (Grand Rapids: Eerdmans, 1976); idem, *Through Peasant Eyes* (Grand Rapids: Eerdmans, 1980); idem, "Informal Controlled Oral Tradition and the Synoptic Gospels," 34–54; idem, "Informal Controlled Oral Tradition and the Synoptic Tradition," 4–11; idem, "Middle Eastern Oral Tradition," 563–67.
41 Dunn, *Jesus Remembered*.
42 Gerhardsson, *Memory and Manuscript*, 283. The concept of eyewitnesses has recently received substantial confirmation by Samuel Byrskog and Richard Bauckham. Byrskog (*Story as History*) gave an exquisitely informed and detailed accounting of *autopsy* (eyewitnessing information processing) in Greek and Roman historiography as comparative basis for eyewitness transmission in the narrative Gospels. Bauckham (*Jesus and the Eyewitnesses*), relying on early patristic sources and internal gospel evidence, argued for a close association between an official body of apostolic eyewitnesses and the gospel tradition, especially Mark and John.

43   Gerhardsson, "Secret of the Transmission," 11, emphasis in original.
44   Gerhardsson, "Secret of the Transmission," 11.
45   Gerhardsson, *Reliability*, 23.
46   Gerhardsson, *Reliability*, 105–07, 131.
47   Gerhardsson, *Memory and Manuscript*, 331.
48   Gerhardsson, *Reliability*, 35.
49   Gerhardsson, *Reliability*, 53, emphasis in original.
50   Gerhardsson, "Secret of the Transmission," 13.
51   Gerhardsson, *Reliability*, 120, is not happy with the concept of "performance." While it may not be the ideal designation, it is by now thoroughly institutionalized in orality-scribality studies. It connotes the complex dynamics of oral delivery in the ancient world, including the roles of speaker and audience, social location, material context, emotive and kinetic dimensions, etc. See especially David Rhoads, "Performance Criticism: An Emerging Methodology in Second Testament Studies—Part I," *BTB* 36 (2006): 118–33; idem, "Performance Criticism: An Emerging Methodology in Second Testament Studies—Part II," *BTB* 36 (2006): 164–84.
52   Andersen, "Oral Tradition," 17–58 (29): "Oral tradition consists of varieties. One should not say 'variations', because that entails the idea of an 'original' which the transmitters or performers are playing with and on."
53   Rhoads, "Performance Criticism—Part I," 126–31; Ong, *Orality and Literacy*, 47; Foley, *How to Read*, 130–33; Finnegan, *Oral Poetry*, 28–29; and Andersen, "Oral Tradition," 18–20.
54   Gerhardsson, *Reliability*, 129–30.
55   Gerhardsson, *Reliability*, 56, 79; idem, "Secret of the Transmission," 16.
56   Gerhardsson, *Reliability*, 50.
57   Alan Kirk and Tom Thatcher, "Jesus Tradition as Social Memory," in *Memory, Tradition, and Text*, 25–42 (31).
58   Pieter J. J. Botha, "Mark's Story as Oral Traditional Literature: Rethinking the Transmission of Some Traditions about Jesus," *Hervormde Teologiese Studies* 47 (1991): 304–31; Joanna Dewey, "Oral Methods"; idem, "Mark as Interwoven Tapestry: Forecasts and Echoes for a Listening Audience," *CBQ* 52 (1991): 221–36; idem, "Mark as Aural Narrative: Structures as Clues to Understanding," *Sewanee Theological Review* 36 (1992): 45–56; idem, "The Gospel of Mark as Oral/Aural Event: Implications for Interpretation," in *The New Literary Criticism and the New Testament* (ed. Elizabeth Struthers Malbon and Edgar V. McKnight; Sheffield: Sheffield University Press, 1994), 145–63; idem, "Mark—A Really Good Oral Story: Is That Why the Gospel of Mark Survived?" *JBL* 123 (2004): 495–507; Horsley, *Hearing the Whole Story*, 53–78; Whitney Shiner, *Proclaiming the Gospel: First-Century Performance of Mark* (Harrisburg: Trinity Press International, 2003).
59   Gerhardsson, *Reliability*, 130.
60   Joanna Dewey, "Textuality in an Oral Culture: A Survey of the Pauline Traditions," *Semeia* 65 (1995): 37–65; Pieter J. J. Botha, "Letter Writing and Oral Communication in Antiquity: Suggested Implications for the Interpretation of Paul's Letter to the Galatians," *Scriptura* (1992): 17–34.
61   Gerhardsson, *Memory and Manuscript*, 290.
62   Gerhardsson, *Memory and Manuscript*, 295.
63   Gerhardsson, *Memory and Manuscript*, 295.
64   Gerhardsson, *Memory and Manuscript*, 301.

65 Gerhardsson, *Memory and Manuscript*, 300; cf. also 296, 297, 306, 321.
66 Gerhardsson, *Memory and Manuscript*, 297–98.
67 Gerhardsson, *Memory and Manuscript*, 299–300.
68 Gerhardsson, *Memory and Manuscript*, 300.
69 Richard Reitzenstein, *Hellenistic Mystery-Religions: Their Basic Ideas and Significance* (Pittsburgh Theological Monograph Series 15; Pittsburgh: Pickwick Press, 1978 [original German 1910]); Wilhelm Bousset, *Kyrios Christos: A History of the Belief in Christ from the Beginnings of Christianity to Irenaeus* (Nashville: Abingdon, 1970 [original German 1913]).
70 Gerhardsson, *Memory and Manuscript*, 309, 311.
71 Jens Schröter, "Jesus and the Canon: The Early Jesus Traditions in the Context of the Origins of the New Testament Canon," in Horsley, Draper, and Foley, *Performing the Gospel*, 104–22 (109).
72 Schröter, "Jesus and the Canon," 120; cf. 120–22.
73 Gerhardsson, *Memory and Manuscript*, 309.
74 Schröter, "Jesus and the Canon," 109.
75 Gerhardsson, *Memory and Manuscript*, 319.
76 Gerhardsson, *Memory and Manuscript*, 303.
77 Gerhardsson, *Memory and Manuscript*, 320.
78 Gerhardsson, *Memory and Manuscript*, 291, emphasis in original. Cf. also 295.
79 Schröter, "Jesus and the Canon," 110.
80 It is a frequently unacknowledged function of the narrative gospel that it located the sayings material in the literary frame of Jesus' life and thus firmly fixed their identity as sayings of the earthly Jesus. On this, see also Schröter, "Jesus and the Canon," 110: "The explicit attribution of the whole tradition to Jesus and its incorporation within his earthly activity constituted a historicizing of the primitive Christian tradition."
81 James M. Robinson, "LOGOI SOPHON: On the Gattung of Q," in *Trajectories through Early Christianity* (Philadelphia: Fortress, 1971), 71–113 (97 n. 57); idem, "Kerygma and History in the New Testament," in *Trajectories through Early Christianity*, 37–46.
82 Helmut Koester, "One Jesus and Four Primitive Gospels," in *Trajectories through Early Christianity*, 158–204 (186 and 166–68); idem, "GNOMAI Diaphoroi: The Origin and Nature of Diversification in the History of Early Christianity," in *Trajectories through Early Christianity*, 114–57 (149–51).
83 Heinz-Wolfgang Kuhn, "Der irdische Jesus bei Paulus als traditionsgeschichtliches und theologisches Problem," *ZTK* 67 (1970): 295–320.
84 Gerhardsson, *Memory and Manuscript*, 22–25, 158.
85 Gerhardsson, *Memory and Manuscript*, 79.
86 Gerhardsson, *Memory and Manuscript*, 80.
87 Gerhardsson, *Memory and Manuscript*, 141, emphasis in original.
88 Gerhardsson, *Memory and Manuscript*, 80.
89 For a summary of Neusner's principal works on the documentary method, see his *The Documentary Foundation of Rabbinic Culture* (South Florida Studies in the History of Judaism 113; Atlanta: Scholars Press, 1995), xvi–xx; idem, "Oral Torah and Oral Tradition," 59–78; idem, *Oral Tradition in Judaism*.
90 Neusner, *Documentary Foundation*, 21.
91 Neusner, "Oral Torah and Oral Tradition," 60.
92 Neusner, *Documentary Foundation*, 31.
93 Neusner, "Oral Torah and Oral Tradition," 69–75.

94   Neusner, "Oral Torah and Oral Tradition," 63 n. 3.
95   Peter Schäfer, *Hekhalot-Studien* (TSAJ 19; Tübingen: Mohr Siebeck, 1988).
96   Schäfer, "Research," 139–52 (149).
97   Schäfer, *Hekhalot-Studien*, 16, emphasis in original.
98   Schäfer, "Research," 149.
99   Schäfer, "Research," 139–52.
100 Schäfer, "Research," 150.
101 Schäfer, "Research," 151.
102 Schäfer, "Research," 151.
103 The ancient manuscript evidence of the pre-Masoretic tradition of the Hebrew Bible, the early Jesus tradition, and the rabbinic tradition all point to oral-scribal pluriformity as the rule rather than the exception. Regarding the pre-Masoretic tradition, see Eugene Ulrich, *The Dead Sea Scrolls and the Origins of the Bible* (Grand Rapids: Eerdmans, 1999). Regarding the early Jesus tradition, see Eldon Jay Epp, "The Oxyrhynchus New Testament Papyri: 'Not without Honor except in Their Hometown'?," *JBL* 123 (2004): 5–55; idem, "It's All about Variants: A Variant-Conscious Approach to New Testament Textual Criticism," *HTR* 100 (2007): 275–308; and David C. Parker, *The Living Text of the Gospels* (Cambridge: Cambridge University Press, 1997). Two features underscore the significance of the text-critical work undertaken by Ulrich, Epp, Parker, and Schäfer. One, the understanding of an early textual pluriformity in the three traditions has been arrived at independently and without direct scholarly interchange, as far as I can see. Two, independently from each other, all four scholars have called for a reconsideration of the project of text criticism.
104 Fraade, *From Tradition to Commentary*.
105 Fraade, *From Tradition to Commentary*, 63.
106 Fraade, *From Tradition to Commentary*, 19.
107 Fraade, *From Tradition to Commentary*, 22.
108 Fraade, *From Tradition to Commentary*, 65.
109 Fraade, *From Tradition to Commentary*, 64.
110 Fraade, *From Tradition to Commentary*, 21.
111 Fraade, *From Tradition to Commentary*, 19.
112 Fraade, *From Tradition to Commentary*, 19.
113 Fraade, *From Tradition to Commentary*, 18.
114 Jaffee, *Torah in the Mouth*, 101.
115 Jaffee, *Torah in the Mouth*, 124.
116 Jaffee, *Torah in the Mouth*, 101.
117 Jaffee, *Torah in the Mouth*, 124.
118 Gerhardsson, *Memory and Manuscript*, 76–77, 100, 126, 150, 158, 163. It bears mentioning that it was under the directorship of Martin Hengel that Samuel Byrskog, Gerhardsson's prominent student, wrote *Story as History*, which treats information-gathering techniques (particularly eyewitness testimony) among ancient Greek and Roman, as well as Jewish historians such as Herodotus, Thucydides, Polybius, Josephus, and Tacitus, among others.
119 Foley, *How to Read*, 79.
120 Foley, *How to Read*, 26, 114–17.
121 On the concept of *Erinnerungsfigur*, see Assmann, *Das kulturelle Gedächtnis*, 37–42, passim.
122 Kirk and Thatcher, "Jesus Tradition as Social Memory," 29.

123 Regarding recent views on the role and identity of scribes, in addition to Carr, see Haines-Eitzen, *Guardians*; Richard A. Horsley, *Scribes, Visionaries and the Politics of Second Temple Judaism* (Louisville, Ky.: Westminster John Knox, 2007), esp. chaps. 4–6.

124 Horsley, *Scribes, Visionaries*, 104.

125 Lothar Ruppert, *Der leidende Gerechte: Eine motivgeschichtliche Untersuchung zum Alten und zwischentestamentlichen Judentum* (FB 5; Würzburg: Echter Verlag, 1972); idem, *Jesus als der leidende Gerechte?* (SBS 59; Stuttgart: KBW, 1972); idem, *Der leidende Gerechte und seine Feinde: Eine Wortfelduntersuchung* (Würzburg: Echter Verlag, 1973).

126 Nickelsburg, "Genre and Function," 153–84 (reprint in idem, *Resurrection, Immortality, and Eternal Life in Intertestamental Judaism and Early Christianity* [HTS 56; Cambridge, Mass.: Harvard University Press, 2006], 249–79).

127 Arthur J. Dewey, "The Locus for Death: Social Memory and the Passion Narrative," in Kirk and Thatcher, *Memory, Tradition, and Text*, 119–28.

128 Dewey, "Locus for Death," 127, emphasis in original.

129 On the topic of memory place, see the classic work by Frances A. Yates, *The Art of Memory*.

Bibliography

Abel, Ernest L. "The Psychology of Memory and Rumor Transmission and Their Bearing on Theories of Oral Transmission in Early Christianity." *JR* 51 (1971): 270–81.
Abramowski, Luise. "Die 'Erinnerungen der Apostel' bei Justin." Pages 341–53 in *Das Evangelium und die Evangelien: Vorträge vom Tübinger Symposium 1982* (WUNT 28). Edited by Peter Stuhlmacher. Tübingen: Mohr Siebeck, 1983.
Achtemeier, Paul J. "*Omne Verbum Sonat*: The New Testament and the Oral Environment of Late Western Antiquity." *JBL* 109 (1990): 3–27.
Aland, Kurt. *Synopsis Quattuor Evangeliorum*. 5th ed. Stuttgart: Bible Societies, 1967.
Albeck, Hanoch, ed. *The Six Orders of the Mishnah: Order Mo'ed*. Jerusalem: Bialik and Dvir, 1973.
Alexander, Elizabeth Shanks. "The Fixing of Oral Mishnah and the Displacement of Meaning." *Oral Tradition* 14 (1999): 100–139.
———. *Transmitting Mishnah: The Shaping Influence of Oral Tradition*. Cambridge: Cambridge University Press, 2006.
Alexander, Loveday. "Acts and Ancient Intellectual Biography." Pages 43–68 in *Acts in Its Ancient Literary Context: A Classicist Looks at the Acts of the Apostles*. Library of New Testament Studies 289. London: Clark, 2006.
———. "Ancient Book Production and the Circulation of the Gospels." Pages 71–111 in *The Gospels for All Christians: Rethinking the Gospel Audiences*. Edited by Richard Bauckham. Grand Rapids: Eerdmans, 1998.
———. "Canon and Exegesis in the Medical Schools of Antiquity." Pages 115–53 in *The Canon of Scripture in Jewish and Roman Tradition*. PIRSB 4. Edited by Philip S. Alexander and Jean-Daniel Kaestli. Lausanne: du Zèbre, 2007.
———. "Community and Canon: Reflections on the Ecclesiology of Acts." Pages 45–78 in *Einheit der Kirche im Neuen Testament*. WUNT 218. Edited by Anatoly A. Alexeev, Christos Karakolis, and Ulrich Luz. Tübingen: Mohr Siebeck, 2008.

———. "The Living Voice: Scepticism Towards the Written Word in Early Christian and in Greco-Roman Texts." Pages 220–47 in *The Bible in Three Dimensions: Essays in Celebration of Forty Years of Biblical Studies in the University of Sheffield*. JSOTSup 87. Edited by David J. A. Clines, Stephen E. Fowl, and Stanley E. Porter. Sheffield: Sheffield Academic Press, 1990.

———. *The Preface to Luke's Gospel: Literary Convention and Social Context in Luke 1.1-4 and Acts 1.1*. SNTSMS 78. Cambridge: Cambridge University Press, 1993.

———. "Schools, Hellenistic." *ABD* 5:1005–11.

Alexander, Loveday, and Philip Alexander. *The School of Moses and the School of Christ: Essays in Early Jewish and Christian Scholasticism*. Tübingen: Mohr Siebeck, forthcoming.

Alexander, Philip S. "Orality in Pharisaic-Rabbinic Judaism at the Turn of the Eras." Pages 159–84 in Wansbrough, *Jesus and the Oral Gospel Tradition*.

———. "Rabbinic Biography and the Biography of Jesus: A Survey of the Evidence." Pages 19–50 in *Synoptic Studies: The Ampleforth Conferences of 1982 and 1983*. JSNTSup 7. Edited by Christopher M. Tuckett. Sheffield: JSOT Press, 1984.

Allert, Craig. *A High View of Scripture? The Authority of the Bible and the Formation of the New Testament Canon*. Grand Rapids: Baker Academic, 2007.

Allison, Dale. "The Pauline Epistles and the Synoptic Gospels: The Pattern of the Parallels." *NTS* 28 (1982): 1–32.

Andersen, Øivind. "Oral Tradition." Pages 17–58 in Wansbrough, *Jesus and the Oral Gospel Tradition*.

Aragione, Gabriella. "Justin, 'Philosophe' chrétien et les '*Mémoires des Apôtres* qui sont appelés *Évangiles*.'" *Apocrypha* 15 (2004): 41–55.

Asmis, Elizabeth. "Basic Education in Epicureanism." Pages 209–39 in *Education in Greek and Roman Antiquity*. Edited by Yun Lee Too. Leiden: Brill, 2001.

Assmann, Jan. "Form as a Mnemonic Device: Cultural Texts and Cultural Memory." Pages 67–82 in Horsley, Draper, and Foley, *Performing the Gospel*.

———. *Das kulturelle Gedächtnis: Schrift, Erinnerung und politische Identität in frühen Hochkulturen*. Munich: Beck, 1992.

———. *Religion und kulturelles Gedächtnis: Zehn Studien*. Munich: Beck, 2000.

Aune, David E. "Assessing the Historical Value of the Apocryphal Jesus Traditions: A Critique of Conflicting Methodologies." Pages 243–72 in *Der historische Jesus: Tendenzen und Perspektiven der gegenwärtigen Forschung*. BZNW 114. Edited by Jens Schröter and Ralph Brucker. Berlin: de Gruyter, 2002.

———. "The Judgment Seat of Christ (2 Cor. 5:10)." Pages 68–86 in *Pauline Conversations in Context: Essays in Honor of Calvin J. Roetzel*. JSNTSup 221. Edited by Janice Capel Anderson, Philip Sellew, and Claudia Setzer. Sheffield: Sheffield University Press, 2002.

———. "Oral Tradition and the Aphorisms of Jesus." Pages 211–65 in Wansbrough, *Jesus and the Oral Gospel Tradition*.

———. "Prolegomena to the Study of Oral Tradition in the Hellenistic World." Pages 59–105 in Wansbrough, *Jesus and the Oral Gospel Tradition*.

———. *Prophecy in Early Christianity and the Ancient Mediterranean World*. Grand Rapids: Eerdmans, 1983.

Avery-Peck, Alan J. "Oral Tradition (Judaism)." *ABD* 5:34–37.

Babylonian Talmud Codex Munich 95: A Limited Facsimile Edition of 400 Copies. Vol. 1. Jerusalem: Sefer Publishing, 1971.

Baddeley, Alan D. *Essentials of Human Memory*. East Sussex: Psychology Press, 1999.

Bailey, Kenneth E. "Informal Controlled Oral Tradition and the Synoptic Gospels." *AJT* 5:1 (1991): 34–54.

———. "Informal Controlled Oral Tradition and the Synoptic Tradition." *Themelios* 20:2 (1995): 4–11.
———. "Middle Eastern Oral Tradition and the Synoptic Gospels." *ExpT* 106 (1995): 363–67.
———. *Poet and Peasant: A Literary-Cultural Approach to the Parables in Luke*. Grand Rapids: Eerdmans, 1976.
———. *Through Peasant Eyes*. Grand Rapids: Eerdmans, 1980.
Bar-Ilan, Meir. "Illiteracy in the Land of Israel in the First Centuries C.E." Pages 46–61 in *Essays in the Social Scientific Study of Judaism and Jewish Society*. Edited by Simcha Fishbane, Stuart Schoenfeld, and Alain Goldschlaeger. New York: KTAV, 1992.
———. "Scribes and Books in the Late Second Commonwealth and Rabbinic Period." Pages 21–38 in *Mikra: Text, Translation, Reading and Interpretation of the Hebrew Bible in Ancient Judaism and Early Christianity*. Edited by Martin Jan Mulder. Peabody, Mass.: Hendrickson, 2004.
Barclay, Craig R. "Autobiographical Remembering: Narrative Constraints on Objectified Selves." Pages 94–125 in Rubin, *Remembering Our Past*.
Barns, John. "A New *Gnomologium*: With Some Remarks on Gnomic Anthologies: II." *CQ* 1 (1951): 1–19.
Bartlett, Frederic C. *Remembering: A Study in Experimental and Social Psychology*. Cambridge: Cambridge University Press, 1995.
Bauckham, Richard. *Jesus and the Eyewitnesses: The Gospels as Eyewitness Testimony*. Grand Rapids: Eerdmans, 2006.
Bergemann, Thomas. *Q auf dem Prüfstand: Die Zuordnung des Mt/Lk-Stoffes zu Q am Beispiel der Bergpredigt*. FRLANT 158. Göttingen: Vandenhoeck & Ruprecht, 1993.
Berger, Klaus. *Formgeschichte des Neuen Testaments*. Heidelberg: Quelle & Mayer, 1984.
———. "Hellenistische Gattungen im Neuen Testament." *ANRW* II.25.2 (1984): 1245–47.
Bikerman, Elias. "La chaîne de la tradition pharisienne." *RB* 59 (1952): 44–54.
Bird, Michael F. "The Formation of the Gospels in the Setting of Early Christianity: The Jesus Tradition as Corporate Memory." *WTJ* 67 (2005): 113–34.
Blank, Reiner. *Analyse und Kritik der formgeschichtlichen Arbeiten von Martin Dibelius und Rudolf Bultmann*. Basel: Friedrich Reinhardt Kommissionsverlag, 1981.
Bloomer, W. Martin. *Valerius Maximus and the Rhetoric of the New Nobility*. London: Duckworth, 1992.
Blum, Herwig. *Die Antike Mnemotechnik*. Hildesheim: Olms, 1969.
Bokser, Baruch. *Post-Mishnaic Judaism in Transition: Samuel on Berakhot and the Beginning of the Gemara*. Chico, Calif.: Scholars Press, 1980.
———. *Samuel's Commentary on the Mishnah. Part One: Mishnayot in the Order of Zera'im*. Leiden: Brill, 1976.
Bonanno, George. "Remembering and Psychotherapy." *Psychotherapy* 27 (1990): 175–86.
Bormann, Lukas. "Autobiographische Fiktionalität bei Paulus." Pages 106–24 in *Biographie und Persönlichkeit des Paulus*. WUNT 187. Edited by Eve-Marie Becker and Peter Pilhofer. Tübingen: Mohr Siebeck, 2005.
Botha, Pieter J. J. "Letter Writing and Oral Communication in Antiquity: Suggested Implications for the Interpretation of Paul's Letter to the Galatians." *Scriptura* (1992): 17–34.
———. "Mark's Story as Oral Traditional Literature: Rethinking the Transmission of Some Traditions about Jesus." *Hervormde Teologiese Studies* 47 (1991): 304–31.

Bousset, Wilhelm. *Kyrios Christos: A History of the Belief in Christ from the Beginnings of Christianity to Irenaeus.* Nashville: Abingdon, 1970.
Boyarin, Daniel. *A Radical Jew: Paul and the Politics of Identity.* Berkeley: University of California Press, 1994.
Braund, David, and John Wilkins, eds. *Athenaeus and His World: Reading Greek Culture in the Roman Empire.* Exeter: University of Exeter Press, 2000.
Bregman, Marc. "An Early Fragment of Avot de Rabbi Nathan from a Scroll (Heb.)." *Tarbiz* 52 (1982–1983): 201–22.
———. "Non-Biblical Scrolls: The State of the Question." Unpublished paper, 2005.
Brenk, Frederick E. "Setting a Good Exemplum: Case Studies in the Moralia, the Lives as Case Studies." Pages 195–215 in *With Unperfumed Voice: Studies in Plutarch, in Greek Literature, Religion and Philosophy, and in the New Testament Background.* Potsdamer altertumswissenschaftliche Beiträge 21. Stuttgart: Franz Steiner Verlag, 2007.
Brewer, William F. "What Is Recollective Memory?" Pages 19–66 in Rubin, *Remembering Our Past.*
Brody, Robert. *The Geonim of Babylonia and the Shaping of Medieval Jewish Culture.* New Haven: Yale University Press, 1998.
Bruner, Jerome, and Carol Fleisher Feldman. "Group Narrative as a Cultural Context of Autobiography." Pages 291–317 in Rubin, *Remembering Our Past.*
Buechler, Adolph. *Types of Jewish-Palestinian Piety from 70 BCE to 70 CE.* 1922. Repr., New York: KTAV, 1968.
Bultmann, Rudolf. *History and Eschatology.* Edinburgh: University of Edinburgh Press, 1975.
———. *The History of the Synoptic Tradition.* New York: Harper & Row, 1963.
Burridge, Richard A. *What Are the Gospels? A Comparison with Graeco-Roman Biography.* 2d ed. Grand Rapids: Eerdmans, 2004.
Byrskog, Samuel. "A Century with the *Sitz im Leben*: From Form-Critical Setting to Gospel Community and Beyond." *ZNW* 98 (2007): 1–27.
———. *Jesus the Only Teacher: Didactic Authority and Transmission in Ancient Israel, Ancient Judaism and the Matthean Community.* ConBNT 24. Stockholm: Almqvist & Wiksell International, 1994.
———. "A New Perspective on the Jesus Tradition: Reflections on James D. G. Dunn's *Jesus Remembered.*" *JSNT* 26 (2004): 459–71.
———. Review of Rudolf Bultmann, *The History of the Synoptic Tradition*, in *JBL* 122 (2003): 549–55.
———. *Story as History—History as Story: The Gospel Tradition in the Context of Ancient Oral History.* WUNT 123. Tübingen: Mohr Siebeck, 2002.
Campbell, Robin. *Seneca: Letters from a Stoic.* Harmondsworth: Penguin, 1969.
Carr, David M. *Writing on the Tablet of the Heart: Origins of Scripture and Literature.* Oxford: Oxford University Press, 2005.
Carruthers, Mary J. *The Book of Memory: A Study of Memory in Medieval Culture.* Cambridge Studies in Medieval Literature 10. Cambridge: Cambridge University Press, 1990.
Casey, Edward S. *Remembering: A Phenomenological Study.* Bloomington: Indiana University Press, 1987.
Clark, Donald L. *Rhetoric in Greco-Roman Education.* New York: Columbia University Press, 1957.
Clay, Diskin. *Paradosis and Survival: Three Chapters in the History of Epicurean Philosophy.* Ann Arbor: University of Michigan Press, 1998.
Connolly, Joy. "The Problems of the Past in Imperial Greek Education." Pages 339–72 in Too, *Education in Greek and Roman Antiquity.*

Conway, Martin A. "Autobiographical Knowledge and Autobiographical Memories." Pages 67–93 in Rubin, *Remembering Our Past.*
Cribiore, Raffaela. "The Grammarians' Choice: Euripides' *Phoenissae* in Hellenistic and Roman Education." Pages 241–59 in Too, *Education in Greek and Roman Antiquity.*
———. *Gymnastics of the Mind: Greek Education in Hellenistic and Roman Egypt.* Princeton: Princeton University Press, 2001.
Crossan, John Dominic. *The Historical Jesus: The Life of a Mediterranean Jewish Peasant.* San Francisco: HarperSanFrancisco, 1991.
Dagenais, John. *The Ethics of Reading in Manuscript Culture: Glossing the* Libro de buen Amor. Princeton: Princeton University Press, 1994.
Dalby, Andrew. "Lynceus and the Anecdotists." Pages 372–94 in Braund and Wilkins, *Athenaeus and His World.*
Davids, Peter H. "The Gospels and Jewish Tradition: Twenty Years after Gerhardsson." Pages 75–99 in *Gospel Perspectives: Studies of History and Tradition in the Four Gospels.* Edited by Richard T. France and David Wenham. Sheffield: JSOT Press, 1980.
Davies, W. D. *Jewish and Pauline Studies.* Philadelphia: Fortress, 1984.
———. "The Moral Teaching of the Early Church." Pages 277–88 in *Jewish and Pauline Studies.*
———. *Paul and Rabbinic Judaism: Some Rabbinic Elements in Pauline Theology.* Rev. ed. New York: Harper & Row, 1955.
———. "Paul and the Law: Reflections on Pitfalls in Interpretation." Pages 91–122 in *Jewish and Pauline Studies.*
———. "Reflections on a Scandinavian Approach to 'the Gospel Tradition.'" Pages 14–34 in *Neotestamentica et Patristica: Freundesgabe Oscar Cullmann.* NovTSup 6. Leiden: Brill, 1962.
———. *The Setting of the Sermon on the Mount.* Cambridge: Cambridge University Press, 1964.
Desbordes, Bernadette Anne. "Introduction à Diogène Laërce: Exposition de l'Altertumswissenschaft servant de préliminaries critiques à une lecture de l'œuvre." Ph.D. diss., Onderwijs Media Instituut, Utrecht, 1990.
Dewey, Arthur J. "The Locus for Death: Social Memory and the Passion Narrative." Pages 119–28 in Kirk and Thatcher, *Memory, Tradition, and Text.*
Dewey, Joanna. "The Gospel of Mark as Oral/Aural Event: Implications for Interpretation." Pages 145–63 in *The New Literary Criticism and the New Testament.* Edited by Elizabeth Struthers Malbon and Edgar V. McKnight. Sheffield: Sheffield University Press, 1994.
———. "Mark—A Really Good Oral Story: Is That Why the Gospel of Mark Survived?" *JBL* 123 (2004): 495–507.
———. "Mark as Aural Narrative: Structures as Clues to Understanding." *Sewanee Theological Review* 36 (1992): 45–56.
———. "Mark as Interwoven Tapestry: Forecasts and Echoes for a Listening Audience." *CBQ* 52 (1991): 221–36.
———. "Oral Methods of Structuring Narrative in Mark." *Int* 43 (1989): 32–44.
———. "Textuality in an Oral Culture: A Survey of the Pauline Traditions." *Semeia* 65 (1995): 37–65.
DeWitt, Norman W. *Epicurus and His Philosophy.* Minneapolis: University of Minnesota Press, 1954.
Dibelius, Martin. *From Tradition to Gospel.* London: Ivor Nicholson and Watson, 1934.

Diels, Hermann, and Walther Kranz, eds. *Die Fragmente der Vorsokratiker*. 9th ed. Berlin: Weidmann, 1964.
Doane, A. N. "Oral Texts, Intertexts, and Intratexts: Editing Old English." Pages 75–113 in *Influence and Intertextuality in Literary History*. Edited by Jay Clayton and Eric Rothstein. Madison: University of Wisconsin Press, 1991.
Dodd, C. H. "The Framework of the Gospel Narratives." Pages 1–11 in *New Testament Studies*. Manchester: Manchester University Press, 1953.
———. "The 'Primitive Catechism' and the Sayings of Jesus." Pages 11–29 in *More New Testament Studies*. Grand Rapids: Eerdmans, 1968.
Döring, Klaus. *Exemplum Socratis: Studien zur Sokratesnachwirkung in der kynisch-stoischen Popularphilosophie der frühen Kaiserzeit und im frühen Christentum*. Hermes Einzelschriften 42. Wiesbaden: Steiner, 1979.
Dunn, James D. G. "Altering the Default Setting: Re-envisaging the Early Transmission of the Jesus Tradition." *NTS* 49 (2003): 139–75.
———. *Jesus Remembered*. Grand Rapids: Eerdmans, 2003.
———. "Jesus Traditions in Paul." Pages 155-78 in *Studying the Historical Jesus*. Edited by Bruce Chilton and Craig A. Evans. Leiden: Brill, 1994.
———. "On History, Memory and Eyewitnesses: In Response to Bengt Holmberg and Samuel Byrskog." *JSNT* 26 (2004): 473–87.
———. *The Theology of Paul the Apostle*. Grand Rapids: Eerdmans, 1998.
Düring, Ingemar. *Aristotle in the Ancient Biographical Tradition*. Studia Graeca et Latina Gothoburgensia 5. Göteborg: Elanders, 1957.
Easton, B. S. *The Gospel before the Gospels*. London: Allen & Unwin, 1928.
Eisenstein, Elizabeth L. *The Printing Press as an Agent of Change: Communications and Cultural Transformations in Early-Modern Europe*. New York: Cambridge University Press, 1979.
Ellis, E. Earle. "New Directions in Form Criticism." Pages 237–53 in *Prophecy and Hermeneutic in Early Christianity: New Testament Essays*. WUNT 18. Tübingen: Mohr, 1978.
Elman, Yaakov. *Authority and Tradition: Toseftan Baraitot in Talmudic Babylonia*. Hoboken, N.J.: KTAV, 1994.
———. "Babylonian Baraitot in the Tosefta and the 'Dialectology' of Middle Hebrew." *AJS Review* 16 (1991): 1–29.
———. "Orality and the Redaction of the Babylonian Talmud." *Oral Tradition* 14 (1999): 52–99.
———. "Order, Sequence, and Selection: The Mishnah's Anthological Choices." Pages 53–80 in Stern, *The Anthology in Jewish Literature*.
———. "The Small Scale of Things: The World Before the Geniza." *PAAJR* 63 (2001): 49–85.
Epp, Eldon Jay. "It's All about Variants: A Variant-Conscious Approach to New Testament Textual Criticism." *HTR* 100 (2007): 275–308.
———. "The Oxyrhynchus New Testament Papyri: 'Not without Honor except in Their Hometown'?" *JBL* 123 (2004): 5–55.
Fairweather, Janet. "Fiction in the Biographies of Ancient Writers." *Ancient Society* 4 (1974): 231–75.
Fascher, Erich. *Die formgeschichtliche Methode: Eine Darstellung und Kritik. Zugleich ein Beitrag zur Geschichte des synoptischen Problems*. Giessen: Alfred Töpelmann, 1924.
Feldman, Carol Fleisher. "Oral Metalanguage." Pages 47–65 in *Literacy and Orality*. Edited by David R. Olson and Nancy Torrance. Cambridge: Cambridge University Press, 1991.
Finnegan, Ruth. "How Oral is Oral Literature?" *BSOAS* 37 (1974): 52–64.

———. *Literacy and Orality: Studies in the Technology of Communication.* Oxford: Blackwell, 1988.
———. *Oral Poetry: Its Nature, Significance, and Social Context.* Bloomington: Indiana University Press, 1977.
Fishbane, Michael. *Biblical Interpretation in Ancient Israel.* Oxford: Clarendon, 1985.
Fitzmyer, Joseph A. "Memory and Manuscript: The Origins and Transmission of the Gospel Tradition." *TS* 23 (1961): 442–47.
Foley, John Miles. "Editing and Translating Traditional Oral Epic: The South Slavic Songs and Homer." Pages 3–27 in *Epea and Grammata: Oral and Written Communication in Ancient Greece.* Supplements to Mnemosyne 230. Edited by Ian Worthington and John Miles Foley. Leiden: Brill, 2002.
———. *How to Read an Oral Poem.* Urbana: University of Illinois Press, 2002.
———. *Immanent Art: From Structure to Meaning in Traditional Oral Epic.* Bloomington: Indiana University Press, 1991.
———. "Memory in Oral Tradition." Pages 83–96 in Horsley, Draper, and Foley, *Performing the Gospel.*
———. *The Singer of Tales in Performance.* Bloomington: Indiana University Press, 1995.
———. *The Theory of Oral Composition: History and Methodology.* Bloomington: Indiana University Press, 1988.
Fraade, Steven D. *From Tradition to Commentary: Torah and Its Interpretation in the Midrash Sifre to Deuteronomy.* Albany: State University of New York, 1991.
———. "Literary Composition and Oral Performance in Early Midrashim." *Oral Tradition* 14 (1999): 33–51.
Friedman, Shamma. "Uncovering Literary Dependencies in the Talmudic Corpus." Pages 35–57 in *The Synoptic Problem in Rabbinic Literature.* BJS 326. Edited by Shaye J. D. Cohen. Providence: Brown Judaic Studies, 2000.
Funk, Robert W. "The Apostolic Parousia: Form and Significance." Pages 249–68 in *Christian History and Interpretation: Studies Presented to John Knox.* Edited by William R. Farmer, C. F. D. Moule, and R. R. Niebuhr. Cambridge: Cambridge University Press, 1967.
Gallo, Italo. *Frammenti Biografici da Papiri.* Vol. 2: *La biografia dei filosofi.* Roma: Edizioni dell' Ateneo & Bizzarri, 1980.
Gerhardsson, Birger. *Die Anfänge der Evangelientradition.* Glauben und Denken 919. Wuppertal: Brockhaus, 1977.
———. "Die Boten Gottes und die Apostel Christi." *SEÅ* 27 (1962): 89–131.
———. *The Ethos of the Bible.* Philadelphia: Fortress, 1981.
———. *Fader vår i Nya testamentet.* Lund: Novapress, 2003.
———. *Fridrichsen, Odeberg, Aulén, Nygren: Fyra teologer.* Lund: Novapress, 1994.
———. *The Good Samaritan—The Good Shepherd?* ConNT 16. Lund: Gleerup, 1958.
———. *The Gospel Tradition.* ConBNT 15. Lund: Gleerup, 1986.
———. "The Gospel Tradition." Pages 497–545 in *The Interrelations of the Gospels.* BETL 95. Edited by David L. Dungan. Leuven: Leuven University Press and Peeters, 1990.
———. "Gottes Sohn as Diener Gottes." *ST* 27 (1973): 73–106.
———. "If We Do Not Cut the Parables Out of Their Frames." *NTS* 37 (1991): 321–35.
———. "Illuminating the Kingdom: Narrative Meshalim in the Synoptic Gospels." Pages 266–309 in Wansbrough, *Jesus and the Oral Gospel Tradition.*
———. "Innan evangelierna skrevs." *SEÅ* 69 (2004): 167–89.
———. *Jesu liknelser.* Lund: Novapress, 1999.
———. *Jesu Maktgärningar i Matteusevangeliet.* Lund: Novapress, 1991.

———. *Kristi uppståndelse*. Lund: Novapress, 2001.

———. *Memory and Manuscript: Oral Tradition and Written Transmission in Rabbinic Judaism and Early Christianity, with Tradition and Transmission in Early Christianity*. ASNU 22. Lund: Gleerup. 1961. Repr., Grand Rapids: Eerdmans, and Livonia: Dove, 1998.

———. *The Mighty Acts of Jesus According to Matthew*. Scripta Minora 1978–1979:5. Lund: Gleerup, 1979.

———. *The Origins of the Gospel Traditions*. Philadelphia: Fortress, 1979.

———. "The Path of the Gospel Tradition." Pages 75–96 in *The Gospel and the Gospels*. Edited by Peter Stuhlmacher. Grand Rapids: Eerdmans, 1991.

———. *The Reliability of the Gospel Tradition*. Peabody, Mass.: Hendrickson, 2001.

———. "The Secret of the Transmission of the Unwritten Jesus Tradition." *NTS* 51 (2005): 1–18.

———. *The Shema in the New Testament: Deut 6:4–5 in Significant Passages*. Lund: Novapress, 1996.

———. *The Testing of God's Son (Matt 4:1-11 & Par): An Analysis of an Early Christian Midrash*. ConBNT 2.1. Lund: Gleerup, 1966.

———. *Tradition and Transmission in Early Christianity*. ConNT 20. Lund: Gleerup, 1964.

———. "Der Weg der Evangelientradition." Pages 79–102 in *Das Evangelium und die Evangelien: Vorträge vom Tübinger Symposium 1982*. WUNT 28. Edited by Peter Stuhlmacher. Tübingen: Mohr Siebeck, 1983.

Gerhardsson, Birger, and Per Erik Persson. *Kyrkans bekännelsefråga*. Malmö: Liber, 1984.

Gilliard, Frank D. "More Silent Reading in Antiquity: *Non Omne Verbum Sonabat*." *JBL* 112 (1993): 689–94.

Goodblatt, David. "The Babylonian Talmud." Pages 154–60 in *The Study of Ancient Judaism*. Vol. 2: *The Palestinian and Babylonian Talmuds*. Edited by Jacob Neusner. New York: KTAV, 1981.

———. *Rabbinic Instruction in Sasanian Babylonia*. Leiden: Brill, 1975.

Goody, Jack. *The Power of the Written Tradition*. Washington: Smithsonian Institution Press, 2000.

Goody, Jack, and Ian Watt. "The Consequences of Literacy." Pages 27–68 in *Literacy in Traditional Societies*. Edited by Jack Goody. Cambridge: Cambridge University Press, 1968.

Goppelt, Leonhard. *Theology of the New Testament*. 2 vols. Grand Rapids: Eerdmans, 1982.

Graham, William A. "Scripture as Spoken Word." Pages 129–69 in *Rethinking Scripture: Essays from a Comparative Perspective*. Edited by Miriam Levering. Albany: State University of New York Press, 1989.

Green, William Scott. "Palestinian Holy Men: Charismatic Leadership and Rabbinic Tradition." *ANRW* II.19 (1978): 619–47.

Greenlee, J. Harold. *A New Testament Greek Morpheme Lexicon*. Grand Rapids: Zondervan, 1983.

Güttgemanns, Erhardt. *Candid Questions Concerning Gospel Form Criticism: A Methodological Sketch of the Fundamental Problematics of Form and Redaction Criticism*. The Pittsburgh Theological Monograph Series 26. Pittsburgh: Pickwick Press, 1979.

Hagner, Donald A. Preface to *The Reliability of the Gospel Tradition*, by Birger Gerhardsson, vii–xvi. Peabody, Mass.: Hendrickson, 2001.

Haines-Eitzen, Kim. *Guardians of Letters: Literacy, Power, and the Transmitters of Early Christian Literature*. Oxford: Oxford University Press, 2000.

Halbwachs, Maurice. *The Collective Memory*. New York: Harper & Row, 1980.
———. *On Collective Memory*. Edited by Lewis A. Coser. Chicago: University of Chicago Press, 1992.
Harris, William V. *Ancient Literacy*. Cambridge, Mass.: Harvard University Press, 1989.
Harvey, John D. *Listening to the Text: Oral Patterning in Paul's Letters*. Grand Rapids: Baker Books, 1998.
Hauptman, Judith. *Rereading the Mishnah: A New Approach to Ancient Jewish Texts*. Tübingen: Mohr Siebeck, 2005.
Häusser, Detlef. *Christusbekenntnis und Jesusüberlieferung bei Paulus*. WUNT 2.210. Tübingen: Mohr Siebeck, 2006.
Havelock, Eric A. *The Literate Revolution in Greece and Its Cultural Consequences*. Princeton: Princeton University Press, 1982.
Haverly, Thomas P. "Oral Traditional Literature and the Composition of Mark." Ph.D. diss., University of Edinburgh, 1983.
Heard, R. G. "The APOMNHMONEUMATA in Papias, Justin, and Irenaeus." *NTS* 1 (1954–1955): 122–29.
Hearon, Holly. "The Implications of Orality for Studies of the Biblical Text." Pages 3–20 in Horsley, Draper, and Foley, *Performing the Gospel*.
Henaut, Barry W. *Oral Tradition and the Gospels: The Problem of Mark 4*. JSNTSup 82. Sheffield: JSOT Press, 1993.
Henderson, Ian. "Didache and Orality in Synoptic Comparison." *JBL* 111 (1992): 283–306.
Hengel, Martin. *Judaism and Hellenism: Studies in Their Encounter in Palestine during the Early Hellenistic Period*. 2 vols. London: SCM Press, 1974.
Hezser, Catherine. *Jewish Literacy in Roman Palestine*. TSAJ 81. Tübingen: Mohr Siebeck, 2001.
———. "The Mishnah and Ancient Book Production." Pages 182–87 in *The Mishnah in Contemporary Perspective*. Part One. Edited by Alan J. Avery-Peck and Jacob Neusner. Leiden: Brill, 2002.
———. *The Social Structure of the Rabbinic Movement in Palestine*. TSAJ 66. Tübingen: Mohr Siebeck, 1997.
Hirst, William, and David Manier. "Remembering as Communication: A Family Recounts Its Past." Pages 271–90 in Rubin, *Remembering Our Past*.
Hock, Ronald F., and Edward N. O'Neil. *The Chreia in Ancient Rhetoric*. Vol. 1: *The Progymnasmata*. SBLTT 27. Atlanta: Scholars Press, 1986.
Holmberg, Bengt. *Paul and Power: The Structure of Authority in the Primitive Church as Reflected in the Pauline Epistles*. Philadelphia: Fortress, 1980.
———. *Sociology and the New Testament: An Appraisal*. Minneapolis: Fortress, 1990.
Holtz, Traugott. "Paul and the Oral Gospel Tradition." Pages 380–93 in Wansbrough, *Jesus and the Oral Gospel Tradition*.
Horsley, Richard A. *Hearing the Whole Story: The Politics of Plot in Mark's Gospel*. Louisville, Ky.: Westminster John Knox, 2001.
———. *Scribes, Visionaries and the Politics of Second Temple Judaism*. Louisville, Ky.: Westminster John Knox, 2007.
Horsley, Richard A., and Jonathan A. Draper. *Whoever Hears You Hears Me: Prophets, Performance, and Tradition in Q*. Harrisburg: Trinity Press International, 1999.
Horsley, Richard A., Jonathan Draper, and John Miles Foley, eds. *Performing the Gospel: Orality, Memory, and Mark*. Minneapolis: Fortress, 2006.
Hubbell, Harry M. *The Rhetorica of Philodemus*. Pages 243–382 in Transactions of the Connecticut Academy of Arts and Sciences 23. New Haven: Yale University Press, 1920.

Hultgren, Stephen. *Narrative Elements in the Double Tradition: A Study of Their Place within the Framework of the Gospel Narrative.* BZNW 113. Berlin: de Gruyter, 2002.
Humphrey, J. H., ed. *Literacy in the Roman World.* Journal of Roman Archaeology Supplementary Series 3. Ann Arbor, Mich.: Journal of Roman Archaeology, 1991.
Hunter, Ian M. L. "Lengthy Verbatim Recall: The Role of Text." Pages 207–34 in *Progress in the Psychology of Language.* Vol. 1. Edited by Andrew W. Ellis. London: Erlbaum, 1985.
Jacob, Christian. "Athenaeus the Librarian." Pages 85–110 in Braund and Wilkins, *Athenaeus and His World.*
Jaeger, Werner. *Aristotle: Fundamentals of the History of His Development.* 2d ed. Oxford: Clarendon, 1948.
Jaffee, Martin S. "Gender and Otherness in Rabbinic Oral Culture: On Gentiles, Undisciplined Jews, and Their Women." Pages 21–43 in Horsley, Draper, and Foley, *Performing the Gospel.*
———. "Oral Tradition in the Writings of Rabbinic Oral Torah: On Theorizing Rabbinic Orality." *Oral Tradition* 14 (1999): 3–32.
———. "Oral Transmission of Knowledge as a Rabbinic Sacrament." Pages 65–79 in *Study and Knowledge in Jewish Thought.* Edited by Howard Kreisel. Beer Sheva: Ben-Gurion University of the Negev Press, 2006.
———. "A Rabbinic Ontology of the Written and Spoken Work: On Discipleship, Transformative Knowledge, and the Living Text of the Oral Torah." *JAAR* 65 (1997): 525–49.
———. *Torah in the Mouth: Writing and Oral Tradition in Palestinian Judaism, 200 BCE–400 CE.* Oxford: Oxford University Press, 2001.
———. "What Difference Does the Orality of Rabbinic Writing Make for the Interpretation of Rabbinic Writings?" Pages 11–33 in *How Should Rabbinic Literature Be Read in the Modern World?* Edited by Matthew A. Kraus. Piscataway, N.J.: Gorgias, 2006.
———. "Writing and Rabbinic Oral Tradition: On Mishnaic Narrative, Lists and Mnemonics." *Journal of Jewish Thought and Philosophy* 4 (1994): 123–46.
Jenkins, Philip. *The New Faces of Christianity: Believing the Bible in the Global South.* Oxford: Oxford University Press, 2006.
Kalmin, Richard. *The Redaction of the Babylonian Talmud: Amoraic or Saboraic?* HUCM 12. Cincinnati: Hebrew Union College Press, 1989.
Kanarfogel, Ephraim. *Jewish Education and Society in the High Middle Ages.* Detroit: Wayne State University Press, 1992.
Kelber, Werner H. "The Case of the Gospels: Memory's Desire and the Limits of Historical Criticism." *Oral Tradition* 17 (2002): 55–86.
———. "The Generative Force of Memory: Early Christian Tradition as a Process of Remembering." *BTB* 36 (2006): 15–22.
———. *The Oral and the Written Gospel: The Hermeneutics of Speaking and Writing in the Synoptic Tradition, Mark, Paul, and Q.* With a new introduction by the author. Voices in Performance and Text. Bloomington: Indiana University Press, 1997.
———. "The Oral-Scribal-Memorial Arts of Communication in Early Christianity." Pages 235–62 in *Jesus, the Voice, and the Text: Beyond the Oral and the Written Gospel.* Edited by Tom Thatcher. Waco, Tex.: Baylor University Press, 2008.
———. "Rethinking the Oral-Scribal Transmission/Performance of the Jesus Tradition." Grand Rapids: Eerdmans, forthcoming.
———. "The Work of Walter Ong and Biblical Scholarship." In *Language, Culture, and Identity: The Legacy of Walter Ong, S.J.* Edited by Sara van den Berg and Thomas M. Walsh. Cresskill, N.J.: Hampton, forthcoming.

———. "The Works of Memory: Christian Origins as Mnemo-History—A Response." Pages 221–48 in Kirk and Thatcher, *Memory, Tradition, and Text.*
Kennedy, George A. *Progymnasmata: Greek Textbooks of Prose Composition and Rhetoric.* Leiden: Brill, 2003.
Kindstrand, Jan Fredrik. "Diogenes Laertius and the *Chreia* Tradition." *Elenchos: Rivista di studi sul pensiero antico* 7 (1986): 219–43.
Kirk, Alan, and Tom Thatcher. "Jesus Tradition as Social Memory." Pages 25–42 in *Memory, Tradition, and Text.*
Kittel, Gerhard. *Die Problem des palästinischen Spätjudentums und das Urchristentum.* Stuttgart: Kohlhammer, 1926.
———, eds. *Memory, Tradition, and Text: Uses of the Past in Early Christianity.* SemeiaSt 52. Atlanta: Society of Biblical Literature, 2005.
Kloppenborg, John S. *The Formation of Q: Trajectories in Ancient Wisdom Collections.* Philadelphia: Fortress, 1987. Repr., Harrisburg: Trinity Press International, 1999.
———. *Excavating Q: The History and Setting of the Sayings Gospel.* Minneapolis: Fortress, 2000.
Klutz, Todd. *The Exorcism Stories in Luke-Acts: A Sociostylistic Reading.* SNTSMS 129. Cambridge: Cambridge University Press, 2004.
Koester, Helmut. *Ancient Christian Gospels: Their History and Development.* London: SCM Press, 1990.
———. "From the Kerygma-Gospel to Written Gospels." *NTS* 35 (1989): 36–81.
———. "GNOMAI Diaphoroi: The Origin and Nature of Diversification in the History of Early Christianity." Pages 114–57 in *Trajectories through Early Christianity*: Fortress, 1971.
———. "Gospels and Gospel Traditions in the Second Century." Pages 27–44 in *Trajectories through the New Testament and the Apostolic Fathers.* Edited by Andrew Gregory and Christopher Tuckett. Oxford: Oxford University Press, 2005.
———. "One Jesus and Four Primitive Gospels." Pages 158–204 in *Trajectories through Early Christianity.* Philadelphia: Fortress, 1971.
———. *Synoptische Überlieferung bei den apostolischen Vätern.* TUGAL 65. Berlin: Akademie-Verlag, 1957.
Krueger, Derek. "The Bawdy and Society: The Shamelessness of Diogenes in Roman Imperial Culture." Pages 222–39 in *The Cynics: The Cynic Movement in Antiquity and Ist Legacy.* Edited by R. Bracht Branham and Marie-Odile Goulet-Cazé. Berkeley: University of California Press, 1996.
Krupp, Michael. "Manuscripts of the Babylonian Talmud." Pages 346–66 in *The Literature of the Sages.* Edited by Samuel Safrai. Assen: Van Gorcum, 1987.
Kubler, George. *The Shape of Time: Remarks on the History of Things.* New Haven: Yale University Press, 1962.
Kuhn, Heinz-Wolfgang. "Der irdische Jesus bei Paulus als traditionsgeschichtliches und theologisches Problem." *ZTK* 67 (1970): 295–320.
Lefkowitz, Mary. *The Lives of the Greek Poets.* London: Duckworth, 1981.
Liddell, H. G., R. Scott and H. S. Jones, eds. *A Greek-English Lexicon.* 9th rev. ed. Oxford: Clarendon, 1940.
Lieberman, Saul. *Hellenism in Jewish Palestine: Studies in the Literary Transmission, Beliefs, and Manners of Palestine in the I Century B.C.E.–IV Century C.E.* New York: The Jewish Theological Seminary of America, 1950.
Lohfink, Gerhard. "Die Vermittlung des Paulinismus zu den Pastoralbriefen." *BZ* 32 (1988): 169–88.
Lord, Albert B. "The Gospels as Oral Traditional Literature." Pages 33–91 in *The Relationships Among the Gospels: An Interdisciplinary Dialogue.* Edited by William O. Walker Jr. San Antonio: Trinity University Press, 1978.

———. *The Singer of Tales*. Harvard Studies in Comparative Literature 24. 1960. 2d ed. Cambridge, Mass.: Harvard University Press, 2000.
Louw, Johannes P., and Eugene A. Nida. *Greek-English Lexicon of the New Testament Based on Semantic Domains*. 2 vols. New York: United Bible Societies, 1988.
Lowenthal, David. *The Past Is a Foreign Country*. New York: Cambridge University Press, 1985.
Lyons, George. *Pauline Autobiography: Toward a New Understanding*. SBLDS 73. Atlanta: Scholars Press, 1985.
MacDonald, Dennis Ronald. "From Audita to Legenda: Oral and Written Miracle Stories." *Forum* 2:4 (1986): 15–26.
MacDonald, James I. H. *Kerygma and Didache: The Articulation and Structure of the Earliest Christian Message*. Cambridge: Cambridge University Press, 1980.
Mack, Burton. *A Myth of Innocence: Mark and Christian Origins*. Philadelphia: Fortress, 1988.
Mack, Burton, and Vernon K. Robbins. *Patterns of Persuasion in the Gospels*. Sonoma: Polebridge, 1989.
Malkki, Liisa H. *Purity and Exile: Violence, Memory, and National Cosmology among Hutu Refugees in Tanzania*. Chicago: University of Chicago Press, 1995.
Mandel, Paul. "Between Byzantium and Islam: The Transmission of a Jewish Book in the Byzantine and Early Islamic Periods." Pages 74–106 in *Transmitting Jewish Traditions: Orality, Textuality, and Cultural Diffusion*. Edited by Yaakov Elman and Israel Gershoni. New Haven: Yale University Press, 2000.
Mansfeld, Jaap. *Studies in the Historiography of Greek Philosophy*. Assen: van Gorcum, 1990.
Manson, T. W. "The Quest of the Historical Jesus—Continued." Pages 3–12 in *Studies in the Gospels and Epistles*. Manchester: Manchester University Press, 1962.
Marrou, Henri-Irenée. *History of Education*. New York: Sheed & Ward, 1956.
McCown, C.C. *The Testament of Solomon*. Leipzig: J. C. Hinrichs, 1922.
McIver, Robert K., and Marie Carroll. "Experiments to Develop Criteria for Determining the Existence of Written Sources, and Their Potential Implications for the Synoptic Problem." *JBL* 121 (2002): 667–87.
McKnight, Edgar V. *What Is Form Criticism?* Philadelphia: Fortress, 1969.
McLuhan, Marshall. *The Gutenberg Galaxy: The Making of Typographic Man*. Toronto: University of Toronto Press, 1962.
Mejer, Jørgen. *Diogenes Laertius and His Hellenistic Background*. Hermes Einzelschriften 40. Wiesbaden: Steiner, 1978.
Mensching, Eckart. *Favorin von Arelate, Memorabilien und Omnigena Historia*. Texte und Kommentare 3. Berlin: de Gruyter, 1963.
Meyer, Ben F. "Some Consequences of Birger Gerhardsson's Account of the Origins of the Gospel Tradition." Pages 424–40 in Wansbrough, *Jesus and the Oral Gospel Tradition*.
Millard, Alan R. *Reading and Writing in the Time of Jesus*. New York: New York University Press, 2000.
Miller, Stuart S. *Sages and Commoners in Late Antique 'Erez Israel: A Philological Inquiry into Local Traditions in Talmud Yerushalmi*. Tübingen: Mohr Siebeck, 2006.
Moeser, Marion. *The Anecdote in Mark, the Classical World and the Rabbis*. JSNTSup 227. Sheffield: Sheffield Academic Press, 2002.
Momigliano, Arnaldo. *The Development of Greek Biography*. Expanded ed. Cambridge, Mass.: Harvard University Press, 1993.
Morgan, Teresa. "Literate Education in Classical Athens." *CQ* 49 (1999): 46–61.
———. *Literate Education in the Hellenistic and Roman Worlds*. Cambridge: Cambridge University Press, 1998.

———. *Popular Morality in the Early Roman Empire*. Cambridge: Cambridge University Press, 2007.
Morgenthaler, Robert. *Statistische Synopse*. Zurich: Gotthelf-Verlag, 1971
Moscovitz, Leib. *Talmudic Reasoning: From Casuistics to Conceptualization*. Tübingen: Mohr Siebeck, 2002.
Mournet, Terence C. *Oral Tradition and Literary Dependency: Variability and Stability in the Synoptic Tradition and Q*. WUNT 2.195. Tübingen: Mohr Siebeck, 2005.
Naeh, Shlomo. "The Art of Memory: Structures of Memory and the Construction of Texts in Rabbinic Literature (Heb.)." Pages 543–90 in *Mehqerei Talmud: Talmudic Studies Dedicated to the Memory of Professor Ephraim E. Urbach*. Vol 2. Edited by Yaakov Zussman and David Rozental. Jerusalem: Magnes Press, 2005.
Nagy, Gregory. *Homeric Questions*. Austin: University of Texas Press, 1996.
Namer, Gérard. *Mémoire et société*. Paris: Méridiens Lincksieck, 1987.
Neirynck, Franz. "Paul and the Sayings of Jesus." Pages 267–321 in *L'Apôtre Paul: Personnalité, style et conception du ministère*. BETL 73. Edited by Albert Vanhoye and Jean-Noël Aletti. Leuven: Leuven University Press and Peeters, 1986.
Nelson, W. David. "Oral Orthography: Oral and Written Transmission of Parallel Midrashic Tradition in the *Mekhilta of Rabbi Simon b. Yohai* and the *Mekhilta of Rabbi Ishmael*." *AJS Review* 29 (2005): 1–32.
Neusner, Jacob. *The Documentary Foundation of Rabbinic Culture: Mopping Up after Debates with Gerald L. Bruns, S. J. D. Cohen, Arnold Maria Goldberg, Susan Handelman, Christine Hayes, James Kugel, Peter Schaefer, Eliezer Segal, E. P. Sanders, and Lawrence H. Schiffman*. South Florida Studies in the History of Judaism 113. Atlanta: Scholars Press, 1995.
———. Foreword to *Memory and Manuscript*, by Birger Gerhardsson. xxv–xlvi.
———. *Form-Analysis and Exegesis: A Fresh Approach to the Interpretation of the Mishnah*. Minneapolis: University of Minnesota Press, 1980.
———. "Gerhardsson's *Memory and Manuscript* Revisited: Introduction to a New Edition." *Approaches to Ancient Judaism* NS 12 (1997): 171–94.
———. *The Memorized Torah: The Mnemonic System of the Mishnah*. BJS 96. Chico, Calif.: Scholars Press, 1985.
———. "Oral Torah and Oral Tradition: Defining the Problematic." Pages 59–75 in *Method and Meaning in Ancient Judaism*. Chico, Calif.: Scholars Press, 1979.
———. *Oral Tradition in Judaism: The Case of the Mishnah*. New York: Garland, 1987.
———. "The Rabbinic Traditions about the Pharisees before 70 A.D.: The Problem of Oral Tradition." *Kairos* 14 (1972): 57–70.
———. *The Redaction and Formulation of the Order of Purities in the Mishnah and Tosefta*. Vol. 21 of *A History of the Mishnaic Law of Purities*. Leiden: Brill, 1977.
Nickelsburg, George W. E. "The Genre and Function of the Markan Passion Narrative." *HTR* 73 (1980): 153–84.
———. *Resurrection, Immortality, and Eternal Life in Intertestamental Judaism and Early Christianity*. HTS 56. Cambridge, Mass.: Harvard University Press, 2006.
Nineham, Dennis E. "Eyewitness Testimony and the Gospel Tradition." *JTS* n.s. 9 (1958): 13–25, 243–52; *JTS* n.s. 11 (1960): 253–64.
———. "The Order of Event in St. Mark's Gospel—An Examination of Dr. Dodd's Hypothesis." Pages 223–39 in *Studies in the Gospels: Essays in Memory of R. H. Lightfoot*. Edited by Dennis E. Nineham. Oxford: Blackwell, 1955.
Nora, Pierre. "From *Lieu de mémoire* to Realms of Memory." Pages xv–xxiv in *Realms of Memory*. Vol. 1.
———. "General Introduction: Between Memory and History." Pages 1–20 in *Realms of Memory*. Vol. 1.

———, ed. *Les Lieux de mémoire*. 3 vols. in 7. Paris: Gallimard, 1984–1992.
———, ed. *Realms of Memory: Rethinking the French Past*. 3 vols. New York: Columbia University Press, 1996–1998.
Okpewho, Isidore. *African Oral Literature*. Indianapolis: Indiana University Press, 1992.
Olick, Jeffrey K. "Collective Memory: The Two Cultures." *ST* 17 (1999): 333–48.
Olson, David R. *The World on Paper: The Conceptual and Cognitive Implications of Writing and Reading*. Cambridge: Cambridge University Press, 1994.
Ong, Walter J. *Orality and Literacy: The Technologizing of the Word*. London: Methuen, 1982. 2d ed. London: Routledge, 2002.
Parker, David C. *The Living Text of the Gospels*. Cambridge: Cambridge University Press, 1997.
Parks, Ward. "Orality and Poetics: Synchrony, Diachrony, and the Axes of Narrative Transmission." Pages 511–32 in *Comparative Research on Oral Traditions: A Memorial for Milman Parry*. Edited by John Miles Foley. Columbus, Ohio: Slavica, 1987.
———. "The Textualization of Orality in Literary Criticism." Pages 46–61 in *Vox intexta: Orality and Textuality in the Middle Ages*. Edited by A. N. Doane and Carol Braun Pasternack. Madison: University of Wisconsin Press, 1991.
Parry, Milman. "Studies in the Epic Technique of Oral Verse-Making. I: Homer and Homeric Style." *HSCP* 41 (1930): 73–147.
———. "Whole Formulaic Verses in Greek and Southslavic Heroic Song." *TAPA* 64 (1933): 179–97.
Perrin, Norman. *Rediscovering the Teaching of Jesus*. New York: Harper & Row, 1967.
Pinault, Jody Rubin. *Hippocratic Lives and Legends*. Studies in Ancient Medicine 4. Leiden: Brill, 1992.
Prager, Jeffrey. *Presenting the Past: Psychoanalysis and the Sociology of Misremembering*. Cambridge, Mass.: Harvard University Press, 1998.
Rabbinovicz, Raphael. *Diqduqei Sofrim*. Repr., New York: MP Press, 1976.
Reitzenstein, Richard. *Hellenistic Mystery-Religions: Their Basic Ideas and Significance*. Pittsburgh Theological Monograph Series 15. Pittsburgh: Pickwick Press, 1978.
Resch, Alfred. *Der Paulinismus und die Logia Jesu in ihrem gegenwärtigen Verhältnis untersucht*. Texte und Untersuchungen zur Geschichte der altchristlichen Literatur, NF 12. Leipzig: Hinrichs, 1904.
Rhoads, David. "Performance Criticism: An Emerging Methodology in Second Testament Studies—Part I." *BTB* 36 (2006): 118–33.
———. "Performance Criticism: An Emerging Methodology in Second Testament Studies—Part II." *BTB* 36 (2006): 164–84.
Richards, Randolph E. *Paul and First-Century Letter Writing: Secretaries, Composition, Collection*. Downers Grove, Ill.: InterVarsity, 2004.
———. *The Secretary in the Letters of Paul*. WUNT 2.42. Tübingen: Mohr Siebeck, 1991.
Riesenfeld, Harald. "The Gospel Tradition and Its Beginnings." *SE* 1 (TU 73) (1959): 43–65.
Riesner, Rainer. *Jesus als Lehrer: Eine Untersuchung zum Ursprung der Evangelien-Überlieferung*. WUNT 2.7. 3d ed. Tübingen: Mohr Siebeck, 1988.
Robbins, Vernon K. "Form Criticism: New Testament." *ABD* 2:841–43.
———, ed. *Ancient Quotes and Anecdotes*. Sonoma: Polebridge Press, 1989.
———. "*Chreia* and Pronouncement Story in Synoptic Studies." Pages 1–29 in *Patterns of Persuasion in the Gospels*.
Robinson, James M. "Kerygma and History in the New Testament." Pages 37–46 in *Trajectories through Early Christianity*. Philadelphia: Fortress, 1971.

———. "LOGOI SOPHON: On the Gattung of Q." Pages 71–113 in *Trajectories through Early Christianity*. Philadelphia: Fortress, 1971.
Rodriguez, Rafael. "Jesus and His Traditions: Memory, Performance, History." Ph.D. diss., Sheffield, 2008.
Rordorf, Willy. "Does the Didache Contain Jesus Tradition Independently of the Synoptic Gospels?" Pages 394–423 in Wansbrough, *Jesus and the Oral Gospel Tradition*.
Rosché, Theodore. "The Words of Jesus and the Future of the 'Q' Hypothesis." *JBL* 79 (1960): 210–20.
Rosenzweig, Roy, and David Thelen. *The Presence of the Past: Popular Uses of History in American Life*. New York: Columbia University Press, 1998.
Rubenstein, Jeffrey. *The Culture of the Babylonian Talmud*. Baltimore: The Johns Hopkins University Press, 2003.
———. *Rabbinic Stories*. New York: Paulist, 2002.
Rubin, David C. *Memory in Oral Traditions: The Cognitive Psychology of Epic, Ballads, and Counting-out Rhymes*. Oxford: Oxford University Press, 1995.
———, ed. *Remembering Our Past: Studies in Autobiographical Memory*. Cambridge: Cambridge University Press, 1996.
Ruppert, Lothar. *Jesus als der leidende Gerechte?* SBS 59. Stuttgart: KBW, 1972.
———. *Der leidende Gerechte: Eine motivgeschichtliche Untersuchung zum Alten und zwischentestamentlichen Judentum*. FB 5. Würzburg: Echter Verlag, 1972.
———. *Der leidende Gerechte und seine Feinde: Eine Wortfelduntersuchung*. Würzburg: Echter Verlag, 1973.
Russo, Joseph. "Prose Genres for Performance of Traditional Wisdom in Ancient Greece: Proverb, Maxim, Apothegm." Pages 49–64 in *Poet, Public, and Performance in Ancient Greece*. Edited by Lowell Edmunds and Robert W. Wallace. Baltimore: The Johns Hopkins University Press, 1997.
Sanders, E. P. *The Tendencies of the Synoptic Tradition*. SNTSMS 9. Cambridge: Cambridge University Press, 1969.
Sanders, E. P., and Margret Davies. *Studying the Synoptic Gospels*. London: SCM Press, 1989.
Sandt, Huub van de, and David Flusser. *The Didache: Its Jewish Sources and Its Place in Early Judaism and Christianity*. CRINT 5. Assen: Van Gorcum, 2002.
Schäfer, Peter. *Hekhalot-Studien*. TSAJ 19. Tübingen: Mohr Siebeck, 1988.
———. "Once Again the Status Quaestionis of Research in Rabbinic Literature: An Answer to Chaim Milikowsky." *JJS* 40 (1989): 89–94.
———. "Research into Rabbinic Literature: An Attempt to Define the Status Quaestionis." *JJS* 37 (1986): 139–52.
Schmidt, Karl Ludwig. *The Place of the Gospels in the General History of Literature*. Columbia: University of South Carolina Press, 2002.
———. *Der Rahmen der Geschichte Jesu: Literarkritische Untersuchungen zur ältesten Jesusüberlieferung*. Berlin: Trowitzsch, 1919.
———. "Die Stellung der Evangelien in der allgemeinen Literaturgeschichte." Pages 50–134 in ΕΥΧΑΡΙΣΤΗΡΙΟΝ: *Studien zur Religion und Literatur des Alten und Neuen Testaments*. Vol. 2. Göttingen: Vandenhoeck und Ruprecht, 1923.
Schmithals, Walter. "Kritik der Formkritik." *ZTK* 77 (1980): 149–85.
Schröter, Jens. "Jesus and the Canon: The Early Jesus Traditions in the Context of the Origins of the New Testament Canon." Pages 104–22 in Horsley, Draper, and Foley, *Performing the Gospel*.
Schwartz, Barry. *Abraham Lincoln and the Forge of National Memory*. Chicago: University of Chicago Press, 2000.

———. "Frame Image: Towards a Semiotics of Collective Memory." *Semiotica* 121 (1998): 1–38.

———. "Jesus in First-Century Memory—A Response." Pages 249–61 in Kirk and Thatcher, *Memory, Tradition, and Text*.

———. "The Social Context of Commemoration: A Study in Collective Memory." *Social Forces* 61 (1982): 374–402.

Segal, Eliezer. "Anthological Dimensions of the Babylonian Talmud." Pages 81–107 in Stern, *The Anthology in Jewish Literature*.

Sellars, Walter C., and Robert J. Yeatman. *1066 and All That: A Memorable History of England, Comprising All the Parts You Can Remember Including One Hundred and Three Good Things, Five Bad Kings and Two Genuine Dates*. Methuen: London, 1930.

Shiner, Whitney. "Memory Technology and the Composition of Mark." Pages 147–65 in Horsley, Draper, and Foley, *Performing the Gospel*.

———. *Proclaiming the Gospel: First-Century Performance of Mark*. Harrisburg: Trinity Press International, 2003.

Skidmore, Clive. *Practical Ethics for Roman Gentlemen: The Work of Valerius Maximus*. Exeter: University of Exeter Press, 1996.

Small, Jocelyn Penny. *Wax Tablets of the Mind: Cognitive Studies of Memory and Literacy in Classical Antiquity*. London: Routledge, 1997.

Smith, Morton. "A Comparison of Early Christian and Early Rabbinic Tradition." *JBL* 82 (1963): 169–76.

Spiegel, Yaakov. *Chapters in the History of the Jewish Book: Scholars and Their Annotations* (Heb.). Ramat Gan: Bar-Ilan University Press, 1996.

Squire, Larry R., and Eric R. Kandel. *Memory: From Mind to Molecules*. New York: Scientific American Library, 1999.

Staden, Heinrich von. "Haireseis and Heresy: The Case of the *haireseis iatrikai*." Pages 76–100 in *Jewish and Christian Self-Definition 3: Self-Definition in the Graeco-Roman World*. Edited by Ben F. Meyer and E. P. Sanders. London: SCM Press, 1982.

Stanton, Graham N. "Form Criticism Revisited." Pages 13–27 in *What about the New Testament? Essays in Honour of Christopher Evans*. Edited by Morna Hooker and Colin Hickling. London: SCM Press, 1975.

———. *Jesus and Gospel*. Cambridge: Cambridge University Press, 2004.

Starr, Raymond J. "The Circulation of Literary Texts in the Roman World." *CQ* 37 (1987): 213–23.

Stern, David. "Anthology and Polysemy in Classical Midrash." Pages 108–39 in *The Anthology in Jewish Literature*.

———, ed. *The Anthology in Jewish Literature*. Oxford: Oxford University Press, 2004.

Sternbach, Leo. *Gnomologium Vaticanum e Codice Vaticano Graeco 743*. Berlin: de Gruyter, 1963.

Stollenberger, Michael G. "The Lives of the Peripatetics: An Analysis of the Contents and Structure of Diogenes Laertius' 'Vitae philosophorum' Book 5." *ANRW* II 36:6 (1992): 3793–3879.

Strack, H. L., and Günter Stemberger. *Introduction to the Talmud and Midrash*. 2d ed. Minneapolis: Fortress, 1996.

Stroker, William D. *Extracanonical Sayings of Jesus*. SBLRBS 18. Atlanta: Scholars Press, 1989.

Swain, Simon. *Hellenism and Empire: Language, Classicism and Power in the Greek World, A.D. 50–250*. Oxford: Clarendon, 1996.

Sweeny, Armin. *A Full Hearing: Orality and Literacy in the Malay World*. Berkeley: University of California Press, 1987.

Talmon, Shemaryahu. "Oral Tradition and Written Transmission, or the Heard and the Seen Word in Judaism of the Second Temple Period." Pages 121–58 in Wansbrough, *Jesus and the Oral Gospel Tradition*.
Taylor, Nicholas H. *Paul, Antioch and Jerusalem: A Study in Relationships and Authority in Earliest Christianity*. JSNTSup 66. Sheffield: JSOT Press, 1992.
Taylor, Vincent. *The Formation of the Gospel Tradition*. London: Macmillan, 1933.
Telford, William R. "The Pre-Markan Tradition in Recent Research (1980–1990)." Pages 693–723 in *The Four Gospels 1992: Festschrift Frans Neirynck*. Vol. 2. BETL 100. 3 vols. Edited by F. Van Segbroeck, C. M. Tuckett, G. van Belle and J. Verheyden [et al.] Leuven: Leuven University Press and Peeters, 1992.
Thatcher, Tom. *Why John Wrote A Gospel: Jesus—Memory—History*. Louisville, Ky.: Westminster John Knox, 2006.
Theissen, Gerd. *The Gospels in Context: Social and Political History in the Synoptic Tradition*. Edinburgh: Clark, 1992.
———. "The Wandering Radicals." Pages 33–59 in *Social Reality and the Early Christians: Theology, Ethics, and the World of the New Testament*. Edinburgh: Clark, 1992.
Theissen, Gerd, and Anette Merz. *The Historical Jesus*. London: SCM Press, 1998.
Thomas, Rosalind. *Literacy and Orality in Ancient Greece*. Cambridge: Cambridge University Press, 1992.
Thompson, Michael B. "The Holy Internet: Communication Between Churches in the First Christian Generation." Pages 49–70 in *The Gospels for All Christians: Rethinking the Gospel Audiences*. Edited by Richard Bauckham. Grand Rapids: Eerdmans, 1998.
Tonkin, Elizabeth. *Narrating Our Pasts: The Social Construction of Oral History*. Cambridge Studies in Oral and Literate Culture 22. Cambridge: Cambridge University Press, 1992.
Too, Yun Lee, ed. *Education in Greek and Roman Antiquity*. Leiden: Brill, 2001.
———. "The Walking Library: The Performance of Cultural Memories." Pages 111–23 in Braund and Wilkins, *Athenaeus and His World*.
Toorn, Karel Van Der. *Scribal Culture and the Making of the Hebrew Bible*. Cambridge, Mass.: Harvard University Press, 2007.
Travis, Stephen H. "Form Criticism." Pages 153–64 in *New Testament Interpretation*. Edited by I. Howard Marshall. Exeter: Paternoster, 1977.
Trobisch, David. *Die Entstehung der Paulusbriefsammlung: Studien zu den Anfängen christlicher Publizistik*. NTOA 10. Freiburg: Universitätsverlag, 1989.
Tropper, Amram. *Wisdom, Politics, and Historiography: Tractate Avot in the Context of the Graeco-Roman Near East*. Oxford: Oxford University Press, 2004.
Tuckett, Christopher M. "Jesus and the Sabbath." In *Jesus in Continuum*. Edited by Tom Holmén. Tübingen: Mohr Siebeck, forthcoming.
———. "Paul and the Synoptic Mission Discourse?" *ETL* 60 (1984): 376–81.
———. Review of Stephen Hultgren, *Narrative Elements in the Double Tradition: A Study of Their Place within the Framework of the Gospel Narrative*, in *JTS* 54 (2003): 691–94.
Ulrich, Eugene. *The Dead Sea Scrolls and the Origins of the Bible*. Grand Rapids: Eerdmans, 1999.
Uro, Risto. "*Thomas* and Oral Gospel Tradition." Pages 8–32 in *Thomas at the Crossroads: Essays on the Gospel of Thomas*. Edited by Risto Uro. Edinburgh: Clark, 1998.
Vansina, Jan. *Oral Tradition as History*. Madison: University of Wisconsin Press, 1985.
Vegge, Tor. *Paulus und das antike Schulwesen: Schule und Bildung bei Paulus*. BZNW 134. Berlin: de Gruyter, 2006.

Wagner-Pacifici, Robin. "Memories in the Making: The Shape of Things that Went." *QS* 19 (1996): 301–21.

Walfish, Avraham. "Approaching the Text and Approaching God: The Redaction of Mishnah and Tosefta Berakhot." *Jewish Studies* 43 (2005–2006): 22–25.

Walter, Nikolaus. "Paulus und die urchristliche Jesustradition." *NTS* 31 (1985): 498–522.

Wansbrough, Henry, ed. *Jesus and the Oral Gospel Tradition.* JSNTSup 64. Sheffield: JSOT Press, 1991.

Webb, Ruth. "The Progymnasmata as Practice." Pages 289–316 in Too, *Education in Greek and Roman Antiquity.*

Wehrli, Fritz. "Gnome, Anekdote und Biographie." *Museum Helveticum* 30 (1973): 193–208.

Weiss-Halivni, David. *Midrash, Mishnah, and Gemara: The Jewish Predilection for Justified Law.* Cambridge, Mass.: Harvard University Press, 1986.

Weldon, Mary Susan, and Krystal D. Bellinger. "Collective Memory: Collaborative and Individual Processes in Remembering." *Journal of Experimental Psychology: Learning, Memory, and Cognition* 23 (1997): 1160–75.

Wenham, David. *Paul: Follower of Jesus or Founder of Christianity?* Grand Rapids: Eerdmans, 1995.

Worthington, Ian. "Greek Oratory and the Oral/Literate Division." Pages 165–77 in *Voice into Text: Orality and Literacy in Ancient Greece.* Edited by Ian Worthington. Leiden: Brill, 1996.

Wright, N. T. *Jesus and the Victory of God.* Christian Origins and the Question of God 2. Minneapolis: Fortress, 1996.

Yates, Frances A. *The Art of Memory.* Chicago: University of Chicago Press, 1966.

Young, Frances M. "Christian Teaching." Pages 91–104 in *The Cambridge History of Early Christian Literature.* Edited by Frances M. Young, Lewis Ayres, and Andrew Louth. Cambridge: Cambridge University Press, 2004.

Zerubavel, Yael. *Recovered Roots: Collective Memory and the Making of Israeli National Tradition.* Chicago: University of Chicago Press, 1997.

Zlotnick, Dov. *The Iron Pillar Mishnah: Redaction, Form, and Intent.* Jerusalem: Bialik Institute, 1988.

Zumthor, Paul. *Oral Poetry: An Introduction.* Theory and History of Literature 70. Minneapolis: University of Minnesota Press, 1990.

Zuntz, Günther. *Persephone: Three Essays on Religion and Thought in Magna Graecia.* Oxford: Clarendon, 1971.

Zussman, Yaakov. "Oral Torah Means Just What It Says (Heb.)." Pages 209–384 in *Mehqerei Talmud: Talmudic Studies Dedicated to the Memory of Professor Ephraim E. Urbach.* Edited by Yaakov Zussman and David Rozental. Jerusalem: Magnes Press, 2005.

List of Contributors

LOVEDAY ALEXANDER is emeritus professor of biblical studies at Sheffield University and Canon-Theologian at Chester Cathedral. She was trained as a classicist at Sommerville College, Oxford, and has retained an overriding interest in the boundaries between the New Testament and its Greco-Roman matrix. Future plans include a joint-authored volume on the School of Moses and the School of Christ (with Philip Alexander), and a commentary on Hebrews.

DAVID E. AUNE is Walter Professor of New Testament and Christian Origins at the University of Notre Dame and a fellow of the Royal Norwegian Society of Sciences and Letters (*Det Kongelige Norske Videnskabers Selskab*) and of the Norwegian Academy of Science and Letters (*Det Norske Vitenskaps-Akademi*). Among his books are *Apocalypticism, Prophecy and Magic in Early Christianity* (2006), *The Westminster Dictionary of New Testament and Early Christian Literature and Rhetoric* (2003), and a three-volume commentary on Revelation (1997–1998).

SAMUEL BYRSKOG is the successor of Birger Gerhardsson on the chair as professor of New Testament Studies at the University of Lund, Sweden. His main publications include *Jesus the Only Teacher* (1994), *Story as History – History as Story* (2000), and *Romarbrevet 1–8* (2006). He has also authored numerous essays and articles dealing with various aspects of tradition and transmission in early Christianity and its Jewish and Greco-Roman environment.

MARTIN S. JAFFEE holds the Samuel and Althea Stroum Chair in Jewish Studies at the University of Washington. He is the author of *Torah in the Mouth: Writing and Oral Tradition in Palestinian Judaism, ca. 200 BCE–400 CE* in addition to many other books and essays. His most recent book is *The End of Jewish Radar: Snapshots of Postethnic American Judaism* (2009).

WERNER H. KELBER is the Isla Carroll and Percy E. Turner Professor Emeritus of Biblical Studies at Rice University. His principal work is *The Oral and the Written Gospel* (Philadelphia, 1983; Paris, 1990; Bloomington, 1997). His other publications have focused on the search for the historical Jesus, gospel narrativity, orality-scribality studies, memory and rhetoric, text criticism, and the media history of the Bible.

ALAN KIRK is chair of the department of philosophy and religion, James Madison University, Virginia. His research interests are ancient gospels, and most currently, applications of cognitive and cultural memory theory to problems in the origins and history of the gospel tradition. Recent publications include *Memory, Tradition, and Text: Uses of the Past in Early Christianity*, co-edited with Tom Thatcher (2005); "Memory Theory and Jesus Research," in *Handbook of the Study of the Historical Jesus*, edited by Tom Holmén and Stanley E. Porter (2009); "Tradition and Memory in the Gospel of Peter," in *Das Evangelium nach Petrus: Text, Kontexte, Intertexte*, edited by Tobias Nicklas and Thomas Kraus (2007).

TERENCE C. MOURNET is associate professor of New Testament and director of educational technology at Sioux Falls Seminary, Sioux Falls, South Dakota, and the author of *Oral Tradition and Literary Dependency: Variability and Stability in the Synoptic Tradition and Q* (2005). His current research is in the area of early Christianity and the New Testament with special interest in the following areas: the formation of the Synoptic tradition, orality and literacy in antiquity and postmodernity, oral performance and storytelling, folklore, historical Jesus research, and methodological questions relating to the study of Early Christianity.

CHRISTOPHER TUCKETT is professor of New Testament Studies in the University of Oxford. He has published widely across a range of New Testament (and related) topics, with particular research interests in the history and development of Jesus traditions in early Christianity. His main publications as single-authored works include *The Revival of the Griesbach Hypothesis* (1982), *Q and the History of Early Christianity* (1996), *Christology and the New Testament* (2001), and *The Gospel of Mary* (2007).

Index of Ancient Sources

HEBREW BIBLE/OLD TESTAMENT	
Numbers	
12:3	104
1 Kings	
17	104
Job	
22:28	106
Psalms	
127	106, 108, 109
127:1	106
Proverbs	
23:25	101, 103
25:21	189
Habakkuk	
2:1	99

NEW TESTAMENT	
Matthew	
5:9	189
5:11	189
5:43-44	73
5:44	24, 77, 189
17:20	77, 189
24:43	77, 189
Mark	
2:1–3:6	213
2:1-12	215
2:18-22	215
2:18-20	211
2:23-28	215
4:1-34	213
6:6b-13	75
7:14	70
7:15	73, 77
8–16	14
9:33-50	75
9:50	77, 189
10:45	78
11:22-23	189
12:17	73
12:28-34	73
14:61-62	78
Luke	
1:1-4	220
1:2	152
1:30-35	78
1:32-35	78
2:21-51	78
4:18-30	78
4:18-21	78
6:27-38	75
6:27-28	73, 77
6:27	189
6:35	189
11:41	73
14:11	78

22:19-20	73	13:22	238		
24	78, 115	13:39	238		
24:7	78	13:48	238		
24:34	78	13:52	238		
24:36ff.	78	14:1	238		
24:48	238	14:3	238		
Acts		14:20	238		
1	78, 115	14:22	238		
1:1	238	14:23	238		
1:8	238	14:28	238		
1:22	238	15:5	238		
2–13	115	15:7	238		
2:32	238	15:10	238		
2:42	238	15:35	238		
2:44	238	16:1	238		
3:15	238	16:31	238		
4:2	238	16:34	238		
4:4	238	17:12	238		
4:18	238	17:19	238		
4:32	238	17:34	238		
4:33	238	18:8	238		
5:14	238	18:11	238		
5:21	238	18:23	238		
5:28	238	18:25	238		
5:32	238	18:27	238		
5:42	238	19:1	238		
6:1-6	114	19:2	238		
6:1	238	19:4	238		
6:2	238	19:9	238		
6:7	238	19:18	238		
8:12	238	19:30	238		
8:13	238	20:1	238		
8:37	238	20:20	238		
9:1	238	20:30	238		
9:10	238	20:35	210		
9:19	238	21:4	238		
9:25	238	21:16	238		
9:26	238	21:20	238		
9:36	238	21:21	238		
9:38	238	21:25	238		
9:42	238	21:28	238		
10:34-43	69, 71	22:15	238		
10:37-38	28	22:19	238		
10:39	238	22:20	238		
10:41	238	23:11	238		
10:43	238	26:16	238		
11:17	238	28:31	238		
11:21	238	Romans			
11:26	238	1	78		
11:29	238	1:3-4	77, 78		
13:1	238	1:9	81		
13:12	238	2:21	84		

7:14	82	2 Corinthians	
12:7	84	1:12–2:17	80
12:14	24, 73, 77, 189	3:1-6	71
12:20	189	3:2-3	71
13:7	73	7:15	81
13:8-10	73	Galatians	
14:14	24, 77, 189	1	68
14:20	70	1–2	68
15:15	81	1:9	83
16:22	66	1:11–2:21	80
1 Corinthians		1:12	83, 84
1:16	82	1:14	83
4:12-13	73	1:18	78, 185, 248
4:16	82	1:19	78
4:17	81, 84	2:6-9	248
5	70	4	78
6:2	82	4:4-5	77, 78
6:15	82	5:6	70
7:9	24	5:14	73
7:10-12	70	6:6	247
7:10-11	73, 76, 186, 188	6:11	66
7:10	75, 188	6:15	70
7:12-16	188	Ephesians	
7:12	188, 189	2:11	81
7:19	70	4:21	84
7:25	186, 189	5:1	82
8	70	Philippians	
9:4-18	70	1:3	81
9:14	73, 75, 76, 186, 188	2:6-11	77, 78
9:15-18	188	3:4-16	80
10:16	188	3:17	82
11:1	82	4:9	83
11:2	81, 83	Colossians	
11:14	84	1:28	84
11:23-26	186	2:6	69, 83
11:23-25	70, 73, 75, 78, 188	2:7	84
11:23	83	2:8	83
11:23a	73	3–4	75
11:24	81	3:16	84
11:25	81	4:16	81
13:2	77, 188	4:17	83
14	70	4:18	81
14:14	73	1 Thessalonians	
14:37	75	1:2–3:13	80
15	70, 78	1:2-3	82
15:1	83	1:2	81
15:3ff.	185	1:3	81
15:3-8	69, 77, 78	1:5	82
15:3-7	248, 252	1:6	82
15:3-5	186	2:9	81
15:3	83	2:13	83
		2:14	82

3:4	82	**MISHNAH, TALMUD, AND RELATED**	
3:6	81	**LITERATURE**	
4–5	75	MISHNAH	
4:1-8	70	*Abot*	
4:1	82, 83	1:1	87, 103, 141
4:2	83	1:8-9	103
4:3	82	2:8	3
4:13–5:11	73	*Abodah Zarah*	
4:15-17	84–85, 228	1:3	69
4:15-16	75	*Parah*	
4:15	186, 187	3:1-11	236
4:16-18	188	*Peah*	
4:17	70	2:6	102, 103
5:2, 4	77, 189	*Sukkah*	
5:13	77, 189	5:4	233
5:27	81	4:9	236
2 Thessalonians		*Taanit*	
2:5	81	3:8	91, 99, 101, 102, 104, 105
2:15	83, 84	*Yadayim*	
3:6	83	4:2	103
3:7	82	*Yoma*	
3:9	82	1:3-7	236
1 Timothy		*Yebamot*	
2:12	84	16:7	103
4:11	84		
6:2	84	TOSEPHTA	
2 Timothy		*Kippurim*	
1:3	81	1:8	236
1:4	81	*Parah*	
1:5	81	3:1-14	236
1:6	81	*Peah*	
2:2	84	3:8	233
2:8	81	*Sukkah*	
2:14	81	3:16	236
Titus		4:2	233
1:11	84	*Taanit*	
3:1	81	2/3:13	233, 237
OLD TESTAMENT PSEUDEPIGRAPHA		THE BABYLONIAN TALMUD	
Letter of Aristeas		*Baba Batra*	
1	220	4a–5b	229
154	247	29a-b	229
		Berakot	
Philo		57b	69
On Agriculture		*Erubin*	
132	148	54b	232
On the Life of Moses		*Horayot*	
1.1.4	220	12a	231
On the Special Laws		*Hullin*	
4.107	148, 247	101a–105a	229
		Ketubbot	
		62b	237

Megillah
| 7b | 232 |
| 27a | 232 |

Pesahim
| 32b | 231 |

Shabbat
| 31a | 104 |
| 63a | 232 |

Taanit
7a	232
8a	232
19a	91
23a	99, 102, 104, 105, 236, 237

THE JERUSALEM TALMUD
Taanit
| 66d | 101, 104 |
| 67a | 102, 237 |

OTHER RABBINIC WORKS
Abot de Rabbi Nathan
| A:15 | 104 |
| A:33 | 236 |

APOSTOLIC FATHERS
Didache
| 1:3 | 73 |

NEW TESTAMENT APOCRYPHA AND PSEUDEPIGRAPHA
Gospel of Thomas
6	246
12	246
13	246
18	246
20	246
21	246
22	246
24	246
37	246
43	246
51	246
52	246
53	246
60	246
72	246
79	246
91	246
99	246
100	246
104	246
113	246
114	246

CLASSICAL AND ANCIENT CHRISTIAN WRITINGS

Aristotle
Eudemian Ethics
| 7.12, 1245b20 | 242 |

Nicomachean Ethics
| 9.10.6, 1171a15–17 | 242 |

Soul
| 405a19–21 | 241 |

Athenaeus
Deipnosophistae
4.162	123, 240
9.9	240
11.116	123, 240
14.614d	122

Clement of Alexandria
Adumbrationes ad 1 Peter
| 5.13 | 247 |

Hypotyposeis
| 6 | 247 |

Diogenes Laertius
The Lives and Opinions of the Philosophers
1.63	123
2.29	123
2.34	240
2.48–49	126
2.48	121, 140
2.57	121
2.122	246
2.123	246
3.20	123
3.34	121
4.47	242
5.3	243
5.17–21	127, 242
5.18	124, 126, 243
5.34	127, 242
6.20–83	133
6.30	133
6.40	241
6.51	241
6.55	241
7.4	123
7.36	123
7.163	123

Index of Ancient Sources

Eusebius
Ecclesiastical History
2.15.1–2	247
3.28.6	247
3.39.1–4	117
3.39.1–3	147
3.39.1	118, 247
3.39.2	117
3.39.3	118
3.39.4	248
3.39.7	247
3.39.15	117
3.39.16	117
4.14.6	247
5.20.5–7	147
6.14.5–7	247

Galen
On the Passions and Errors of the Soul
38–39	243

On Sects
1 (SM 3.2.3–11)	245
2 (SM 3.3.9–20)	245
4 (SM 3.7.6)	245
4 (SM 3.8.20–21)	245
8 (SM 3.20.8–17)	245

Harpocration
Lexeis of the Ten Orators
Δ 85	240
E 123	240
Θ 25	240
Φ 1	240

Herodotus
Histories
3.55.2	221
4.76.6	221
9.16.1	221

Hermogenes
Progymnasmata
3	124, 243
3.1	243

Hesiod
Theogony
53–63	2
133–36	2

Homer and the Homeric tradition
To Hermes
429–30	2

Justin
First Apology
2.11	120
18	120
26	247
30	246
33.5	116
46	116
66.3	115, 116
67.3	116

Second Apology
3	120
7	120
10	120

Dialogue with Trypho
10.2	116
18.1	239
88.3	116, 239
100.1	116, 239
100.3	239
100.4	239
103.6	239
103.8	116, 239
104.1	239
105.5	116
105.6	239
106.1	239
106.3	116, 239
106.4	239
107.1	239

Lucian
Life of Demonax
1–2	140
67	141, 239

Nicias
1.524a	123

Nikolaus
Progymnasmata
20	242

Pausanias
Description of Greece
9.39.8–13	2

Philodemus
Volumina rhetorica
II 50 col. 36	243
II 55 col. 40	244

Plato

Index of Ancient Sources

Parmenides
127a–c	241

Phaedrus
275a	2
275d–e	122

Protagoras
342–43	243
343a8–b2	243

Sophist
217c	241

Pliny the Elder
Natural History
7.24.88	3

Plutarch
Moralia
172c	129, 242, 243
172d	243
172e	131, 243
1129a	245

Priscian
De usu
30–35	243

Quintilian
Institutio Oratoria
1.9.2–6	128
1.9.3	129, 243
1.9.4	129
1.9.5	129
10.7.32	2
11.2	244
11.2.40	245

Seneca the Elder
Controversiae
1 pref. 2	3

Seneca the Younger
Epistulae morales
95.65–66	130
95.72–73	130
95.72	130
104.21–22	131

Theon
Progymnasmata
64.29–30	244
66.15	240
96–97	128
96	243
97	242
98–99	243
98	242
99	243
101–2	243
101	243
102	133, 244
126.34	240

Thucydides
History of the Peloponnesian War
1.138.6	221
2.5.5–6	221
2.48.2	221
2.88.3	221
6.2.2	221

Xenophon
Memorabilia
1.2.2–3	132
1.2.17ff.	246
1.2.21	246
1.2.31	245
1.2.62–63	246
1.2.62	245
1.3.1	121, 140
1.4.2	245
2.4.1	245
2.5.1	245
3.14	121
4.1	140
4.2	245
4.5.2	246
4.6.1	246
4.7.1	245
4.8.1	245

Index of Modern Authors

Abel, E. L., 221
Abramowski, L., 239
Achtemeier, P. J., 221
Aland, K., 247, 248
Albeck, H., 233
Alexander, E. S., 163, 230, 232, 234, 235, 237, 251
Alexander, L., 51, 113, 198–201, 220, 239, 240, 241, 243, 244, 246, 247, 248
Alexander, P. S., 66, 150, 224, 225, 239, 244, 246, 248
Allert, C., 228
Allison, D., 75, 76, 226, 227
Andersen, Ø., 257
Aragione, G., 239, 240
Asmis, E., 241, 245
Assmann, J., 160, 168, 170, 238, 250, 251, 253, 254, 259
Aune, D. E., 63, 185, 188–89, 220, 228, 229
Avery-Peck, A. J., 224, 231

Baddeley, A. D., 253
Bailey, K. E., 40, 41, 52–56, 61, 119, 120, 143, 221, 240, 246, 256
Bar-Ilan, M., 220, 249
Barclay, C. R., 253
Barns, J., 241
Bartlett, F. C., 252, 253
Bauckham, R., 64, 120, 152, 212, 213, 215, 216, 217, 223, 224, 239, 240, 248, 252, 256
Bellinger, K. D., 168, 253, 254
Bergemann, T., 42, 217
Berger, K., 214, 239
Bikerman, E., 238, 246
Bird, M. F., 221
Blank, R., 212, 215
Bloomer, W. M., 241
Blum, H., 244
Bokser, B., 235
Bonanno, G., 252, 253
Bormann, L., 227
Botha, P. J. J., 257
Bousset, W., 258
Boyarin, D., 225
Bregman, M., 229

Brenk, F. E., 241, 243
Brewer, W. F., 253
Brody, R., 229
Bruner, J., 167, 253, 254
Buechler, A., 233
Bultmann, R., 4, 22, 23, 27, 29–37, 40, 41, 44–46, 52, 55, 155, 176, 178, 186, 202, 209, 210, 212, 213, 214, 215, 216, 217, 218, 248, 255
Burridge, R. A., 217
Byrskog, S., 1, 31, 37, 119, 174, 175, 201, 202, 210, 211, 212, 214, 215, 216, 217, 222, 223, 229, 238, 240, 256, 259

Campbell, R., 243
Carr, D. M., 178–79, 181, 200, 205, 219, 249, 251, 256, 260
Carroll, M., 252
Carruthers, M. J., 234, 251
Casey, E. S., 169, 254
Clark, D. L., 241
Clay, D., 245
Connolly, J., 244
Conway, M. A., 253
Cribiore, R., 238, 242, 244, 249
Crossan, J. D., 218

Dagenais, J., 251
Dalby, A., 122, 240, 244
Davids, P. H., 209, 210
Davies, M., 210, 211, 212, 213, 214, 215
Davies, W. D., 64, 75, 77, 223, 227
Desbordes, B. A., 240
Dewey, A. J., 206, 260
Dewey, J., 217, 257
DeWitt, N. W., 241, 245
Dibelius, M., 4, 5, 10, 22, 23, 27, 29–31, 33, 35–37, 44–46, 209, 210, 212, 213, 214, 215, 216
Doane, A. N., 250
Dodd, C. H., 213, 226
Döring, K., 242
Draper, J. A., 220, 221, 223
Dunn, J. D. G., 11, 34, 52, 53, 54, 56, 61, 77, 181, 210, 215, 216, 218, 221, 222, 223, 225, 227, 240, 256

Index of Modern Authors

Düring, I., 240, 241, 243, 244

Easton, B. S., 212, 214
Eisenstein, E. L., 218
Ellis, E. E., 214, 215
Elman, Y., 229, 231, 232, 237, 251
Epp, E. J., 204, 259

Fairweather, J., 243
Fascher, E., 212
Feldman, C. F., 167, 252, 253, 254
Finnegan, R., 219, 250, 257
Fishbane, M., 254
Fitzmyer, J. A., 64, 224
Flusser, D., 221
Foley, J. M., 49, 58, 180, 219, 223, 226, 228, 234, 245, 252, 254, 256, 257, 259
Fraade, S. D., 161, 195–96, 232, 251, 259
Friedman, S., 233
Funk, R. W., 70, 225

Gallo, I., 240, 241
Gerhardsson, B., *passim*
Gilliard, F. D., 221
Goodblatt, D., 231, 235
Goody, J., 216, 222, 250, 251
Goppelt, L., 226
Graham, W. A., 225
Green, W. S., 102, 105, 236
Greenlee, J. H., 228
Güttgemanns, E., 212, 215, 255

Hagner, D. A., 208, 218
Haines-Eitzen, K., 224, 260
Halbwachs, M., 79, 167, 227, 253
Harris, W. V., 51, 158, 220, 249
Harvey, J. D., 67, 73–74, 225, 226
Hauptman, J., 232, 233
Häusser, D., 77–78, 227
Havelock, E. A., 47, 218, 219
Haverly, T. P., 219
Heard, R. G., 121, 239, 240
Hearon, H., 219, 240, 246
Henaut, B. W., 218
Henderson, I., 221
Hengel, M., 30, 214, 259
Hezser, C., 51, 158, 220, 229, 231, 248, 249
Hirst, W., 253
Hock, R. F., 214, 242, 243, 244

Holmberg, B., 212, 216, 222
Holtz, T., 67, 72–73, 75, 225, 226
Horsley, R. A., 220, 221, 223, 257, 260
Hubbell, H. M., 243, 244
Hultgren, S., 213
Hunter, I. M. L., 254

Jacob, C., 244, 255
Jaeger, W., 131, 243
Jaffee, M. S., 65, 87, 145, 150, 161, 162, 163, 178, 181, 191, 196–97, 222, 224, 228, 230, 231, 232, 247, 248, 250, 251, 256, 259
Jenkins, P., 249

Kalmin, R., 235
Kanarfogel, E., 234
Kandel, E. R., 166, 253, 254
Kelber, W. H., 16, 64, 65, 67, 70–72, 173, 208, 210, 211, 214, 215, 217, 222, 223, 224, 225, 226, 237, 248, 249, 250, 254, 255
Kennedy, G. A., 242, 243, 244
Kindstrand, J. F., 240, 241, 242, 243
Kirk, A., 155, 183, 202, 203, 223, 257, 259
Kittel, G., 210
Kloppenborg, J. S., 144, 213, 246, 247
Klutz, T., 248
Koester, H., 151, 221, 239, 240, 246, 248, 258
Krueger, D., 242
Krupp, M., 229
Kubler, G., 254
Kuhn, H.-W., 90, 258

Lefkowitz, M., 131, 243
Lieberman, S., 231, 232
Lohfink, G., 228
Lord, A. B., 49, 74, 180, 219, 234, 256
Louw, J. P., 228
Lowenthal, D., 254
Lyons, G., 227

MacDonald, D. R., 221
MacDonald, J. I. H., 226
Mack, B., 214, 253
Malkki, L. H., 168, 253, 254
Mandel, P., 251
Manier, D., 253
Mansfeld, J., 241
Manson, T. W., 212

Marrou, H.-I., 238
McCown, C. C., 225
McIver, R. K., 252
McKnight, E. V., 212
McLuhan, M., 218
Mejer, J., 125, 240, 241, 242, 243
Mensching, E., 240
Merz, A., 216
Meyer, B. F., 209, 210, 217
Millard, A. R., 220
Miller, S. S., 229, 231, 232
Moeser, M., 143, 246
Momigliano, A., 242, 243
Morgan, T., 135, 145, 153, 158, 239, 241, 242, 243, 244, 247, 248, 249
Morgenthaler, R., 42, 217
Moscovitz, L., 235
Mournet, T. C., 34, 39, 53, 56, 61, 181, 215, 217, 218, 220, 221, 222, 223, 256

Naeh, S., 230, 232
Nagy, G., 135, 244
Namer, G., 253
Neirynck, F., 76, 227
Nelson, W. D., 230, 232, 237
Neusner, J., 64, 65, 66, 87, 110, 174, 184, 193, 194, 196, 197, 207, 210, 211, 218, 222, 223, 224, 228, 230, 234, 255, 258, 259
Nickelsburg, G. W. E., 205, 214, 260
Nida, E. A., 228
Nineham, D. E., 163, 164, 169, 213, 252
Nora, P., 79, 80, 227, 228

Okpewho, I., 218
Olick, J. K., 254
Olson, D. R., 162, 251
O'Neil, E. N., 214, 242, 243, 244
Ong, W. J., 50, 56, 219, 222, 255, 257

Parker, D. C., 204, 259
Parks, W., 254
Parry, M., 49, 74, 218, 226, 254
Perrin, N., 64, 66, 223, 224
Pinault, J. R., 245
Prager, J., 253

Rabbinovicz, R., 234, 236
Reitzenstein, R., 258
Resch, A., 75, 226

Rhoads, D., 257
Richards, R. E., 224
Riesenfeld, H., 5, 207
Riesner, R., 208
Robbins, V. K., 212, 214, 215
Robinson, J. M., 190, 258
Rodriguez, R., 238
Rordorf, W., 221
Rosché, T., 42, 217
Rosenzweig, R., 253
Rubenstein, J., 102, 105, 230, 233, 235, 236
Rubin, D. C., 170, 253, 254
Ruppert, L., 205, 260
Russo, J., 160, 164, 250, 252

Sanders, E. P., 33, 210, 211, 212, 213, 214, 215, 218, 225
Sandt, H. van de, 221
Schäfer, P., 194–95, 251, 259
Schmidt, K. L., 22, 23, 120, 209, 217, 239, 240
Schmithals, W., 208, 212
Schröter, J., 187, 190, 258
Schwartz, B., 168, 253, 254
Segal, E., 229, 251, 252
Sellars, W. C., 238
Shiner, W., 215, 251, 257
Skidmore, C., 241
Small, J. P., 136, 161, 244, 247, 248, 251
Smith, M., 11, 25, 64, 174, 209, 210, 211, 218, 222, 223, 224, 248, 255
Spiegel, Y., 229
Squire, L. R., 166, 253, 254
Staden, H. von, 241
Stanton, G. N., 212, 213, 216
Starr, R. J., 158, 249
Stemberger, G., 229, 231, 235, 250, 251
Stern, D., 229
Sternbach, L., 241
Stollenberger, M. G., 240, 242
Strack, H. L., 229, 231, 235, 250, 251
Stroker, W. D., 228
Swain, S., 244
Sweeny, A., 162, 251

Talmon, S., 219
Taylor, N. H., 212
Taylor, V., 56, 215
Telford, W. R., 213
Thatcher, T., 202, 254, 257, 259
Theissen, G., 36, 213, 215, 216, 217

Thelen, D., 253
Thomas, R., 251
Thompson, M. B., 220
Tonkin, E., 160, 250, 252, 253, 254
Too, Y. L., 244
Toorn, K. Van Der, 220
Travis, S. H., 212
Trobisch, D., 228
Tropper, A., 246
Tuckett, C. M., 21, 175, 218, 226

Ulrich, E., 259
Uro, R., 219

Vansina, J., 34, 143, 151, 152, 216, 222, 246, 248
Vegge, T., 239

Wagner-Pacifici, R., 167, 253
Walfish, A., 233

Walter, N., 75–76, 227
Watt, I., 216, 222
Webb, R., 242, 244, 247
Wehrli, F., 241, 247
Weiss-Halivni, D., 110, 235
Weldon, M. S., 168, 253, 254
Wenham, D., 76, 227
Worthington, I., 74, 226
Wright, N. T., 52, 221, 225

Yates, F. A., 79, 227, 260
Yeatman, R. J., 238
Young, F. M., 247

Zerubavel, Y., 254
Zlotnick, D., 230
Zumthor, P., 252
Zuntz, G., 207
Zussman, Y., 230, 231

CPSIA information can be obtained
at www.ICGtesting.com
Printed in the USA
LVHW031816241022
731421LV00003B/238